FROM HELL TO HOLLYWOOD

OUR ALL-PUPORSE WARRIOR: John Wayne became the key cinematic symbol of the American fighting man—-Army, navy, Air Force, Seabees--seen here as a marine in *The Sands of Iwo Jima*.

FROM HELL TO HOLLYWOOD

An Encyclopedia of World War II Films

Volume 2

by Douglas Brode

BearManor Media

2019

From Hell To Hollywood: An Encyclopedia of World War II Films
Volume 2

Published in the United States of America by:

BearManor Media

1317 Edgewater Dr. #110
Orlando, FL 32804

BearManorMedia.com

Printed in the United States.

Typesetting and layout by John Teehan

Special thanks to 'Tony' and the entire crew at the Sundance Copy Center in San Antonio, TX, for their time, skills, and enthusiasm!

ISBN—978-1-62933-522-3

For my grandson,

TYLER REESE BRODE

Table of Contents

Introduction
"Which World War II Are You Referring To?"

To **CLAIM THAT THE 1960S** was a period of confusion, change, and at times chaos in America--among the citizenry and in the pop-culture that constantly reflects our ever-evolving world--would be to understate the situation. A brief-lived era of optimism followed the election of John Fitzgerald Kennedy as president at the decade's cusp; this turned to dust following the attractive, witty, inspiring president's assassination in November, 1963. For our purposes, it's important to note that this occurred only months after the theatrical release of *P.T. 109*. The Warner Bros. film had been self-consciously crafted to project a pure, heroic image of J.F.K. in World War II. A glossy, superficial tribute and at best a modest box-office success *P.T. 109* presented a simple vision of The Big One that recalled the overtly propagandistic combat movies distributed while our Crusades in Europe and the Pacific still raged.

Yet another major film dealing with that war premiered while the nation continued to reel after suspected Kennedy-assassin Lee Harvey Oswald was himself shot dead (on live TV) by a minor crime figure, Jack Ruby. *The Victors*, apparently intended as a blockbuster holiday release, had been directed, written, and produced by Carl Foreman (1914-1984); two years earlier, he had served as screenwriter for *The Guns of Navarone*. That film paid off its audience with everything expected in 1961 from a WWII epic: An all-star cast, action sequences in state-of-the-art color and enormous widescreen, a tragic romance, and an explosive ending in which the good-guys won the day. The great adventure had been so convincingly wrought that most viewers never realized the narrative was absolute fabrication. What no one could guess at that moment: *The Guns*

1

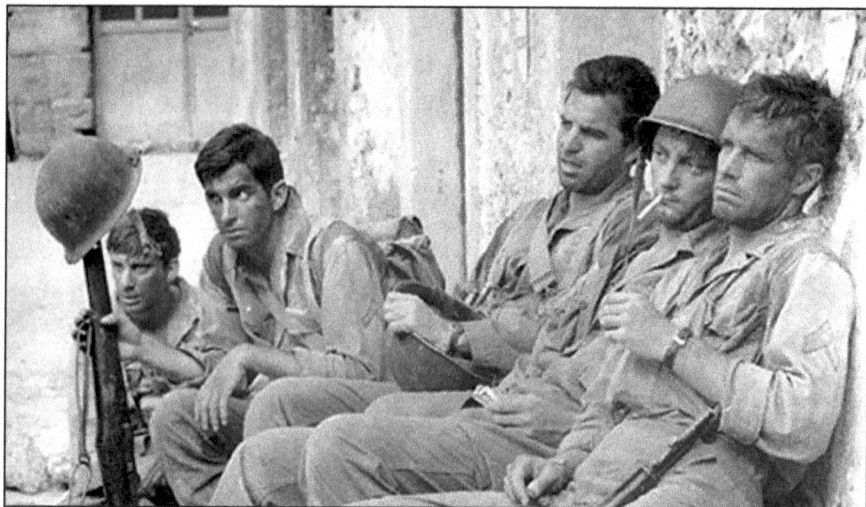

THE LAST GOOD WAR?: Infantrymen appear dejected, rather than uplifted, by their experience in combat as rendered in Carl Foreman's pessimistic *The Victors* (1963), a box-office flop that nonetheless set the pace for most combat films to follow.

of Navarone (and the equally enormous docu-drama *The Longest Day,* premiering early in 1962) marked the final times in which WWII stories would successfully be displayed as what author James Jones (*From Here to Eternity, The Thin Red Line,* etc.) hailed as "the last good war"; i.e., the final conflict which allowed Americans to believe that we were unquestionably the good-guys; therefore, anyone we opposed… evil incarnate.

Not that such films would never again be made. Yet when *Tora! Tora! Tora!* (directed by Robert Wise, and providing for Pearl Harbor what *T.L.D.* had for the Normandy Invasion) was released in 1970, audiences revealed little interest despite its considerable qualities. Simply, that sort of approach now seemed stodgy. Some seven years later, Richard Attenborough's massive, expensive, all-star *A Bridge Too Far* received a lukewarm reception, owing to the filmmaker's awkward attempt to mount an old-fashioned *Longest Day* style saga about what had been a disaster on the level of Custer's Last Stand.

To risk over-simplification, the nation (and the world) had changed. Radically so, necessitating that our movies alter as well. In 1969, no one could have foreseen that the latest Julie Andrews musical *Darling Lili* might flop, or that a low budget biker flick, *Easy Rider,* would appeal to the public. Still, none of this is meant to suggest that history could no longer 'work.' Indeed, the number one box-office hit of 1967 (domestic and international) had not been *Bonnie and Clyde* or *The Graduate* but the anti-heroic WWII film *The Dirty Dozen*.

As the 1970s began, and in contrast to the simultaneously distributed *Tora! Tora! Tora!*, *Patton* (directed by Hollywood veteran Franklin J. Schaffner; written by Francis Coppola who would shortly helm *The Godfather* (1972)), swept the Oscars and scored as a popular favorite. Mostly, that had to do with the irony inherent in its opening image of the title character (played by George C. Scott), dwarfed under an enormous red, white, and blue flag, allowing his rough and ready patriotic pronouncements to appear comedic owing to the sharp visual contrast. The film refused to portray Patton as either hero or villain, rather a three-dimensional person. How much more appropriate this seemed to a citizenry that had suffered through the still-ongoing war in Southeast Asia and intense, angry divisiveness on the home-front.

"Why are we in Vietnam?" many people asked. No one was able to offer a fully satisfying answer, then or now.

For here was an altogether different America. We could never go home again to the way we were before our communal innocence was shattered by a war that seemingly made no sense, Civil Rights activism which transformed from idealistic to violent, a youth movement that degenerated into a nationwide drug culture and, among other myriad elements, the continuing assassinations of admired political leaders. In this altered context, *The Godfather* announced that crime figures were not the crazed hoods featured on television's *The Untouchables* (1959-1963) but loving family men whose business happened to be bootlegging. Perhaps if the WWII biopic *MacArthur* (1977) had followed *Patton's* example, playing to a populace that had grown increasingly more sceptical of traditional morality following exposure to *Midnight Cowboy* (1969) and *Taxi Driver* (1976), this might have been a hit. Rather, the approach was conventional rah-rah hero worship, long out of style.

Not that there's necessarily anything wrong with such an approach. Only the public paid scant attention, while critics dismissed *MacArthur* as too conventional for ticket-buyers who had adjusted to a New Normal. For a WWII film to succeed, it had to feature a postmodern sensibility, the case with *Kelly's Heroes* (1970). Eventually, that film's star Clint Eastwood emerged as one of our significant directors. Often thought to be the most conservative filmdom personality since John Wayne, in truth C.E. offered a notably different sensibility. In 2006, he directed two WWII films back to back, avoiding in each any retro elements. Whereas Republic's *Sands of Iwo Jima* (1949; directed by Allan Dwan) had glorified the flag-raising atop Mt. Suribachi, Eastwood's *Flags of Our Fathers* revealed this to have been a staged photo-op followed by a bond selling tour. Wayne's film reduced the Japanese enemy to non-human clichés; Eastwood's *Letters from Iwo Jima* focused on the courage, decency, and humanity of the Japanese to whom that battle had been an Alamo-like last stand.

The point of Clint Eastwood's films on the subject: In war, every soldier is a victim. There are no victors.

The first film to ever press this point is the one eluded to earlier. *The Victors* (1963) followed a typical infantry squad from their first days in Italy through the Normandy invasion to the war's end and era of occupation. An ensemble piece, the immense anti-heroic epic proceeded as a series of vignettes, some inter-related, others singular in subject matter. All were shot in a grim black-and-white aesthetic that denied glorification, quite a departure from the popular film which *The Victors'* auteur had recently penned. A flag-waver directed by J. Lee Thompson, *The Guns of Navarone* focused on a special squad of carefully picked warriors who completed their mission against all odds; the two survivors (Gregory Peck and David Niven) laugh and joke as they safely swim away... despite the brutal deaths of all their companions.

How different *T.G.O.N.* appeared from Foreman's earlier, grittier WWII projects: *Home of the Brave* (1949; Mark Robson, dir.), about the difficult integration of a marine unit, and *The Men* (1950; Fred Zinnemann), depicting the tragic plight of amputee vets. Noteworthy: During the 1950s, Foreman had been blacklisted during Sen. Joseph McCarthy's era of Red Baiting; 'alleged' associations with leftish organizations destroyed many a gifted writer's reputation. Perhaps, then, *T.G.O.N.* served as Foreman's attempt to prove once and for all that he was as patriotic as anyone in Tinseltown. In this light, *The Victors* might be considered his mea culpa for the previous release. For here ordinary, average 'dogface' G.I.s pray less for communal victory than individual survival. Compared to the triumphant conclusion of *T.G.O.N.*, *T.V.* ends as a pair of Allies, one American and one Russian, kill one another in a drunken brawl over a minor misunderstanding in a dirty street.

Speaking to that work's box-office failure, co-star George Hamilton has argued that "it was way too dark"--not as a piece, mind you, but for that moment. Then again, *The Victors* may be thought of as the necessary lamb for sacrifice on our movie marketplace. As Hamilton added, the film surely "foreshadow(ed) the great paranoid movies of the sixties." Often, the artistic work that heralds an emergent movement is under-appreciated in its time and afterwards forgotten. How important to note, though, that a year and a half later, our Zeitgeist had caught up with this 'ahead of its time' movie. Few viewers 'got the joke' when the historical execution of Pvt. Eddie Slovik was depicted while "Have Yourself a Merry Little Christmas" (the Frank Sinatra version) played on The *Victors'* soundtrack. Yet when Stanley Kubrick opted for such ironic contrast between the image of a mid-air plane refuelling and "Try a Little Tenderness" (causing the mechanical process to resemble sex), audiences bellowed. By 1970, the producers of *Patton* were rightly assured that their own ironic opening would play to the vast mainstream.

Like all other movies on every imaginable subject and belonging to each existing genre, WWII films are not all 'of a piece.' Any one reflects the period during which it was made. The same holds true for, say, Westerns: In *They Died With Their Boots On* (1941), released even as America entered WWII, the 1876 Battle of the Little Big Horn is depicted as a glorious self-sacrifice on the order of Thermopylae Pass or, for that matter, Bataan; in *Little Big Man* (1970), which reached theatres at the height of our national paranoia over Vietnam, the 'massacre' is portrayed as a military failure.

So it goes with the subject of this encyclopedia, which hopefully explains why so much attention is granted to each film's distribution date, even when movies like *The Guns of Navarone* and *The Victors* are separated by only a few years *and* written by the same scribe. Considering the two together: How wonderful it would be to escape, in glorious color and with patriotic symphonic music on the soundtrack, from destruction of the enemy's big guns? *That* would be a WWII experience most Americans could enjoy.

Then again, who among us would want to lie face down in the mud of a Berlin alley, dying in gruesome black and white, accompanied only by the sounds of silence, with a sense of having accomplished absolutely nothing?

The point is: There is no single WWII with hundreds of different films about it. Each specific WWII movie creates its own self-contained experience. Uniforms and guns, the planes and tanks consistently look the same. Capturing the surface of events is easy enough to do with just a little homework. But the war itself--what it meant then, what it means now, what it will mean tomorrow and tomorrow and (to quote

Shakespeare) tomorrow--must be examined as a product of its time: The way in which we some artist envisions the ever-changing world of 'today,' then imposes that sensibility on a past that has long since become more mythic than historic in mists of time.

GOING AWAY, COMING HOME: In *Peyton Place*, young American men report for induction into the army and head off to camps by bus; in *The Best Years of Our Lives*, one such fellow (Harold Russell) returns with hooks in place of hands and must attempt to readjust.

Oceana: The Mediterranean and Aegean

ANGRY HILLS, THE (1959)

CREDITS:
Raymond Prods.; Robert Aldrich, dir.; Leon Uris (novel), A. I. Bezzerides, scr.; Raymond Stross, pro.; Richard R. Bennett, mus.; Stephen Dade, cin.; Peter Tanner, ed.; B&W; 2.35:1; 105 min.

CAST:
Robert Mitchum (*Mike Morrison*); Stanley Baker (Conrad); Peter Illing (*Leonides*); Gia Scala (*Eleftheria*); Theodore Bikel (*Dimitrios*); Sebastian Cabot (*Chesney*); Donald Wolfit (*Dr. Stergion*).

Rating: * 1/2
A war correspondent (Mitchum) is drawn into action when the Allies ask him to use his neutral status to enter Greece and seek out collaborators who betrayed resistance members. One of those rare cases in which a talented cast and crew were unable to produce a worthwhile film. Lacks suspense or intrigue despite on-location work in Athens. Slow, sluggish pace; utterly unrewarding.

ANZIO (1968)

CAST:

Columbia; Duilio Coletti, Edward Dmytryk, dir.; Wynford Vaughan-Thomas (book), Coletti, Harry Craig, Frank De Felitta, Giuseppe Mangione, scr.; Dino De Laurentiis, pro.; Riz Ortolani, mus.; Giuseppe Rotunno, cin.; Alberto Gallitti, Peter Taylor, ed.; C; 2.35:1; 117 min.

CAST:

Robert Mitchum (*Dick Ennis*), Peter Falk (*Rabinoff*); Robert Ryan (*Gen. Carson*); Earl Holliman (*Sgt. Stimmler*); Arthur Kennedy (*Gen. Lesley*); Reni Santoni (*Movie*).

Rating: * 1/2

HIT THE BEACH: Robert Mitchum leads his men on a deadly attack in the less than memorable 'quasi-epic' *Anzio.*

Awful faux epic does no justice to the well-known attack on western Italy. Early scenes promise a *Longest Day*–style docudrama. The operation's commander (Ryan) and the officer in charge (Kennedy) fail to reach a working agreement on whether troops should push inland swiftly or hunker down. The focus shifts to an Ernie Pyle–like correspondent (Mitchum) and a not-so-magnificent-seven ranger squad. Informed by a Vietnam-era antiwar attitude, which is undercut by an old-fashioned rah-rah theme song. Lacks the big battle scenes that make *The Battle of the Bulge* watchable on a comic-book level. The officers in charge were modeled after real-life generals Mark W. Clark and John P. Lucas.

BATTLE OF SAN PIETRO, (THE) (1945)

CREDITS:
US Army Pictorial Services; John Huston, dir.; Huston, scr.; Huston, Frank Capra, pro.; Dimitri Tiomkin, mus.; Huston, Julies Buck, cin.; Gene Fowler, Jr., ed.; B&W; 1.31:1; 32 min.

CAST:
Mark W. Clark (*himself/introductory comments*); John Huston (*narrator*).

Rating: *****

Writer-director Huston—assigned to the 143rd Regiment of the 36th Division—and his crew captured the combat (beginning on December 8 and continuing for ten days) at San Pietro Infine, halfway between Naples to the south and Rome in the north. The costly victory against the Nazis' "winter line" opened the way for an occupation of Rome. Huston had been asked to create a movie that would educate soldiers back home about what they would shortly experience. Accepting that at face value, he included images of Americans in death throes, the camera later lingering on body bags. The film was shelved after being viewed by army brass who thought it offered such an unsparing vision of war that soldiers who saw it might refuse to ship overseas. Gen. George Marshall felt otherwise: a strong dose of reality was needed as a sobering answer to romanticized war films. Objective in its imagery, Huston's subjective artistic vision

REALITY CHECK: John Huston's *The Battle of San Pietro* caught the true horror of war thanks to his on-location camera crew.

does shine through: as young bodies are buried, "Red River Valley" in the soundtrack creates continuity between these modern warriors and heroes of the American frontier.

BELL FOR ADANO, A (1945)

CREDITS:

20th Century Fox; Henry King, dir.; John Hersey (novel), Lamar Trotti, Norman Reilly Raine, scr.; Trotti, Louis D. Lighton, pro.; Alfred Newman, mus.; Joseph LaShelle, cin.; Barbara McLean, ed.; B&W; 1.37:1; 103 min.

CAST:

John Hodiak (*Maj. Victor P. Joppolo*); Gene Tierney (*Tina Tomasino*);

William Bendix (*Sgt. Roth*); Richard Conte (*Nicolo*); Harry Morgan (*Capt. Purvis*).

Rating: ****

As US troops move northward into Sicily, a fair-minded major is assigned to restore order in a small town. He does so by replacing the now-missing, once-beloved church bell. Mildly propagandistic pro-American democracy piece features none of the jingoism found in Hollywood films from a year earlier. The verisimilitude that novelist Hersey captured among citizens is effectively transferred to the screen for this charming heartwarmer. Tierney wasn't a wise choice to play an Italian peasant; the role all but begs for Anna Magnani or Silvana Mangano. Hodiak proves acceptable in a role that really ought to have gone to Henry Fonda.

BOLD AND THE BRAVE, THE (1956)

CREDITS:
Filmmakers Producing Co./RKO; Lewis R. Foster, dir.; Robert Lewin, scr.; Hal E. Chester, pro.; Herschel Burke Gilbert, mus.; Sam Leavitt, cin.; Aaron Stell, ed.; B&W; 2.00:1; 87 min.

CAST:
Wendell Corey (*Fairchild*); Don Taylor (*Preacher*); Mickey Rooney (*Dooley*); Nicole Maurey (*Fiamma*); John Smith (*Smith*); Race Gentry (*Hendricks*).

Rating: ****

During the Italian campaign, a rivalry develops between a cynical soldier (Taylor)—whose religious convictions cause him to condemn his squad members' weaknesses for wine, women, and song—and a quiet idealist (Corey). Rooney, as the company "character," received an Oscar nomination, as did the script. Over time, this film—once thought to be lost and rarely revived on TV—gained a reputation as an overlooked masterpiece. In truth, it is a solid B-budget war movie—nothing more,

MAN VS. MACHINE: An American hero (Don Taylor) attempts to take out a German tank single-handedly in *The Bold and the Brave.*

nothing less. Its impact might be stronger if Corey and Taylor, each miscast, had switched roles. Still, a mano-a-mano duel between a soldier and a Nazi tank shows cult director Foster's ability to breath rich cinematic life into a tightly budgeted project.

CAPTAIN CORELLI'S MANDOLIN (2001)

CREDITS:
Universal/Miramax; John Madden, dir.; Louis de Bernières (novel), Shawn Slovo, scr.; Tim Bevan, Mark Huffam, Kevin Loader, pro.; Stephen Warbeck, mus.; John Toll, cin.; Mick Audsley, ed.; C; 2.35:1; 131 min.

CAST:

Penelope Cruz (*Pelagia*); Nicolas Cage (*Corelli*); John Hurt (*Dr. Iannis*); Christian Bale (*Mandras*); Irene Pappas (*Drosoula*); Gerasimos Skiadaressis (*Stamatis*).

Rating: **

Italy's 33rd Infantry Division *Acqui* occupies a charming Greek island, Cephalonia. A protofeminist (Cruz) despises the situation but falls in love with an easygoing captain (Cage). Bernières's 1995 novel offers a memorable portrait of war and the people it affects via sweet-spirited romance. This reductive film jettisons any grand scope by focusing on the conventional chick-flick love affair. Gorgeously photographed, easy to enjoy on a lighthearted level. One excellent performance on view: the always amazing Pappas!

CITTA PRIGIONIERA, LA (1962)

CREDITS:

Joseph Antony, dir.; Eric Bercovici, Mark Brandel, Guy Elmer, scrs./prod; Mario Bonotti, Michael Billingsley, Raymond Poullon, ed; Leonida Barboni, cin.; Piero Picconi, mus.; Galatea Films/Lux-Maxima; 110 min. (director's cut); 87 min. (American release); B&W; 35 mm.

CAST:

David Niven (*Maj. Peter Whitfield*); Ben Gazzara (*Capt. George Stubbs*); Lea Massari (*Leila Mendores);* Martin Balsam *(Joseph Feinberg)*; Daniela Rocca (*Doushka*); Michael Craig (*Eliott);* Percy Herbert *(Reed).*

Rating: ** ½

Rugged American and English troops push toward Rome, meeting with Italian partisans (mainly beautiful women) to chase out the Nazis. But things go wrong; any among the seeming heroes may be a traitor. This little known (and perhaps lost) film resembles a less than successful combination of two concurrent Carl Foreman WWII epics, the entertaining blockbuster *(The) Guns of Navarone* and the grim message movie *The Victors*. Also released as *The Conquered City* and *The Captive City* (not to be confused with a far more famous 1952 crime film of that name). Eventually cut down to less than 90 min., with all complex characterization trimmed away, released as a minor action flick, double-billed with a horror movie at Drive Ins.

CONFORMISTA, IL, aka CONFORMIST, THE (1970)

CREDITS:
Mars Films/Marianne Prods./Paramount; Bernardo Bertolucci, dir.; Alberto Moravia (novel), Bertolucci, scr.; Maurizio Lodi-Fè, pro.; Georges Delerue, mus.; Vittorio Storaro, cin.; Franco Arcalli, ed.; C; 1.66:1; 111 min. (director's cut), 106 min. (original international cut).

CAST:
Jean-Louis Trintignant (*Marcello Clerici*); Stefania Sandrelli (*Giulia*); Gastone Moschin (*Manganiello*); Dominique Sanda (*Anna Quadri*); Enzo Tarascio (*Prof. Quadri*).

Ratings: ***** (director's cut)
**** 1/2 (original international cut)

Italian-French-West German coproduction dramatizes the rise of Fascism in Italy during the 1930s. The lead's name represents his outlook: a clerk, he's all but invisible, surviving day to day by determining which way the wind blows and going with it—politically, emotionally, sexually. Sensing he was born homosexual, Clerici represses his natural urges and marries, hoping to become another face in the crowd, anonymity ensuring existence. His ugly, empty situation contrasts with the era's colorful/gauche artwork, visually (rather than didactically) informing his ironic, tragic, darkly comic status. In his final test of loyalty to Nazi authority, Clerici must assassinate the professor who earlier taught him liberal values. One remarkably erotic moment: two beauties—Sandrelli and Sanda—dance what might be thought of as the First Tango in Rome

FIRST TANGO IN ROME: The Italian elite surrender to divine decadence and, with it, the Nazi value system in Bernardo Bertolucci's *The Conformist*.

during a quasi-lesbian interlude, prefiguring this filmmaker's more (in) famous work to come.

FIGHTER ATTACK (1953)

CREDITS:
Allied Artists; Lesley Selander, dir.; Shimon Wincelberg, scr.; William A. Calihan, Jr., pro.; Marlin Skiles, mus.; Harry Neumann, cin.; Stanley Rabjohn, ed.; C; 1.37:1; 80 min.

CAST:
Sterling Hayden (*Steve*); J. Carroll Naish (*Bruno*); Joy Page (*Nina*); Kenneth Tobey (*George*); Arthur Caruso (*Aldo*); Frank DeKova (*Benedetto*).

Rating: **

An American pilot (Hayden), flying his final mission over Italy, is shot down. Partisans, led by a gorgeous woman (Joy), ensure his survival and escape. Naish chews the scenery as a bold priest. The last film shot in Cinecolor, a dreadful process with painfully washed-out hues.

5 PER L'INFERNO, aka FIVE FOR HELL (1969)

CREDITS:
Film Star; Gianfranco Parolini, dir.; Sergio Garrone, Renato Izzo, Gianfranco Parolini, scr.; Aldo Addobbati, Paolo Moffa, pro.; Elsio (Vasco) Mancuso, mus.; Sandro Mancori, cin.; Giuseppe Bellecca, ed.; C; 2.35:1; 95 min.

CAST:
John (Gianni) Garko (*Lt. Glenn Hoffmann*); Klaus Kinski (*Col. Hans Mueller*); Aldo Canti, aka Nick Jordan (*Nick Amadori*); Margaret Lee (*Helga Richter*).

Rating: **
Yet another raunchy/goofball team-action flick shot in the wake of *The Dirty Dozen*'s stunning success. The leader (Garko) and his goofy volunteers trek behind enemy lines to steal a cache of Nazi secrets. High point: Kinski, wonderfully mad as an SS officer. A better cast might have transformed the lovable lunatics into something special. A cut above the ordinary spaghetti actioner, explaining why it did receive an international release.

FORCE OF ARMS (1951)

CREDITS:
Warner Bros.; Michael Curtiz, dir.; Orin Jannings, Richard Tregaskis, scr.; Anthony Veiller, pro.; Max Steiner, mus.; Ted D. McCord, cin.; Owen Marks, ed.; B&W; 1.37:1; 99 min.

CAST:
William Holden (*Sgt. Joe Peterson*); Nancy Olson (*Lt. Eleanor Mackay*); Frank Lovejoy (*Maj. Blackford*); Gene Evans (*Smiley McFee*); Dick Wesson (*Kleiner*).

Rating: ** 1/2

A tough American sergeant serving in the 36th Division distinguishes himself during the 1943 Battle of San Pietro. On leave, he meets and falls in love with a WAC lieutenant. Back at the front, his abilities are tempered by memories of the woman. Inspired by Hemingway's WWI classic *A Farewell to Arms*, the result is a typical studio program picture, released as the top half of a double bill. This, despite the impressive star and world-class director. Routine, ordinary, dull.

GENERAL DELLA ROVERE (1959)

CREDITS:
Zebra Film; Roberto Rossellini, dir.; Indro Montanelli (novel), Rossellini, Sergio Amidei, Diego Fabbri, scr.; Alain Poiré, pro.; Renzo Rossellini, mus.; Carlo Carlini, cin.; Cesare Cavagna, Anna Maria Montanari, ed.; B&W; 1.66:1; 132 min. (director's cut), 129 min. (US theatrical print).

CAST:
Vittorio De Sica (*Bardone/Grimaldi*); Hannes Messemer (*Col. Mueller*); Vittorio Caprioli (*Aristide Banchelli*); Mary Greco (*Vera*); Sandra Milo (*Olga*); Giovanna Ralli (*Valeria*).

Ratings: ***** (director's cut)
**** 1/2 (US theatrical)

A petty thief scams Italy's most vulnerable citizens. Sad people whose relatives have been taken away by Nazis will desperately pay anyone who claims to be able to help. The Germans take him into custody; the thief is a double for a top-ranking Italian officer. If he will impersonate that man, employing his new identity to join Milan's Partisans, he'll be able to learn the identity of the resistance's leader and report back. Something unexpected occurs. Once the thief dons the uniform, he realizes this is the kind of person he'd always wanted to be. Against his better judgment, he turns the tables on the Reich. As always, Rossellini's subject is the human face, sometimes as a mask, at other moments a source of revelation. De Sica captures and crystalizes every human nuance, reaction, and gesture.

GUERRA CONTINUA, LA, aka *WARRIORS 5* (1962)

CREDITS:
American International Pictures (US); Leopoldo Savona, dir.; Gino De Santis, Ugo Pirro, Leopoldo Savona, scr.; Fulvio Lucisano, pro.; Les Baxter, Ronald Stein, mus. (US); Claudio Racca, cin.; Gabriele Varriale, ed.; B&W; 84 min. (US).

CAST:
Jack Palance (*Jack*); Giovanna Ralli (*Italia*); Franco Balducci (*Conti*); Miha Baloh (*Sansone*); Guido Bertone (*Carlo*); Folco Lulli (*Marzi*); Serge Reggiani (*Libero*).

Rating: **

A French-funded/Italian-lensed action flick, picked up for distribution in America (slightly retooled for the drive-in circuit) by the now-famous exploitation company owing to its American "star." One paratrooper survives a massive drop, attempting to knock out a bridge all by himself, until a motley group of anti-Mussolini Partisans and a gorgeous pick-up girl join him. Minor league. Sparked by some well-staged battle sequences. European titles: *La Guerra Continua* (Italy), *La Derriere Attack* (France).

GUNS OF NAVARONE, THE (1961)

CREDITS:
Columbia; J. Lee Thompson, Alexander Mackendrick, dir.; Alistair MacLean (novel), Carl Foreman, scr.; Foreman, pro.; Dimitri Tiomkin, mus.; Oswald Morris, cin.; Alan Osbiston, ed.; C; 2.35:1; 157 min.

CAST:
Gregory Peck (*Capt. Mallory*); David Niven (*Cpl. Miller*); Anthony Quinn (*Andrea Stavros*); Stanley Baker (*Butcher Brown*); Anthony Quayle (*Maj. Franklin*); James Darren (*Spyros*); Irene Papas (*Maria*); Gia Scala (*Anna*); James Robertson Justice (*Commodore Jensen/Narrator*).

Rating: *****

Six volunteers—including a battle-seasoned commando (Peck), a Greek resistance fighter (Quinn), and an explosives expert (Niven)—manage a daring night landing by sea on a Greek island. Then, they traverse a high cliff to knock out German artillery. A film that redefined WWII movies for a new decade, *Navarone* features an immense screen image, impactful stereo sound, a strong female role (Papas), a duplicitous beauty (Scala) worthy of the era's upcoming Bond films, and a young pop star (Darren) to attract teenagers. It also involves a complicated espionage plot with large-scale action, an uneasy relationship between the three leads (and a traitor in their midst), heightened realism in terms of violence, ticking-clock suspense, a rousing symphonic score, and a wisp of the cynicism that would take hold during that decade. If *Navarone* seems less impressive today, it's because it has been imitated so often. Note: there never were guns on Navarone as Navarone does not exist.

HELL RAIDERS (1968)

CREDITS:
Azalea Pictures; Larry Buchanan, dir.; Buchanan, Lou Rusoff, scr.; Buchanan, Edwin Tobolowsky, pro.; Robert C. Jessup, cin.; James Ferguson, ed.; B&W/C; 1.33:1; 80 min.

THE GREATEST MISSION THAT NEVER WAS: An intrepid band of heroes set out to destroy two immense enemy cannons in The *Guns of Navarone*; in truth, no such artillery ever existed.

CAST:

John Agar (*Maj. Ronald Paxton*); Richard Webb (*Lieutenant*); Joan Huntington (*Laura Grant*); Bill Thurman (*Tex*); Annabelle Weenick (*Pretty Girl*).

Rating: *

Worthless remake of *Suicide Battalion* (not great to begin with), reset in Italy: GIs are assigned to locate and destroy important papers before the Germans find them. Shot in color in and around Dallas. Preceded by a ten-minute B&W documentary about the need for the US Air Force to make dangerous daytime bombing runs—which has nothing whatsoever to do with the film that follows!

HORNETS' NEST (1970)

CREDITS:

Triangle Prods./Delphus; Phil Karlson, Franco Cirino, dir.; S. S. Schweitzer, Stanley Colbert, scr.; Stanley S. Canter, pro.; Ennio Morricone, mus.; Gábor Pogány, cin.; Terry Williams, ed.; C; 1.85:1; 110 min.

CAST:

Rock Hudson (*Turner*); Sylva Koscina (*Bianca*); Sergio Fantoni (*Von Hecht*); Giacomo Rossi-Stuart (*Schwalberg*); Jacques Sernas (*Maj. Taussig*); Mark Colleano (*Aldo*).

Rating: *** 1/2

An American unit parachutes into occupied Italy to blow up a dam. The survivor is hidden in nearby caves by starving kids who wish to serve as Partisans. Production values are top drawer; expensive-looking battle sequences will please action fans. The script is at best so-so, including an unnecessary sequence in which the hero suddenly rapes a female doctor. Were it not for this and some nasty language, *Hornet's Nest* might have been a solid WWII film for adults to watch with their kids.

LAST NOTE, THE (2017)

CREDITS:
TakovisidFilm; Pantelis Voulgaris, dir.; Voulgaris, Ionna Karystiani, scrs.; Yiannis Takovidis, pro.; C; Alexander Voulgaris, mus.; Simos Sarketzis, cin.; Takis Giannopoulos, ed.; 117 min.

CAST:
Andreas Konstantinou (*Napoleon Soukatzidis*); Andre Hennicke (*Karl*); Melia Kreiling (*Hara Lioudaki*); Tasos Dimas *(Kostas);* Aineias Tsamatis (*Christos*); Vassilis Koukalani (*Sarantos*); Loukas Kyriazis *(Kovats)*; Lefteris Lambrakis *(Chaidari).*

RATING: ****

During the totalitarian rein of Metaxas over Greece between 1936-1941, communists were regularly rounded up by a Gestapo- like police force and ensconsed in Kaisariani prison camp. In 1944, occupying German forces were outraged at an ambush by Resistance forces. To teach the nation a lesson, the S.S. removed 200 of the prisoners and at Chaidari executed all of them. The day--May 1--was chosen ironically on the part of Nazis, who thought it appropriate to murder these working class rebels on labor day. Voulgaris' film pays remarkable attention to realistic details and employs the fact-based story to rally today's democratic Greeks. Impressively mounted though truly a grueling experience for audiences as we are spared absolutely nothing as to the butchery. At moments, the writing verges on soap-opera yet the overall impact is certainly impressive.

MALTA STORY, (THE) (1953)

CREDITS:
Arthur Rank Film; Brian Desmond Hurst, dir.; Hugh P. Lloyd (book), William Fairchild, Nigel Balchin, scr.; Peter De Sarigny, pro.; William Alwyn, mus.; Robert Krasker, cin.; Michael Gordon, ed.; B&W; 1.37:1; 103 min. (UK), 97 min. (US).

CAST:

Alec Guinness (*Flight Lt. Peter Ross*); Jack Hawkins (*Air CO Frank*); Anthony Steel (*Wing Cmdr. Bartlett*); Muriel Pavlow (*Maria Gonzar*); Renée Asherson (*Joan*); Hugh Burden (*Eden*); Nigel Stock (*Ricardi*).

Ratings: *** 1/2 (UK cut)
*** (US cut)

Located less than sixty miles from the Sicilian coast, Malta offers a strategic base coveted by the Allied and Axis powers. A British officer (Guinness) is assigned to aerial reconnaissance. This becomes complicated when he meets a local woman (Pavlow) and romance takes precedence. The love story is subpar, bringing the film down a notch from its otherwise solid depiction of daily bombing raids. Documentary footage of the SS *Ohio's* historic attempt to break through enemy fire and keep the population from starving adds authenticity. Unfortunately, Hurst has his cast perform in an off-putting way, making emotional involvement difficult.

MIRACLE AT ST. ANNA (2008)

CREDITS:

Touchstone/40 Acres and a Mule; Spike Lee, dir.; James McBride (novel), scr.; Lee, Roberto Cicutto, Luigi Musini, pro.; Terence Blanchard, mus.; Matthew Libatique, cin.; Barry Alexander Brown, ed.; C; 2.35:1; 160 min.

CAST:

Derek Luke (*Sgt. Aubrey Stamps*); Michael Ealy (*Bishop* Cummings); Laz Alonso (*Cpl. Hector Negron*); Omar Benson Miller (*Sam Train*); Pierfrancesco Favino (*Peppi/"The Butterfly"*); John Leguizamo (*Enrico*), D. B. Sweeney (Col. *Driscoll*).

Rating: *

Prior to Christmas 1983, a distraught postal worker (Alonso) pulls a gun and shoots a customer. The killing was motivated by an event from four decades earlier: he was among a quartet of African American members of

THE AFRICAN AMERICAN SOLDIER IN ACTION!: Spike Lee mounted what he hoped would serve as a tribute to our black fighting men in *Miracle of St. Ana.*

the "Buffalo Brigade" serving in Tuscany, surrounded in Colognora by a nonarticlate child who may be Jesus, a beautiful feminist, Partisans, and Mussolini diehards. A tribute to the 92nd Division's action at the Serchio River was overdue. However, this maudlin, pretentious, and by the end laugh-out-loud silly (not to mention long!) would-be epic hardly serves that purpose. Most offensive: though African American himself, director Lee reduces the black characters to racial stereotypes.

NIGHT AMBUSH, aka *ILL MET BY MOONLIGHT* (1958)

CREDITS:

Rank/Vega Film; Michael Powell, Emeric Pressburger, dir.; W. Stanley Moss (book), Powell, Pressburger, scr.; Powell, Pressburger, pro.; Mikis Theodorakis, mus.; Christopher Challis, cin.; Arthur Stevens, ed.; B&W; 1.85:1; 93 min.

CAST:

Dirk Bogarde (*Maj. Patrick Leigh Fermor/Philedem*); Marius Goring (*Maj. Gen. Kreipe*); David Oxley (*Capt. W. Stanley Moss*); Cyril Cusack (*Sandy*); Michael Gough (*Zoidakis*); Christopher Lee (*Nazi*).

Rating: **** 1/2

In occupied Crete, a Partisan network stretches across the island, doing damage to the enemy. A Brit special agent (Bogarde) arrives with an ambitious plan: kidnap the ranking general (Goring) from under the noses of his guards (along with his Mercedes), drive the Nazi to the coast, and spirit him off to Cairo. Solid storytelling with a hint of droll English humor underlining the thrills, suspense, and unexpected plot turns, all apparently fact based. Underplayed but potent is the cat-and-mouse game that develops between the Brit and the German. The Powell-Pressburger team convinces us we're watching a cinematic tour of Crete, enhanced by evocative folk music, though the film was shot at Pinewood Studios (UK) and carefully chosen locations in the Alpes-Maritimes in France and Italy.

NOTTE DI SAN LORENZO, LA, aka *NIGHT OF THE SHOOTING STARS, THE* (1982)

CREDITS:

RAI/UA Classics; Paolo Taviani, Vittorio Taviani, dir.; Taviani brothers, Giuliani G. De Negri, Tonino Guerra, scr.; De Negri, pro.; Nicola Piovani, mus.; Franco Di Giacomo, cin.; Roberto Perpignani, ed.; C; 1.66:1; 105 min.

CAST:

Omero Antonutti (*Galvano*); Margarita Lozano (*Concetta*); Claudio Bigagli (*Corrado*); Miriam Guidelli (*Belindia*); Massimo Bonetti (*Nicola*); Enrica Maria Modugno (*Mara*).

Rating: **** 1/2

Germans occupy Tuscany, imposing Nazism on simple people in small villages. The Americans finally advance, but the horrors aren't over yet. Word gets out that the rustic folk are to congregate in a church, the Nazis insisting that this building alone will not be bombed. The citizens must decide for themselves: Do as the fascists command, or scatter and help the oncoming liberators? Influenced by Fellini's distinct style, the Taviani brothers combine ultrarealism with bizarre fantasy. Masterful creation of an eerie mood and wonderfully developed characters. Ironically, the 1944 bombing of San Miniato's church, which inspired the script, was not (as believed when the film was made) done by Nazis; rather, it was mistakenly carried out by the Americans. Winner of the Special Jury Prize at Cannes.

PAISÀ (1946)

CREDITS:
Metro-Goldwyn-Mayer; Roberto Rossellini, dir.; Sergio Amidei, Klaus Mann, Federico Fellini, Marcello Pagliero, Alfred Hayes, Vasco Pratolini (stories), Rossellini, Rod E. Geiger, scr.; Geiger, Rossellini, Mario Conti, pro.; Renzo Rossellini, mus.; Otello Martelli, cin.; Eraldo Da Roma, ed.; B&W; 1.37:1; 134 min. (director's cut), 120 min. (US print).

CAST:
Carmela Sazio (*Carmela*); Robert Van Loon (*Joe*); Dots Johnson (*MP*); Alfonsino Pasca (*Pasquale*); Maria Michi (*Francesca*); Gar Moore (*Fred*); Harriet Medin (*Harriet*); Giulietta Masina (*Young Woman*).

Ratings: **** 1/2 (director's cut)
**** (US cut)

July 10, 1943: the American fleet fires on German-held positions along Sicily's southern tip. Shortly after, troops land and, for ten months, travel north past Naples to Rome and on to Venice. Rossellini's sweeping, intimate epic is less concerned with great battles—which are depicted—than with human stories. Each episode was penned by a different writer; all offer variations on tragic failures to communicate. More like anecdotes than full stories, several deal with romantic liaisons, and none offer a happy ending. The most endearing tale involves several Catholic priests at an isolated monastery who invite American chaplains to dinner only to realize one is a rabbi. The spontaneous, improvised, realistic style conceals the fact that the movie was carefully scripted. Even what might appear to be liabilities in a Hollywood picture—amateurish acting, awkward dialogue—add to a sense of authenticity.

PIGEON THAT TOOK ROME, THE (1962)

CREDITS:
Llenoc Pictures/Paramount; Melville Shavelson, dir.; Donald Downes (novel), Shavelson, scr.; Shavelson, pro.; Alessandro Cicognini, mus.; Daniel L. Fapp, cin.; Frank Bracht, ed.; B&W; 2.35:1; 103 min.

CAST:
Charlton Heston (*Capt. Paul MacDougall*); Elsa Martinelli (*Antonella Massimo*); Harry Guardino (*Sgt. Contini*); Salvatore Baccaloni (*Ciccio Massimo*); Gabriella Pallotta (*Rosalba*); Brian Donlevy (*Col. Harrington*).

Rating: *

Bumbling soldiers turned spies (Heston, Guardino) move in with an Italian family and, from the apartment, send carrier pigeons to headquarters. They pair off with two daughters (Martinelli, Pallotta) to the chagrin of their father (Baccaloni). A bust: supposed to be funny and most decidedly isn't. Guardino is fine as a horny Italian American, though the part smacks of ethnic caricaturing. Heston—so perfect for epic drama—has no idea how to deliver a funny line. Long out of print; difficult to locate.

QUICK AND THE DEAD, THE (1963)

CREDITS:
Manson Corp./Beckman Film; Robert Totten, dir.; Totten, Sheila Lynch, scr.; Sal Altonian, pro.; Jaimie Mendoza-Nava, mus.; John Arthur Morrill,

cin.; Marvin Walowitz, ed.; B&W; 1.37:1; 92 min.

CAST:
Larry D. Mann (*Parker*); Victor French (*Milo Riley*); John Cedar (*Lt. Rogers*); James Almanzar (*Giorgio*); Majel Barrett (*Teresa*); Louis Massad (*Donatelli*).

Rating: *

Caught behind enemy lines, American soldiers attempt to fight their way back to safety in the company of two women (pro-Allies Partisans). The premise was hoary even when John Ford used it for *The Lost Patrol* (1934) and has been endlessly dragged out ever since (*Sahara, Bataan*). A low-budget item that makes Corman's WWII films from the late fifties and early sixties appear classy. Rarely dull. Barrett would appear in *Star Trek* and marry Gene Roddenberry.

RAPPRESAGLIA, aka MASSACRE IN ROME (1973)

CREDITS:
Surf Film; George (Pan) Cosmatos, dir.; Robert Katz (book), Cosmatos, Fabio Mauri, Lucio De Cara, scr.; Philip M. Breen, Carlo Ponti, Marcello D'Amico, pro.; Ennio Morricone, mus.; Marcello Gatti, cin.; Françoise Bonnot, Roberto Silvi, ed.; C; 1.66:1; 103 min.

CAST:
Richard Burton (*Lt. Col. Herbert Kappler*); Marcello Mastroianni (*Father Pietro Antonelli*); Leo McKern (*Gen. Kurt Maelzer*); John Steiner (*Dollmann*).

Rating: ****

Burton delivers one of his best later performances as the occupying German officer who gave the order that, following a Partisan attack on the SS, ten randomly picked Roman citizens must be executed for each

German life lost. A bold priest (Mastroianni) hurries about the city, as the clock ticks closer to the terrible moment, trying to prevent the coming holocaust. Exciting on the level of suspense and moving on the emotional plane, this international coproduction relates a true tale of horror by daylight. Kappler would later be played by Christopher Plummer in a 1983 TV movie *The Scarlet and the Black*. The "300 lives for 30" command is faithfully dramatized here.

STORY OF GI JOE, THE (1945)

CREDITS:
United Artists; William A. Wellman, dir.; Ernie Pyle (books), Guy Endore, Leopold Atlas, Philip Stevenson, scr.; Lester Cowan, pro.; Louis Applebaum, mus.; Russell Metty, cin.; Albrecht Joseph, ed.; B&W; 1.37:1; 108 min.

CAST:
Burgess Meredith (*Ernie Pyle*); Robert Mitchum (*Lt. Walker*); Freddie Steele (*Sgt. Warnicki*); Wally Cassell (*Pvt. Dondaro*); Jimmy Lloyd (*Spencer*); John R. Reilly (*Murphy*).

Rating: *****

The everyday life of a dogface foot soldier, as seen through the eyes of Scripps-Howard news correspondent Ernie Pyle (1900–1945), played to perfection by Meredith. Authentic to the point of being excruciating. Like the equally monumental *A Walk in the Sun*, this was shot during the final days of the war, allowing for a less patriotic, grittier, unromanticized approach. One sequence in which a stressed soldier hears the voice of his child on a record will haunt you for the rest of your life. Reconstructed battle scenes will leave you convinced they are newsreel footage. Individual gag lines are lifted directly (no credit given) from Bill Mauldin's *Up Front* cartoons. The outfit is the C Company, 18th Infantry, but the movie is about every ordinary guy who ever put on a uniform in this or any other war.

STRATEGIA DEL RAGNO, aka *SPIDER'S STRATAGEM, THE* (1970)

CREDITS:

RAI/Red Film; Bernardo Bertolucci, dir.; Jorge Luis Borges (story), Bertolucci, Eduardo de Gregorio, Marilù Parolini, scr.; Giovanni Bertolucci, pro.; Franco Di Giacomo, Vittorio Storaro, cin.; Roberto Perpignani, ed.; C; 1.37:1; 100 min.

CAST:

Giulio Brogi (*Athos Magnani, elder and junior*); Alida Valli (*Draifa*); Pippo Campanini (*Gaibazzi*); Tino Scotti (*Costa*); Franco Giovanelli (*Rasori*).

Rating: **** 1/2

"You can't go home again," Thomas Wolfe wrote. Either it will have changed beyond recognition or your subjective memories will not jibe with objective reality. A successful white-collar Italian (Brogi) learns that the hard way. Thirty-five years after his father (Brogi) was murdered in a small village for having led Partisans, this spitting image of his deceased dad embarks on a memory trip to the provinces. Rather than welcome him with open arms, the villagers turn away, causing him to become obsessed with understanding why and learning what really happened in the past. The way Storaro captures the natural and man-made beauties of the Po Valley contrasts vividly with the smallness and smugness of its people. An Italian variation on John Ford's *The Man Who Shot Liberty Valance* (1962): "When the legend becomes a fact, print the legend." But should we? In the finale, viewers realize the film we thought we were watching is not the film we were watching. Derived from Borges's exquisite "Tema del Traidor y del Héroe."

TANK COMMANDOS (1959)

CREDITS:

American International Pictures; Burt Topper, dir.; Topper, scr.; Topper, pro.; Ronald Stein, mus.; John M. Nickolaus, Jr., cin.; Asa Boyd Clark, ed.;

35 mm; B&W; 79 min.

CAST:
Donato Farretta (*Diano*); Robert Barron (*Lt. Blaine*); Maggie Lawrence (*Jean*); Wally Campo (*Pvt. Lazzotti*); Maria Monay (*Italian Woman*); Carmen D'Antonio (*Teresa*).

Rating: * 1/2

Should've been called "*Anti*-Tank Commandos." With the help of an Italian youth (Farretta), a US demolitions team blows up an underwater bridge which the Germans had been using to move armored equipment. A whiz kid at grim B&W low-budget fare, Topper keeps the action rolling. Pathetic script bogs down as soldiers romance an American nurse (Lawrence) and a local (Monay), who look like a pair of fashion models. The depiction of a child's death, intended as realism, is in terrible taste.

THEY WHO DARE (1954)

CREDITS:
British Lion/Mayflower Pictures/Allied Artists; Lewis Milestone, dir.; Robert Westerby, scr.; Aubrey Baring, Maxwell Setton, pro.; Robert Gill, mus.; Wilkie Cooper, cin.; Vladimir Sagovsky, ed.; C; 1.37:1; 107 min.

CAST:
Dirk Bogarde (*Lt. David Graham*); Denholm Elliott (*Corcoran*); Akim Tamiroff (*Capt. George One*); Gérard Oury (*Capt. George Two*); Lisa Gastoni (*George II's Girlfriend*); Kay Callard (*Nightclub Singer*).

Rating: ** 1/2

On Rhodes, German and Italian forces set up an air base and rain down bombs on Egypt. English commandos and Greek patriots slip into the compound to blow it up. Based on an incident that occurred in the Dodecanese islands. Familiar material. The producers thought color might increase interest, though it actually detracts from the grim sensibility. Elliott has an early opportunity to reveal his great gifts. WWII buffs will appreciate the real Savoia-Marchetti SM.79 bombers, a rare sight on-screen. A letdown from the director of *All Quiet on the Western Front* and *A Walk in the Sun!*

TIME OF DESTINY, A (1988)

CREDITS:
Alive Films; Gregory Nava, dir.; Nava, Anna Thomas, scr.; Thomas, pro.; Ennio Morricone, mus.; James Glennon, cin.; Betsy Blankett Milicevic, ed.; C; 118 min.

CAST:
William Hurt (*Martin Larraneta*); Timothy Hutton (*Jack*); Melissa Leo (*Josie Larraneta*); Francisco Rabal (*Jorge*); Concha Hidalgo (*Sebastiana*); Stockard Channing (*Margaret*).

Rating: *

Based on the source material that inspired Verdi's opera *La Forza del Destino* (1862), this pretentious mess concerns a fiery Basque (Hurt) obsessed with murdering the man (Hutton) who eloped with his young sister. The motive: that event led to the accidental death of the siblings' father. A miracle on the battlefield turns them into friends, though as the war's end approaches, hostility returns. Utterly unconvincing.

UP FRONT (1951)

CREDITS:
Universal; Alexander Hall, dir.; Bill Mauldin (book), Stanley Roberts, Ring Lardner, Jr., scr.; Leonard Goldstein, pro.; Joseph Gershenson, mus.; Russell Metty, cin.; Milton Carruth, ed.; B&W; 1.37:1; 92 min.

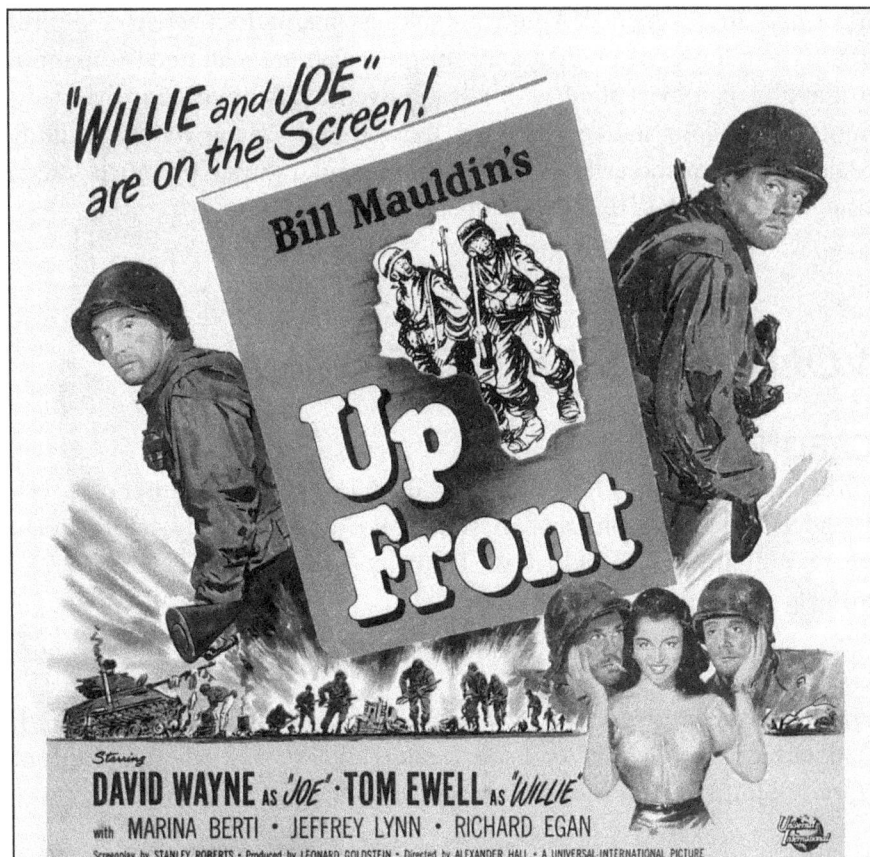

IN TRIBUTE TO MR. MAULDIN: David Wayne and Tom Ewell incarnate the cartoon characters 'Willie and Joe' in *Up Front*.

CAST:

David Wayne (*Joe*); Tom Ewell (*Willie*); Marina Berti (*Emi Rosso*); Jeffrey Lynn (*Capt. Ralph Johnson*); Richard Egan (*Capa*); Silvio Minciotti (*Poppa Rosso*).

Rating: *** 1/2

"I can't get no lower, Joe," Willie sighs. "Me buttons is in da way." That line, spoken by one dogface to another as enemy rockets explode, was accompanied in *Yank* magazine by an indelible sketch of guys hoping to make it through the night. Bill Mauldin (1921–2003), an infantryman with the 45th Division, created this cartoon duo. Their appearances in

Stars and Stripes helped American soldiers maintain a sense of humor about their desperate plight. Sadly, the great gags are scattered throughout a maudlin B movie filled with silly, conventional hijinks involving yet another gorgeous Italian girl (Berti). Ewell and Wayne vividly embody Mauldin's down-to-earth (in every sense) regular guys. Too much screen time wasted on WWII Hollywood clichés.

VON RYAN'S EXPRESS (1965)

CREDITS:
20th Century Fox; Mark Robson, dir.; David Westheimer (novel), Wendell Mayes, Joseph Landon, scr.; Saul David, pro.; Jerry Goldsmith, mus.; William H. Daniels, cin.; Dorothy Spencer, ed.; C; 2.35:1; 117 min.

CAST:
Frank Sinatra (*Col. Joseph L. Ryan*); Trevor Howard (*Maj. Eric Fincham*); Raffaella Carrà (*Gabriella*); Brad Dexter (*Sgt. Bostick*); Sergio Fantoni (*Oriani*); John Leyton (*Orde*); Edward Mulhare (*Capt. Costanzo*).

Rating: ****

A downed American pilot (Sinatra) finds himself the ranking officer in an Italian prison camp. Most are members of a crack Brit outfit, the 9th Fusiliers, led by a hard-liner (Howard). The English are offended by their new commander, whom they "heil" as a dictator. When Italy surrenders, a sympathetic Axis officer (Fantoni) offers to help them steal a train and escape. Appealing, well-paced action entertainment only if you can buy the Italian American star as a blustery Irishman. Supporting cast is superb, suspense ploys work, battle sequences are well staged. Surface entertainment, compared to the similarly structured if more ambitious *The Train*. The most harrowing moment: our hero's need to shoot down a gorgeous girl (Carrà)—something that almost occurred in *The Guns of Navarone*.

CAUGHT!: Allied soldiers are herded into freight cars in *Von Ryan's Express,* though an unlikely anti-hero (Frank Sinatra, off-screen) will shortly lead a great escape.

WALK IN THE SUN, A (1945)

CREDITS:

Superior Pictures; Lewis Milestone, dir.; Harry Brown (novel), Robert Rossen, scr.; Milestone, Samuel Bronston, pro.; Freddie Rich, mus.; Russell Harlan, cin.; Duncan Mansfield, ed.; B&W; 1.37:1; 117 min.

TOWARD A MORE REALISTIC COMBAT FILM: At war's end, films about the conflict became less propagandistic, more grimly honest: Robert Mitchum in *The Story of G.I. Joe;* a machine gun squad takes on an occupied farmhouse in *A Walk in the Sun.*

CAST:

Dana Andrews (*Sgt. Bill Tyne*); Richard Conte (*Rivera*); John Ireland (*Windy Craven*); Lloyd Bridges (*Ward*); George Tyne (*Friedman*); Sterling Holloway (*McWilliams*); Norman Lloyd (*Archimbeau*); Huntz Hall (*Carraway*); George Offerman, Jr. (*Tinker*); Burgess Meredith (*Narrator*).

Rating: *****

The 1943 predawn sea-to-land assault on the Salerno beachhead includes the fifty-three men of the Lee Platoon, Texas Division. Their orders: proceed inland and capture a farmhouse that might be in enemy hands. Their young lieutenant is killed, and command passes to an ordinary Joe (Andrews). One of the first such films to avoid heroics and propaganda, showing how everyday people rose to the occasion and performed heroically without realizing it. The iambic pentameter dialogue and leftish politics are a holdover from 1930s-style 'group theatre.' The score features what were then called Negro spirituals and authentic folk songs. Ties with *Story of GI Joe*, released the same year, as the *Iliad* of its time. Not one character is a stereotype; each comes to vivid life before our eyes. The manner in which a private (Ireland) self-censors his mental letters to his sister serves as a central metaphor for what occurs in combat and what those at home can handle.

WHAT DID YOU DO IN THE WAR, DADDY? (1966)

CREDITS:

Mirisch Corporation; Blake Edwards, dir.; Edwards, William Peter Blatty, Maurice Richlin, scr.; Edwards, Dick Crockett, Owen Crump, pro.; Henry Mancini, mus.; Philip H. Lathrop, cin.; Ralph E. Winters, ed.; C; 2.35:1; 116 min.

CAST:

James Coburn (*Lt. Christian*); Dick Shawn (*Capt. Lionel Cash*); Sergio Fantoni (*Capt. Oppo*); Giovanna Ralli (*Gina*); Aldo Ray (*Rizzo*); Harry Morgan (*Pott*); Carroll O'Connor (*Gen. Bolt*).

Rating: **

Italian troops holding a strategically located village agree to surrender if they can celebrate a local feast. When an information officer (Morgan) shows up, the commanding officers (Shawn, Fantoni) decide they must pretend to be fighting. Meanwhile, a US lieutenant (Coburn) and the local beauty (Ralli) could cause the faux combat to become real. Lukewarm attempt by Edwards to create a bridge between the easygoing service comedies of the late 1950s and the hard-edged ones (*MASH*) to follow. Wannabe black comedy defeats itself by being shot in bright color. The situation and gags sound funnier when described than they actually come off on-screen.

WHICH WAY TO THE FRONT? (1970)

CREDITS:
Warner Bros.; Jerry Lewis, dir.; Gerald Gardner, Dee Caruso, Dick Miller, scr.; Lewis, pro.; Lou Brown, Pete King, mus.; W. Wallace Kelley, cin.; Russel Wiles, ed.; C; 1.85:1; 96 min.

CAST:
Jerry Lewis (*Brendan Byers/Field Marshal Kesselring*); Jan Murray (*Sid Hackle*); John Wood (*Finkel*); Steven Franken (*Bland*); Dack Rambo (*Love*); Robert Middleton (*Colonico*); Kay Ballard (*Senora Messina*).

Rating: NO STARS

Frustrated at receiving 4-F classification, a rich playboy forms his own miniarmy and heads to Italy. His plan is to impersonate a field marshal. In cameo appearances, Martin Kosleck and Richard Loo play, for the final time, the German and Japanese villains they'd patented during the war years. Screenwriter Miller, a scene stealer from B pictures, also has a one-line bit. Unfunny in impact, embarrassingly inept on all technical levels.

ON THE LIGHTER SIDE: Giovanna Ralli, James Coburn, Sergio Fantoni, and Dick Shawm in *What Did You Do in the War Daddy?*; Jerry Lewis (right) dons a disguise in *Which Way to the Front?*

BRITS IN STIR: Courageous English captives accept their grim fate in *Albert R.N.*; David Niven plays one such victim in *The Best of Enemies*.

Behind Barbed Wire:
Prisoners of War

ALBERT R.N. (1953)

CREDITS:
Angel Prods./Eros Films/Rank; Lewis Gilbert, dir.; Guy Morgan (play), Edward Sammis (play), Morgan, Vernon Harris, scr.; Daniel M. Angel, pro.; Malcolm Arnold, mus.; Jack Asher, cin.; Charles Hasse, ed.; B&W; 1.37:1; 88 min.

CAST:
Anthony Steel (*Lt. Geoffrey Ainsworth*); Jack Warner (*Capt. Maddox*); William Sylvester (*Texas Norton*); Guy Middleton (*Barton*); Anton Diffring (*Capt. Schultz*).

Rating: ****

Members of the Royal Navy are held captive in a POW camp lorded over by a nasty Nazi (Diffring). The bedraggled (and fact-based) heroes devise a unique plan: assemble a human-sized dummy (the title character) that can be broken down into small pieces. Whenever they are led out of the barbed-wire confines for a shower, one escapes as others reassemble Albert and carry him back for the head count. One of many Brit-produced POW films, a subgenre of WWII cinema during the 1950s. A tidy, exciting example of edge-of-your-seat suspense.

BEST OF ENEMIES, THE (1961)

CREDITS:

Columbia; Guy Hamilton, dir.; Suso Cecchi D'Amico, Jack Pulman, Agenore Incrocci, Furio Scarpelli, scr.; Dino De Laurentiis, pro.; Nino Rota, mus.; Giuseppe Rotunno, cin.; Bert Bates, Tatiana Casini Morigi, ed.; C; 2.35:1; 104 min.

CAST:

David Niven (*Maj. Richardson*); Alberto Sordi (*Capt. Blasi*); Michael Wilding (*Lt. Burke*); Harry Andrews (*Capt. Rootes*); Noel Harrison (*Lt. Hilary*); Ronald Fraser (*Prefect*).

Rating: **** 1/2

In Africa, an Italian officer (Sordi) becomes locked in a battle of wits with a high-minded Brit commander (Niven). As the two try to outfox one another, enmity transforms into respect, respect into mutual liking. When the English are captured, the anti-Nazi Italian decides to aid in an escape. Sadly, this delightful film is near impossible to locate. Uplifted by a tender approach to tough material and a winning way of conveying its theme: that nationalism ought to mean nothing; people should relate to one another based on individual worthiness. Many bright bits of comic business.

BOMBER'S MOON (1943)

CREDITS:

Edward Ludwig, Harold D. Schuster, dirs..; Kenneth Ganet, Leonard Lee, Aubrey Wisberg, scrs.; Sol (M.) Wurtzel, Aubrey Wisberg, prod.; Robert Fritch, ed.; Lucien Ballard, cin.; David Buttolph, mus.; 20th Century Fox; 1.37:1; B&W: 67 min.

CAST:

George Montgomery (*Capt. Jeff Dakin*); Annabella (*Alexandra Zorich*); Kent Taylor (*Capt. Paul von Block*); Martin Kosleck (*Maj. Von Streicher*); Walter Kingsford (*Prof. Frederich Mueller*); Robert Barrat (*Ernst*).

Rating: **

In an 'inescapable' P.O.W. camp, an American R.A.F. volunteer seethes at the memory of his younger brother being shot dead while parachuting out of a burning craft. He (Montgomery) vows to somehow escape and bring that Nazi (Kosleck) to justice. But might one of his fellow conspirators actually be an enemy agent? Minor, forgettable studio program-picture bolstered by Annabella's radiance, Ballard's inventive cinematography, and anti-Nazi Kosleck's over-the-top performance as The Enemy.

BRIDGE ON THE RIVER KWAI, THE (1957)

CREDITS:
Columbia; David Lean, dir.; Pierre Boulle (novel), Carl Foreman, Michael Wilson, scr.; Sam Spiegel, pro.; Malcolm Arnold, mus.; Jack Hildyard, cin.; Peter Taylor, ed.; C; 2.35:1; 161 min.

CAST:
William Holden (*Shears*); Alec Guinness (*Col. Nicholson*); Jack Hawkins (*Maj. Warden*); Sessue Hayakawa (*Col. Saito*); James Donald (*Maj. Clipton*); Geoffrey Horne (*Lt. Joyce*); Ann Sears (*The Nurse*).

Rating: *****

Burmese jungle, 1942: an American POW (Holden) escapes, even as recently captured soldiers, led by an idealistic martinet (Guinness), arrive. A battle of wills develops between the camp commander (Hayakawa) and the colonel. The escapee is persuaded by a commando (Hawkins) to scout for a force planning to devastate the bridge upon completion. In actuality, no Americans were in the camp, and the bridge, despite such efforts, was never blown up. An audience seeking entertainment first, history second, wanted a grand finale and a charismatic star. Holden even gets to have a brief romance with a beautiful nurse (Sears). The perfect balance between a high-concept product international viewers found irresistible and a work of consummate craftsmanship, even art, with an antiwar message. "Madness," a survivor

THE MEN AND THE MISSION: Alec Guinness (Oscar winner, Best Actor) and William Holden in *The Bridge on the River Kwai.*

(Donald) screams at the end, as the pulled-back camera offers audiences an enticing CinemaScope vision of mass carnage. Swept the Oscars, winning seven, including Best Actor (Guinness), Director, and Picture.

BRYLCREEM BOYS, THE (1998)

CREDITS:
Isle of Man/Opix; Terence Ryan, dir.; Ryan, Jamie Brown, scr.; Ryan, Bernie Stampfer, Alan Latham, Paul Madigan, pro.; Richard Hartley, mus.; Gerry Lively, cin.; Emma F. Hickox, ed.; C; 1.33:1; 106 min.

CAST:
Bill(y) Campbell (*Miles Keogh*); Chris Ryan (*Colin Parker*); Jean Butler (*Mattie Guerin*); Gabriel Byrne (*Commandant O'Brien*); Hal Fowler (*Winthrop*); Anders Jillybo (*Larsen*).

Rating: *** 1/2

A decision by Éamon de Valera's Irish government to remain neutral creates an awkward situation for Allied and Axis soldiers captured on the Emerald Isle. They are "held" in a single camp, Curragh (County Kildare), until hostilities end. A Canadian (Campbell) and German (Ryan) pilot both fall for a lovely village lass (Butler). The film (shot on the Isle of Man) employs this odd situation in the service of the most simple sort of romantic comedy (in the popular lexicon, a chick flick). It works well enough on that level. Such issues as the nature of romance and whom we are or are not attracted to (and why) are avoided to create an easygoing, unambitious light entertainment.

CAMP ON BLOOD ISLAND, THE (1958)

CREDITS:
Hammer/Columbia; Val Guest, dir.; Guest, Jon Manchip White, scr.; Anthony Hinds, pro.; Gerard Schurmann, mus.; Jack Asher, cin.; Bill

Lenny, ed.; B&W; 2.35:1; 81 min.

CAST:
Andre Morell (*Col. Lambert*); Carl Möhner (*Piet Van Elst*); Walter Fitzgerald (*Beattie*); Edward Underdown (*Dawes*); Barbara Shelley (*Kate*); Michael Marne Maitland (*Sakamura*).

Rating: *** 1/2

In a remote Malaya camp, the Japanese commandant takes cruel pleasure in having his guards mistreat POWs. This B movie was rushed into production to capitalize on the vast international success of *Bridge on the River Kwai*. A moneymaker (on a modest level), with the British Maitland playing the vicious Asian. At times, the film's aesthetics have more in common with lurid 1950s men's action magazine than a serious project, with gorgeous women interred as well. On a pulp fiction level, it pays off for its audience.

CAPTIVE HEART, THE (1946)

CREDITS:
Ealing Studios; Basil Dearden, dir.; Angus MacPhail, Guy Morgan, Patrick Kirwan, scr.; Michael Balcon, pro.; Alan Rawsthorne, mus.; Douglas Slocombe, cin.; Charles Hasse, ed.; B&W; 1.37:1; 108 min. (director's cut), 86 min. (US cut).

CAST:
Michael Redgrave (*Capt. Karel Hasek*); Rachel Kempson (*Cecilia Mitchell*); Frederick Leister (*Mowbray*); Mervyn Johns (*Evans*); Rachel Thomas (*Mrs. Evans*); Jack Warner (*Horsfall*).

Ratings: **** 1/2 (director's cut)
*** 1/2 (US theatrical cut)

Interred in the Dachau concentration camp, a Czech officer (Redgrave) attempts an escape. He switches identities with a dead Brit and, when recaptured, is placed in a POW camp. Sensing this new arrival isn't one of their own, the English assume he's a plant. To prove them wrong, he begins a casual correspondence with the deceased soldier's distant wife that blossoms into deep love. Quite marvelous in the ultra-low-key manner UK studios, especially Ealing, are known for. Thrilling, though the emphasis is on poignancy, with rich character development that is, sadly, lost in the shorter cut. Redgrave's complex performance is one of his finest, Kempson a perfect match. The first WWII POW movie. Derek Bond and Sam Kydd, in supporting roles, were actual camp survivors.

COLDITZ STORY, THE (1955)

CREDITS:
Ivan Foxwell/British Lion; Guy Hamilton, dir.; P. R. Reid (novel), Hamilton, Ivan Foxwell, William Douglas-Home, scr.; Foxwell, pro.; Francis Chagrin, mus.; Gordon Dines, cin.; Peter Mayhew, ed.; B&W; 1.37:1; 94 min.

CAST:
John Mills (*Pat Reid*); Christopher Rhodes ("*Mac*" *McGill*); Lionel Jeffries (*Harry Tyler*); Bryan Forbes (*Winslow*); Theodore Bikel (*Vandy*); Anton Diffring (*Fischer*).

Rating: ****

An ancient castle located on a strategic river becomes a last-resort prison where Nazis dump incorrigible Allies. On arrival, P. R. Reid and fellow Englishmen scheme to get out. Bizarre, ingenious, occasionally successful gambits include costuming one of their own as a German officer. Most of what appears on-screen is true, though Reid's movie-like 1953 book, written as a novel, is a work of fiction, not memoir. Most intriguing: the need for the various Allies to overcome language barriers that initially have them running off on contradictory projects. A smart sense of humor is achieved through dialogue additions by Douglas-Home. Major liability: a lack of character development or evolving relations between the POWs.

THE CAUSE THAT WOULD NOT DIE: A freedom fighter (Gene Kelly) attempts to escape his Nazi captors in *Cross of Lorraine*.

CROSS OF LORRAINE, THE (1943)

CREDITS:

Metro-Goldwyn-Mayer; Tay Garnett, dir.; Hans Habe (book), Michael Kanin, Ring Lardner, Jr., Alexander Esway, Robert Hardy Andrews, Lilo Dammert, scr.; Edwin H. Knopf, pro.; Bronislau Kaper, Eric Zeisl, mus.; Sidney Wagner, cin.; Dan Milner, ed.; B&W; 1.37:1; 90 min.

CAST:
Jean-Pierre Aumont (*Paul*); Gene Kelly (*Victor*); Sir Cedric Hardwicke (*Sebastian*); Richard Whorf (*Francois*); Joseph Calleia (*Rodriguez*); Peter Lorre (*Berger*); Hume Cronyn (*Duval*).

Rating: **** 1/2

Following Marshal Philippe Pétain's surrender, several soldiers—believing that with defeat they'll be sent home—are interred. Brutal beatings, administered by an insane sergeant (Lorre), force most into submission. One (Aumont) appears to welcome such sadistic treatment; this savior-like figure contrasts sharply with self-serving collaborator Cronyn. A confused everyman (Kelly) must decide which one to emulate. Religious allegory combined with patriotic fervor, so sincerely directed by Garnett that nothing seems hokey—not back then, not now. Based in part on *A Thousand Shall Fall* (1941), a novel from two years earlier by refugee Habe, intended to convince uncertain Americans to join the fray. Early noir shadow play adds to the power.

DESPERATE JOURNEY (1942)

CREDITS:
Warner Bros.; Raoul Walsh, dir.; Arthur T. Horman, scr.; Hal B. Wallis, pro.; Max Steiner, mus.; Bert Glennon, cin.; Rudy Fehr, ed.; B&W; 1.37:1; 107 min.

CAST:
Errol Flynn (*Flight Lt. Terrence Forbes*); Ronald Reagan (*Johnny Hammond*); Nancy Coleman (*Kaethe Brahms*); Raymond Massey (*Maj. Otto Baumeister*); Alan Hale (*Sgt. Edwards*); Arthur Kennedy (*Jed Forrest*).

Rating: ****

An Allied aircraft that had been bombing German bases is shot down. Captured survivors become prisoners of war and then escape, only to be captured again. In addition to traveling westward by any means possible, they have confiscated enemy secrets. Critics weren't crazy about the first big-budget film to portray dangerous action as an ongoing prank. Audiences, however, couldn't get enough, owing to Walsh's spirited playing of adventure with glib humor. Holds up today in a way that Warner's more intense/didactic pieces (*The Purple Heart*, for example) do not. Flynn and Reagan make a terrific team in what might be perceived as a predecessor to the Bond films.

ELUSIVE CORPORAL, THE (1962)

CREDITS:
Les Films du Cyclope/Omnia Films; Jean Renoir, dir.; Jacques Perret (novel), Renoir, Charles Spaak, Guy Lefranc, scr.; Roland Girard, Adry De Carbuccia, pro.; Joseph Kosma, mus.; George Leclerc, cin.; Renee Lichtig, ed.; B&W; 1.66:1; 90 min.

CAST:
Jean-Pierre Cassel (*The Corporal*); Claude Brasseur (*Papa*); O. E. Hasse (*Man on Train*); Claude Rich (*Ballochet*); Jacques Jouanneau (*Penche-à-gauche*); Sacha Briquet (*The Girl*).

Rating: *** 1/2

Occupying Germans seize all men who might cause problems and toss them into a camp. One corporal is upper class; others range from a dairy farmer to a big-city intellectual. Purposefully similar in concept to Renoir's classic WWI POW/great escape film *Grand Illusion* (1937), in which wartime confinement serves to address the longstanding yet doomed European class system. Lightning failed to strike twice. The follow-up lacks its predecessor's complex theme and bravura moviemaking. Several attempts at escape do provide solid laughs.

ESCAPE BY NIGHT (1960)

CREDITS:
International Goldstar/Lux Film/Dismage; Roberto Rossellini, dir.; Rossellini, Brunello Rondi, Sergio Amidei, Diego Fabbri, scr.; G. B. Romanengo, pro.; Renzo Rossellini, mus.; Carlo Carlini, cin.; Roberto Cinquini, ed.; 1.66:1; 151 min. (director's cut), 138 min. (original Italian theatrical print), 82 min. (original US theatrical/TV print).

CAST:
Leo Genn (*Maj. Michael Pemberton*); Giovanna Ralli (*Esperia Belli*); Sergey Bondarchuk (*Sgt. Fyodor Nazukov*); Peter Baldwin (*Lt. Peter Bradley*); Hannes Messemer (*Von Kleist*); Sergio Fantoni (*Don Valerio*).

Ratings: **** 1/2 (director's cut);
   **** (original Italian theatrical);
   *** 1/2 (original US cut)

An Englishman (Genn), a Russian (Bondarchuk), and an American (Baldwin) escape from a Nazi camp in Rome. They head off in different directions, each hoping to make his way back to his outfit. Rossellini magically segues from an ultrarealistic POW movie into something more powerful: a metaphor about the need for all Allies to stick together now and after the war. A decade and a half following the Armistice, the auteur informs this 1945 story with the social reality of the Cold War. More commercial in nature than the director's earlier Neorealist classics. The girl (Ralli) who helps them is "movie-star beautiful" rather than a believable everyday woman. No one is likely to mind as the pace is swift (despite the length), the characters well defined, and the geography absolutely authentic (thanks to on-location shooting). Vivid and impressive.

ESCAPE IN THE DESERT (1945)

CREDITS:
Warner Bros.; Edward A. Blatt, dir.; Robert E. Sherwood (play), Marvin Borowsky, Thomas Job, scr.; Alex Gottlieb, pro.; Adolph Deutsch, mus.;

Robert Burks, cin.; Owen Marks, ed.; B&W; 1.37:1; 79 min.

CAST:

Jean Sullivan (*Jane*); Philip Dorn (*Philip Artveld*); Irene Manning (*Lora Tedder*); Helmut Dantine (*Capt. Becker*); Alan Hale (*Dr. Tedder*); Samuel S. Hinds (*Gramp*); Kurt Kreuger (*Lt. Von Kleist*).

Rating: ** 1/2

A different kind of POW movie: this time, it's the Nazis who are held on American soil. The leader (Dantine) manages a break, and they head off into the middle of nowhere, guessing no one will find them amid the sand and rock. They happen upon an isolated gas station where a pretty girl (Sullivan) has fallen for a Dutch serviceman (Dorn). It's *The Petrified Forest* all over again, updated for WWII's closing days. Sherwood's poetic language is stripped away; the suspense never really takes hold. Dantine, as always, makes an impression.

ESCAPE TO ATHENA (1979)

CREDITS:

ITC/Astral; George P. Cosmatos, dir.; Edward Anhalt, Richard Lochte, scr.; Sir Lew Grade, Jack Weiner, David Niven, Jr., pro.; Lalo Schifrin, mus.; Gilbert Taylor, cin.; Ralph Kemplen, ed.; C; 2.35:1; 125 min.

CAST:

Roger Moore (*Maj. Otto Hecht*); Stefanie Powers (*Dottie*); Telly Savalas (*Zeno*); David Niven (*Prof. Blake*); Claudia Cardinale (*Eleana*); Richard Roundtree (*Judson*); Sonny Bono (*Rotelli*); Elliott Gould (*Charlie*).

Rating: *

Prisoners held in Stalag Luft VII-Z on the island of Rhodes dig for ancient artifacts. The wicked commandant (Moore) picks over them, saving the most valuable for himself. One of the many failed, big-budget, all-star extravaganzas produced by Grade in the 1970s. A disastrous attempt to bring back the class and glamour of old, long-gone Hollywood. Everyone is terribly miscast. William Holden provides a supposedly "clever" one-line cameo that spits on his classic roles in *Stalag 17* and *Bridge on the River Kwai*. Empty, glossy, embarrassing.

GREAT ESCAPE, THE (1963)

CREDITS:
United Artists; John Sturges, dir.; Paul Brickhill (book), James Clavell, W. R. Burnett, scr.; Sturges, Clavell, Walter Mirisch, pro.; Elmer Bernstein, mus.; Daniel L. Fapp, cin.; Ferris Webster, ed.; C; 2.35:1; 172 min.

CAST:
Steve McQueen (*Hilts*); James Garner (*Hendley*); Richard Attenborough (*Bartlett/X*); James Donald (*Ramsey*); Charles Bronson (*Danny*); Donald Pleasence (*Blythe*); James Coburn (*Sedgwick*); Hannes Messemer (*Von Luger*); David McCallum (*Ashley-Pitt*); Gordon Jackson (*MacDonald*).

Rating: *****

An inescapable prison is built for Allied POWs with reputations for breaking out. Upon arrival, the Allied mavericks plan their great escape: 250 prisoners via tunnels. Among such films, this one is tied with *Bridge on the River Kwai* for popularity. As with that earlier classic, no Americans were historically involved but were added for box-office appeal. Dramatic and comedic bits involving individuals and relationships, inspired casting with each actor in a neatly defined role, and a last-minute inspiration (the motorcycle, supposedly McQueen's idea) all result in high-style entertainment via meticulous craftsmanship. The story was told less spectacularly, if more accurately, in *The Wooden Horse*. Proof positive that nearly twenty years after the fact, WWII still spoke to international audiences.

AN ICONIC MOMENT: Steve McQueen, in the image that transformed a popular actor into a superstar, on his beloved motorcycle in *The Great Escape*.

GREAT RAID, THE (2005)

CREDITS:
Mirimax; John Dahl, dir.; William B. Breuer (book), Hampton Sides (book), Carlo Bernard, Doug Miro, scr.; Lawrence Bender, Marty Katz,

pro.; Trevor Rabin, mus.; Peter Menzies, Jr., cin.; Scott Chestnut, Pietro Scalia, ed.; C; 2.35:1; 132 min.

CAST:

Benjamin Bratt (*Lt. Col. Mucci*); James Franco (*Capt. Prince*); Robert Mammone (*Fisher*); Max Martini (*Wojo*); James Carpinello (*Aliteri*); Mark Consuelos (*Guttierez*); Joseph Fiennes (*Maj. Gibson*).

Rating: ****

Following the infamous Death March, American survivors were herded into Philippine prison camps and intentionally starved. When the tide of the war turned three years later, the Japanese determined to liquidate all captives. The 6th American Ranger Battalion, working in conjunction with Filipino volunteers, staged a raid on Cabanatuan to save 500 prisoners. The film cuts back and forth between prisoners, advancing troops, and

AMERICAN PATRIOTISM LIVES!: Steve McQueen, Jud Taylor, and James Garner celebrate the fourth of July sequence in *The Great Escape*.

civilians—both Asian and American, including many women—who work behind the scenes. Solid re-creation of a little-known story. Too bad the participants' complex personalities are never explored. The final battle competes with that of *Saving Private Ryan*.

HANNIBAL BROOKS (1969)

CREDITS:
United Artists/Scimitar Films; Michael Winner, dir.; Winner, Tom Wright, Dick Clement, Ian La Frenais, scr.; Winner, pro.; Francis Lai, mus.; Robert Paynter, cin.; Lionel Selwyn, Peter Austen-Hunt, ed.; C; 1.85:1; 101 min.

CAST:
Oliver Reed (*Stephen Brooks*); Michael J. Pollard (*Packy*); John Alderton (*Bernard*); Wolfgang Preiss (*Col. Von Haller*); Helmut Lohner (*Willi*); Peter Carsten (*Kurt*); Karin Baal (*Vronia*).

Rating: ****

A captured Brit (Reed) is assigned to the Munich Zoo, where he develops a friendship with an Asian elephant. When he escapes, he brings her along over the Alps. To make this relevant for a 1969 audience, Pollard plays a variation on his *Bonnie and Clyde* character. The plot combines two real-life stories: screenwriter Wright did care for an elephant named Lucy while captured; another elephant, Olga, was rescued from the Vienna zoo. Laughs neatly interspersed with suspense/drama as a Nazi officer (Preiss) pursues the ramshackle company. The finest work from a mediocre-at-best director, mainly known for the *Death Wish* films.

HART'S WAR (2002)

CREDITS:
Cheyenne Ent./Metro-Goldwyn-Mayer; Gregory Hoblit, dir.; Billy Ray, Tony George, scr.; Hoblit, David Foster, David Ladd, Arnold Rifkin,

pro.; Rachel Portman, mus.; Alar Kivilo, cin.; David Rosenbloom, ed.; C; 2.35:1; 125 min.

CAST:

Bruce Willis (*Col. William McNamara*); Colin Ferrell (*Lt. Thomas Hart*); Terrence Howard (*Lt. Lincoln Scott*); Cole Hauser (*Sgt. Vic Bedford*); Marcel Iures (*Col. Visser*).

Rating: *** 1/2

During the brutal winter of 1945, a vicious racist is murdered in the American compound of a German POW camp. Everyone assumes the guilty party must be an African American flyboy (Howard). As the old-fashioned commanding officer (Willis) oversees a trial, a lieutenant (Ferrell) assumes the job of defense attorney. Well produced on all levels, with fine performances and a powerfully grim vision of camp life. Too bad the second half is less convincing than the gripping opening. Worthwhile for its accurate portrait of the generalized resentment—among officers as well as enlisted men—regarding the newly integrated military. Based on an acclaimed 1999 novel by John Katzenbach.

HILL, THE (1965)

CREDITS:

Metro-Goldwyn-Mayer/Seven Arts; Sidney Lumet, dir.; Ray Rigby (play), R. S. Allen (play), scr.; Kenneth Hyman, pro.; Oswald Morris, cin.; Thelma Connell, ed.; B&W; 1.66:1; 123 min.

CAST:

Sean Connery (*Roberts*); Harry Andrews (*Wilson*); Ian Bannen (*Harris*); Alfred Lynch (*Stevens*); Ossie Davis (*Jacko*); Roy Kinnear (*Bartlett*); Jack Watson (*McGrath*); Ian Hendry (*Sgt. Williams*); Michael Redgrave (*Doc*).

Rating: *****

A POW film with a difference: the prisoners and those in charge are all British. This is a "glass-house": a camp located in the Libyan desert, not for captured enemies but insubordinate countrymen. The commander's (Andrews) theory about how to "cure" such rebels: run them up and down a man-made hill, hour after hour, until they break, and then begin rehabilitation. A rough Welshman (Connery) takes up the challenge,

CONFRONTATION IN CONFINEMENT: Harry Andrews goes up against Sean Connery in *The Hill*; James Fox and George Segal become tender comrades *King Rat*.

refusing to be "tamed." As in the original play, the hill symbolizes the establishment's desire/need to reduce anyone who dares to cling to individuality to rubble. Connery's greatest performance. Each costar brings his character to full, vivid life, even as heat threatens to smother all. Shot near Almeria, Spain, by a director whose forte was always grim realism.

KING RAT (1965)

CREDITS:
Coleytown Prods./Columbia; Bryan Forbes, dir.; James Clavell (novel), Forbes, scr.; Marvin Miller, James Woolf, pro.; John Barry, mus.; Burnett Guffey, cin.; Walter Thompson, ed.; B&W; 1.85:1; 134 min.

CAST:
George Segal (*Corporal King*); Tom Courtenay (*Lt. Robin Grey*); James Fox (*Peter Marlowe*); Patrick O'Neal (*Max*); Denholm Elliott (*Larkin*); James Donald (*Dr. Kennedy*); John Mills (*Col. Smedley-Taylor*).

Rating: **** 1/2

Like Clavell's 1962 novel, this film is set at Changi, a Japanese camp in Singapore for English, Australian, and American POWs. With most prisoners near starving, a cocky American corporal (Segal) turns the grim situation to his advantage by creating a black market. With a naïve Brit (Fox) under his wing, he harvests the one "crop" that's plentiful—rats—secretly butchers them, and then sells the "meat" to hungry soldiers. Effectively shot in a depressing black-and-white style. The King–Marlowe relationship is presented as a love-at-first sight homoerotic romance—an innovation at the time. The film also expresses the antiwar sensibility of the Vietnam era. Only flaw: Segal is too mild mannered to be believed; Steve McQueen, the first choice, would have been perfect.

MAN IN THE MIDDLE (1965)

CREDITS:
Pennebaker Productions; Guy Hamilton, dir.; Howard Fast (novel), Willis Hall, Keith Waterhouse, scr.; Walter Seltzer, pro.; John Barry, mus.; Wilkie Cooper, cin.; John Bloom, ed.; B&W; 2.35:1; 94 min.

CAST:
Robert Mitchum (*Lt. Col. Barney Adams*); France Nuyen (*Kate Davray*); Barry Sullivan (*Gen. Kempton*); Trevor Howard (*Maj. Kensington*); Keenan Wynn (*Lt. Winston*).

Rating: ****

India, 1944: a joint English–American camp is rocked when a US officer (Wynn) marches into a Brit barracks and shoots a soldier. The American commander (Sullivan) wants a quick court-martial, a guilty verdict, and an execution to appease the English. Meeting the confessed killer, the defense lawyer (Mitchum) realizes he might be insane and, as such, shouldn't face the death penalty. Intelligent, quietly forceful rendering of Fast's *The Winston Affair* (1963), however compromised as a result of censorship that toned down its warning about the military's aim to do the expedient thing rather than the right thing. Raises the issue of altered race relations toward the war's end. One of Wynn's best roles.

McKENZIE BREAK, THE (1970)

CREDITS:
Levy-Gardner-Laven; Lamont Johnson, dir.; Sidney Shelley (novel), William W. Norton, scr.; Arthur Gardner, Jules V. Levy, pro.; Riz Ortolani, mus.; Michael Reed, cin.; Tom Rolf, ed.; C; 1.85:1; 108 min.

CAST:
Brian Keith (*Capt. Jack Connor*); Helmut Griem (*Kapitän Willi Schluetter*); Ian Hendry (*Maj. Perry*); Jack Watson (*Gen. Kerr*); Horst Janson (*Lt. Neuchl*).

Rating: **** 1/2

At a POW camp in Scotland, a determined German officer (Griem) concocts an intricate escape plan for twenty-eight men who are desperately needed to pilot U-boats. To thwart the plan, a maverick officer (Keith) initiates a cat-and-mouse game. No big action-adventure fireworks here, a la *The Great Escape*; none of the stinging humor of *Stalag 17*. It's a subtle, nuanced piece, low key all the way, involving on a cerebral level. Contains not a single clichéd character, stereotypical situation, or overly familiar line of dialogue. Refreshingly unique conflicts arise between Luftwaffe and U-boat officers among the Germans and, among the Englishmen, between by-the-book Geneva Convention followers and those who seek to win at any cost. Understated and powerful.

MERRY CHRISTMAS, MR. LAWRENCE, aka *FURYO* (1982)

CREDITS:
Recorded Pictures; Nagisa Ôshima, dir.; Ôshima, Paul Mayersberg, scr.; Jeremy Thomas, pro.; Ryûichi Sakamoto, mus.; Tôichirô Narushima, cin.;

WAR CRIMES: A Brit captive (Jack Thompson) awaits execution in *Merry Christmas, Mr. Lawrence.*

Tomoyo Oshima, ed.; C; 1.85:1; 123 min.

CAST:
Tom Conti (*Col. John Lawrence*); David Bowie (*Maj. Jack Celliers*); Ryûichi Sakamoto (*Capt. Yonoi*); Takeshi Kitano (*Sgt. Hara*); Jack Thompson (*Hicksley*); Johnny Ohkura (*Kanemoto*); Alistair Browning (*De Jong*); Yûya Uchida (*Commander*).

Rating: ***

A stiff-upper-lip Brit (Bowie) is held in a Japanese POW camp lorded over by a by-the-book officer (Sakamoto). The two play a virtual chess game based less on military issues than the deep, dark desires each sparks in the other. Confusing where it means to be complicated. Divides viewers on whether it is meaningful or pretentious, effectively stylized or embarrassingly arty, intriguingly oblique or annoyingly obscure. Far more accessible is the theme of communication, in terms of both language and culture: If the two sides can't grasp each other's world views, how are they to form a relationship? Unique, but not necessarily in a good way. From the director of the infamous *In the Realm of the Senses* (1976).

PILOT RETURNS, A (1942)

CREDITS:
Alleanza Films; Roberto Rossellini, dir.; Vittorio Mussolini (story), Rossellini, Michelangelo Antonioni, Rosario Leone, Massimo Mida, scr.; Franco Bartoli, pro.; Renzo Rossellini, mus.; Vincenzo Seratrice, cin.; Eraldo de Roma, ed.; B&W; 1.37:1; 80 min.

CAST:
Massimo Girotti (*Gino Rossati*); Michela Belmonte (*Anna*); Gaetano Masier (*Trisotti*); Elvira Betrone (*Signora Rossati*); Piero Lulli (*De Santis*).

Rating: ****

Among the oddest WWII films in conception and execution. Mussolini's own son had written a propaganda piece about an Italian flyer who, attacking the Allies, is shot down and becomes a POW. The original idea was to show his courage, endurance, and desperate desire to escape. Secretly antifascist, Rossellini and his team reshaped the material. The finished film reverses the theme: the Brits who take the youth captive are gentlemen to a fault, causing the hero to realize that Italy never should have followed Mussolini. Hardly a great film, but the story behind the story makes it a must-see.

PURPLE HEART, THE (1944)

CREDITS:
20th Century Fox; Lewis Milestone, dir.; Darryl F. Zanuck (aka Melville Crossman), Jerome Cady, scr.; Zanuck, pro.; Alfred Newman, mus.; Arthur C. Miller, cin.; Douglass Biggs, ed.; B&W; 1.37:1; 99 min.

IN ENEMY HANDS: Dana Andrews on far left, Richard Conte and Farley Granger on far right, in *The Purple Heart*.

CAST:

Dana Andrews (*Capt. Ross*); Richard Conte (*Lt. Canelli*); Farley Granger (*Clinton*); Kevin O'Shea (*Skvoznik*); Don "Red" Barry (*Vincent*); Sam Levene (*Greenbaum*); Richard Loo (*Gen. Mitsubi*).

Rating: ***

Well-intentioned misfire in which eight Americans, downed after a bombing raid on Tokyo, are (illegally) brought before a Japanese civil court and tried for murder. Between daily sessions, they are mercilessly tortured, such acts occurring offscreen. With no action sequences, we are left with only drama and dialogue; the former is uninspired, the latter transparent. The only way to make this work would have been to provide well-rounded characters; other than Levene as a roughhewn intellectual, they are at best suggested. Based on the trial of eight survivors from the Doolittle Raid, three of whom were executed. Calls in the movie for Japan's annihilation helped prepare ordinary Americans for the upcoming nuclear bombings. Attending reporters are played as a Greek chorus.

RAILWAY MAN, THE (2013)

CREDITS:

Archer St./Lionsgate; Jonathan Teplitzky, dir.; Eric Lomax (book), Frank Cottrell Boyce, Andy Paterson, scr.; Chris Brown, Bill Curbishley, Paterson, pro.; David Hirschfelder, mus.; Garry Phillips, cin.; Martin Connor, ed.; C; 2.35:1; 116 min.

CAST:

Colin Firth (*Eric*); Jeremy Irvine (*Young Eric*); Nicole Kidman (*Patti*); Stellan Skarsgård (*Finlay*); Michael MacKenzie (*Sutton*); Jeffrey Daunton (*Burton*); Bryan Probets (*York*).

Rating: **** 1/2

A middle-aged man (Firth) encounters the love of his life (Kidman) while riding on a railway train. Their whirlwind romance is challenged when he suffers sudden fits as a result of horrific WWII experiences. A gifted engineer, captured by the Japanese, he was sent north of the Malay Peninsula. For daring to build a radio, Eric Lomax was tortured by the Kempeitai. Hoping to save his marriage, he sets out to confront the man who devastated his life—not for revenge but forgiveness. Story elements recall *Bridge on the River Kwai* while predating *Unbroken*. This is its own film, however, with unique rewards. Firth's and Kidman's (notably deglamorized) performances are memorable. Framing device purposefully recalls the classic *Brief Encounter* (1945).

RETURN FROM THE RIVER KWAI (1989)

CREDITS:
Roadshow Prod./Warner Bros.; Andrew V. McLaglen, dir.; Joan Blair (book), Clay Blair, Jr. (book), Sargon Tamimi, Paul Mayersberg, scr.; Kurt Unger, pro.; Lalo Schifrin, mus.; Arthur Wooster, cin.; Alan Strachan, ed.; 35; C; 101 min.

CAST:
Timothy Bottoms (*Miller*); Nick Tate (*Lt. Commander Hunt*); George Takei (*Lt. Tanaka*); Edward Fox (*Maj. Benford*); Denholm Elliott (*Grayson*); Anna Maria Tirol (*Girl*).

Rating: *

In 1945, Allied prisoners learn they will be transferred to Japan and plan an escape. In this (fictional) version, the pilot who blew up the bridge is shot down on his attempted flight home, joins the Meo warriors, and initiates a local resistance movement. David Lean's talent brought *Bridge on the River Kwai* to life; McLaglen's lack thereof kills any possibilities here. Belated faux sequel to a true classic is not worth watching.

SECRET OF BLOOD ISLAND, THE (1964)

CREDITS:
Hammer/Rank/Universal; Quentin Lawrence, dir.; John Gilling, scr.; Anthony Nelson Keys, pro.; James Bernard, mus.; Jack Asher, cin.; Tom Simpson, ed.; 1.75:1; B&W/C; 84 min.

CAST:
Jack Hedley (*Crewe*); Barbara Shelley (*Elaine*); Patrick Wymark (*Maj. Jocomo*); Charles Tingwell (*Maj. Dryden*); Bill Owen (*Bludgin*); Michael Ripper (*Tojoko*).

Rating: ★★★

Flying from Kuala Lumpur back to London, a Brit aviator/agent (Shelley) experiences engine trouble and lands in Malaya. A POW (Hedley) rescues the beauty from the jungle and smuggles her into a camp where he and others are cruelly treated by the commandant (Ripper). A bit farfetched and not on par with its companion piece, *The Camp on Blood Island*. Entertaining all the same as Allies disguise the breathtaking woman as a man, with unexpected consequences. English actors play Japanese torturers with fiendish relish. Garish.

SECRET WAR OF HARRY FRIGG, THE (1968)

CREDITS:
Universal; Jack Smight, dir.; Peter Stone, Frank Tarloff, scr.; Hal E. Chester, pro.; Carlo Rustichelli, mus.; Russell Metty, cin.; J. Terry Williams, ed.; C; 2.35:1; 110 min.

CAST:
Paul Newman (*Pvt. Harry Frigg*); Sylva Koscina (*Countess De Montefiore*); Andrew Duggan (*Gen. Armstrong*); Tom Bosley (*Gen. Pennypacker*); John Williams (*Gen. Mayhew*); James Gregory (*Prentiss*).

Rating: *

Five Allied generals are captured and held prisoner in an Italian chateau. The army promotes a lovable loser to two-star major general, with plans to infiltrate the chateau and free the officers. However, his dalliance with an aristocratic beauty (Koscina) slows down the process. Maybe this read well in script form, but it fails in making the leap from page to screen. Perhaps a gifted director might have helped. Despite his enormous gifts, Newman never excelled at this type of light, fluffy comedy.

STALAG 17 (1953)

CREDITS:
Paramount; Billy Wilder, dir.; Edmund Trzcinski (play), Donald Bevan, Wilder, Edwin Blum, scr.; Wilder, William Schorr, pro.; Leonid Raab, mus.; Ernest Laszlo, cin.; George Tomasini, ed.; B&W; 1.37:1; 120 min.

A GREEK CHORUS IN MODERN TIMES: Robert Strauss, William Holden, and Harvey Lembeck observe and comment on all around them in *Stalag 17*.

THE COMEDY OF HORRORS: William Holden as 'Sefton' Academy award winner, Best Actor) in Billy Wilder's dark comedy, *Stalag 17*.

CAST:

William Holden (*Sefton*); Don Taylor (*Lt. Dunbar*); Otto Preminger (*Col. von Scherbach*); Robert Strauss (*Animal*); Harvey Lembeck (*Shapiro*); Richard Erdman (*Hoffy*); Peter Graves (*Price*); Neville Brand (*Duke*).

Rating: *****

A self-serving louse (Holden) is suspected of being a traitor when would-be US escapees are killed by Nazi guards. A ticking clock warns that the time is nigh for a young pilot (Taylor) to make the next try. Graves finally got to show the darker side of his clean-cut image. Strauss and Lembeck provide fine comic support. Ostensibly a comedy, though that limiting genre label hardly describes this dramatic situation that flirts with the tragic. Preminger is well cast (some might say typecast) as the sadistic Nazi commander. Holden initially turned down the lead fearing that Sefton's sleaziness might ruin his career. He won the Best Actor Oscar, and superstardom followed.

TARGET UNKNOWN (1951)

CREDITS:
Universal-International; George Sherman, dir.; Harold Medford, scr.; Aubrey Schenck, pro.; Milton Rosen, mus.; Maury Gertsman, cin.; Frank Gross, ed.; B&W; 1.37:1; 90 min.

jCAST:
Mark Stevens (*Capt. Jerome Stevens*); Alex Nicol (*Sgt. Al Mitchell*); Robert Douglas (*Col. von Broeck*); Don Taylor (*Lt. Frank Webster*); Gig Young (*Capt. Reiner*).

Rating: ** 1/2

Another B film about American flyers who bail out over occupied France and are then captured and interrogated by Nazis. Rather than torture these men, the Germans have casual conversations with them, putting them at ease so they'll reveal bits of information. A remake of a military film, Bernard Vorhaus's *Resisting Enemy Interrogation* (1944), created to warn troops about how subtle the enemy can be. Viewed by servicemen about to head overseas, that sixty-two-minute item boasts prestigious stars—Arthur Kennedy, Lloyd Nolan, Peter Van Eyck—who outclass the contract players in this studio reworking. An escape sequence was added to make the material more commercial.

TO END ALL WARS (2001)

CREDITS:
Argyll Films; David L. Cunningham, dir.; Ernest Gordon (book), Brian Godawa, scr.; Cunningham, pro.; Greg Gardiner, cin.; Tim Silano, ed.; C/B&W; 1.85:1; 125 min.

CAST:
Ciarán McMenamin (*Capt. Ernest Gordon*); Robert Carlyle (*Maj. Ian Campbell*); Kiefer Sutherland (*Jim Reardon*); Mark Strong (*Dusty Miller*); Yugo Saso (*Takashi Nagase*).

Rating: *** 1/2

Captured Scotch soldiers, along with an obligatory American (Sutherland), are forced by Japanese captors to build the Thailand–Burma railway. Plotwise, this is *Bridge on the River Kwai* without the bridge. Sequences depicting harsh treatment recall that classic. But with that and the expansive scenery, all comparisons end. The script does not know whether it wants to be a docudrama about what really happened or offer a moral lesson. Acting is solid, but there's no penetration of characters' motives: why the Yank goes from a self-interested King Rat type to a martyr for the others is never made clear.

VICTORY (1981)

CREDITS:
Lorimar Films; John Huston, dir.; Evan Jones, Yabo Yablonsky, scr.; Freddie Fields, pro.; Bill Conti, mus.; Gerry Fisher, cin.; Roberto Silvi, ed.; C; 2.35:1; 116 min.

CAST:
Sylvester Stallone (*Robert Hatch*); Michael Caine (*Capt. John Colby*); Pelé (*Luis*); Max von Sydow (*Maj. Karl Von Steiner*); Daniel Massey (*Col. Waldron*).

TIME OUT FOR ATHLETICS: Contemporary sports star Pele plays a P.O.W. in John Huston's *Victory.*

Rating: **

A diverse group of Allies, led by a stiff-upper-lip officer (Caine), agrees to play a soccer game with German captors, hoping an American (Stallone) can escape. On paper, it must've sounded like a winning cross between *The Great Escape* and *The Longest Yard.* On screen? An overlong, meandering variation on the timeworn breakout theme. Sly looks and sounds absurdly anachronistic while Caine rises above the weak material. Pelé provides the film's only delight. Conti's *Rocky*-like score is insufferable. A great director's worst film.

WAY BACK, THE (2010)

CREDITS:
Exclusive Films; Peter Weir, dir.; Slawomir Rawicz (book), Weir, Keith R. Clarke, scr.; Duncan Henderson, Joni Levin, Nigel Sinclair, Weir, pro.;

Burkhard von Dallwitz, mus.; Russell Boyd, cin.; Lee Smith, ed.; C/B&W; 2.35:1; 133 min.

CAST:

Dragos Bucur (*Zoran*); Colin Farrell (*Valka*); Ed Harris (*Smith*); Alexandru Potocean (*Tomasz*); Saoirse Ronan (*Irena*); Gustaf Skarsgård (*Voss*); Mark Strong (*Khabarov*); Jim Sturgess (Janusz); Sebastian Urzendowsky (*Kazik*).

Rating: **** 1/2

Soviet forces roll into Poland, supposedly to safeguard it by keeping the Nazis out. This quickly turns into an armed occupation, leading to a reign of terror. When a member of the Polish military (Sturgess) is falsely accused of being an enemy spy, he's arrested and sent to a gulag. There, he and a small group of friends plan their escape and then attempt the 4,000-mile journey home. Slawomir Rawicz's 1956 book has been alternately regarded as an honest memoir and a work of fiction. Either way, the film is near perfect but not in the manner of Hollywood blockbusters. It downplays crowd-pleasing entertainment, similar to other placid Weir films, beginning with *Picnic at Hanging Rock* (1975). The cinematography is stunning enough to carry the narrative, creating a visual essay of a trek that eventually leads to India. Understated, subtle.

WOODEN HORSE, THE (1950)

CREDITS:

London Films/British Lion; Jack Lee, dir.; Eric Williams (book), scr.; Clifton Parker, mus.; C. M. Pennington, cin.; John Seabourne, Sr., ed.; 35 mm.; B&W; 1.37:1; 101 min.

CAST:

Leo Genn (*Peter*); David Tomlinson (*Phil*); Anthony Steel (*John);* David Greene *(Bennett*); Peter Burton (*Nigel*); Michael Goodliffe *(Robbie);* Bryan Forbes (*Paul);* Peter Finch (*Australian*).

Rating: **** 1/2

Sickened by their dull existence, British POWs held in Stalag Luft III consider an escape. One man recalls the ploy that ended the Trojan War, wondering if a piece of exercise equipment might serve such a purpose. Entertaining qualities—such as the sharp humor of *Stalag 17* and the epic scope of *Bridge on the River Kwai*—are absent here. A docudrama approach to a fact-based if fictionalized tale. Lee cast several men who had never acted so they would seem like soldiers rather than polished performers. Based on the same incident that inspired *The Great Escape*. Professionally executed; satisfying in its grim manner.

HISTORY REPEATS ITSELF: British Prisoners of War hoping to escape rely on an idea borrowed from the ancient Greeks.

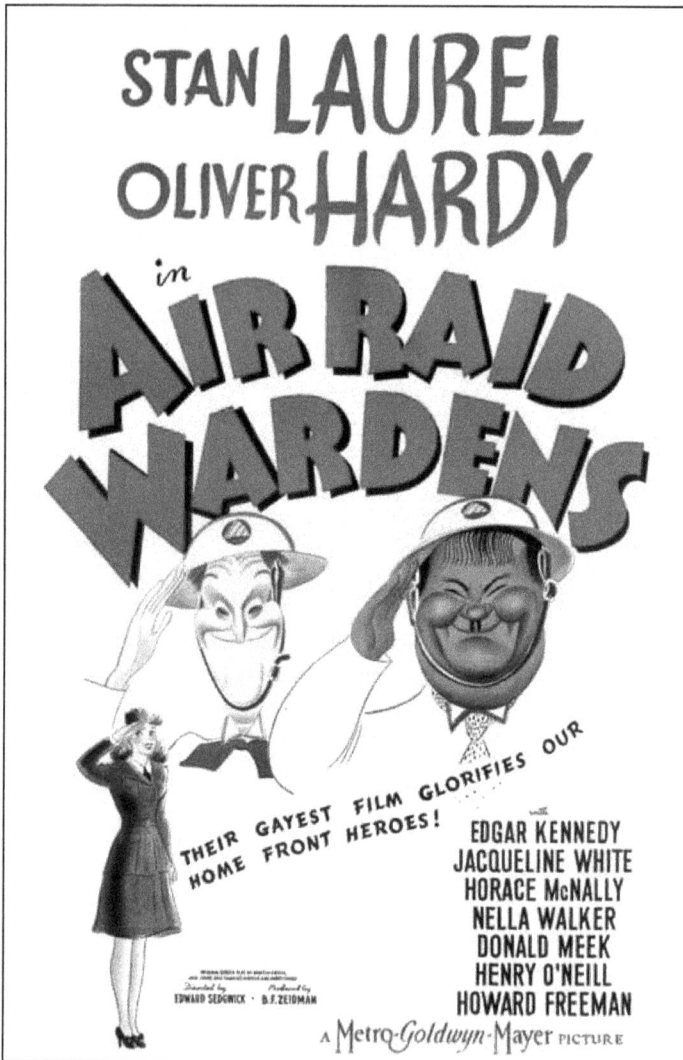

NEVER LOSE YOUR SENSE OF HUMOR: One way Americans survived the stressful early-1940s was by laughing at their difficulties with comedy stars such as Stan Laurel and Oliver Hardy.

"Wish You Were Here": The Home Front

AIR RAID WARDENS (1943)

CREDITS:
Metro-Goldwyn-Mayer; Edward Sedgwick, dir.; Jack Jevne, Charley Rogers, Harry Crane, scr.; B. F. Zeidman, pro.; Nathaniel Shilkret, mus.; Walter Lundin, cin.; B&W; 1.37:1; 67 min.

CAST:
Stan Laurel (*Stanley*); Oliver Hardy (*Oliver*); Edgar Kennedy (*Joe Bledsoe*); Jacqueline White (*Peggy Parker*); Stephen McNally (*Dan Madison*); Nella Walker (*Millicent*).

Rating: * 1/2

Classified 4-F, the skinny one and his plump partner search for other ways to serve their country. In their small hometown, they work at a radio plant and volunteer to be air-raid wardens in the least likely place to be bombed. Even with a solid cast of scene-stealing comics—including Kennedy, master of the slow burn—the great comedy team can do nothing with the dreadful script. Propaganda abounds, though laughs are few and far between.

ALL THROUGH THE NIGHT (1941)

CREDITS:
Warner Bros.; Vincent Sherman, dir.; Leo Rosten, Leonard Spigelgass, Edwin Gilbert, scr.; Jerry Wald, pro.; Adolph Deutsch, Max Steiner, mus.; Sidney Hickox, cin.; Rudi Fehr, ed.; B&W; 1.37:1; 107 min.

CAST:
Humphrey Bogart (*Gloves Donahue*); Conrad Veidt (*Franz*); Kaaren Verne (*Leda*); Jane Darwell (*Ma*); Peter Lorre (*Pepi*); Judith Anderson (*Madame*); William Demarest (*Sunshine*); Jackie Gleason (*Starchy*); Phil Silvers (*Louie*).

EVEN GANGSTERS CAN BE GOODGUYS: Humphrey Bogart joins the Crusade against fascism in *All Through the Night*.

Rating: ****

Reasonable facsimiles of Damon Runyon's Sky Masterson (Bogart), Nathan Detroit (Demarest), and Nicely-Nicely Johnson (Gleason) try to rescue a young foreigner (Verne) from German saboteurs planning to blow up New York City. Early evidence that WB was the studio most willing to take on the American Bundt by revealing the fifth columnists among us. Lighthearted approach to the thrills works, even today, though once-"clever" racial jokes date the material.

BAMBOO BLONDE, THE (1946)

CREDITS:
RKO; Anthony Mann, dir.; Wayne Whittaker, Olive Cooper, Lawrence Kimble, scr.; Herman Schlom, pro.; Frank Redman, cin.; Les Millbrook, ed.; C. Bakaleinikoff, mus.; B&W; 1.37:1; 67 min.

CAST:
Frances Langford (*Louise Anderson*); Ralph Edwards (*Eddie*); Russell Wade (*Patrick Ransom, Jr.*); Iris Adrian (*Montana Jones*); Jane Greer (*Eileen Sawyer*).

Rating: ** 1/2

On the eve of departure for the South Pacific, a wealthy lieutenant (Wade) falls hard for a lovable lower-class chorine (Langford). His B-29 crew paints an idealized image of her on their bomber. When they return as heroes for a bond-drive tour, she's invited to come along as a singer. The concept sounds better than the final picture. Second-string stars and tight production values have Langford perform the same song twice to cut royalty costs. Sweetly sentimental during its best moments, but thin and shallow.

THE GIRL WE LEFT BEHIND: Flyboys paint a portrait of their dream girl on planes in *The Bamboo Blonde*.

CHOSEN, THE (1981)

CREDITS:

Chosen Film Co./Analysis Releasing; Jeremy (Paul) Kagan, dir.; Chaim Potok (novel), Edwin Gordon, scr.; Eli Landau, Edie Landau, pro.; Elmer Bernstein, mus.; Arthur J. Ornitz, cin.; David Garfield, ed.; C; 1.85:1; 108 min.

CAST:

Maximilian Schell (*Prof. David Malter*); Barry Miller (*Reuven Malter*); Rod Steiger (*Rabbi Reb Saunders*); Robby Benson (*Dan Saunders*); Hildy Brooks (*Mrs. Saunders*); Kaethe Fine (*Shaindel Saunders*).

Rating: **** 1/2

Two Jewish boys, living near each other in Brooklyn, inhabit different universes. One (Miller), the son of a professor (Schell), embraces contemporary American life. The other (Benson) has a conservative rabbi (Steiger) and is steeped in Hasidic tradition. An odd-couple friendship develops via a combination of comedy and drama. Quietly effective, as is Potok's 1967 bestseller. "Major" differences on such issues as dietary laws seem insignificant when they watch newsreel accounts of the Holocaust. This is precisely the manner in which most Americans—Jewish or gentile—first confronted the Final Solution: at the movies. Atmospheric and exceptionally well acted.

CLOCK, THE (1945)

CREDITS:

Metro-Goldwyn-Mayer; Vincente Minnelli, dir.; Paul Gallico (story), Pauline Gallico (story), Robert Nathan, Joseph Schrank, scr.; Arthur Freed, pro.; George Bassman, mus.; George J. Folsey, cin.; George White, ed.; B&W; 1.37:1; 90 min.

CAST:

Judy Garland (*Alice Mayberry*); Robert Walker (*Cpl. Joe Allen*); James Gleason (*Al Henry*); Keenan Wynn (*Drunk*); Marshall Thompson (*Bill*); Lucile Gleason (*Mrs. Henry*); Ruth Brady (*Helen*).

Rating: ****

One of the few films to attempt a serious analysis of the war brides phenomenon. A young woman who recently moved to Manhattan "meets cute" with a genial GI (Walker), and they spend an all-day odyssey in glorious New York. They cap it off by deciding to marry (to enjoy sex morally before he leaves), running into a bureaucracy that creates a ticking clock. The writing is charming. This might have been a classic were it not for MGM's annoying tendency to shoot exterior scenes on obvious studio sets, undercutting this fable's potential to be a realistic fairy tale.

COWBOY CANTEEN (1944)

CREDITS:
Columbia; Lew Landers, dir.; Felix Adler, Paul Gangelin, scr.; Jack Fier, pro.; John Leipold, mus.; George Meehan, cin.; Aaron Stell, ed.; B&W; 1.37:1; 72 min.

CAST:
Charles Starrett (*Steve Bradley*); Jane Frazee (*Connie*); Tex Ritter (*Tex*); Barbara Jo Allen (*Vera Vague*); Dub Taylor (*Cannonball*); Guinn "Big Boy" Williams (*Spud*).

Rating: ** 1/2

Vaudeville performers, including a snappy blonde (Frazee), head west to turn a ranch into a rural version of the Stage Door/Hollywood Canteens. Columbia's B-pictures unit, known for its B westerns, reoriented itself for the war cause and came up with this pleasant item, existing mainly to show off country–western performers. Most fascinating: the "integration" of African American singers The Mills Bros. into an otherwise all-Anglo mix, reflecting the parallel integration of the armed forces.

DECEMBER (1991)

CREDITS:
LRS Media; Gabe Torres, dir.; Torres, scr.; Richard C. Berman, Donald Paul Pemrick, pro.; Deborah Holland, mus.; James Glennon, cin.; Carol Kravetz, Rick Hinson, ed.; 35 mm; C; 93 min.

CAST:

Allister Gibbs (*Balthazar Getty*); Brian Krause (*Tim Mitchell*); Jason London (*Russell Littlejohn*); Will Wheaton (*Kipp Gibbs*); Chris Young (*Stuart Brayton*).

Rating: ***

On that infamous Sunday, December 7, 1941, most citizens hear about Pearl on their radios. Over the next twenty-four hours, individuals must decide what to do. This indie film focuses on five boys attending a New England prep school. Their reactions are diverse, from rushing out to join up to waiting for further developments. Several reverse their decisions during a long night's journey into day. At its best, this obvious labor of love comes across as sensitive to the manner in which young minds deal with calamity. Too often, however, the film seems as uncomprehending as the boys.

FOCUS (2001)

CREDITS:

Carros Pictures; Neal Slavin, dir.; Kendrew Lascelles, scr., Arthur Miller, novel); Slavin, Robert A. Miller, prod.; Mark Adler, mus.; Juan Ruiz Anchia, cin.; Tariq Anwar, David B. Cohen, ed.; 1.85:1; C; 106 min.

CAST:

William H. Macy (*Lawrence Newman*); Laura Dern (*Gertrude Hart*); David Paymer (*Finkelstein*) Meat Loaf Aday (*Fred*); Kay Hawtrey (*Mrs. Newman*); Michael Copeman (*Carlson*); Kenneth Welsh (*Father Crighton*); Joseph Ziegler (*Gargan*).

Rating: *** ½

A veteran (Macy) returns home to his Brooklyn neighborhood and, owing to poor eyesight, must purchase glasses owing to his desk job at a local company. Shock sets in when co-workers and even longtime neighbors suspect him of being a Jew as his appearance is notably altered. A moral test occurs when he must decide if, as a non-Jew, he will welcome the block's first Jewish family or, for self-protection and even survival, he will side with the anti-Semites. A labor of love for Slavin based on an early novel by playwright Miller. Strong acting, particularly by Dern as the anti-hero's wife. Unfortunately, the script offers only skin-deep characterizations, while the decision to film this in a cheery, appealing area negates the fact that this is set in what the police considered one of the Brooklyn's nastiest areas diminishes the overall impact. Deeply heart-felt.

FORT McCOY (2014)

CREDITS:
Marzipan Ent.; Kate Connor, Michael Worth, dirs.; Connor, scr.; Connor, Eric Stoltz, pro.; Dana Nin, mus.; Neil Lisk, cin.; Robert Brakey, ed.; C; 100 min.

CAST:
Eric Stoltz (*Frank Stirn*); Kate Connor (*Ruby*); Lyndsey Fonesca (*Anna*); Andy Hirsch (*Sam*); Camryn Manheim (*Florie);* Seymour Cassel (*Father Mivkovek*); Brendan Fehr (*Sgt.Rossi);* Gerta Lonning (*Gertie*); Johnny Pacar (*Texas Slim).*

Rating: *** ½

Depressed after being rejected for military service as a 4-F, a barber (Stoltz) contributes to the war cause by plying his trade at Fort McCoy WI: shaving American servicemen as well as P.O.W.s. His teenage daughter (Fonesca) falls for a Jewish-American soldier; the younger girl befriends a juvenile German prisoner; the husband suspects that his wife finds men in uniform more attractive/masculine than he. An indie labor of love for Connor, who based the script on her family's experiences. Occasionally hits the heartwarming high notes everyone labored to achieve, though the Norman Rockwell-like visuals tend to bury a sometimes intriguing tale with schmaltz. Stoltz is highly effective in a complex role.

49th PARALLEL, aka INVADERS, THE (1941)

CREDITS:
Ortus Films/Columbia; Michael Powell, dir.; Rodney Ackland, Emeric Pressburger, scr.; Powell, George H. Brown, pro.; Ralph Vaughan Williams, mus.; Freddie Young, cin.; David Lean, ed.; B&W; 1.37:1; 123 min. (UK), 95 min. (US).

CAST:
Laurence Olivier (*Johnnie*); Raymond Massey (*Brock*); Richard George (*Bernsdorff*); Eric Portman (*Lt. Hirth*); Niall MacGinnis (*Vogel*); Finlay Currie (*Factor*); Glynis Johns (*Anna*); Anton Walbrook (*Peter*); Leslie Howard (*Scott*).

Ratings: **** 1/2 (UK)
**** (US)

German U-boats slip along the Canadian coast, wreaking havoc to distract the English. One such submarine, sailing underwater to join the Battle of St. Lawrence, comes close to shore. Six crew members procure needed food and water; while they are gone, the U-boat is sunk in Hudson Bay. They attempt to make their way south, by foot and on a stolen airplane, to the still-neutral US. Canadians who ordinarily live and let live—English, French, Inuit, and others—come together as a community prevent this escape. Superb blend of edge-of-your-seat thriller and propaganda, aimed at the US audience to make the case that it was time to join the cause: the Nazis Are Coming! Criticized in England for depicting several "decent" Germans. Story and screenplay Oscars went to the gifted Pressburger. The cinematography/editing team of Young and Lean ensures that every image is take-your-breath-away beautiful, the pace near perfect.

GANGWAY FOR TOMORROW (1943)

CREDITS:
RKO; John H. Auer, dir.; Aladar Laszlo, Arch Oboler, scr. John H. Auer, pro.; Roy Webb, mus.; Nicholas Musuraca, cin.; George Crone, ed.; B&W; 1.37:1; 69 min.

CAST:
Margo (*Lisette Rene*); John Carradine (*Mr. Wellington*); Robert Ryan (*Joe Dunham*); William Terry (*Bob Nolan*); James Bell (*Burke*); Alan Carney, Wally Brown ("*The Boys*").

Rating: *** 1/2

Five diverse workers share a ride to a local war plant. They know virtually nothing about one another. A French refugee (Margo) served with the resistance; a would-be air force flyer (Ryan) remains bitter about his rejection; a former prison warden (Bell) had to send his brother to the chair; a onetime Miss America (Ward) broke her lover's heart; a philosopher-hobo (Carradine) wishes to rejoin the human community. How each came to be in this carpool is illustrated via flashbacks. A one-of-a-kind movie thanks to writer Oboler, avatar of radio's famous *Lights Out*. Bell's story, the strangest, contains a flashback within a flashback. Interesting, if uneven qualitywise.

GHOSTS ON THE LOOSE (1943)

CREDITS:
Monogram; William Beaudine, dir.; Kenneth Higgins, scr.; Jack Dietz, Sam Katzman, pro.; Mack Stengler, cin.; Carl Pierson, ed.; B&W; 1.37:1; 66 min.

CAST:
Leo Gorcey (*Mugs*); Huntz Hall (*Glimpy*); Bobby Jordan (*Danny*); Bela Lugosi (*Emil*); Ava Gardner (*Betty*); Rick Vallin (*Jack*); Ernest Morrison (*Scruno*); Billy Benedict (*Benny*).

Rating: * 1/2

Nazis use an isolated mansion as their base, spreading rumors that the house is haunted. The vicious Dead End Kids have morphed into the mischievous if well-meaning Gas House Gang, integrated thanks to "Sunshine Sammy" Morrison. Best line? Gorcey to Hall: "I'm gonna send you to an optimist to get yer eyes examined!" Hungarian accent intact, Lugosi plays the German leader. Casting coup: Gardner as Huntz Hall's sister! And the "nightmare" takes place on…Elm Street! Objective quality: nil. Nostalgia value? Immeasurable.

HOLLYWOOD CANTEEN (1944)

CREDITS:
Warner Bros.; Delmer Daves, dir.; Daves, scr.; Alex Gottlieb, pro.; M. K. Jerome, mus.; Bert Glennon, cin.; Christian Nyby, ed.; B&W; 1.37:1; 124 min.

CAST:
Robert Hutton (*"Slim" Green*); Joan Leslie (*Herself*); Dane Clark (*"Brooklyn"*); Janis Paige (*Angela*); Bette Davis (*Herself*); John Garfield (*Himself*).

Rating: ***

Wounded in the Pacific, a sweet-hearted hick (Hutton) and his streetwise pal (Clark) get leave time in LA. They visit the title establishment, greeted by creators Davis and Garfield. While the fast talker chases after a faux star (Paige), the hero sets his sights on a real one (Leslie). Endless cameos by Warner contract players. In reality, the Canteen was manned by people from every studio. The long string of acts grows tiresome. And it's a bit self-promoting as Jack Warner has the vets visit his studio. This detracts from the single-set appeal of its predecessor, *Stage Door Canteen*. Music by The Andrews Sisters and the Jimmy Dorsey Orchestra, among others. Most embarrassing line, though it encapsulates the bygone era: "I could be one of our Russian friends…or even one of our own colored boys!"

ANYTHING FOR THE BOYS: Stars Bette Davis (with a real G.I.) and Joan Crawford (with Dane Clark playing a soldier) roll up their sleeves and entertain servicemen in *Hollywood Canteen.*

HUMAN COMEDY, THE (1943)

CREDITS:
Metro-Goldwyn-Mayer; Clarence Brown, dir.; William Saroyan (story), Howard Estabrook, scr.; Clarence Brown, pro.; Herbert Stothart, mus.; Harry Stradling, Sr., cin.; Conrad A. Nervig, ed.; B&W; 1.37:1; 118 min.

CAST:
Mickey Rooney (*Homer Macauley*); Frank Morgan (*Willie Grogan*); James Craig (*Tom Spangler*); Marsha Hunt (*Diana Steed*); Fay Bainter (*Mrs. Macauley*); Ray Collins (*Macauley*); Van Johnson (*Marcus*); Donna Reed (*Bess*).

Rating: ****

Saroyan kick-started the nostalgia movement with his popular novel, here handsomely filmed by MGM. A poor boy (Rooney) works at the local telegraph station. His job: deliver messages from the military, informing people their husbands or sons are dead. He senses that in time, such a missive will arrive about his brother (Johnson), which he'll have to deliver to their mom (Bainter). Many of the era's top songs are included, adding to the verisimilitude. Best described as anecdotal, this appealing patchwork quilt of happy and sad moments takes us everywhere, reminiscent of Wilder's *Our Town*. *The Human Comedy* offers a vision of a way of life that Americans communally believed they were fighting to preserve. Embodies the term "Americana."

IN THE MEANTIME, DARLING (1944)

CREDITS:
Metro-Goldwyn-Mayer; Otto Preminger, dir.; Arthur Kober, Michael Uris, scr.; Preminger, pro.; Cyril J. Mockridge, mus.; Joseph MacDonald, cin.; Louis R. Loeffler, ed.; B&W; 1.37:1; 77 min.

CAST:
Jeanne Crain (*Maggie Preston*); Frank Latimore (*Lt. Daniel Ferguson*); Eugene Pallette (*Henry Preston*); Mary Nash (*Mrs. Preston*); Gale Robbins

THE BOY NEXT DOOR?: Mickey Rooney as an all-American kid in *The Human Comedy*; Skip Homier as an adopted Nazi youth in *Tomorrow the World.*

(*Shirley*); Clarence Muse (*Hotel porter*).

Rating: ***

One of several films to deal with a unique problem during the war years: newlywed girls' need to find temporary housing near their husbands' bases. The focus is on a pampered woman (Crain) from a upper-class home and her problems adjusting to other women, mostly middle class. Terrible opening, played as raucous comedy, though things settle down for a more serious (and pleasurable) form of humor that reveals a great deal about the lifestyle of that time, from its music to long-gone manners.

ITHACA (2015)

CREDITS:
Co-Op Ent.; Meg Ryan, dir.; Eric Jendressen, scr., William Saroyan (novel); Jendressen, Janet Brenner, Laura Ivey, prods.; John Mellancamp, mus.; Andrew Dann, cin.; John F. Lyons, ed.; C; 2.35:1; 96 min.

CAST:
Alex Neustaedter (*Homer Macauley*); Meg Ryan (*Mom*); Tom Hanks (*Dad*); Sam Shepard (*Willie Grogan*); Hamish Linklater (*Tom Spangler*); Jack Quaid (*Marcus*); Spencer Howell (*Ulysses*); Christine Nelson (*Bess*); Gabriel Basso (*Tobey*).

Rating: ** ½

A fourteen-year-old (Neustaedter), living in what appears to be Main Street, U.S.A. from a Disney theme park, delivers telegrams that families fear, informing them loved ones died overseas. His great fear: Someday, one will arrive informing him of his older brother's passing. Saroyan's 75+ year old work won the Pulitzer in its time, largely for capturing an abiding combination of melancholia and good-will on the home-front. This production unaccountably eliminates what was truly timeless--the parents' (Ryan, Hanks) complex relationship with one another and their off-spring--leaving little for a modern viewer other than overdone sentimentality of a

Norman Rockwell order. Well-intentioned avatar Ryan brings nothing new to the piece while missing the intensity of the 1943 film version.

JANIE (1944)

CREDITS:
Warner Bros.; Michael Curtiz, dir.; Herschel V. Williams, Jr. (play), Josephine Bentham, Charles Hoffman, Agnes Christine Johnston, scr.; Alex Gottlieb, pro.; Heinz Roemheld, Franz Waxman, Frank Perkins, mus.; Carl E. Guthrie, cin.; Owen Marks, ed.; B&W; 1.37:1; 102 min.

CAST:
Joyce Reynolds (*Janie Conway*); Robert Hutton (*Pfc. Dick Lawrence*); Edward Arnold (*Charles*); Ann Harding (*Lucille*); Alan Hale (*Prof. Reardon*); Robert Benchley (*John Van Brunt*).

Rating: ***

WB's attempt to create a female Andy Hardy for the WWII era. Reynolds appears perkily unmemorable as the title teenager who goes "uniform mad" when military maneuvers are scheduled near her small town. A soldier (Hutton) moves in with her family, which includes the curmudgeonly dad (Arnold) and civil defense volunteer mom (Harding). Enjoyable idiocy provides a genial time capsule of the jitterbug/jive-talking era. The film that introduced the term "smooching" to the public. Hattie McDaniel appears as yet another black maid; Benchley does one more variation on his fidgety cynic. Smart dialogue, snappy direction.

JOE SMITH, AMERICAN (1942)

CREDITS:
Metro-Goldwyn-Mayer; Richard Thorpe, dir.; Allen Rivkin, scr.; Jack Chertok, Dore Schary, pro.; Daniele Amfitheatrof, mus.; Charles Lawton, Jr., cin.; Elmo Veron, ed.; B&W; 1.37:1; 63 min.

CAST:

Robert Young (*Joe Smith*); Marsha Hunt (*Mary Smith*); Harvey Stephens (*Dunhill*); Darryl Hickman (*Johnny*); Jonathan Hale (*McKettrick*); Noel Madison (*Schricker*); Ava Gardner (*Bit*).

Rating: **

A plant worker (Young) is abducted by enemy agents and tortured. Inspired by history's Nathan Hale and his own son (Hickman), he refuses to give information, miraculously escapes, and then helps authorities track down the Nazis. Absurd plot. Claustrophobic interrogation scenes might be powerful if they weren't continuously interrupted by useless flashbacks. The most harrowing aspect is not the bad guys beating our hero but the manner in which the US government tosses out the Bill of Rights, questioning the victim about everything from his religious beliefs to his bank account. From a *Cosmopolitan* story by Paul Gallico.

LETTER FOR EVIE, A (1946)

CREDITS:

Metro-Goldwyn-Mayer; Jules Dassin, dir.; Blanche Brace (short story), DeVallon Scott, Alan Friedman, scr.; William H. Wright, pro.; George Bassman, mus.; Karl Freund, cin.; Chester W. Schaeffer, ed.; B&W; 1.37:1; 89 min.

CAST:

Marsha Hunt (*Evie O'Connor*); John Carroll (*Edgar "Wolf" Larson*); Hume Cronyn (*John McPherson*); Spring Byington (*Mrs. McPherson*); Norman Lloyd (*DeWitt Pynchon*); Cameron Mitchell (*Wounded Soldier*).

Rating: *** 1/2

Hungry to find "a real man," a uniform-factory worker (Hunt) slips a note to an unknown soldier into a size 16 1/2 shirt pocket, hoping some big handsome lug responds. The elegant recipient (Carroll) isn't interested, but his skinny sidekick (Cronyn) is, and he sends her his buddy's pic with the expected complications. Similar in plot, though not tone, to the tragic *Love Letters*, this modestly pleasant farce is bolstered by Hunt's charms and Cronyn's comic timing. Diminished, however, by Carroll's inability to portray a Gable-like playboy. Nicely captures the meet-and-marry mood of the war years, as well as the changing sexual mores.

LITTLE BOY (2015)

CREDITS:
Metanoia/Open Road; Alejandro Monteverde, dir.; Monteverde, Pepe Portillo, scr.; Leo Severino, pro.; Stephan Altman, Mark Foster, mus.; Andrew Cadelago, cin.; Meg Ramsay, Joan Sobel, Fernando Villena, ed.; C; 2.35:1; 106 min.

CAST:
Jakob Salvati (*Pepper Flynt Busbee*); Emily Watson (*Emma*); Michael Rapaport (*James*); David Henrie (*London*); Ted Levine (*Sam*); Cary-Hiroyuki Tagawa (Hashimoto); Kevin James (*Dr. Fox*); Barry Ford (*Narrator*).

Rating: ****

When his father (Rapaport) volunteers and then goes missing in action, a boy (Salvati) in a small California town draws on a comic-book/movie-serial magician's supposed powers to continue believing life is essentially good while learning from experience that all Japanese people aren't our enemies. Executive producer Roma Downey (of TV's *Touched by an Angel*) oversaw this faith-based movie, which has appeal beyond that limited target audience. Similar in tone to the 1950s live-action films of Walt Disney, with a touch of *The Twilight Zone*. Happily, a Norman Rockwell *Saturday Evening Post*-cover visualization does not sentimentalize the material to a point that serious issues are avoided. The child star is superb, Watson a great talent. Sweet-spirited and smart.

LITTLE TOKYO, USA (1942)

CREDITS:
20th Century Fox; Otto Brower, dir.; George Bricker, scr.; Bryan Foy, pro.; Joseph MacDonald, cin.; Harry Reynolds, ed.; B&W; 1.37:1; 64 min.

CAST:
Preston Foster (*Michael Steele*); Brenda Joyce (*Maris*); *Hanover*); Harold Huber (*Takimura*); Donald Douglas (*Hendricks*); June Duprez (*Teru*); George E. Stone (*Kingoro*); Abner Biberman (*Satsuma*).

Rating: NO STARS

Shortly after Pearl, an LA cop launches an investigation into the Japanese American community. Virtually everyone living in Little Tokyo is a saboteur. The worst of Asian fifth columnists are those claiming to be loyal citizens. A vicious attack on an ethnic subculture, the likes of which was never unleashed on German or Italian Americans. This artless if widely seen film was designed to condition the public to accept the relocation of Japanese Americans.

MEET THE PEOPLE (1944)

CREDITS:
Metro-Goldwyn-Mayer; Charles Reisner, dir.; Louis Lantz (story), Sol Barzman, Ben Barzman, S. M. Herzig, Fred Saidy, scr.; E. Y. Harburg, Arthur Freed, pro.; Lennie Hayton, mus.; Robert Surtees, cin.; Alex Troffey, ed.; B&W; 1.37:1; 100 min.

CAST:
Lucille Ball (*Julie Hampton*); Dick Powell (*William Swanson*); Virginia O'Brien (*Peg*); Bert Lahr (*Commander*); Rags Ragland (*Smith*); June Allyson (*Annie*).

Rating: **

Unmemorable, occasionally spunky minor musical undercut by mediocre songs. A shipyard worker (Powell) hopes to convince a snooty Broadway star (Ball) to appear in a show timed with the launching of a destroyer. The play-within-the-play's title is the same as the film's, its ideology a throwback to New Deal–era movies lionizing the common man. Vaughn Monroe and His Orchestra and Spike Jones and His City Slickers appear as themselves. Populism meets patriotism.

MIRACLE IN THE RAIN (1956)

CREDITS:
Warner Bros.; Rudolph Maté, dir.; Ben Hecht (novel), scr.; Frank P. Rosenberg, pro.; Franz Waxman, mus.; Russell Metty, cin.; Thomas Reilly, ed.; B&W; 1.37:1; 107 min.

CAST:
Jane Wyman (*Ruth Wood*); Van Johnson (*Arthur Hugenon*); Peggie Castle (*Millie*); Fred Clark (*Jalonik*); Eileen Heckart (*Grace*); Josephine Hutchinson (*Agnes*); Marcel Dalio (*Marcel*); Alan King (*Gil*).

Rating: *** 1/2

During a downpour in New York City, a shy office worker bumps into a PFC on leave and a romance buds. Afterward, while caring for her ill mother, she receives word he's been killed in combat. Yet, she still believes that somehow, some way, they'll meet again. One of Hecht's hard-boiled yet sentimental Big Apple fables, this intriguing if improbable piece might have been better served by a less treacly approach to direction, music, etc. Vivid characterizations—including Heckart as a gum-snapping gal pal and Castle as a gorgeous secretary involved with her boss (Clark)—elevate this above simplistic soap opera. Religious aspects are extremely heavy handed.

MIRACLE OF MORGAN'S CREEK, THE (1944)

CREDITS:
Paramount; Preston Sturges, dir.; Sturges, scr.; Sturges, Buddy G. DeSylva, pro.; Charles Bradshaw, Leo Shuken, Gil Grau, mus.; John F. Seitz, cin.; Stuart Gilmore, ed.; B&W; 1.33:1; 98 min.

CAST:
Eddie Bracken (*Norval Jones*); Betty Hutton (*Trudy Kockenlocker*); Diana Lynn (*Emmy*); William Demarest (*Const. Kockenlocker*); Porter Hall (*Justice*); Emory Parnell (*Tuerck*); Al Bridge (*Johnson*); Chester Conklin (*Pete*).

Rating: *****

Accelerated dialogue drives an appropriately absurd story: a small-town virgin (Hutton) heads to the USO hall to dance with GIs. Soon, she's pregnant but has no idea who the father might be. Sturges stock-company member Demarest is suitably gruff as her dad who feared this would happen after reading about war brides marrying strangers. Bracken is a pudding-faced whiner who can't get into uniform but loves the lady. Strong satire of small minds in middle America. Sturges keeps the tone so genial that there was no outrage regarding the central theme (a defense of bigamy). This provided a needed corrective to *The Clock* and others that romanticized love at first sight during the war. Of the great comedy auteurs (Capra, Wilder, Lubitsch, Hawks), none caught the spirit of this era so perfectly as Sturges.

1941 (1979)

CREDITS:
Universal; Steven Spielberg, dir.; Robert Zemeckis, Bob Gale, John Milius, scr.; Buzz Feitshans, pro.; John Williams, mus.; William A. Fraker, cin.; Michael Kahn, ed.; C; 2.35:1; min.

THE NEW AMERICAN WOMAN: In Preston Sturges' *The Miracle at Morgan's Creek*, Betty Hutton (with William Demarest) flaunts The New Morality: in Woody Allen's *Radio Days*, Diane Keaton moves up the ladder to media stardom.

A TIME FOR PANIC: Angelenos fear that,, following Pearl Harbor, they may be the enemy's next target in *1941*.

CAST:

Dan Aykroyd (*Sgt. Frank Tree*); Ned Beatty (*Ward Douglas*); John Belushi (*Wild Bill Kelso*); Murray Hamilton (*Crumn*); Christopher Lee (*Capt. Kleinschmidt*); Tim Matheson (*Loomis*); Toshirô Mifune (*Cmdr. Mitamura*); Warren Oates (*Madman Maddox*); Robert Stack (*Gen. Joseph Stilwell*); Treat Williams (*Stretch*); John Candy (*Foley*); Slim Pickens (*Wood*); Lionel Stander (*Angelo*).

Rating: *

Following Pearl, an Axis sub is spotted off the California coast. A cross-section of the public—civvies and military—goes berserk fearing imminent invasion. The director's first flop is a resounding one: expensive, elaborate gags that were supposed to be uproariously funny fall flat. A once-in-a-lifetime cast, squandered on an empty project. Full of sound and fury, signifying nothing. Only plus: detailed attention to the period. Stack's role as a real-life general had originally been offered to John Wayne.

ON THE SUNNY SIDE (1942)

CREDITS:
20th Century Fox; Harold D. Schuster, dir.; Lillie Hayward, George Templeton, scr., Mary C. McCall Jr. (magazine story); Lou T. Ostrow, pro.; David Raksin, mus.; Lucien N. Andriot, cin.; Red Allen, ed.; B&W; 1.37:1; 69 min.

CAST:
Roddy McDowall (*Hugh Aylesworth*); Jane Darwell (*Annie*); Stanley Clements (*Tom Sanders*); Katharine Alexander *(Mary Andrews)*; Ann (E.) Todd (*Betty*); Donald Douglas (*George);* Freddie Mercer (*Don*); Jill Esmond *(Mrs. Aylesworth).*

Rating: * ½

For safety's sake, Brit children are transported to the U.S. and placed with host families. One near-perfect 12-year-old (McDowall) arrives in an Ohio small-town right out of Norman Rockwell, where the local kids resemble an upscale version of The Little Rascals. Low-key, broadly-played, utterly clichéd vision of a subject worthy of serious study. One bright point for today's viewers: the village bully and his 'toady' appear to be models for their counterpart characters in *A Christmas Story* (1983), including a funny fight sequence by a fence.

PEYTON PLACE (1957)

CREDITS:
20th Century Fox; Mark Robson, dir.; Grace Metalious (novel), John Michael Hayes, scr.; Jerry Wald, pro.; Franz Waxman, mus.; William C. Mellor, cin.; David Bretherton, ed.; C; 2.35:1; 157 min.

CAST:
Lana Turner (*Constance MacKenzie*); Lee Philips (*Michael Rossi*); Lloyd Nolan (*Dr. Swain*); Arthur Kennedy (*Lucas Cross*); Russ Tamblyn (*Norman Page*); Terry Moore (*Betty Anderson*); Hope Lange (*Selena Cross*); Diane Varsi (*Allison*); Barry Coe (*Rodney*).

Rating: ****

Domestic epic waters down the scandalous novel by Metalious (1924–1964). A sensitive teenage writer (Varsi) observes the seamy underbelly of a New England town between the late 1930s and early 1950s. Warrants interest because of its accurate portrayal of how a faraway war changed everything. The area's richest, most conventionally masculine young man (Coe) dies overseas; local momma's boy (Tamblyn) comes into his own as a hero. Vivid depictions of small-town young men leaving on a bus and of burial services for those who shortly return. Memorable moment: a postwar meeting of two once-close friends, each so changed that they momentarily fail to recognize each other.

PIN UP GIRL (1944)

CREDITS:
20th Century Fox; H. Bruce Humberstone, Libbie Block, Robert Ellis, Helen Logan, Earl Baldwin, scr.; William LeBaron, pro.; Arthur Lange, Cyril J. Mockridge, mus.; Ernest Palmer, cin.; Robert L. Simpson, ed.; C; 1.37:1; 83 min.

CAST:
Betty Grable (*Lorry Jones*); John Harvey (*Tommy Dooley*); Martha Raye (*Molly McKay*); Joe E. Brown (*Eddie Hall*); Eugene Pallette (*Barney*); Dorothea Kent (*Kay*); Nat "King" Cole (*Canteen Pianist*).

Rating: *** 1/2

A blonde from Missoula and her silly sidekick travel to DC, taking government jobs as stenographers. Ridiculously contrived, mounted in the gloriously muted-pastel Fox color process, serving mainly to show off the famed photograph of Grable in a one-piece bathing suit. The real value here is provided by art directors James Basevi and Joseph C. Wright, who idealize the era; by specialty dancers the Condo Brothers as high-jacking hicks; and by Angela Blue as a definitive Parisienne Apache dancer. A representation of the new morality has women of dubious sexual morality suddenly tolerated for "supporting the troops." Most memorable number: a spectacular ice-skating sequence in red, white, and blue.

POWDER TOWN (1942)

CREDITS:
Rowland V. Lee, dir.; David Boehm, John Twist, scr.; Cliff Reid, pro.; Samuel E. Beetley, ed.; Frank Redman, cin.; Roy Web, mus.; RKO Radio Pictures; 79 min.; B&W; 1.37:1.

CAST:
Victor McLaglen (*Jeems O'Shea*); Edmond O'Brien (*J. Quincy Pennant*); June Havoc (*Dolly*); Dorothy Lovett (*Sally*): Eddie Foy Jr. (*Billy Meeker*); Damian O'Flynn (*Lindsay*).

Rating: *

Big, brawling Irishman O'Shea is assigned to watch over the meek, milk-toast absent minded professor 'Pennie' when the latter is assigned to the title area, a swiftly built city where blue collar Americans work at preparing state of the art munitions. Occasional newsreel footage of men on their way to work or labouring adds spice to a mostly dull comedy/ adventure/ romance featuring a hopelessly miscast O'Brien opposite a gross caricature of Gallic excess. Odd in that the war itself is never once mentioned. Based on a novel by Max Brand, best known for *Destry Rides Again*. Unrewarding.

RADIO DAYS (1987)

CREDITS:
Orion Pictures; Woody Allen, dir.; Allen, scr.; Robert Greenhut, Charles H. Joffe, Jack Rollins, pro.; Dick Hyman, mus.; Carlo Di Palma, cin.; Susan E. Morse, ed.; C; 1.85:1; 88 min.

CAST:

Mia Farrow (*Sally White*); Dianne Wiest (*Bea*); Danny Aiello (*Rocco*); Julie Kavner (*Mother*); Wallace Shawn (*Masked Avenger*); Seth Green (*Joe*); Michael Tucker (*Father*); Josh Mostel (*Abe*); Diane Keaton (*Jazz Singer*); Woody Allen (*Narrator*).

Rating: *****

Glorious salute to radio's golden age, when drama and comedy, as well as music and news, made the medium central to American lives by creating an aural community among people of diverse locations and ethnicities. Parallel plots cut between an aspiring star (Farrow) and an Allenesque child (Green) who, in his naïve imagination, reinvents these less-than-perfect radio stars as gods and goddesses. Various life situations in New York's Rockaway Beach are vividly re-created. The child's experience while watching out for enemy submarines just off the coast—as he's instructed to do by on-air announcers—is one of those magical movie moments you cherish forever. Kitty Carlisle, Don Pardo, and Tito Puente play variations of themselves. One of Woody's most sentimental, nostalgic, and unpretentiously appealing films.

RATIONING (1944)

CREDITS:

Metro-Goldwyn-Mayer; Willis Goldbeck, dir.; Harry Ruskin, Grant Garrett, Robert E. Hopkins, William R. Lipman, scr.; Orville O. Dull, pro.; David Snell, Sol Kaplan, mus.; Sidney Wagner, cin.; Ferris Webster, ed.; B&W; 1.37:1; 93 min.

CAST:

Wallace Beery (*Ben Barton*); Marjorie Main (*Iris Tuttle*); Donald Meek (*Wilfred Ball*); Dorothy Morris (*Dorothy*); Howard Freeman (*Cash*); Connie Gilchrist (*Mrs. Porter*).

Rating: ***

Boozy, bleary-eyed Beery was always best when teamed (in seven films) with his natural nemesis, Main, the middle-American shrew with a high-pitched voice that could break glass. Here he's a local butcher in Anytown, USA, who tries to procure the necessary coupons from the local rationing board headed by arch-enemy Main. Adding to the mounting consternation, his adopted son wants to marry her daughter. The extant black market for meat is revealed in this broad, lowbrow comedy. Jokes about the color coding of various meats, prime in their time, will have little meaning for younger viewers. A product of its age; to be enjoyed, it must be seen from that perspective.

SECRET COMMAND (1944)

CREDITS:
Edward Sutherland, dir.; Roy Chanslor, scr.; Pat O'Brien, Phil L. Ryan, prods.; Viola Lawrence, ed.; Franz Planer, cin.; Paul Sawtell, mus.; Columbia; B&W; 1.37:1 82 min.

CAST:
Pat O'Brien (*Sam Gallagher*); Carole Landis (*Jill McGann*); Chester Morris (*Jeff Gallager*); Ruth Warrick *(Lea)*; Tom Tully *('Brownie')*; Barton MacLane *('Red')*; Carol Nugent *(Joan)*.

Rating: *** ½

Alcoholic former reporter Sam Gallagher asks his more solid brother Jeff for a job working on the docks where our ships are launched. Jeff fears that Sam may hope to rekindle a romance with Lea, the girl they both love, also wondering if Sam might be a Nazi agent. Actually, he's with our government and hopes to infiltrate, then expose undercover Nazis planning to sabotage the process. Film's biggest weakness: ordinary guy Pat O'Brien disastrously cast as a lover boy. Landis shines as a blonde, buxom, ballsy F.B.I. agent. Interesting in that (at O'Brien's insistence) this film challenges then-widespread prejudices toward Irish Americans. Otherwise, solid though unsurprising program picture from Columbia's B unit. From a *Saturday Evening Post* short story by John & Ward Hawkins.

SEPARATE PEACE, A (1972)

CREDITS:

Paramount; Larry Peerce, dir.; John Knowles (novel), Fred Segal, scr.; Robert A. Goldston, Otto Plaschkes, pro.; Charles Fox, mus.; Frank Stanley, cin.; John C. Howard, ed.; C; 1.33:1; 104 min.

CAST:

John Heyl (Finny); Parker Stevenson (*Gene*); William Roerick (*Mr. Patchwithers*); Peter Brush (*Leper*); Victor Bevine (*Brinker*); Scott Bradbury (*Chet*).

Rating: *

Knowles's 1959 coming-of-age novel takes its title from Hemingway's *A Farewell to Arms*: you can't hide from war, which seeks out the most innocent, even when they attempt to create a separate peace. Boys at Devon Prep School, fearing they'll be drafted, try to do so with tragic results. Two friends (Heyl, Stevenson) learn about life and death the hard way. What is understated in the novel (e.g., the homoerotic element) is made explicit on-screen by one of Hollywood's worst directors, his cinematic canvas awash in grotesque pastels. A fine book reduced to a flat film.

SHERLOCK HOLMES IN WASHINGTON (1943)

CREDITS:

Universal; Roy William Neill, dir.; Arthur Conan Doyle (characters), Bertram Millhauser, Lynn Riggs, scr.; Howard Benedict, Neill, pro.; Frank Skinner, mus.; Lester White, cin.; Otto Ludwig, ed.; B&W; 1.37:1; 71 min.

CAST:

Basil Rathbone (*Sherlock Holmes*); Nigel Bruce (*Doctor Watson*); Marjorie Lord (*Nancy Partridge*); Henry Daniell (*William Easter*); George Zucco (*Stanley*).

Rating: *** 1/2

A Brit courier passes microfilm to an unsuspecting American deb (Lord), causing Nazis (Daniell, Zucco) to abduct her. Holmes and Watson fly to Washington. The sleuth realizes the missing MacGuffin has been inserted into a "V for Victory" matchbook. Clever fish-out-of-water premise (Watson discovers chewing gum) is never fully developed in a so-so script *not* derived from a Doyle original. Best moment: Holmes passing himself off as an eccentric art dealer, a precedent to Bogart's similar rare-book expert in *The Big Sleep*. This film—begun before the US officially entered the war but completed after—is a hybrid: in the first half, bad spies are identified only as "the enemy." Later, they're clearly posited as German.

SINCE YOU WENT AWAY (1944)

CREDITS:
Vanguard/Selznick International; John Cromwell, dir.; Margaret Buell Wilder (book), David O. Selznick, scr.; Selznick, pro.; Max Steiner, mus.; Stanley Cortez, Lee Garmes, cin.; John Faure, Arthur Fellows, Marsh Hendry, ed.; B&W; 1.37:1; 130 min.

CAST:
Claudette Colbert (*Mrs. Anne Hilton*); Jennifer Jones (*Jane*); Joseph Cotten (*Lt. Tony Willett*); Shirley Temple (*Bridget*); Monty Woolley (*Col. William G. Smollett*); Lionel Barrymore (*Clergyman*); Robert Walker (*Cpl. William G. Smollett II*); Hattie McDaniel (*Fidelia*); Agnes Moorehead (*Mrs. Hawkins*).

Rating: ****

Like many wives, Mrs. Wilder wrote to her overseas husband. Unlike others, she kept copies and published them in book form. Selznick, always on the lookout for material for his next superproduction, bought the rights. An upscale mother (Colbert) of two growing girls (Jones, Temple) maintains her home with help from her loyal maid (McDaniel). Difficulties include a huffy Brit boarder (Woolly) and her old flame

(Cotten). Alternately hokey and touching, this film's considerable virtues outweigh the flaws of overproduction, including Steiner's weepy score. The best moments occur when Cromwell's camera drifts off to ordinary Americans at USO dances and train stations. The parting of Jones and her beau (Walker) would be later satirized in *Airplane!* A true time capsule.-

STAGE DOOR CANTEEN (1943)

CREDITS:
Sol Lesser Productions; Frank Borzage, dir.; Delmer Daves, scr.; Frank Borzage, Sol Lesser, pro.; Freddie Rich, mus.; Harry J. Wild, cin.; B&W; 1.37:1; 132 min.

CAST:
Cheryl Walker (*Eileen Burke*); William Terry (*Dakota Smith*); Marjorie Riordan (*Jean*); Lon McCallister (*California Jack*); Margaret Early (*Ella Sue*).

Rating: ****

A troop train reaches the East Coast, where soldiers head for a canteen to enjoy food, dancing, entertainment. This being the Big Apple, the place is filled with stars from radio, downtown dens, upscale cabarets, and the theater: Tallulah Bankhead slips over from her latest play, and Gypsy Rose Lee performs a modified strip. The boys are treated to a kitschy combination of high-, middle-, and lowbrow pop culture. Out-of-work actresses share their evenings with lonely GIs. An African American soldier joins, hinting at postwar integration. Outside, "every night until victory, this light will be gleaming." With peace at hand, such canteens closed as the sense of a true American community somehow slipped through our collective fingers like sand.

SUMMER OF '42 (1971)

CREDITS:
Warner Bros.; Robert Mulligan, dir.; Herman Raucher, scr.; Richard A. Roth, pro.; Michel Legrand, mus.; Robert Surtees, cin.; Folmar Blangsted, cd.; C; 1.85:1; 103 min.

CAST:
Jennifer O'Neill (*Dorothy*); Gary Grimes (*Hermie*); Jerry Houser (*Oscy*); Oliver Conant (*Benjie*); Christopher Norris (*Miriam*); Maureen Stapleton (*Hermie's mother, voice only*); Robert Mulligan (*Narrator*).

Rating: ****

Popular coming-of-age story about a teenager (Grimes) who hangs out with his plump pal (Hauser) and their brainy buddy (Conant) on an

AN END TO INNOCENCE: On the home-front, a teenage boy (Gary Grimes) and his innocent pals come to terms with the adult world in *Summer of '42*.

island where it's easy to forget that war rages overseas. Then, a gorgeous war bride (O'Neill) arrives; the boys are smitten. Shot in the Norman Rockwell style, with an appropriately nostalgic score. When the woman's husband dies overseas, Hermie finds himself at the right place at the right time to live his wildest dreams. What seemed sweetly spontaneous on the woman's part when this film was released would today likely land her in jail for child molestation. Sexy and sentimental.

SUNDAY DINNER FOR A SOLDIER (1944)

CREDITS:
20th Century Fox; Lloyd Bacon, dir.; Martha Cheavens (story), Melvin Levy, Wanda Tuchock, scr.; Walter Morosco, pro.; Alfred Newman, mus.; Joseph MacDonald, cin.; J. Watson Webb, ed.; B&W, 1.37:1; 85 min.

CAST:
Anne Baxter (*Tessa Osborne*); John Hodiak (*Sgt. Eric Moore*); Charles Winninger (*Grandfather*); Anne Revere (*Agatha*); Connie Marshall (*Mary*); Chill Wills (*Mr. York*); Bobby Driscoll (*Jeep*); Jane Darwell (*USO lady*).

Rating: ****

Had the term "heartwarming" not existed, it would've had to have been created for this slice of Americana. In a small Florida community, a young woman (Baxter) raises her siblings (Marshall, Driscoll) while caring for her lovably dotty father (Winninger) on a houseboat. The area's other families invite soldiers over for a special meal; these people scrimp and save to do the same. The invitation never reaches the army base. Then, a forlorn GI (Hodiak) happens along. Revere is memorable as a nosy neighbor. Few films capture the era's spirit of self-sacrifice so exquisitely. Marred by obvious studio sets for exterior scenes. Theme song: "I'll See You in My Dreams" (1924) by Isham Jones and Gus Kahn.

SUN VALLEY SERENADE (1941)

CREDITS:

20th Century Fox; H. Bruce Humberstone, dir.; Art Arthur, Robert Harari, Robert Ellis, Helen Logan, scr.; Milton Sperling, pro.; Mack Gordon, mus.; Edward Cronjager, cin.; James B. Clark, ed.; B&W; 1.37:1; 86 min.

CAST:

Sonja Henie (*Karen Benson*); John Payne (*Ted Scott*); Glenn Miller (*Phil Corey*); Milton Berle (*Nifty*); Joan Davis (*Miss Carstairs*); Dorothy Dandridge (*Dancer*); the Nicholas Bros., The Modernaires, Fred "Snowflake" Toones (*themselves*).

Rating: ****

A pianist romances a gorgeous but temperamental jazz singer to convince her she should join him, his bandleader, and their agent for a Christmas Eve performance at an Idaho ski resort. A romantic triangle forms when the Scandinavian refugee he's agreed to care for turns out to be a beauty. The charmingly nonsensical plot well serves Miller's music, his great wartime hits on display. Henie's ice skating is superbly sensuous. All the era's good spirits are evident but also its limiting prejudices: Dandridge and the Nicholas Bros. are never allowed to mix with other entertainers, and Toones plays his stereotyped background porter for the umpteenth time. Of more interest to fans of the musical genre than WWII buffs. Mostly a delightful entertainment. One question: Why wasn't the film shot in color?

TENDER COMRADE (1943)

CREDITS:

RKO; Edward Dmytryk, dir.; Dalton Trumbo, scr.; David Hempstead, pro.; Leigh Harline, mus.; Russell Metty, cin.; Roland Gross, ed.; B&W; 1.37:1; 102 min.

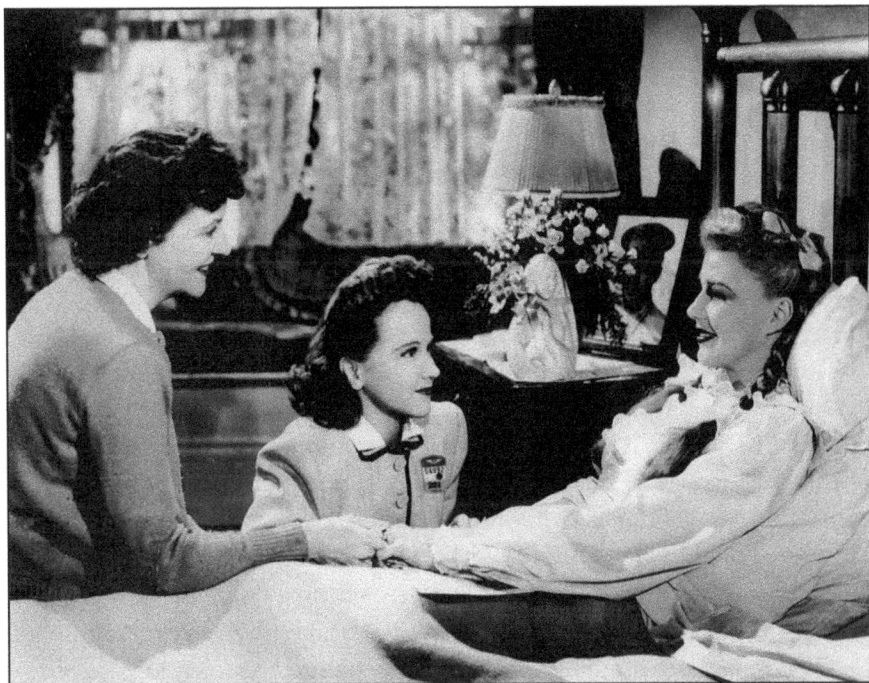

THE EMERGENCE OF AMERICAN SISTERHOOD: While her husband is overseas, other women become close friends and full supporters of a war bride (Ginger Rogers); letters from the front draw together females of various ages in a single family in *Since You Went Away*: Jennifer Jones, Claudette Colbert, Shirley Temple.

CAST:

Ginger Rogers (*Jo Jones*); Robert Ryan (*Chris Jones*); Ruth Hussey (*Barbara*); Patricia Collinge (*Helen*); Mady Christians (*Manya*); Kim Hunter (*Doris*); Jane Darwell (*Mrs. Henderson*).

Rating: ***

When her new husband ships out, a young bride moves in with a diverse group of women, all eager to do whatever they can to support the cause. The only major movie shot during WWII to focus entirely on the war bride syndrome is, sadly, a disappointment, owing to its simplistic tone and sentimental girly-girl small talk. After combat ended, a confederacy of dunces formed to blacklist the writer and director for a purportedly communist (consider the title) and feminist (women together, in group fashion, sharing what little they have) confection. Red-baiting accusers failed to consider that the film's title derives from a quote by Robert Louis Stevenson, referring to true love. Most memorable shot: cinematographer Metty's surreal dream image of the sadly separated couple.

THRILL OF A ROMANCE (1945)

CREDITS:

Metro-Goldwyn-Mayer; Richard Thorpe, dir.; Richard Connell, Gladys Lehman, scr.; Joe Pasternak, pro.; George E. Stoll, mus.; Harry Stradling, Sr., cin.; George Boemler, ed.; C; 1.37:1; 105 min.

CAST:

Van Johnson (*Major Thomas Milvaine*); Esther Williams (*Cynthia Glenn*); Frances Gifford (*Maude*); Henry Travers (*Glenn*); Spring Byington (*Nona Glenn*); Lauritz Melchior (*Nils*); Tommy Dorsey and his Orchestra (*themselves*).

Rating: ***

Glossy, song-laden vehicle for swimming star Williams, playing a small-town girl swept off her feet by a rich businessman. He offers to marry her, taking his overwhelmed virgin bride to a Redwoods resort. Before the marriage can be consummated, he's called away on business, and she falls for a war hero on leave. Censorship kept the stars from kissing, considering her awkward situation. Though the affair remains platonic (in the film if not in its real-life parallels), this pushed the limits of a Code-approved release for suggesting that there's nothing wrong with an intense flirtation—a notion that would not have been acceptable before the war changed everything.

TOMORROW IS FOREVER (1946)

CREDITS:

International Pictures; Irving Pichel, dir.; Gwen Bristow, Lenore J. Coffee, scr.; David Lewis, pro.; Max Steiner, mus.; Joseph A. Valentine, cin.; Ernest J. Nims, ed.; B&W; 2.37:1; 104 min.

CAST:

Claudette Colbert (*Elizabeth Hamilton*); Orson Welles (*John Andrew MacDonald/Erik Kessler*); George Brent (*Lawrence Hamilton*); Lucile Watson (*Aunt Jessica*); Natalie Wood (*Margaret*).

Rating: ** 1/2

Handsomely mounted, sincerely acted, impossibly contrived three-handkerchief weeper. Married to a businessman, a loyal wife has no idea that her "deceased" first husband, disfigured in WWI, works for her spouse's company as scientist, also caring for a war orphan. The intent was to create a domestic tragedy of fate, but this plays more like a soap opera. Melodramatic resolutions worthy of grand opera seem unintentionally funny in the realistic context.

TOMORROW, THE WORLD! (1944)

CREDITS:

United Artists; Leslie Fenton, dir.; James Gow (play), Arnaud d'Usseau (play), Ring Lardner, Jr., Leopold Atlas, scr.; Lester Cowan, pro.; Louis

Applebaum, mus.; Henry Sharp, cin.; Anne Bauchens, ed.; B&W; 1.37:1; 86 min.

CAST:

Fredric March (*Mike Frame*); Betty Field (*Leona Richards*); Agnes Moorehead (*Aunt Jessie*); Joan Carroll (*Pat*); Edit Angold (*Frieda*); Skip(py) Homeier (*Emil Bruckner*).

Rating: ** 1/2

A college professor, working for the war cause and about to marry his Jewish fiancée, agrees to adopt an orphan whose antifascist parents died in a concentration camp. He and his sister are shocked when the child (Homeier, repeating his acclaimed Broadway performance) marches around in a Hitler Youth uniform. Fascinating concept is undermined by a false insistence that America is entirely free of ethnic prejudice and religious bigotry. To enhance this, the story is played out on a studio set that idealizes the small town in Norman Rockwell fashion. Does not pass the test of time.

VERY THOUGHT OF YOU, THE (1944)

CREDITS:

Warner Bros.; Delmer Daves, dir.; Daves, Alvah Bessie,
Lionel Wiggam, scr.; Jerry Wald, pro.; Franz Waxman, mus.; Bert Glennon, cin.; Alan Crosland, Jr., ed.; B&W; 1.37:1; 99 min.

CAST:

Dennis Morgan (*Sgt. David Stewart*); Eleanor Parker (*Janet Wheeler*); Dane Clark (*Fixit*); Faye Emerson (*Cuddles Colton*); Beulah Bondi (*Harriet*); Henry Travers (*Pop*).

Rating: **** 1/2

Home in Pasadena for a three-day leave before shipping out, a lonely GI meets a nice girl from a middle-class home, wrangling an invitation to dinner. Before he leaves, the two marry. Similar in concept, though not execution, to *The Clock*, this tough, honest, moving film opts not for schmaltz but integrity. Daves's expert filming on real locations aids immensely, as does a superb script that avoids the expected clichés about a big happy family. It offers, instead, a group of dysfunctional kinfolk who more resemble relatives in a Lillian Hellman play. This objective film refuses to romanticize whirlwind wartime marriage or offer a cautionary fable, analyzing the abruptly altered meaning of the word "love." Only disappointment: an ending that's predictable in a way nothing else in this fine film is.

VOICE OF THE TURTLE, THE (1947)

CREDITS:
Warner Bros.; Irving Rapper, dir.; John Van Druten (play), Charles Hoffman, scr.; Charles Hoffman, pro.; Max Steiner, mus.; Sol Polito, cin.; Rudi Fehr, ed.; B&W; 1.37:1; 103 min.

CAST:
Ronald Reagan (*Sgt. Bill Page*); Eleanor Parker (*Sally Middleton*); Eve Arden (*Olive Lashbrooke*); Wayne Morris (*Comm. Ned Burling*); Kent Smith (*Kenneth Bartlett*).

Rating: *** 1/2

On a snowy December eve in 1944, a lonely sergeant heads into the Big Apple planning to see a Broadway star who offered a "mercy date." When she dumps him for an officer, a young actress picks up the slack. Filled with the smart, sophisticated dialogue that made Van Druten's play (its title references the long-awaited coming of spring) a hit. By-the-book director Rapper films the play unimaginatively. The unique experience of passion in Manhattan during those nostalgic years comes through only fitfully, with exteriors of famed landmarks rendered via obvious back projection. Reagan and Parker do have a tangible chemistry. TV title: *One for the Book*.

WAKE UP AND DREAM (1946)

CREDITS:

20th Century Fox; Lloyd Bacon, dir.; Robert Nathan (novel), Elick Moll, scr.; Walter Morosco, pro.; Cyril J. Mockridge, mus.; Harry Jackson, cin.; Robert Fritch, ed.; C; 1.37:1; 92 min.

CAST:

John Payne (*Jeff Cairn*); June Haver (*Jenny*); Charlotte Greenwood (*Sara March*); Connie Marshall (*Nella*); John Ireland (*Howard Williams*); Clem Bevans (*Pecket*); Lee Patrick (*The Blonde*).

Rating: *** 1/2

From the 1936 novel *The Enchanted Voyage* by the author of the better-known *Portrait of Jenny* comes this strange, sometimes surreal film. A little girl (Marshall) learns that her brother (Payne) is missing in action. Unable to grasp geography, the child sets out with an elderly sailor (Bevans) in a crude sloop on wheels. They're joined by the soldier's sweetheart (Haver) and a moody youth (Ireland). The child's faith proves so overpowering that adults lose touch with reality and subscribe to her unwavering belief. "Give Me the Simple Life" is the theme song. Not entirely successful, as the book's darker edges were cut to keep this in tune with wartime optimism. Occasionally touching.

WAR AGAINST MRS. HADLEY, THE (1942)

CREDITS:

Metro-Goldwyn-Mayer; Harold S. Bucquet, dir.; George Oppenheimer, scr.; Irving Asher, pro.; David Snell, mus.; Karl Freund, cin.; Elmo Veron, ed.; B&W; 1.37:1; 86 min.

CAST:

Fay Bainter (*Stella*); Edward Arnold (*Fulton*); Richard Ney (*Theodore*);

Jean Rogers (*Patricia*); Sara Allgood (*Mrs. Fitzpatrick*); Spring Byington (*Cecilia*).

Rating: ****

When war breaks out, a DC society matron who never accepted the election of FDR considers it a mere nuisance. Mrs. Hadley refuses to dim her house lights during a blackout, trying to live in a cocoon until the impossibility of doing so becomes apparent even to her. This could've been a simplistic put-down of isolationists. Instead, it's a fine human drama in which, thanks to the underrated Bainter, Mrs. Hadley never degenerates into a cartoon. We can't help but like her, even if we detest her attitudes. Admirable in its aim to induce viewers to set aside old political and even class rivalries for the general good. One of the "smart" projects liberal-progressive Dore Schary initiated at MGM.

WAY WE WERE, THE (1973)

CREDITS:
Columbia; Sydney Pollack, dir.; Arthur Laurents, David Rayfiel, scr.; Ray Stark, pro.; Marvin Hamlisch, mus.; Harry Stradling, Jr., cin.; John F. Burnett, ed.; C; 2.35:1; 118 min.

CAST:
Barbra Streisand (*Katie Morosky*); Robert Redford (*Hubbell Gardner*); Bradford Dillman (*J.J.*); Lois Chiles (*Carol Ann*); Patrick O'Neal (*George*); Viveca Lindfors (*Paula*).

Rating: ****

An elegant but macho soldier from an elite WASP family becomes intrigued by a Jewish American working-class liberal. Painstaking attention paid to period detail, with a smart script that makes this odd-couple romance click. At its best when it deals with the war years, capturing the charming way in which Americans set old differences aside during the crusade. The striking contrast between the mellow war years and the suspicious

THE GOOD OL' DAYS: A social activist (Barbra Streisand) and her writer-boyfriend (Robert Redford) naively believe the war-time sense of community will continue into the postwar period.

antiwar period is sadly diminished by the last-minute cutting of the Red Scare hearings in the second half, leaving viewers unable to grasp what's happening.

YOUNG WIDOW (1946)

CREDITS:

United Artists; Edwin L. Marin, dir.; Hunt Stromberg, pro. Richard Macauley, Margaret Buell Wilder, scr., Clarisse Fairchild Cushman (novel); Hunt Stromberg, pro.; Carmen Drago, mus.; Lee Garmes, cin.; John M. Foley, ed.; 1.37:1; B&W; 100 min.

CAST:

Jane Russell *(Joan Kenwood)*; Louis Hayward *(Lt. Jim Cameron)*; Faith Dommergue *(Gerry)*; Marie Wilson *('Mac')*; Kent Taylor *(Waring)*; Penny Singleton *(Peg)*; Connie Gilchrest *(Cissie);* Norman Lloyd *(Sammy)*; Cora Witherspoon *(Emeline)*; Louise Beavers *(Rosie)*.

Rating: *** ½

When her husband is killed in combat, the title character (Russell) tries to go home again but even her loving family can't relieve the lady of her heartache and belief that her life is, for all intents and purposes, over. Then a young officer (Hayward) woos her; though she's attracted, there is the fear that the entire syndrome may repeat itself. By far Russell's finest performance ever, subtle and restrained; yet she did not like the finished film. Marred by some overly arch painting-like visual schemes and a tendency toward soap-opera. Still, the most poignant film on this particular aspect of war to be shot at the time, though released after combat ended.

"HOW'D *YOU* LIKE TO TUSSEL WITH RUSSELL?": Howard Hughes' insistence on reducing Jane to a sex symbol in films like *The Outlaw* would have to make way as she successfully essayed a more complex role in the ambitious *Young Widow*.

AN ALL PURPOSE HERO: John Mills, England's answer to John Wayne, played the courageous commander in numerous war films including *Above Us The Waves*.

Operation Undersea: The Silent Service

ABOVE US THE WAVES (1955)

CREDITS:
J. Arthur Rank/London Independent Prods.; Ralph Thomas, dir.; Charles Esme Thornton Warren (book), James (D.) Benson (book), Robin Estridge, scr.; William MacQuitty, pro.; Arthur Benjamin, mus.; Ernest Steward, cin.; Gerald Thomas, ed.; B&W; 1.66:1; 99 min.

CAST:
John Mills (*Cmdr. Fraser*); John Gregson (*Lt. Alec Duffy*); Donald Sinden (*Lt. Corbett*); James Robertson Justice (*Admiral* Ryder); Michael Medwin (*Smart*); Anthony Newley (*Engineer*).

Rating: ****

Germany's battleship the *Tirpitz* menaces Brit convoys in the Norwegian fjords. An innovative officer suggests a radical solution: create minisubmarines to rise up under the monstrous ship's keel and place bombs on its sides. Another soft-spoken postwar Brit film of the type that replaced vitriolic patriotism with documentary realism. Though the minisubs did not turn out to be the salvation everyone had hoped for, the effort was deemed worthy—precisely the tone this film adopts toward the experiment. No punches pulled regarding the loss of Allied lives, yet the violence never turns exploitive. The human drama is solid if never exceptional, the action scenes powerful. This historical naval encounter was called Operation Source.

BELOW (2002)

CREDITS:
Dimension Films; David Twohy, dir.; Lucas Sussman, Darren Aronofsky, David Twohy, scr.; Aronofsky, Sue Baden-Powell, Eric Watson, pro.; Graeme Revell, Tim Simonec, mus.; Ian Wilson, cin.; Martin Hunter, ed.; C; 1.85:1; 105 min.

CAST:
Matthew Davis (*Odell*); Bruce Greenwood (*Brice*); Olivia Williams (*Claire*); Holt McCallany (*Loomis*); Scott Foley (*Coors*); Zach Galifianakis (*Weird Wally*); Nick Hobbs (*Winters*).

Rating: *** 1/2

Well-crafted thriller takes the hoary haunted-house genre and resets it underwater. The WWII era is employed exclusively as the backdrop to a ghost story. Her ship torpedoed, a nurse (Williams) is taken aboard a cursed sub. Could it be that the captain did not die in an unlikely accident but was murdered? The visual style of *Das Boot* is combined with a storyline vaguely reminiscent of *Twilight Zone*'s "The Thirty-Fathom Grave." Entertaining enough on a shallow level (pun intended) for fans of dark thrillers.

BOOT, DAS (1981)

CREDITS:
Bavarian Film; Wolfgang Petersen, dir.; Lothar G. Buchheim (novel), Petersen, scr.; Gunter Rohrbach, pro.; Klaus Doldinger, mus.; Jost Vacano, cin.; Hannes Nikel, ed.; C; 1.85:1; 209 min. (director's cut), 149 min. (theatrical print).

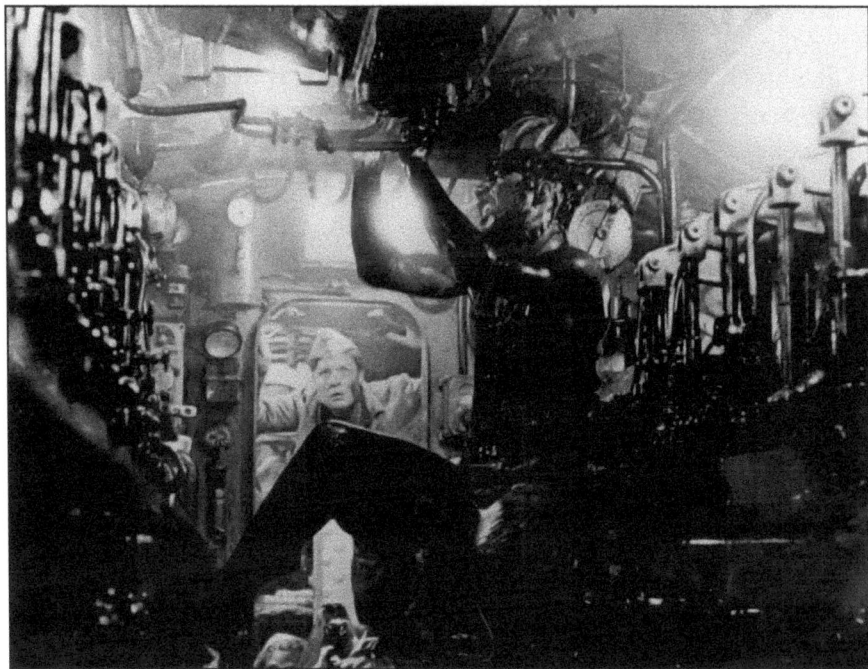

THE OTHER SIDE OF THE STORY: A German captain (Jurgen Prochnow) and his crew board their craft, then set off for action at sea in *Das Boot*.

CAST:

Jürgen Prochnow (*Capt. Henrich Lehmann-Willenbrock*); Herbert Grönemeyer (*Lt. Werner*); Klaus Wennemann (*Chief Engineer Fritz*); Hubertus Bengsch (*1st Lt.*); Martin Semmelrogge (*2nd Lt.*); Bernd Tauber (*Kriechbaum*).

Ratings: ***** (director's cut)
**** 1/2 (theatrical print)

The crew of a VIIC-class U-boat pilots its submarine out of La Rochelle harbor in occupied France but not before a journalist joins them to observe and write propaganda. He realizes, however, that they are complex people, desperate to survive and uninterested in honor or glory. Occasional bursts of vivid violence against the Allies punctuate the exhausting, boring daily routines in a claustrophobic setting. What were supposed to be great victories become embarrassing failures. The captain is emotionally/intellectually torn, dedicated to his crew but not the Reich. No film other than Malick's *The Thin Red Line* has captured with such integrity the long, slow stretches between brutal encounters. The movie and 1973 book are based in part on the memories of Henrich Lehmann-Willenbrock, captain of the U-96 during WWII, as well as Hans-Joachim Krug, first officer aboard the U-219. By combining elements of each man's experiences, this unique film expands beyond the literal reality of a single sub, offering the definitive submarine movie.

CRASH DIVE (1943)

CREDITS:

20th Century Fox; Archie Mayo, dir.; Jo Swerling, W. R. Burnett, scr.; Milton Sperling, pro.; David Buttolph, mus.; Leon Shamroy, cin.; Ray Curtiss, Walter Thompson, ed.; C; 1.37:1; 106 min.

CAST:

Tyrone Power (*Lt. Ward Stewart*); Anne Baxter (*Jean Hewlett*); Dana Andrews (*Lt. Cmdr. Connors*); James Gleason (*Mike McDonnell*); Dame May Whitty (*Grandma*); Harry (Henry) Morgan (*Brownie*).

Rating: *** 1/2

Fred Sersen won a deserved Oscar for Best Visual Effects for his photography of the final battle between an American sub crew and an Axis base. Fox's first WWII epic shot in color, the movie bogs down in a dull romantic triangle. A PT-boater, transferred to the silent service, and a gorgeous schoolteacher "meet cute." Neither knows that her fiancé is her new beau's captain. Too much time wasted away from waterlogged battlefields. Important as one of the first WWII movies to feature an African American as a fully integrated team member.

DESTINATION TOKYO (1943)

CREDITS:
Warner Bros.; Delmer Daves, dir.; Daves, Steve Fisher, Albert Maltz, scr.; Jerry Wald, pro.; Franz Waxman, mus.; Bert Glennon, cin.; Christian Nyby, ed.; B&W; 1.37:1; 135 min.

CAST:
Cary Grant (*Capt. Cassidy*); John Garfield (*Wolf*); Alan Hale (*Cookie*); John Ridgely (*Raymond*); Dane Clark (*Tin Can*); William Prince (*Pills*); Robert Hutton (*Tommy*).

Rating: **** 1/2

The *Copperfin* leaves California on its way to Tokyo Bay. Its mission: gather information about enemy installations for Jimmy Doolittle's raid. Grant is the decent captain; Garfield, a wild womanizer. Despite their joint top billing, this is an ensemble piece, each crew member developed as a distinct personality. Long and deliberately slow moving but never tedious. Hollywood's first attempt to show how a submarine operates, from daily duties to an emergency appendectomy. Several cross-cuts to home violate the claustrophobia so effectively conveyed. Anti-Japanese jargon that was appropriate in 1943 is less so today. Daves's first directorial outing.

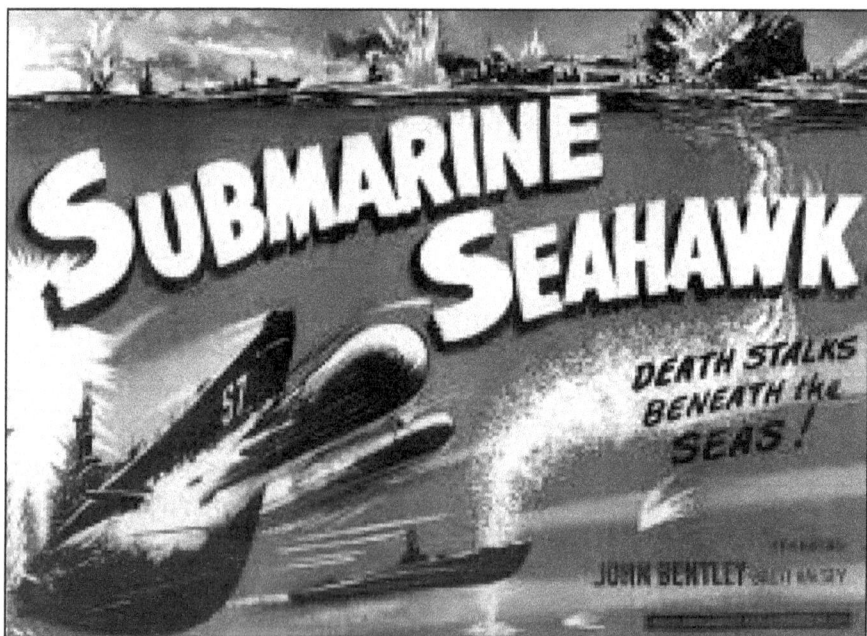

THE SILENT SERVICE: An innovative form of warfare was introduced to the public in such films as *Destination Tokyo* and *Submarine Seahawk*.

ENEMY BELOW, THE (1957)

CREDITS:
20th Century Fox; Dick Powell, dir.; Comdr. D. A. Rayner (novel), Wendell Mayes, scr.; Powell, pro.; Leigh Harline, mus.; Harold Rosson, cin.; Stuart Gilmore, ed.; C; 2.35:1; 98 min.

CAST:
Robert Mitchum (*Capt. Murrell*); Curd Jürgens (*Von Stolberg*); Al (David) Hedison (*Lt. Ware*); Theodore Bikel (*Heinie Schwaffer*); Russell Collins (*Doctor*); Kurt Kreuger (*Von Holem*).

Rating: ****

A new naval captain, fresh from the merchant marines, is assigned to the destroyer/escort USS *Haynes*. His men fear that without combat experience he might not be up to the task. A U-boat commandeered by a world-weary officer tails their craft. Owing to its basis in a 1947 book by a knowing veteran, the movie rings true. Effective moment-by-moment portrayal of the cat-and-mouse strategy in what evolves as a chess-like game, won by the leader able to outthink his opponent. Producer-director Powell achieves verisimilitude in the depiction of life aboard both crafts via parallel plots. Impressive objectivity compared to earlier portrayals of us versus them.

FROGMEN, THE (1951)

CREDITS:
20th Century Fox; Lloyd Bacon, dir.; John Tucker Battle, Oscar Millard, scr.; Samuel G. Engel, pro.; Cyril J. Mockridge, mus.; Norbert Brodine, cin.; William Reynolds, ed.; B&W; 1.37:1; 96 min.

CAST:
Richard Widmark (*Lt. Cmdr. John Lawrence*); Dana Andrews (*Jake Flannigan*); Gary Merrill (*Lt. Cmdr. Pete Vincent*); Jeffrey Hunter (*Pappy Creighton*); Warren Stevens (*Hodges*); Harvey Lembeck (*Mikowsky*).

THE A LIST: More than ten years following war's end, big budget movies like *Run Silent Run Deep* proved that our 20th century 'Crusade' had become as much an ongoing part of American popular culture as The Old West.

Rating: ** 1/2

Members of an underwater demolitions unit come to resent their new commander, less because of his failings than their idealization of the previous leader. Thin drama, shallow characterizations, predictable plot. Value is found in the action scenes, which show how the first frogmen prepared the way for island invasions, leading to lowered casualty rates. A military procedural, educating audiences about the little-known title unit. This first-time-ever depiction of the Frogmen will be largely lost on today's viewers.

HELLCATS OF THE NAVY (1957)

CREDITS:
Morningside Prods./Columbia; Nathan Juran, dir.; Charles A. Lockwood (novel), Hans Christian Adamson (novel), David Lang, Raymond T. Marcus (aka Bernard Gordon), scr.; Charles H. Schneer, pro.; Mischa Bakaleinikoff, mus.; Irving Lippman, cin.; Jerome Thoms, ed.; B&W; 1.85:1; 82 min.

CAST:
Ronald Reagan (*Cmdr. Casey Abbott*); Nancy Davis Reagan (*Lt. Helen Blair*); Arthur Franz (*Lt. Cmdr. Don Landon*); Robert Arthur (*Freddy Warren*); William Leslie (*Paul*).

Rating: *** 1/2

During Operation Barney, a sub commander must locate sea mines (nick-named "hell pots"), which if undetected would destroy Allied ships. As he and his crew go about their jobs, his mind is also on a lovely nurse. Respect-able, solid film offers no inspiration in its love story or the fact-based haz-ardous mission. The 1955 historical book *Hellcats of the Sea*, coauthored by Vice Admiral Lockwood, contains plenty of material for a true epic, which this film is not. Reagan and the missus, in their only theatrical film together, make a memorable team. Notable irony: blacklisted lefty screenwriter Gor-don had to work under a fake name while penning this piece.

NEXT STOP, THE WHITE HOUSE: Ron and Nancy (Davis) Reagan in their only co-starring theatrical film, *Hellcats of the Navy.*

IN ENEMY HANDS (2004)

CREDITS:
Artisan Ent./Splendid; Tony Giglio, dir.; Giglio, John E. Deaver, Johnny Hartmann, scr.; John Brister, Julius R. Nasso, Michael Pierce, pro.; Steven Bramson, mus.; Gerry Lively, cin.; Peter Mergus, Harvey Rosenstock, ed.; C; 1.78:1; 94 min.

CAST:
William H. Macy (*Nathan Travers*); Jeremy Sisto (*Jason Abers*); Til Schweiger (*Herdt*); Thomas Kretschmann (*Ludwig Cremer*); Lauren Holly (*Rachel Travers*).

Rating: ** 1/2

June 1943: American subs make sinking German U-boats in the North Atlantic their top priority. When the USS *Swordfish* is sunk by U-boat 429, survivors are allowed onboard the German craft. They carry meningitis with them, which infects both crews and threatens to wipe out everyone if they don't work together. The film's style is borrowed from *Das Boot*, though this one is no classic, offering familiar material, competently handled. Underwater action scenes are acceptable if ordinary. Interesting story, indifferently told, sparked somewhat by Macy.

INCREDIBLE MR. LIMPET, THE (1964)

CREDITS:
Warner Bros.; Arthur Lubin, dir.; Theodore Pratt (novel), Jameson Brewer, John C. Rowe, Joe DiMona, scr.; John C. Ross, pro.; Frank Perkins, mus.; Harold E. Stine, cin.; Donald Tait, ed.; C; 1.85:1; 99 min.

CAST:
Don Knotts (*Henry Limpet*); Carole Cook (*Bessie*); Jack Weston (*Stickel*); Andrew Duggan (*Harlock*); Larry Keating (*Admiral Spewter*); Oscar Beregi, Jr. (*Nazi Admiral*); Elizabeth MacRae (*Ladyfish, voice*).

Rating: ****

U-boats threaten Allied ships, but no one is certain what to do. All his life, Henry Limpet has been a shy fellow, now classified 4-F. Magic occurs: he becomes a talking fish. Bill Tytla is credited as supervising animation director, but most such work was overseen by Robert McKimson. As one of those cold-water creatures he's always adored, Limpet can help his country track down enemy submarines, even turning Nazi torpedoes about and sending these back at them. Superior songs by Sammy Fain and Harold Adamson add to the appeal. The destroyer on view is the USS *Alfred A. Cunningham*.

MORNING DEPARTURE (1950)

CREDITS:
Rank/JGL; Roy Ward Baker, dir.; Kenneth Woollard (play), W. E. Fairchild, scr.; Jay Lewis, pro.; Desmond Dickinson, cin.; Alan Osbiston, ed.; B&W; 1.37:1; 97 min.

CAST:
John Mills (*Armstrong*); Richard Attenborough (*Snipe*); Nigel Patrick (*Manson*); Peter Hammond (*Oakley*); Andrew Crawford (*McFee*); George Cole (*Marks*); Bernard Lee (*Gates*); Kenneth More (*James*).

Rating: **** 1/2

A submarine sets out from a British port for a routine trip and touches an underwater mine. All onboard are plunged into a life-and-death situation. Based on a one-set play, the film opens our range of perception to include the efforts of a rescue party working against the clock owing to depleting oxygen and bad weather. The men, realizing the odds are against them, ponder their fates. Realistic give-and-take between a classy officer (Mills) and a Cockney coward (Attenborough) eager to redeem himself. Memorable contrast between the ordinariness of the men's onshore lives and their underwater experiences.

MURPHY'S WAR (1971)

CREDITS:
Michael-Deeley-Peter-Yates; Peter Yates, dir.; Max Catto (novel), Stirling Silliphant, scr.; Michael Deeley, pro.; Douglas Slocombe, cin.; John Glen, Frank P. Keller, ed.; C; 2.35:1; 107 min. (US), 105 min. (Argentina).

CAST:
Peter O'Toole (*Murphy*); Siân Phillips (*Dr. Hayden*); Philippe Noiret (*Louis Brezan*); Horst Janson (*Cmdr. Lauchs*); John Hallam (*Lt. Ellis*).

Rating: ****

Sole survivor of a downed merchant marine ship (O'Toole as an Irish seaman) becomes obsessed with destroying the U-boat that killed his mates. He methodically refurbishes, piece by piece, a dilapidated plane. By humanizing the U-boat captain (Janson), the film posits Murphy not as a conventional hero but a man who has surrendered his sanity to the absurdity of war. With taut direction and complex character development, this ironic piece makes clear that the victor belongs to the spoils. The give and take between roughewn Murphy and a proper female doctor recalls Humphrey Bogart and Katharine Hepburn in *The African Queen* (1952).

MYSTERY SUBMARINE (1950)

CREDITS:
Universal-International; Douglas Sirk, dir.; George W. George, George F. Slavin, Ralph Dietrich, scr.; Dietrich, pro.; Milton Rossen, mus.; Clifford Stine, cin.; Virgil W. Vogel, Ralph Dawson, ed.; 35 mm; B&W; 1.37:1; 78 min.

CAST:
Macdonald Carey (*Dr. Brett Young*); Märta Torén (*Madeline Brenner*); Robert Douglas (*Cmdr. Eric von Molter*); Ludwig Donath (*Dr. Adolph Guernitz*); Jacqueline Dalya Hilliard (*Carla von Molter*).

Rating: * 1/2

A minor bread-and-butter film about a naval officer (Carey) who impersonates a Nazi to sink a sub that's moving steadily toward the US. The officer also rescues a doctor (Donath) and an unexpected pair of beauties (Torén and Hilliard). None of the impressively garish flourishes that would characterize Sirk's later work are present here, to the relief or disappointment of his detractors/fans. A misconceived flashback slows down the action. Routine at best.

MYSTERY SUBMARINE, (THE) (1963)

CREDITS:

British Lion; C. M. Pennington-Richards, dir.; Jon Manchip White (play), Bertram Ostrer, Hugh Woodhouse, scr.; Ostrer, pro.; Clifton Parker, mus.; Stanley Pavey, cin.; Bill Lewthwaite, ed.; B&W; 92 min.

CAST:

Edward Judd (*Lt. Cmdr. Tarlton*); James Robertson Justice (*Rear Admiral Rainbird*); Laurence Payne (*Lt. Seaton*); Joachim Fuchsberger (*Cmdr. Scheffler*); Arthur O'Sullivan (*Mike*).

Rating: ★★★

A German crew abandons ship after an on-target bombing raid. The submarine is taken over by Brits who search for enigma-type information. They sail toward other U-boats in the Bay of Biscay to learn their number and location. Story is similar to the later (and superior) *U-571*, loosely based on the same incident. Dramatic confrontations are mainly confined to the ship's interior (this was based on a stage play) as officers Judd and Payne argue about strategy. Neither personality is interesting. Ordinary, acceptable, unexciting, and utterly forgettable.

OPERATION PACIFIC (1951)

CREDITS:

Warner Bros.; George Waggner, dir.; Waggner, scr.; Louis F. Edelman, pro.; Max Steiner, mus.; Bert Glennon, cin.; Alan Crosland, Jr., ed.; B&W; 1.37:1; 111 min.

CAST:

John Wayne (*Lt. Cmdr. Duke E. Gifford*); Patricia Neal (*Lt. Mary Stuart*); Ward Bond (*Cmdr. Perry*); Scott Forbes (*Larry*); Philip Carey (*Bob Perry*); Paul Picerni (*Jonesy*); William Campbell (*The Talker*); Martin Milner (*Caldwell*).

Rating: **

A sub commander deals with torpedoes that fail to fire properly, Asian orphans adrift at sea, enemy ships that appear out of nowhere, and an ex-wife now interested in another officer. Dull and derivative of other far finer, earlier pictures. Worse still, the ultralow budget (rare for Wayne) didn't leave room for big action sequences, provided via stock footage. Director Waggner fails to convey the hedged-in feeling of a submarine. Technical advisor was Charles A. Lockwood, who oversaw all subs in the Pacific during the war. A real disappointment.

OPERATION PETTICOAT (1959)

CREDITS:
Universal-International; Blake Edwards, dir.; Paul King, Joseph Stone, Stanley Shapiro, Maurice Richlin, scr.; Robert Arthur, pro.; David Rose, Henry Mancini, mus.; Russell Harlan, cin.; Frank Gross, Ted J. Kent, ed.; C; 1.85:1; 124 min.

CAST:
Cary Grant (*Lt. Cmdr. Matt T. Sherman*); Tony Curtis (*Lt. Nicholas Holden*); Joan O'Brien (*Lt. Dolores Crandall*); Dina Merrill (*Lt. Barbara Duran*); Gene Evans (*Molumphry*); Dick Sargent (*Stovall*); Madlyn Rhue (*Lt. Reid*).

Rating: ****

One of the better lighthearted Navy service comedies turned out following the success of *Mister Roberts*. Grant is a variation of that title character, Curtis a Pulver-ish go-getter, and O'Brien the gorgeous blonde. Outlandish but believable situation: a sub is painted pink and then plays host to a half dozen stranded nurses. Master of the raised eyebrow, Grant keeps the material from becoming more silly than funny, though things do turn broad at times. Strong incidents include the stealing of a pig and the "sinking" (via torpedo) of a truck on land. The sailors' attitudes toward women are, to put it mildly, old guard—or, more bluntly,

GETTING SERIOUS, GETTIN' SILLY: Sub-mariners John Garfield and Dane Clark find themselves menaced in *Destination Tokyo*; Cary Grant and his crew play host to a bevy of beautiful women in *Operation Petticoat*.

chauvinistic. Clever writing combined with brisk direction, appealingly played. However unlikely it might seem, events here were inspired by real occurrences onboard the *Spearfish*.

RUN SILENT, RUN DEEP (1958)

CREDITS:
Hecht-Hill-Lancaster/United Artists; Robert Wise, dir.; Cmdr. Edward L. Beach (novel), John Gay, scr.; Harold Hecht, pro.; Franz Waxman, mus.; Russell Harlan, cin.; ed.; B&W; 1.85:1; 93 min.

CAST:
Clark Gable (*Cmdr. Rich Richardson*); Burt Lancaster (*Lt. Jim Bledsoe*); Jack Warden (*Mueller*); Brad Dexter (*Cartwright*); Don Rickles (*Ruby*); Nick Cravat (*Russo*); Eddie Foy III (*Larto*).

Rating: **** 1/2

Melville might have admired this WWII version of *Moby Dick*, the great white whale now an enemy destroyer. Captain of a sub once sunk by that craft bides his time. No sooner is he out and away again than his second-in-command, bitter about being passed over for the top job, realizes the crew might be at risk owing to the skipper's obsession. Straightforward underwater adventure. Meticulous attention to the details of daily life adds authenticity. Wise creates the proper sense of claustrophobia, especially when the sub engages a Japanese equivalent in a silent undersea battle of wills. The greatest single sub movie before *Das Boot*, accurate right down to the bizarre noises the men hear.

SEAGULLS OVER SORRENTO, aka *CREST OF THE WAVE* (1954)

CREDITS:
John & Roy Boulting, dirs..; R. Boulting, Frank Harvey, scr.; Boulting Bros., prods.; Max Benedict, ed.; Gilbert Taylor, cin.; Miklos Rosza; MGM British; 1.75:1; B&W; 92 min.

CAST:
Gene Kelly (*Lt. Bradville*); John Justin (*Roger Wharton*); Bernard Lee

('*Lofty*'); Jff Richards ('*Butch*'); Sidney James ('*Badge*'); Fredd Wayne ('*Shorty*'); Ray Jackson ('*Sprog*').

Rating: *

Realizing that state-of-the-art torpedoes will win the war at sea, Britain's greatest munitions experts join an American on an isolated island to iron out the dangerous explosive issues. All too evidently based on a stage play by Hugh Hastings, so almost no underwater action of the type audiences demand from a Silent Service film. As varied men clash and finally come together to get the job done, none rises above the level of a recycled WWII stereotype. Kelly's acting inadequacies in non-dance/musical films is embarrassingly evident here.

SEALED CARGO (1951)

CREDITS:
RKO; Alfred L. Werker, dir.; Edmund Gilligan (novel), Dale Van Every, Oliver H. P. Garrett, Roy Huggins, scr.; Warren Duff, pro.; Roy Webb, mus.; George E. Diskant, cin.; Ralph Dawson, ed.; B&W; 1.37:1; 90 min.

CAST:
Dana Andrews (*Pat Bannon*); Carla Balenda (*Margaret McLean*); Claude Rains (*Capt. Skalder*); Philip Dorn (*Konrad*); Onslow Stevens (*Cmdr. James McLean*); Skip Homeier (*Steve*).

Rating: ****

Halifax, Nova Scotia, is the departure point for most ships crossing the Atlantic with desperately needed supplies for England. A fleet of U-boats hovers near the coastline, awaiting an opportunity to blow up these boats. Also in the area: the Nazi's mother ship, seemingly a neutral schooner, with a supposedly Danish captain (Rains), carrying extra torpedoes. They might have succeeded if not for a New England fisherman (Andrews) who senses something is wrong. But there is, apparently, a spy aboard his own craft—maybe the beautiful young woman (Balenda) he promised to drop off in Trabo (Newfoundland). A tidy thriller with convincing romance, just enough action, and an impressive sense of nautical atmosphere, allowing the viewer to believe this is about to turn into an at-sea ghost story. Satisfying.

SILENT ENEMY, THE (1958)

CREDITS:
Romulus/Remus Films; William Fairchild, dir.; Marshal Pugh (book), Fairchild, scr.; Bertram Oster, pro.; William Alwyn, mus.; Otto Heller, cin.; Alan Osbiston, ed.; B&W; 112 min.

CAST:
Laurence Harvey (*Lt. Lionel Crabbe*); Dawn Addams (*Jill*); Michael Craig (*Seaman Knowles*); Sidney James (*Thorpe*); John Clements (*The Admiral*); Gianna Maria Canale (*Conchita*).

Rating: *** 1/2

Near Gibraltar, Italian frogmen are wreaking havoc on the Brit fleet by swimming up to ships, attaching time bombs to their hulls, and then slipping away. An innovative bomb/mine disposal officer creates a predecessor to (and inspiration for) America's Navy SEALs. The star is perfectly cast as a pompous, vain, brilliant chap who gradually earns our admiration. A bit long but well played, with exciting battle scenes. Realistically filmed, though the incidents are mostly fictional, including an attack on the *Olterra* that never happened. Though the character is named after Lionel Crabbe (1909–1956), the screenplay was drastically altered for entertainment's sake.

SILVER FLEET (1943)

CREDITS:
The Archers; Vernon Sewell, Gordon Wellesley, dir.; Sewell, Wellesley, Emeric Pressburger, scr.; Richardson, Pressburger, Michael Powell, pro.;

Allan Gray, mus.; Erwin Hiller, cin.; Michael C. Chorlton, ed.; B&W; 1.37:1; 88 min.

CAST:
Ralph Richardson (*Jaap van Leyden*); Googie Withers (*Helène van Leyden*); Esmond Knight (*Von Schiffer*); Beresford Egan (*Krampf*); Kathleen Byron (*Teacher*).

Rating: ★★★★

A Dutch collaborator accepts large sums from occupying Nazis to build exquisite U-boats for the Axis cause. Despised by freedom lovers everywhere, he's thrown his reputation away to secretly spy on the enemy. Producer Pressburger has called this the least successful of his wartime films. In truth, it's a strong, solid piece of propaganda, Richardson's superb, understated performance alone worth the effort. One of those rare films to include the term Europeans employed for detested collaborators: *quizlings*. For anyone who has yet to discover the joys of Googie Withers, this provides a good jumping-off point. Superior to its reputation.

SUBCONSCIOUS (2015)

CREDITS:
Hilton Media; Georgia Hilton, dir.; Hilton, scr.; Hilton, Lars Elling Lunde, Peter K. Morrison, pro.; Nate Kohrs, Gary Tash, mus.; Hilton, ed.; C; 122 min.

CAST:
Tim Abell (*Peter Williams*); Aleisha Force (*Stacey*); Tom Stedham (*Garmin*); Naomi Brockwell (*Vicki*); Cambridge Jones (*Sterling*); Mike Beckingham (*Mike*); Peter Barry (*Gant*).

Rating: NO STARS

In 1943, the USS *Lionfish* was removed from action, relocated to a remote pier, and sealed off. Seventy years later, a historian becomes obsessed with finding out why. When he and his research assistants are allowed to board, they find themselves back in the past for a specific purpose. Brutal contemporary horror, blended awfully with WWII action.

SUBMARINE ALERT (1943)

CREDITS:
Pine-Thomas Prods./Paramount; Frank McDonald, dir.; Maxwell Shane, scr.; William H. Pine, William C. Thomas, pro.; Freddie Rich, mus.; Fred Jackman, Jr., cin.; William H. Ziegler, ed.; B&W; 1.37:1; 66 min.

CAST:
Richard Arlen (*Lewis Deerhold*); Wendy Barrie (*Ann*); Nils Asther (*Dr. Huneker*); Roger Pryor (*G. B. Fleming*); Abner Biberman (*Commander Toyo*); Marc Lawrence (*Bela*); Dwight Frye (*Haldine*).

Rating: **

A radio engineer cannot find a job owing to his immigrant status yet needs money to pay for his child's operation. Knowing this, Nazis draw him into a spy circle, employing his skills to stay in contact with their nearby U-boats. One of several films released in 1943 by various Poverty Row indie companies that fueled a widespread silent-scream fear: enemy subs were (supposedly) positioned along our coasts, ready to do damage. Ultracheap but more suspenseful than many other such low-budget products. Frye brings his bizarre horror-movie image to the role of a fifth columnist. Only film of its time to depict the FBI as nastily hassling recent European arrivals about their loyalties, and not just Germans.

SUBMARINE BASE (1943)

CREDITS:
PRC; Albert (H.) Kelley, dir.; George M. Merrick, Arthur St. Claire, scr.; Jack Schwarz, pro.; Charles Dant, mus.; Marcel Le Picard, cin.; Holbrook N. Todd, ed.; B&W; 1.37:1; 65 min.

CAST:

John Litel (*James Xavier Taggart*); Alan Baxter (*Joe Morgan*); Eric Blore (*Spike*); Georges Metaxa (*Kroll*); George Flaherty (*Cavanaugh*); Fifi D'Orsay (*Maria*); Iris Adrian (*Dorothy*).

Rating: *

A big-city wise guy hopes to turn a profit by supplying the Nazis with torpedoes. Or so things appear. At midmovie, we learn that the heel is a hero, pretending to be bad to help destroy enemy submarines. Ultratight budget allowed only for minimal, threadbare action. Weak.

SUBMARINE COMMAND (1951)

CREDITS:

Paramount; John Farrow, dir.; Jonathan Latimer, scr.; Joseph Sistrom, pro.; David Buttolph, cin.; Lionel Lindon, cin.; Eda Warren, ed.; B&W; 1.37:1; 87 min.

CAST:

William Holden (*Lt. Cmdr. Ken White*); Nancy Olson (*Carol*); William Bendix (*CPO Boyer*); Don Taylor (*Morris*); Arthur Franz (*Carlson*); Darryl Hickman (*Wheelwright*); Peggy Webber (*Alice*); Jack Kelly (*Lt. Barton*).

Rating: ** 1/2

On the final day of WWII, a commander must make a decision during ocean combat that will cost dearly in terms of American lives. Devastated by what he believes might have been a failure of courage, he views the sudden Korean conflict as a possibility for redemption. The film's strong point: an honest attempt to dramatize posttraumatic stress disorder and excellent imagery thanks to the Navy's full cooperation. Unfortunately, every character is a cliché drawn from earlier, better films. Even the dialogue mostly sounds recycled. Ordinary, routine, mediocre.

SUBMARINE RAIDER (1942)

CREDITS:
Columbia; Lew Landers, Budd Boetticher, dir.; Aubrey Wisberg, scr.; Wallace MacDonald, pro.; John Leipold, mus.; Franz Planer, cin.; William A. Lyon, ed.; B&W; 1.37:1; 64 min.

CAST:
John Howard (*Comm. Warren*); Marguerite Chapman (*Sue Curry*); Bruce Bennett (*Russell*); Warren Ashe (*Bill*); Eileen O'Hearn (*Vera*); Nino Pipitone (*Capt. Yamanada*); Philip Ahn (*Kawakami*).

Rating: * 1/2

The day before Japan's attack on Pearl, an enemy aircraft carrier moves toward Hawaii, decimating a civilian yacht. The lone survivor (Chapman) is picked up by an American sub that searches for the enemy. Thrown into production as fast as possible after December 7, 1941, this slipshod production more resembles one of the shoestring-budget quickies that indies Monogram and Mascot churned out than a Columbia program picture. Howard is okay as the US sub commander, Pipitone over the top as his Asian counterpart/enemy.

SUBMARINE SEAHAWK (1958)

CREDITS:
American International Pictures/Golden State Prods.; Spencer Gordon Bennet, dir.; Lou Rusoff, Orville H. Hampton, scr.; Rusoff, Samuel Z. Arkoff, James H. Nicholson, pro.; Alexander Laszlo, mus.; Gilbert Warrenton, cin.; Homer Powell, Ronald Sinclair, ed.; B&W; 1.37:1; 83 min.

CAST:
John Bentley (*Lt. Cmdr. Paul Turner*); Brett Halsey (*Lt. David Shore);* Wayne Heffley (*Cmdr. Stoker*); Steve Mitchell (*Flowers);* Henry McCann (*Seaman Ellis*); Nicky Blair (*Sam).*

Rating: * ½

A sub commander (Bentley), ordered to locate the Japanese flotilla, finds himself in the awkward position of not firing back when enemy vessels attack. This creates anger among the crew. One of those early A.I.P. ten day wonders released only as obligatory 'second features.' at Drive Ins. A cut above the average cheapie owng to an impressive job by the editors who transformed stock footage into a halfway decent battle climax.

SUBMARINE X-1 (1969)

CREDITS:
Mirisch; William Graham, dir.; John C. Champion, Edmund H. North, Donald S. Sanford, Guy Elmes, scr.: John C. Champion, pro.; Ron Goodwin, mus.; Paul Beeson, cin.; John S. Smith, ed.; C: 1.66:1; 89 mins.

CAST:
James Caan (*Cmdr. Richard Bolton*); David Sumner (*Davies*); Norman Bowler (*Pennington*); Brian Grellis (*Barquist*); Paul Young (*Quentin*); Diana Beevers (*WRNS Officer*).

Rating: * 1/2

Owing to a reputation for accomplishing difficult tasks at a terrible cost to the latest crew, Bolton is resented by those he must train for an upcoming mission. In Scotland, they are familiarized with experimental midget-subs that will allow for greater maneuverability if also greater vulnerability. The final attack is based on two historical assaults on the Axis warship *Tirpitz*. Despite solid production values, this film is done in by a sluggish script, wooden acting, and lifeless direction of personal moments and action sequences. Caan plays one more of those Canadian roles which allow Americans to get away with parts that rightly should have gone to Brits.

TAMPICO (1944)

CREDITS:

20th Century Fox; Lothar Mendes, dir.; Kenneth Gamet, Richard Macaulay, Fred Niblo Jr, scrs.; Robert Bassler, pro.; David Raksin, mus.; Charles (G.) Clarke, cin.; Robert Fritch, ed.; B&W; 1.37:1; 75 min.

CAST:

Edward G. Robinson (*Capt. Bart Manson*); Lynn Bari (*Kathy Hall*); Victor McLaglen (*Fred Adamson*); Robert Bailey (*Watson)*; Marc Lawrence (*Valdez)*; Mona Maris (*Dolores).*

Rating: ** ½

A fleet of U-boats is dispatched by Germany to prowl undersea between Southern California and Tampico. They randomly torpedo American ships and hope to destroy oil-riggers filled with energy supplies. A captain picks up civilian survivors from another ship. Among them is a charming shady-lady (Bari) whose stories fail to check out; the burly Irish-American first mate (McLaglen) suspects she may be a spy. Solid premise fails to pay off as the film proves to be but a lumbering set-up for an unconvincing final pay-off. The first Hollywood film to admit that some Irish hated the English enough to support the Axis.

TORPEDO ALLEY (1952)

CREDITS:

Allied Artists; Lew Landers, dir.; Warren Douglas, Samuel Roesca, scr., Lindsley Parsons, pro.; William A. Sickener, cin.; W. Donn Hayes, ed.; B&W; 1.37:1; 84 min.

CAST:

Mark Stevens (*Lt. Bob Bingham*); Dorothy Malone (*Lt. Susan Peabody*); Charles Winninger (*Oliver Peabody*); Bill Williams (*Graham*); Douglas Kennedy (*Gates*); James Millican (*Cmdr. Heywood*); William Henry (*Instructor*)

Rating: * ½

Yet another redemption tale: A pilot survives the crash that killed crewmen owing to his freezing at the controls. Rescued at sea by a sub, he believes that the Silent Service will allow him opportunity to re-achieve self-respect. There's a tough but fair officer (Millican), also a pretty Navy nurse (Malone) for romance. When the Korean Conflict breaks out, he sees this as his chance to erase earlier feelings of failure. Routine, mediocre.

TORPEDO RUN (1958)

CREDITS:
Metro-Goldwyn-Mayer; Joseph Pevney, dir.; William Wister Haines, Richard Sale, scr.; Edmund Grainger, prod.; George J. Folsey, cin.; Gene Ruggiero, ed.; C; 2.35:1; 98 mins.

CAST:
Glenn Ford (*Lt. Cmdr. Barney Doyle*); Ernest Borgnine (*Lt. Archie Sloan*);Dean Jones (*'Fuzz' Foley*); L.Q. Jones (*'Hash' Benson*); Philip Ober (*Adm. Setton*); Paul Picerni (*Fisher*); Al Freeman, Jr. (*Cook*).

Rating: *** ½

A commander is assigned to torpedo the *Shinaru*, a Japanese aircraft carrier that brought planes close to Pearl. He gives the command, knowing a Japanese transport on which his wife (Diane Brewster) and daughter (Kimberly Beck) are held captive is perilously close to the target. Believing them to be dead he Ahab-like sets out on a vengeance voyage. Borgnine plays the thoughtful second in command. So-so script, hampered by tedious flashbacks that add nothing. Dialogue contains actual shorthand -lingo which submariners employ to communicate with one another.

TORPEDO ZONE, aka SUBMARINE ATTACK (1955)

CREDITS:
Excelsa Film; Duilio Coletti, dir.; Coletti, Oreste Biancoli, Marc-Antoine Bragadin, Ennio De Concini, scr., Bragidin (novel); Coletti, pro.; Nino Rota, mus.; Leonida Barori, cin.; Giuliana Attenni, ed.; C; 86 min.

CAST:
Lois Maxwell (*Lily Donald*) Renato Baldini (*Commandanti*); Crlo Bellini (*Officer*); Aldo Bufi Landi (*Lt.*); Earl Cameron (*Johnny Brown*); Carlo Delle Piane (*Ciccio*); Edward Fleming (*Cartier*).

Rating: *** ½

An Italian sub commander (Baldini), grown weary of war, would rather save lives than take them. While many German officers in his position allow Allies stranded in the ocean to perish, he dutifully picks up survivors. His craft becomes a virtual microcosm; that, and the decision not to name crew members, suggests a metaphoric approach, as does the Christmastime setting. French-Italian co-production (with English participation, including actress Maxwell). Loosely based on an actual incident; bolstered by Rota's evocative music. Historical stock footage rounds out the action scenes.

TWO-MAN SUBMARINE (1944)

CREDITS:
Columbia; Lew Landers, dir.; Bob Williams, Leslie T. White, Griffin Jay, scr.; Jack Fiers, pro.; Mario Castelnuovo-Tedesco, mus.; James Van Trees, cin.; Jerome Thoms, ed.; B&W; 1.37:1; 62 min.

CAST:
Tom Neal (*Jerry Evans*); Ann Savage (*Pat Benson*); J. Carrol Naish (*Dr. Hadley*); Robert (B.) Williams (*Walt*); Abner Biberman (*Fabian*); George

Lynn *(Fosmer)*; Alex Havier *(Fuzzytop)*.

Rating: *

On an island in the South Pacific, an American hero (Neal) guards a doctor (Naish) who has nearly completed work on a new medicine, penicillin. Problem is, the Axis wants it and sends the title object to unload a Nazi agent. Who could this be? The attractive woman (Savage) who has joined their company, or some other recently arrived stranger? However putrid this grade Z item may be, the film rightly notes that Germany was indeed far ahead of the Allies as to creative use of mini-subs. A year later, Neal and Savage would reunite in one of the most memorable of all B noirs, *Detour*.

U-BOAT PRISONER (1944)

CREDITS:
Columbia; Lew Landers, Budd Boetticher, dir.; Archie Gibbs, Aubrey Wisberg, Malcolm Stuart Boylan, scr.; Wallace MacDonald, pro.; Burnett Guffey, cin.; Paul Borofsky, ed.; Victor Young, Mischa Bakaleinikoff, mus.; B&W; 1.37:1; 66 min.

CAST:
Bruce Bennett *(Archie Gibbs)*; Erik Rolf *(Kapitaen Ganz)*; John Abbott *(Lamont)*; John Wengraf *(Rudehoff)*; Sam Ash *(Engineer)*; Trevor Bardette *(Convoy Commander)*; Sven Hugo Borg *(Dorner)*.

Rating: *** 1/2

A German spy targets an American vessel about to be torpedoed by a Nazi sub, lorded over by a cynical captain and a Gestapo officer. Before they can pick up their man, the villain is overcome by a U.S. sailor who then assumes the spy's identity, hoping to sabotage the U-boat. True-life incident (the lead character shares his name with one of the writers) results in an uninspired second-feature, shot mostly on a single set (the torpedo room), with stock Navy documentary footage rounding out the action. Typical cat-and-mouse heroes-above/enemy-below stuff, sparked by an unusual premise.

U-571 (2000)

CREDITS:
Universal; Jonathan Mostow, dir.; Mostow, Sam Montgomery, David Ayer, scr.; Dino and Martha De Laurentiis, pro(s).; Richard Marvin, mus.; Oliver Wood, cin.; Wayne Wahrman, ed.; C; 2.35:1; 116 min.

CAST:
Matthew McConaughey (*Lt. Andrew Tyler*); Bill Paxton (*Lt. Cmdr. Mike Dahlgren*); Harvey Keitel (*CPO Klough*); Jon Bon Jovi (*Emmett*); David Keith (*Coonan*); Thomas Kretschmann (*Wassner*).

Rating: ****

An Allied sub commander attacks a U-boat, confiscating an Enigma machine on board. When he's killed and his sub sinks, a Lt. must assume command. He has the brains as well as the courage to get the job done. But is he willing to, if necessary, sacrifice his crew for the cause? Solid entertainment, with a strong sense of pace and a camera that rapidly moves through the sub in the tradition of *Das Boot*. Accolades all around for acting, though the script might have developed the men's personalities more fully. That won't matter to fans of WWII action, such sequences impeccably staged. Much criticized by the British, who were the first to capture the all-important Enigma code device.

UP PERISCOPE (1959)

CREDITS:
Warner Bros.; Gordon Douglas, dir.; Robb White (novel), Richard H. Landau, scr.; Aubrey Schenck, pro.; Carl E. Guthrie, cin.; John Schreyer, ed.; C; 2.35:1; 111 min.

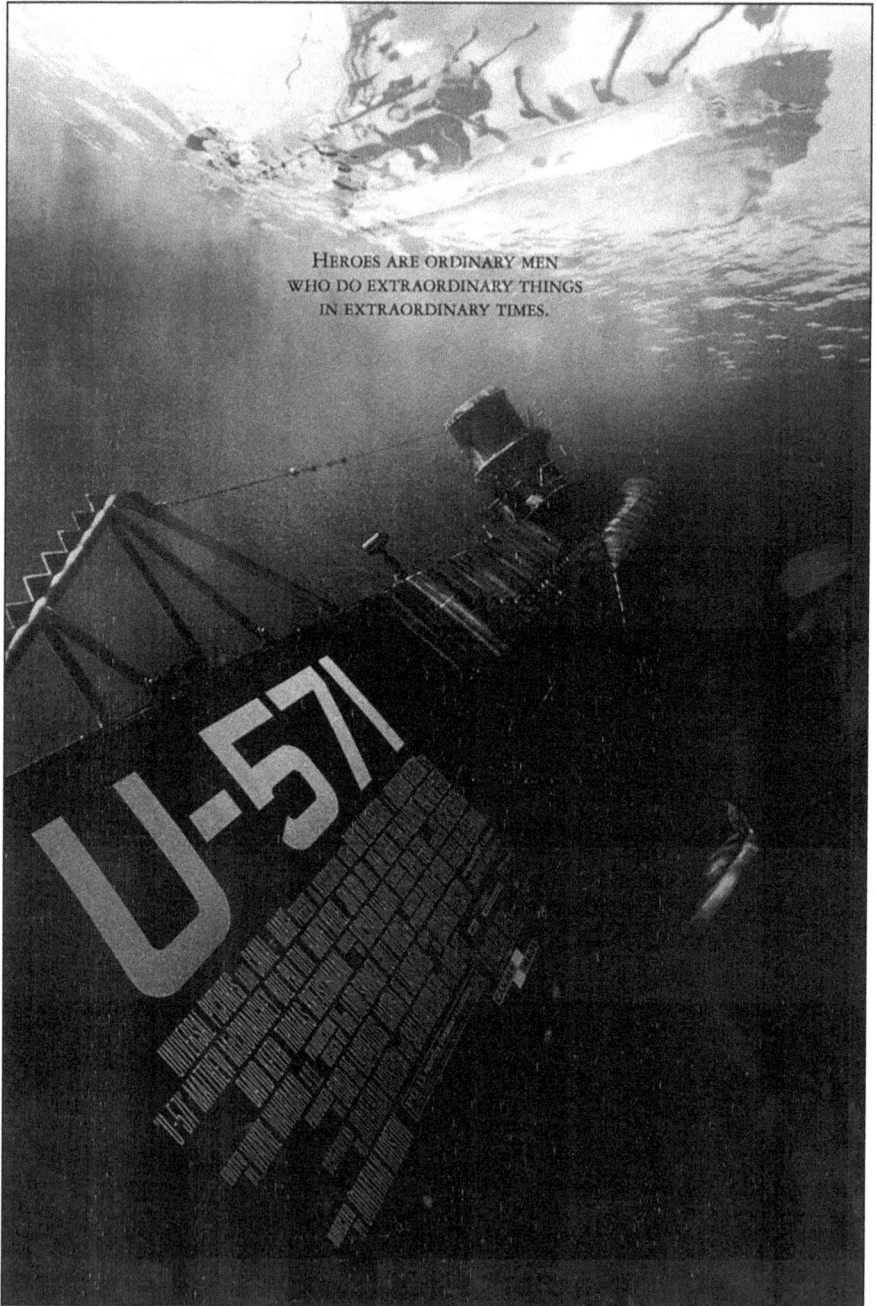

HEROES ARE ORDINARY MEN
WHO DO EXTRAORDINARY THINGS
IN EXTRAORDINARY TIMES.

WORLD WAR II 'LIVES': Films such as *U-571* vividly prove that rather than merely a subject for films, WWII has become the basis of an ongoing film genre with no end in sight.

CAST:

James Garner (*Lt. Ken Braden*); Edmond O'Brien (*Commander Stevenson*); Andra Martin (*Sally*); Alan Hale (Jr.) (*Pat*); Carleton Carpenter (*Carney*); Frank Gifford (*Ensign Mount*); Edd Byrnes (*Ash*); Warren Oates (*Kovacs*).

Rating: *** 1/2

A sub commander inadvertently causes the death of a sailor owing to his by-the-book approach. That attitude is tested when he's assigned to deliver a frogman to an island for a special mission. Familiar material, rendered enjoyable by a fresh-faced cast of Warner's contract players and effective depiction of sea- to-land action as well as state-of-the-art underwater photography. Martin, Garner's love interest, is appealing but her scenes only slow-down an overly long, too predictable project. Moderately suspenseful second half; Garner gets to show off his charisma in an early leading role. Rare acting role for athlete Gifford.

WE DIVE AT DAWN (1943)

CREDITS:

Gainsborough/Gaumont British; Anthony Asquith, dir.; J.B. Williams, Val Valentine, Frank Launder, scr.; Edward Black, pro.; Hubert Bath, mus.; Jack E. Cox, cin.; R.E. Dearing, ed.; B&W; 1.37:1; 98 min.

CAST:

John Mills (*Lt. Taylor*); Louis Bradfield (*Lt. Brace*); Ronald Milar (*Lt. Johnson*); Jack Watling (*Lt. Gordon*); Reginald Purdell (*Dabbs*); Caven Watson (*Duncan*); Naill MacGinnis (*Corrigan*).

Rating: **** ½

The Nazis' latest super-battleship *Brandenburg* is en route to the Kiel Canal where it will receive final testing in the Baltic Sea. A Brit sub commander and his crew head out to eliminate this threat. Considering the patriotic fervor of most early 1940s combat films, it's surprising to encounter this uniquely objective piece. Realistic rather than idealized portrayals of the sailors' home-lives, each man dealing with serious issues. In place of conventional rowdy commaraderie on board, many men dislike others they must work with, for complex motives that reveal convincing personalities. Sailors aren't portrayed as super-professionals, each a master of his unique task, but as fallible humans nervously hoping to do their best. Less time lavished on action here than the manner in which ordinary folks behave under stress. Low-key lighting and subdued acting result in a stand-out film from an age when jingoism ran rampant.

TWO-FACED WOMAN: Yet another vivid portrait from Joan Crawford graced this film about a woman who appears to have sold out to the Nazis though she secretly works as an Allied agent.

Undercover: Spies, Saboteurs & Secret Agents

ABOVE SUSPICION (1943)

CREDITS:
Metro-Goldwyn-Mayer; Richard Thorpe, dir.; Helen MacInnes (novel), Keith Winter, Melville Baker, Leonard Lee, Patricia Coleman, scr.; Leon Gordon, Victor Saville, pro.; Bronislau Kaper, Eric Zeisl, mus.; Robert H. Planck, cin.; George Hively, James E. Newcom, ed.; B&W; 1.37:1; 90 min.

CAST:
Joan Crawford (*Frances Myles*); Fred MacMurray (*Richard Myles*); Conrad Veidt (*Hassert Seidel*); Basil Rathbone (*Sig von Aschenhausen*); Reginald Owen (*Dr. Mespelbrunn*).

Rating: **

The music of Franz Liszt and overripe red roses serve as MacGuffins in this Hitchcock wannabe about an Oxford scholar and his American bride. About to embark on their European honeymoon, the couple is enlisted by the British Foreign Office to locate a mystery man and discover the formula for Hitler's upcoming super-weapon. Perhaps the Master of Suspense might've been able to jell this ever more untenable mélange of suspense, comedy and romance. Without him it all falls flat. MGM's papier-mache Europe, mounted on a sound-stage, hardly adds to the sadly missing sense of believability. Rathbone and Veidt (both anti-Nazis) are in fine form as nasty Germans.

ACROSS THE PACIFIC (1942)

CREDITS:
Warner Bros.; John Huston, Vincent Sherman, dir(s); Robert Carson (original story), Richard Macaulay, scr.; Jack Saper, Jerry Wald, pro.; Adolph Deutsch, Heinz Roemheld, Clifford Vaughan, mus.; Arthur Edeson, cin.; Frank Magee, ed.; B&W; 1.37:1; 97 min.

CAST:
Humphrey Bogart (*Rick Leland*); Mary Astor (*Alberta Marlow*); Sydney Greenstreet (*Dr. Lorenz*); Charles Halton (*Smith)*; Victor Sen Yung

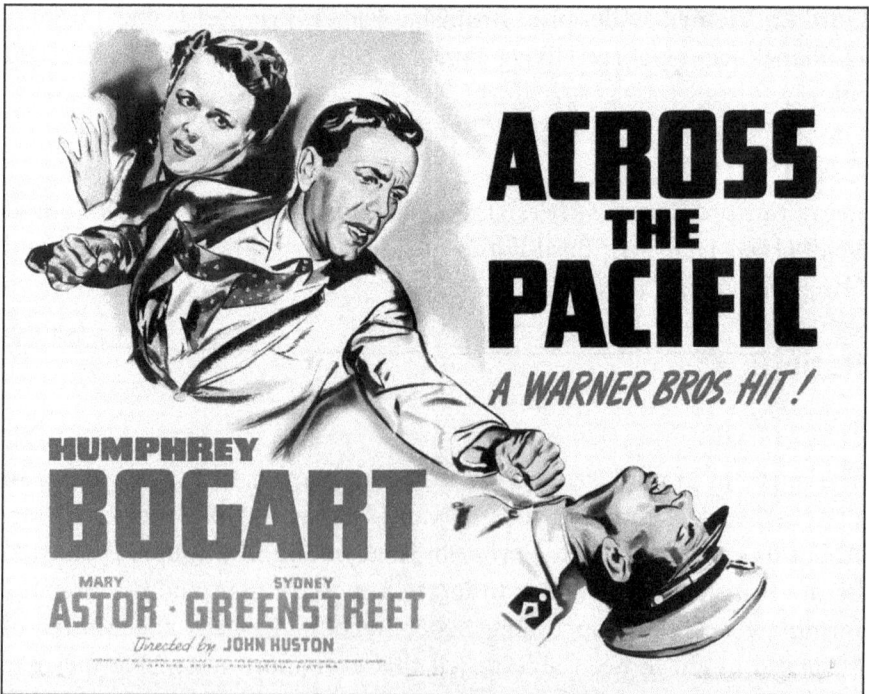

THE CAUSE: Humphrey Bogart starred in almost as many World War II films as John Wayne, *Across the Pacific* among them.

(*Totsuiko*); Roland Got (*Sugi*); Lee Tung Foo (*Sam*); Frank Wilcox (*Capt. Morrison*).

Rating: *** ½

Unofficial follow-up to *The Maltese Falcon* (same director and stars). Bogie (playing 'Rick,' a cross-reference to *Casablanca*; with best friend 'Sam'!), wears his trademark trench-coat. Following court-marial, he's a lone wolf who books passage on a Japanese ship headed for the Panama Canal, pursuing a pretty face (Astor). The rogue finds himself involved in international intrigue via a mysterious stranger (Greenstreet). At mid-movie, we learn what they don't know: the disgrace was a sham. Rick works undercover to determine whether the Japanese are planning to bomb the canal. We know what even he doesn't: This operation will take place on Sunday, Dec. 7. Some smart, sassy dialogue ship-board and a nifty shoot-out in a Panama movie theatre, where a Japanese film plays, qualify this as acceptable.

ADVENTURES OF TARTU, aka *SABOTAGE AGENT* (1941)

CREDITS:
MGM British/Gainsborough; Harol S. Bucquet, dir.; John Lee Mahin, Howard Emmett Rogers, John C. Higgins, Miles Malleson, scr(s).; Irving Asher, pro.; Hubert Bath, Louis Levy, mus.; Jack E. Cox, cin.; Douglas Myers, ed.; B&W; 1.37:1; 111 min. (U.K.), 103 min. (U.S.)

CAST:
Robert Donat (*Terence Stevenson/Jan Tartu*); Valerie Hobson (*Maruschuka Lanova*); Walter Rilla (*Otto Vogel*); Glynis Johns (*Paula Palacek*); Phyllis Morris (*Anna Palacek*); Martin Miller (*Dr. Novotny*).

Rating(s)   **** ½ (U.K. cut)
**** (U.S. cut)

A calm, cool, collected captain nonchalantly goes about his business, defusing unexploded bombs. Then he's tapped for an even more dangerous job: Parachute into occupied Rumania, pass himself off as a Nazi, then slip into Czechoslovakia to locate (then return with) Germany's poison gas formula. The qualities that made Donat such a delight are all on display here, ranging from his remarkable talent at playing serious roles in a lighthearted manner to his chameleon-like ability to morph from one distinctive personality into another. A deadly-serious plot is rendered as entertainment with surprising success. Johns established herself as a star with an indelible performance as a dedicated/ doomed Partisan. Many Hitchcock-like touches on view, the film shot at the master of suspense's old studio. Only liability: several twists are difficult to accept.

AGAINST THE WIND (1948)

CREDITS:
Ealing/Eagle Lion; Charles Crichton, dir.; T.E.B. Clarke, J. Elder Wills, Michael Pertwee, scr.; Michael Balcon, pro.; Leslie Bridgewater, mus.; Lionel Barnes, cin.; alan Osbiston, ed.; B&W; 1.37:1; 96 min.

CAST:
Simone Signoret (*Michèle*); Jack Warner (*Cronk*); Gordon Jackson (Duncan); Robert Beatty (*Father Philip*); Paul Dupuis (*Picquart*); Gisèle Préville (*Julie*).

Rating: *** ½

A tribute to the British Special Operations Executive which trained in secret for special missions behind enemy lines; part spy, part soldier. The task at hand: Seize important documents from a Belgium-based Nazi heaquarters and return home after freeing a key Allied officer held prisoner. It's an oft-told tale; this offering is competent in every way yet hardly ranks with the best (i.e., the fictional *Guns of Navarone)*. Blame a so-so script and overly eclectic cast. Signoret is luminescent, hinting at the great star she would soon become, though her love story fails to click as Jackson doesn't provide the necessary sparks. A tight-budget didn't leave room for much action. Not bad; rather, disappointing.

ALLIED (2016)

CREDITS:
GK Films/Huaha Media/Paramount; Robert Zemeckis, dir.; Steven Knight, scr.; Zemeckis, Knight, Graham King, pros.; Alan Silvestri, mus.; Don Burgess, cin.; Mick Audsley, Jeremiah O'Driscoll, ed.; 2.35:1; C; 124 min.

CAST:
Brad Pitt (*Max Vatan*); Marion Cotillard (*Marianne Beausejour*); Sally Messham (*Margaret*); Jared Harris (*Frank*); Lizzy Caplain (*Bridget*); Charlotte Hope (*Louise*); Marion Bailey (*Mrs. Sinclair*); Matthew Goode (*Guy Sangster*); Matthew Goode (*Sangster*); Iain Batchelor (*Pilot Fleischer*).

Rating: **

UNDERCOVER: An American Brad Pitt has second thoughts about his wartime companion/wife (Marion Cotillard) in *Allied*.

In 1942, a Canadian-born operative (Pitt) joins a former ace of the French Resistance (Cotillard) in Morocco to carry out an Allied mission. The two fall in love and, once relatively safe in wartime London, marry and have a child. Then evidence surfaces implicating her as a Nazi agent. Any attempt to raise a serious moral issue—-the conflicting loyalties between one's country and a dearly beloved person-—gets lost as the plotting becomes increasingly preposterous and at the end melodramatic where it means to be tragic. This rates as a window dressing movie, watchable only for the gorgeously mounted production design (which recalls old Hollywood films including *Casablanca*), theme-park like retro-settings, and dazzlingly nostalgic costumes for breathtaking Cotillard.

ATLANTIC CONVOY (1942)

CREDITS:
Columbia; Lew Landers, dir.; Robert Lee Johnson, scr.; Colbert Clark, pro.; Henry Freulich, cin.; James Sweeney, ed.; B&W; 1.37:1; 66 min.

CAST:
Bruce Bennett (*Capt. Morgan*); Virginia Field (*Linda Adams*); John Beal (*Hansen*); Clifford Severn (*Sandy*); Larry Parks (*Gregory*); Lloyd Bridges (*Bert*); Victor Killian (*Otto*); Hans Schumm (*Cmdr. Von Smith*).

Rating: ** ½

Despite the nautical-sounding title, this is actually a spy/ saboteur yarn. German U-boats devastate Allied convoys in the North Atlantic. The U.S. sends a courageous captain (Bennett) to Iceland; his sea patrols will hopefully knock out enemy subs. Meanwhile, several Germans infiltrate the port to blow up the harbor's entrance. Who among the townsfolk can be trusted, and who cannot? Landers made such ultra-low-budget projects his stock in trade at Columbia's B unit and, like many other of his other unpretentious (to be kind) films, this plays out as a spirited thriller. For once, Bridges is among the good guys, not a Nazi.

BACKGROUND TO DANGER (1943)

CREDITS:
Warner Bros.; Raoul Walsh, dir.; Eric Ambler (novel), W.R. Burnett, William Faulkner, scr.; Jerry Wald, pro.; Friedrich Hollaender, mus.; Tony Gaudio, cin.; Jack Killifer, ed.; B&W; 1.37:1; 80 min.

CAST:
George Raft (*Joe Barton*); Brenda Marshall (*Tamara Zaleshoff*); Sydney Greenstreet (*Col. Robinson*); Peter Lorre *(Nikolai)*; Osa Massen (*Ana Remzi*); Turhan Bey (*Hassan*).

Rating: ** 1/2

A German agent (Greenstreet) schemes to trick leaders of neutral Turkey into joining the Axis. His plan is thwarted by a soldier-of-fortune (Raft) and two Russian spies (Lorre, Marshall). A cut-rate *Casablanca* from Warner's B unit with falsified maps subbing for letters of transit. Toy trains whiz about on tabletops; Raft stalks Nazis through smoke and shadows on a studio-lot back, even reviveing his coin-flipping gambit from *Scarface* (1932). Raft to Marshall about Greenstreet: "We gotta ketch dat Fat Guy!" Far-fetched, fast paced fun.

CAIRO (1942)

CREDITS:
MGM; W.S. Van Dyke, dir.; John McClain, Ladislas Fodor, scr.; Joseph L. Mankiewicz, pro.; Ray June, cin.; James E. Newcom, ed.; B&W; 1.37:1; 101 min.

CAST:
Jeanette MacDonald (*Marcia Wilson*); Robert Young (*Homer Smith);* Ethel Waters *(Cleona);* Reginald Owen *(Cobson);* Lionel Atwill (*German);* Dooley Wison (*Hector);* Mona Barrie (*Mrs. Morrison*); Eduardo Ciannelli (*Ahmed Ben Hassan).*

Rating: *** ½

Through a bizarre (and not always believable) series of circumstances, a bumbling small-town journalist (Young) finds himself in the title city, attempting to stop a Nazi spy from developing a super-weapon: A radio-controlled plane. He assumes that an innocent American chanteuse (MacDonald) is a Black Widow (she isn't) and that a society dame (Barrie) is to be trusted (she's not). The first WWII film to spoof the era's earlier spy films, sometimes effectively. Young has a marvelous comedy bit in which he bumbles from one unexpected trap to the next. Waters, cast as another maid, gets to sing (marvelously), is treated as an equal by her boss, and is fully developed as a character, even enjoying a romance with Wilson (Sam from *Casablanca*). A mixed bag.

CATCHER WAS A SPY, THE (2018)

CREDITS:
Ben Lewin, dir.; Robert Rodat, scr., Nicholas Dawidoff (book); Kevin Scott Frakes, Jim Young, Buddy Patrick, prod.; Howard Shore, mus.; Andrij Parekh, cin.; C; 2.85:1; 98 min.

CAST:
Paul Rudd (*Moe Berg*); Connie Nielsen (*Koranda*); Guy Pearce (*Robert Furman*); Sienna Miller(*Estella Huni*); Paul Giamatti (*Samuel Goudsmit*); Jeff Daniels (*William J. ("Wild Bill") Donovan*); Hiroyuki Sanada (*Kawabata*); Shea Whigham (*Cronin*); Giancarlo Giannini (*Amaldi*).

Rating: *** ½

The legendary Casey Stengel referred to Morris ("Moe") Berg (1902-1972) as "the strangest man ever to play baseball." The Princeton University graduate and White Socks player joined the O.S.S. and become an unlikely agent. One obit claimed the intellectual had been "A third string catcher and a first rate spy." A movie about this fascinating fellow ought to at least try to unlock the abiding enigma; this well-crafted but light-weight work merely presents moments from his life and career without expanding our understanding of Berg. Rudd might have proven impressive in the role if only the script gave him more to work with. Scores neither as a biopic or a generic mystery. As intriguing as it is unsatisfying. The film's problems are reflected by its silly but meaningless Salinger in-joke title.

CIRCLE OF DECEPTION, (A) (1960)

CREDITS:
20th Century-Fox; Jack Lee, dir.; Nigel Balchin, Robert Musil, Alec Waugh (scr.), Anthony Cave Brown (book); Tom Monohan, pro.; Clifton Parker, mus.; Gordon Dines, cin.; Gordon Pilkington, ed.; B&W; 2.35:1; 100 min.

CAST:
Bradford Dillman (*Paul Raine*); Suzy Parker (*Lucy Bowen*); Harry Andrews (*Capt. Rawson*); Robert Stephens (*Capt. Stein*); Paul Rogers (*Spence*).

Rating: *** ½

A Brit spy (Dillman), fearful of his weaknesses, attempts to bite the bullet, refusing to divulge D-Day secrets as, following capture, he's systematically tortured by a Nazi (Stephens). Grim irony: he was selected for this mission because a commander (Andrews) and his seductive assistant (Parker) knew of their agent's psychological flaws, hoping to pass mis-information along to the enemy by counting on him to break. Fascinating fact-based espionage tale, though the results are routine owing to a journeyman director and lack of chemistry between the leads despite their real-life marriage. Occasionally compelling.

CONFIDENTIAL AGENT (1945)

CREDITS:
Warner Bros.; Herman Shumlin, dir.; Graham Greene (novel), Robert Buckner, scr.; Robert Buckner, pro.; Franz Waxman, mus.; James Wong

Howe, cin.; George Amy, ed.; B&W; 1.37:1; 118 min.

CAST:
Charles Boyer (*Luis Denard*); Lauren Bacall (*Rose Cullen*); Victor Francen (*Licata*); Wanda Hendrix (*Else*); George Coulouris (*Captain Currie*); Peter Lorre (*Contreras*); Katina Paxinou (*Mrs. Melandez*).

Rating: **** 1/2

Before there was John le Carre and *The Spy Who Came in From the Cold* (1963), Greene (1904-1991) rated as the master of smart, serious-minded spy stories, presenting espionage as a dull, dirty, dehumanizing trade. Here, a Spanish Civil war survivor (Boyer) slips into England. He hopes to convince the powers that be to cease exporting coal to Franco, however much Brits need the money. Constantly surprising, endlessly rewarding script aligns him with an upper-class brat (Bacall); she transforms into one of the era's strong screen women. They go up against the meanest Nazis (Lorre, Paxinou) ever. Graphic abuse and the death of an innocent child (Hendrix) attests to the project's bleak integrity. Had this been directed by someone on the level of Sir Carol Reed, it might have provided a pre-war *The Third Man*, later adapted from another Green novel.

DANGEROUSLY THEY LIVE (1941)

CREDITS:
Warner Bros.; Robert Florey, dir.; Marion Parsonnet, scr.; Bryan Foy, pro.; L. William O'Connell, cin.; Harold McLernon, ed.; B&W; 1.37:1; 77 min.

CAST:
John Garfield (*Dr. Michael Lewis*); Nancy Coleman (*Jane Graystone*); Raymond Massey (*Ingersoll*); Lee Patrick (*Nurse Johnson*); Moroni Olsen (*John Goodwin*); Esther Dale (*Dawson*).

Rating: **

An amnesiac accident-victim (Coleman) is taken to a manor house outside Manhattan by her doctor (Massey) and a man claiming to be her father (Olsen). In fact, she's a British spy, they Nazi agents who hope to unlock secrets about an Allied convoy off Halifax so their U-boats can destroy it. Garfield is the intern who falls for and rescues her. The film flirts with Hitchcockian themes but misses the mark by the proverbial mile. Despite a stylish noir realization by Florey the results are nondescript.

DECISION BEFORE DAWN (1951)

CREDITS:
20th Century Fox/Bavarian Film; Anatole Litvak, dir.; Peter Viertel, Jack Rollens, Carl Zuckmayer, scr., George Howe (novel); Litvak, Frank McCarthy, pro(s).; Franz Waxman, mus.; Franz Planer, cin.; Dororthy Spencer, ed.; B&W; 1.37:1; 119 min.

CAST:
Richard Basehart (*Lt. Dick Rennick*); Gary Merrill *(Col. Devlin)*; Oskar Werner (*'Happy' Maurer*); Hildegard Knef (*Hilde*); Dominique Blanchar *(Monique)*; O.E. Hasse; H.W. Briggs *(Himself)*.

Rating: **** ½

As Allied armies close in on Berlin from two sides, U.S. intelligence officers come up with a novel way of having their troops arrive first. Carefully selected German POWs have an oportunity to better their lot in the postwar world by becoming spies, infiltrating their own ranks, passing key information back to the Yanks. Among the earliest film to de-demonize the German people, arguing that there were those who didn't support Hitler. Though the storyline and characters are fictional, such a ploy was used during the war's final hours with, as the film illustrates, ironic results. 'Somber' best describes the tone; entertaining despite unpleasant situations the lead (Werner, in a star-making performance) finds himself in. No war movie clichés. Filmed on location in Wurzberg. Nominated for several Oscars including Best Picture; listed by the National Board of Review as one of the year's Ten Best.

EAGLE HAS LANDED, THE (1976)

CREDITS:
Associated GeneralFilms; John Sturges, dir.; Jack Higgins (novel); Tom Mankiewicz, scr.; David Niven Jr., Jack Wiener, pro.; Lalo Schifrin, mus.; Anthony B. Richmond, cin.; Anne V. Coates, ed.; C; 2.35:1; 135 min (145 extended).

CAST:
Michael Caine (*Col. Kurt Steiner*); Donald Sutherland (*Liam Devlin*); Robert Duvall (*Col. Max Radl*); Jenny Agutter (*Molly Prior*); Donald Pleasence (*Himmler*); Anthony Quayle (*Canaris*); Jean Marsh (*Joanna*); Treat Williams (*Clark*).

Rating: **

A Nazi officer (Duvall) plans to kidnap Churchill by planting an IRA agent (Sutherland) in a Brit east-coast township, later parachuting in a maverick commando (Caine). Ken Follett-like 1975 novel transfers terribly to the screen. The characters are detestable, including a 'sensitive' young woman (Agutter) who murders her patriotic fiancee because she

THE PLOT TO KILL CHURCHILL: Spies, counter-spies, and counter-counter spies (including Michael Caine, far right) play a deadly game in *The Eagle Has Landed*.

finds a conspirator more attractive! It doesn't help that Duvall (in black-eye patch) does an over-the-top German accent while most of the others (Quayle, Pleasence) speak in native English voices. Capped by the least satisfying trick ending in movie history.

ESPIONAGE AGENT (1939)

CREDITS:
Warner Bros.; Lloyd Bacon, dir.; Robert Buckner, Warren Duff, Michael Fessier, Frank Donaghue, James Hilton, scr.; Louis F. Edelman,prod;Adolph Deutsch,mus.; Charles Rosher,cin.; Ralph Rosher; ed.; B&W; 1.37:1; 83 min.

CAST:
Joel McCrea *(Barry Corvall)*; Brenda Marshall *(Brenda Ballard)*; Jeffrey Lynn *(Warrington)*; George Bancroft *(Dudley/ Donald)*; Stanley Ridges *(Peyton)*; Martin Kosleck *(Müller)*.

Rating: ** 1/2

An American consul stationed in Tangier aids displaced Europeans to escape early combat. He falls in love with and marries a refugee, unaware she's a Nazi spy. Initially intriguing storyline meanders after the midpoint, losing believability and interest. Bolstered by an accurate depiction of the State Department's role in complex international situations as America still clung to isolationism. A message movie, designed to convince Congress to create the first counter-espionage operation as well as stricter laws to monitor immigration of possible saboteurs.

EYE OF THE NEEDLE (1981)

CREDITS:
United Artists; Richard Marquand, dir.; Ken Follett (novel), Stanley Mann, scr.; Stephen J. Friedman, pro.; Miklós Rózsa, mus.; Alan Hume, cin.; Sean Barton, ed.; C; 1.85:1; 112 min.

(Above and facing page) **THE SPY WHO LOVED ME (OR SO I THOUGHT):** In *Eye of the Needle,* an Irishman (Donald Sutherland) aligned with the Nazis convinces guards he is a harmless bicyclist; he cuts wires to enter into off-limits areas; a loyal Englishman (Christopher Cazenove) comes to realize the threat; the spy's lover (Kate Nelligan) realizes what is happening and alerts the authorities.

CAST:

Donald Sutherland (*Heinrich Faber*); Kate Nelligan (*Lucy Rose*); Christopher Cazenove (*David Rose*); Ian Bannen (*Yard Inspector Godliman*); Jonathan & Nicholas Haley (*Jo Rose*).

Rating: **

A lonely woman inhabiting an isolated Scotch island with her disabled husband and son becomes romantically involved with a soft-spoken stranger washed up by a storm. Gradually, she realizes he's a Nazi spy, on his way back to Germany with secret Allied information. The power of Follett's 1978 novel derived from inner thoughts and emotions of the characters. That's gone; we watch a routine, slow-moving, uninvolving cat-and-mouse thriller unsatisfyingly unfold. Despite notably graphic sex scenes, the two leads provide no screen chemistry.

FALCON'S BROTHER, THE (1942)

CREDITS:

R.K.O.; Stanley Logan, dir.; Michael Arlen (original character), Stuart Palmer, Craig Rice, scr.; Maurice Geraghty, pro.; Roy Webb, mus.; Russell Metty, cin.; Mark Robson, ed.; B&W; 1.37:1; 63 min.

CAST:

George Sanders (*Gay Lawrence*); Tom Conway (*Tom Lawrence*); Jane Randolph (*Marcia*); Don Barclay (*Lefty*); Charlotte Wynters (*Arlette*); Keye Luke (*Jerry*).

Rating: ***

When a super-suave amateur sleuth heads for the New York docks to meet his arriving brother, he's informed the sibling died en route from South America. But the supposed 'corpse' shows up alive and well; the pair set out to foil a plot by Nazi spies. The fourth series entry set the stage for Sanders' real-life brother Conway to assume the title role after Gay sacrifices his life for the American way. A contrived script keeps this programmer from reaching the heights of the best Falcon films. You haven't lived until you've seen the V for Victory gown worn by model Kay Aldrich at a fashion show. Brooklynese sidekick Lefty (Barclay), sassy gal-pal Marcia (Randolph), and houseboy Jerry (Key Luke) as always provide clever comedy relief.

5 FINGERS, aka FIVE FINGERS (1952)

CREDITS:
20th Century Fox; Joseph L. Mankiewicz, dir.; Michael Wilson, scr., L.C. Moyzisch (book); otto Lang, pro.; Bernard Hermann, mus.; Nobert Brodine, cin.; James B. Clark, ed.; B&W; 1.37:1; 108 min.

CAST:
James Mason (*Ulysses Diello*); Danielle Darrieux (*Countess Anna Staviska*); Michael Rennie (*Colin Travers*); Walter Hampden (*Sir Frederic Taylor*); Oskar Karlweis (*Moyzisch*).

THE ULTIMATE SPY: Five *Fingers* offered James Mason (seen here with Danielle Darrieux) the chance to play a fictionalized version of one of the war's most intriguing triple agents.

Rating: **** ½

As the D-Day invasion nears, British authorities realize the Germans have somehow acquired their key strategies. But how? The strange (and mostly true) story behind that incident, as told in the book *Operation Cicero*, is here brought to the screen as an innovative spy movie: Ultra low-key in approach, with no action or chase scenes. Moreover, in comparison to propaganstic spy films from the war years, here the main character is a suave, charming rogue even U.S. audiences can't help but root for. He's a valet to a Brit commander in neutral Turkey and romances a destitute aristocrat (Darrieux, the only fictional figure on view) while playing cat and mouse with an English agent. This strong yet subtle movie re-invented a genre. The real-life character on whom Diello was based was Elyesa Bazlla.

FOREIGN AGENT (1942)

CREDITS:
Monogram; William Beaudine, dir.; John W. Krafft, Martin Mooney, scr.; Mooney, Max King, pro.; Edward J. Kay, mus.; Mack Stengler, cin.; Frederick Bain, ed.; B&W; 1.37:1; 63 min..

CAST:
Gale Storm (*Mitzi Mayo*); John Shelton (*Jimmy*); Ivan Lebedeff (*Okura*); Patsy Moran (*Joanie*); Lyle Latell (*Eddie*); Hans Schumm (*Dr. Werner*).

Rating: *

A patriotic scientist, working on a searchlight filter that could aid as L.A. prepares for a Japanese attack, supposedly commits suicide. His daughter suspects foul play. An eager government agent and a crusading radio journalist help her foil an evil Axis doctor masquerading as a pacifist. The captivating Storm's stunt-woman roommate (Moran) provides low low-comedy relief. Dull and talky, relieved by stock footage of action at sea and in the air. Exaggerated Asian ethnic stereotypes are embarrassing, even for that time. Storm performs the propaganda tune: "Taps for the Japs."

GOLDEN EARRINGS (1947)

CREDITS:

Paramount; Mitchell Leisen, dir.; Abraham Polonsky, frank Butler, Helen Deutsch, scr(s), Yolanda Foldes (novel); Harry Tugend, pro.; Victor Young, mus.; Daniel L. Fapp, cin.; Alma Macrorie, ed.; B&W; 1.37:1; 95 min.

THE GLAMOROUS GYPSY: German born Marlene Dietrich proves her loyalty to the Allied cause in *Golden Earrings*.

CAST:
Marlene Dietrich *(Lydia)*; Ray Milland *(Col. Ralph Denistoun)*; Murvyn Vye *(Zoltan)*; Bruce Lester *(Richard Byrd)*; Dennis Hoey *(Hoff)*; Quentin Reynolds *(Himself)*.

Rating: *** ½

A lonely gypsy travels across Europe, making do as best she can. Fortune throws her in contact with an Allied agent who has escaped the Nazis and must now locate a mysterious doctor. Our hero could never complete his heroic mission were it not for the slinky lady who transforms from innocent bystander to committed democrat. Shot mostly on studio sets, with over- the-top dialogue and broad performances, this plays most effectively if enjoyed on the outre level of High Camp.

HOUSE ON 92nd ST, THE (1945)

CREDITS:
20th Century-Fox; Henry Hathaway, dir.; Barré Lyndon, Charles G. Booth, John Monks Jr., scr.; Louis De Rochemont, pro.; David Buttolph, Emil Newman, mus.; Norbert Brodine, cin.; Harmon Jones, ed.; B&W; 1.37:1; 88 min.

CAST:
William Eythe *(Bill Dietrich)*; Lloyd Nolan *(George A. Briggs)*; Signe Hasso *(Elsa)*; Gene Lockhart *(Roper)*; Leo G. Carroll *(Hammersohn)*; Reed Hadley *(Narrator)*.

Rating: **** ½

Shortly before the U.S. enters the war, a German-American is contacted by Fifth Columnists as a possible recruit. He heads directly to the F.B.I. where a seasoned agent mentors the youth to serve as a double-agent. The assignment: Keep Process 97 (the atomic bomb) secrets from leaking out. Fox, the studio that pioneered the docudrama, made this their first such experiment in the new realism. Everything was shot on location;

F.B.I. agents are played by actual Bureau members with only the leads performed by lesser-known actors. No-nonsense narration, adding to the impact, would be imitated often, including Jack Webb's legendary TV show *Dragnet*. Even the expected spy-vs.-spy romance between handsome hero Eythe and femme fatale Hasso was avoided to make this truly realistic.

INVISIBLE AGENT (1942)

CREDITS:

Universal; Edwin L. Marin, dir.; Curt Siodmak, scr.; Frank Lloyd, George WaGGner, pro(s).; Hans J. Salter, mus.; Lester White, cin.; Edward Curtiss, ed.; B&W; 1.37:1; 81 min.

CAST:

Ilona Massey (*Maria Sorenson*); Jon Hall *(Frank Raymond)*; Peter Lorre (*Ikito*); Cedric Hardwicke *(Stauffer)*; J. Edward Bromberg (*Heiser*); Albert Bassermann (*Arnold Schmidt).*

Rating: ***

A descendant of the Invisible Man is approached by Nazi agents, threatened with torture if he doesn't hand his notebooks over. Instead, he serves America by hecoming the title character. Massey is something to see as the mistress of a high-ranking Nazi, actually an Allied double-agent, Lorre scrumptuously sleazy as a slimy villain. Undone by direction that treats Nazis as the basis for broad comedy (a predecessor to TV's *Hogan's Heroes).* Claude Rains, who played the tragic scientist in the first Universal film from H.G. Wells' novel, can be glimpsed briefly in a wall photograph. Screenwriter Siodmak was himself a refugee from Nazi Germany. Best feature: Academy Award nominated special effects by John P. Fulton.

JOURNEY INTO FEAR (1943)

CREDITS:
R.K.O.; Norman Foster, Orson Welles, dirs.; Eric Ambler (novel), Welles, Joseph Cotten,Ben Hecht, scr.; Welles, George Schaefer, pro.; Roy Webb, Rex Dunn, mus.; Karl Struss, cin.; Mark Robson, ed.; B&W; 1.37:1; 69 min.

CAST:
Joseph Cotten (*Howard Graham*); Ruth Warrick (*Stephanie*); Orson Welles (*Col. Haki*); Agnes Moorehead (*Mrs. Mathews*); Everett Sloane (*Kopeikin*); Dolores del Rio (*Josette*).

Rating: ★★★★

An American munitions salesman (Cotton) cuts deals in Eastern Europe to supply anti-Nazi Turks with guns. He's spirited away from his wife (Warrick) by a warlord (Welles), then forced to travel by sea with a boatload of people who may be friends or enemies, spies or counter-spies. Dazzlingly directed, with the five stars of *Citizen Kane* reunited in a considerably smaller project. The film suffers from severe editing that

JOURNEY INTO FEAR: Fresh from *Citizen Kane*, actor Joseph Cotton again joined forces with director/star Orson Welles for this tale of espionage.

renders this more confusing than complex and a disappointing final trek that leads nowhere. Individual sequences are well staged. Mystery girl Del Rio's Catwoman was a predecessor to Bob Kane's 'Selina Kyle.' More style, sadly, than substance.

MAN WHO NEVER WAS, THE (1956)

CREDITS:
20th Century-Fox; Ronald Neame, dir.; Ewen Montagu (book), Nigel Balchin, scr.; André Hakim, pro.; Alan Rawsthorne, mus.; Oswald Morris, cin.; Peter Taylor, ed.; C; 2.55:1; 103 min.

CAST:
Clifton Webb (*Lt. Cmdr. Ewen Montagu*); Gloria Grahame (*Lucy Sherwood*); Robert Flemyng (*Lt. George Acres*); Josephine Griffin *(Pam)*; Stephen Boyd *(Patrick O'Reilly)*; Laurence Naismith (*Adm. Cross*); Peter Sellers (*Churchill, voice only*).

Rating: **** 1/2

Splendid story, closely following the historic Operation Mincemeat. In 1943, the Allies are about to invade Sicily. A concerned British officer, knowing that the Nazis have dug in, devises a plan to save Allied lives: Create a person, supposedly dead, out of thin air; borrow the body of some recently deceased chap, attach letters indicating the attack will be directed against Spain, then allow the enemy to find the floating corpse. With luck, they'll swiftly re-assign their troops. Fascinating first-half super-realistically chronicles the way in which the ruse is engineered; edge-of-your-seat second focuses on a Nazi spy arriving in London to learn whether the discovered body was planted. One lovesick librarian creates the only link between those two situations, with ironic results. One of those rare times when the film fully captures a complex (1953) book.

MONUMENTS MEN (2014)

CREDITS:

Columbia/Smokehouse; George Clooney, dir.; Clooney, Grant Heslov, scr., Robert M. Edsel, Bret Witter (book); Clooney, Heslov, prods.; Alexandre Desplat, mus.; Phedon Papamichael, cin.; Stephen Mirrione, ed.; 2.35:1; C; 118 min.

CAST:

George Clooney *(Frank Stokes)*; Matt Damon *(James Granger)*; Bill Murray *(Richard Campbell)*; Cate Blanchett *(Claire)*; John Goodman *(Garfield)*; Jean Dujardin *(Clermont)*; Hugh Bonneville *(Jeffries)*; Bob Balaban *(Savitz)*; Dimitri Leonidas *(Epstein)*.

Rating: ★★★

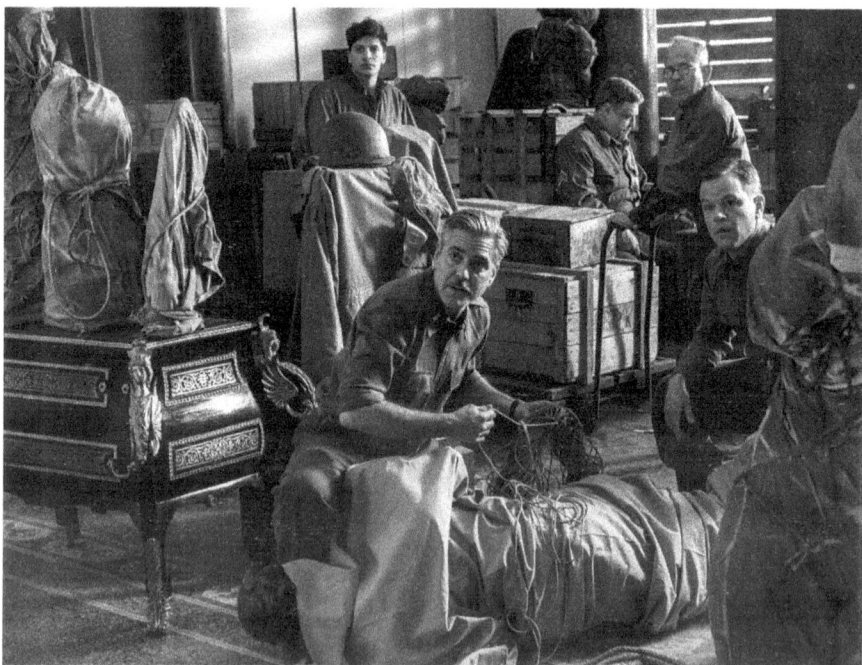

IN SEARCH OF ART: George Clooney leads a special team of agents hoping to recover stolen paintings in *Monuments Men*.

An oddball assortment of intellectuals and academics head off to Europe in 1943, their mission to rescue priceless/classical works of art before retreating Nazis can carry these back to Germany. Blanchett plays a French museum curator willing and able to join their mission. A fascinating true story is too often reduced to the level of filmmaker Clooney's *Ocean's 11* franchise. Attempts to combine the entertaining goofiness of *Kelly's Heroes* with the deadly serious thematic ambitions of *The Train*, though the two elements never really jell into a successful project. Handsome production values certainly help.

NAZI AGENT (1942)

CREDITS:
M.G.M.; Jules Dassin, dir.; Paul Gangelin, John Meehan Jr., Lothar Mendes, scr.; Irving Asher, pro.; Lennie Hayton, mus.; Harry Stradling Sr., cin.; Frank E. Hull, ed.; B&W; 1.37:1; 83 min.

CAST:
Conrad Veidt (*Otto Becker/Baron Hugo Von Detner*); Ann Ayars (*Kaaren De Relle*); Frank Reicher (*Fritz*); Dorothy Tree (*Miss Harper*); William Tannen (*Ludwig*); Martin Kosleck (*Kurt*).

Rating: ***

A loyal German-American is blackmailed by his evil twin hoping to use the good brother's business as a safe-place for nefarious activities. The good twin kills his sibling and assumes his identity (and mistress), sabotaging the saboteurs who follow his orders. Intriguing premise ruined by flat, uninspired writing and a supposedly inspirational ending that makes no sense. Dassin provides shadowy touches that characterized his postwar work; Veidt is fine in both roles. Interesting only in that the film reveals there were indeed 'good Germans' who despised fascism.

NIGHT TRAIN TO MUNICH (1940)

CREDITS:

20th Century Fox; Carol Reed; Gordon Wellesley, Sidney (Sydney) Gilliat, Frank Lanunder, scr.; Edward Black, pro.; Charles Williams, mus.; Otto Kanturek, cin.; R.E. Dearing, ed. B&W; 1.37:1; 95 min.

CAST:

Margaret Lockwood (*Anna Bomasch*); Rex Harison (*Dick Randall/Gus Bennett*); Paul Henreid, aka von Herniid (*Karl Marsen*); Basil Radford (*Chartres*); Naunton Wayne (*Caldicott*); James Harcourt (*Axel Bomasch*); Felix Aylmer (*Dr. Fredericks*).

Rating: **** ½

A scheming Nazi (Henreid) kidnaps a top Czech scientist (Harcourt) and his daughter (Lockwood), forcing them onto the title train. Their only hope for escape: a former street actor (Harrison), now serving as a Brit secret agent. Top-billed star plays a similar role to her part in Hitch's The Lady Vanishes two years earlier; tense script is by the same writing team and, as a charming in-joke, Radford and Wayne embody their beloved "quare fellows" from that classic. Reed keeps the tone considerably more serious this time around. A harrowing escape to Switzerland on a high, creaky cable car was the best such scene until a similar gambit appeared in the 1954 thriller *Second Chance*. Marvelous combination of romance, suspense, and action, with a fine comic undercurrent.

NORTHERN PURSUIT (1943)

CREDITS:

Warner Bros.; Raoul Walsh, dir.; Leslie T. White, Frank Gruber, Alvah Bessie, William Faulkner, scr.; Jack Chertok, pro.; Adolph Deutsch, Max Steiner, mus.; Sidney Hickox, cin.; Jack Killifer, ed.; B&W; 1.37:1; 94 min.

CAST:

Errol Flynn (*Steve Wagner*); Julie Bishop (*Laura*); Helmut Dantine (*Col. von Keller*); John Ridgely (*Jim*); Gene Lockhart (*Ernst*); Tom Tully (*Barnett*); Monte Blue (*Jean*); Jay Silverheels (*Indian*).

Rating: * 1/2

1941; a U-boat gets stuck in the ice near Hudson's Bay. One spy survives an avalanche that kills the others. Hot on his trail: a Mountie of German descent, eager to prove his loyalty. The plot features endless twists and turns, not one even vaguely believable. The big scale action sequences (ski chase, plane crash, etc.) are superior to scenes filled with ridiculously florid dialogue. Endless attempts to create suspense (is Flynn going over to the other side?) fail. As his love interest, Bishop is so loud, abrasive, and erratic it's impossible to grasp why he tolerates her. Least rewarding of Warner's big-budget propaganda dramas.

OPERATION AMSTERDAM (1959)

CREDITS:

Rank Organization; Michael McCarthy, dir.; David E. Walker (book), John Eldridge, Michael McCarthy, scr.; Maurice Cowan, pro.; Philip Green, mus.; Reginald Wyer, cin.; Arthur Stevens, ed.; B&W; 1.66:1; 105 min.

CAST:

Peter Finch (*Jan Smit*); Eva Bartok (*Anna*); Tony Britton (*Maj. Dillon*); Alexander Knox (*Walter Keyser*); Malcolm Keen (*Johan Smit*); Christopher Rhodes (*Alex*).

Rating: ***

May 1940: as Nazis overrun Holland, British Intelligence sends a three-man team to Amsterdam. Their mission: round up industrial diamonds and bring them to England so the Germans can't use them for cutting and boring during plane production. Major roadblock: they have only one day to do so before the enemy cuts off all exit routes. Low key and, at its best moments, effectively so. Sadly ruined by murky character motives and the lack of a genuinely suspenseful tone. Slowgoing, bolstered by Finch.

O.S.S. (1946)

CREDITS:
Paramount; Irving Pichel, dir.; Richard Maibaum, scr.; Maibaum, pro.; Daniele Amfitheatrof, Heinz Roemheld, mus.; Lionel Linden, cin.; William Shea, ed.; B&W; 1.37:1; 105 min.

CAST:
Alan Ladd (*Philip Masson/John Martin*); Geraldine Fitzgerald (*Ellen Rogers/Elaine Duprez*); Patrick Knowles (*Cmdr. Brady*); John Hoyt (*Col. Meister*); Gloria Saunders (*Sparky*).

Rating: *** 1/2

A former thief, recruited for the country's first modern spy unit, is sent on a test mission to blow up a French railroad tunnel to slow down advancing Germans. Problems develop when he realizes his feelings for a female agent run deep. Solid if uninspired film, with several strong suspense scenes. Too often slowed down by talky exposition. One of the first films to acknowledge the practice of photocopying diplomatic papers rather than stealing them outright. Released even as the wartime outfit was transitioning into the Cold War unit to be known as the CIA. On the basis of this film, producer Albert Broccoli hired Maibaum as screenwriter for the early James Bond films.

PACIFIC RENDEZVOUS (1942)

CREDITS:
Metro-Goldwyn-Mayer; George Sidney, dir.; Harry Kurnitz, George Oppenheimer, P. J. Wolfson, scr.; Kurnitz, B. F. Zeidman, pro.; David Snell, mus.; Paul Vogel, cin.; Kurnitz, Ben Lewis, ed.; B&W; 1.37:1; 76 min.

CAST:
Lee Bowman (*Lt. William Gordon*); Jean Rogers (*Elaine Carter*); Mona Maris (*Olivia*); Carl Esmond (*Andre*); Paul Cavanagh (*Cmdr. Brennan*); Blanche Yurka (*Mrs. Savarina*).

Rating: **

A minor film from a major studio. Shot on elaborate sets left over from more spectacular offerings but with lesser stars and a shorter running time. Despite the title, this isn't an action-at-sea epic (though it does begin with stock footage of a battle). Rather, it's a spy caper about a stalwart hero dealing with his dumb-blonde girlfriend and a svelte, seductive spy. Uneven blend of screwball comedy and serious drama. Any merit derives from an accurate portrayal of how decoding experts slowly break down secret messages.

"PIMPERNEL" SMITH, aka MISTER V (1941)

CREDITS:
British National/United Artists; Leslie Howard, dir.; Baroness Emmuska Orczy (novel), Anatole de Grunwald, Roland Pertwee, scr.; Howard, pro.; John Greenwood, mus.; Mutz Greenbaum, cin.; Douglas Myers, ed.; B&W; 1.37:1; 120 min.

CAST:
Leslie Howard (*Horatio Smith*); Ben Williams (*Graubitz*); Allan Jeayes (*Benckendorf*); Peter Gawthorne (*Koslowski*); Ernest Butcher (*Weber*); Joan Kemp-Welch (*Teacher*).

Rating: **** 1/2

In 1941, a hero arrives in Europe to save as many Jews as possible from the Holocaust. He assumes the form of a British professor whose stuffy Oxford image belies his courage. Intense, entertaining, suspenseful. The story behind the story is remarkable. In 1934, Howard starred in *The Scarlet*

Pimpernel (1935) as a Brit fop rescuing French aristocrats. He conceived of this twentieth-century follow-up and saw it through to completion. (Howard was himself Jewish.) The title was changed to *Mister V* for American audiences. A year and a half later, Howard's plane, supposedly carrying messages for the war cause, was shot down by the Luftwaffe. This was Churchill's favorite among the propagandistic films produced to help Brits keep a stiff upper lip through the dark days of the Blitz. Sweden's Raoul Wallenberg (1912–1945) was so impressed by the movie that he played the role in real life, spiriting away Hungarian Jews.

PRIVATE'S PROGRESS (1956)

John Boulting, dir.; Boulting, Alan Hackney, Frank Harvey, prods.; Roy Boulting, pro.; Anthony Harvey, ed.; Eric Cross, cin.; John Addison, mus.; British Lion/Charter Film; 102 min.; B&W; 1.37:1.

CAST:
Ian Carmichael *(Pvt. Stanley Windrush)*; Dennis Price *(Bertram Traepurcel)*; Terry Thomas *(Maj. Hitchcock)*; Miles Malleson *(Windrush Sr.)*; Sally Miles *(Catherine)*; Richard Attenborough *(Cox)*; Jill Adams *(Prudence)*; Ian Bannen *(Horrocks)*.

Rating: **** ½

During the 1950s, the Boulting Bros. became famous for their wry, dry comedies featuring sharp if good-natured satire on the British ruling class. At the time of its release, this WWII spoof was considered a classic of its kind; unaccountably it has become something of a lost film. Carmichael is plu- perfect as the English equivalent of young Jimmy Stewart in his genial/oblivious roles; Terry Thomas, he of the wide evil eyes and twisted grin, equally sublime as a Machiavellian who plans to use the hapless hero in a scheme to recover works of art stolen by the Nazis in 1942. Always engaging, at times sublime U.K. upper-crust humour. Overdue for a revival!

ROMMEL RUFT KAIRO (1959)

CREDITS:
Omega Film GmbH; Wolfgang Schleif, dir.; John Eppler (novel), K. H. Turner, Heinz Oskar Wuttig, scr.; Wolfram Röhrig, mus.; Kurt Grigoleit, cin.; Hermann Ludwig, ed.; B&W; 1.37:1; 105 min.

CAST:
Adrian Hoven (*Capt. Johannes Eppler, alias Hussein Gafaar*); Elisabeth Müller (*Lt. Kay Morrison*); Peter van Eyck (*Capt. Graf von Almassy*); Paul Klinger (*Rommel*); Leila Iman (*Amina*).

Rating: ***

The story of Operation Salaam (see *Foxhole in Cairo*), this time focusing on German spy Eppler rather than the British team out to stop him. From Eppler's own book (a novel, not a memoir). Effective use of Cairo locations as well as the Sahara, where so many of the real incidents occurred. Several actors would repeat their roles in the English film on the same subject a year later. How fascinating to watch the two in tandem as back-to-back "he said, she said" versions. This German project doesn't defend Hitler or Nazism but objectively depicts the cat- and-mouse games involving virtual chess players and the manner in which a spy goes up against a counterspy. The longer running time allows for a more fully developed, therefore comprehensible, retelling.

SABOTEUR (1942)

CREDITS:
Universal; Alfred Hitchcock, dir.; Hitchcock, Dorothy Parker, Joan Harrison, Peter Viertel, scr.; Frank Lloyd, pro.; Joseph A. Valentine, cin.; Otto Ludwig, Edward Curtiss, ed.; B&W; 1.37:1; 109 min.

CAST:
Robert Cummings (*Barry*); Priscilla Lane (*Pat*); Otto Kruger (*Tobin*); Clem Bevans (*Neilson*); Norman Lloyd (*Fry*); Alma Kruger (*Mrs. Sutton*);

VERTIGO: Long before Jimmy Stewarts suffered from a fear of heights in Alfred Hitchcock's famed drama, Norman Lloyd experienced just such a moment in *Saboteur.*

Ian Wolf (*Robert*); Billy Curtis (*Midget*).

Rating: ****

A patriotic young man works at an aircraft factory. When this Glendale, CA, plant is decimated by fire, he—at the wrong place at the wrong time—is unfairly accused. He desperately goes on the run, hoping to unmask the real enemy agents, pursued by them as well as misguided Americans. Hitch's ongoing wrong-man theme, readjusted for the WWII era, with many motifs from the master: the hero's love/hate relationship with a beautiful blonde, curious characters (a trainload of circus freaks), and seemingly respectable upper-class types who are rotten to the core. Hitch had hoped to cast superstars Gary Cooper and Joan Fontaine; they are missed here more than in *Foreign Correspondent.* The grand finale (a vertigo-inducing sequence atop the Statue of Liberty) is marvelously executed but incoherent storywise. Less than top-flight Hitchcock, it's still effective as then-topical entertainment.

SAINT'S VACATION, THE (1941)

CREDITS:
RKO; Leslie Fenton, dir.; Leslie Charteris (novel), Charteris, Jeffrey Dell, scr.; William Sistrom, pro.; Bretton Byrd, mus.; Bernard Knowles, cin.; Al Barnes, Ralph Kemplen, ed.; B&W; 1.37:1; 60 min.

CAST:
Hugh Sinclair (*Simon Templar*); Sally Gray (*Mary Langdon*); Cecil Parker (*Rudolph Hauser*); Arthur Macrae (*Monty Hayward*); Leueen MacGrath (*Valerie*).

Rating: ** 1/2

Charteris's novel *Getaway* becomes a fast-paced espionage tale. In the seventh series entry, Sinclair assumes the suave supersleuth role, heading (with fussy "Man Friday" Macrae) to Paris for some fun, tailed by a sassy blonde reporter (Gray). Once there, a mystery woman (MacGrath) introduces them to a music box (an eventual MacGuffin) containing hidden codes. Car chases, fistfights, and a wild train ride make this a short, relatively sweet theme-park-ride movie. Shot before America entered the war. The bad guys are referred to only as "enemy agents."

SECRET MISSION (1942)

CREDITS:
Independent Prods.; Harold French, dir.; Shaun (Terence) Young, Anatole de Grunwald, Basil Bartlett, scr.; Marcel Hellman, pro.; Mischa Spoliansky, mus.; Bernard Knowles, cin.; Edward B. Jarvis, ed.; B&W; 1.37:1; 94 min.

CAST:
Hugh Williams (*Maj. Peter Garnett*); Carla Lehmann (*Michèle de Carnot*); Michael Wilding (*Clark*); James Mason (*de Carnot*); Herbert Lom (*Nazi*); Stewart Granger (*Jackson*).

Rating: ** 1/2

Three Englishmen and a Free French volunteer travel to occupied France where their mission is to learn key Nazi positions of men and guns to facilitate a bombing raid. If that sounds par for the course, get this: they pass themselves off as champagne salesmen, entering the enemy's offices and proffering bounteous free samples. Dummkopf Germans are suspicious these may be Gestapo agents sent to check on them. Decidedly different, if far from successful. Grim suspense doesn't jell with beyond-the-fringe British comedy. Lehmann is fine as a Gallic girl who has cynically accepted the despised presence of the conquerors. Mason's French accent is, simply, to die for.

SHERLOCK HOLMES AND THE SECRET WEAPON (1943)

CREDITS:
Universal; Roy William Neill, dir.; Arthur Conan Doyle (short story), Edward T. Lowe, Jr., W. Scott Darling, Edmund L. Hartmann, scr.; Howard Benedict, pro.; Frank Skinner, mus.; Lester White, cin.; Otto Ludwig, ed.; B&W; 1.37:1; 68 min.

CAST:
Basil Rathbone (*Sherlock Holmes*); Nigel Bruce (*Dr. John H. Watson*); Lionel Atwill (*Prof. Moriarty*); Kaaren Verne (*Charlotte*); William Post, Jr. (*Dr. Tobel*).

Rating: *** 1/2

Master of disguises Holmes rescues an all-important Zurich scientist from the Gestapo and spirits him off to Blitz-scarred London. When not creating an ingenious bombsight for the RAF, the defector slips away to visit a gorgeous mystery woman and is captured by supercriminal Moriarty, now a Nazi agent. Fourth in the Rathbone–Bruce series, second of this studio's updates from Victorian London to WWII. Modestly budgeted movie is smartly directed; an effectively

"THE GAME'S AFOOT": The World's Greatest Detective (Basil Rathbone) and Dr. Watson (Nigel Bruce) join a pretty mystery girl (Kaaren Verne) in attempting to thwart the Nazis in *Sherlock Holmes and the Secret Weapon*.

paced adaptation of Doyle's Victorian-era "Dancing Men." Torture sequence of the scientist by Moriarty appears grisly considering the era's Production Code. Then again, excess in service of the cause allowed censors to blink. Holmes's closing words about his beloved isle are from Shakespeare's glorious *Richard II*. Few actors have recited "This England..." so enchantingly.

SHINING THROUGH (1992)

CREDITS:
20th Century Fox; David Seltzer, dir.; Susan Isaacs (novel), David Seltzer, scr.; Carol Baum, Howard Rosenbaum, Nigel Wooll, pro.; Michael Kamen, mus.; Jan de Bont, cin.; Craig McKay, ed.; C; 2.35:1; 132 min.

CAST:
Michael Douglas (*Ed Leland*); Melanie Griffith (*Linda Voss*); Liam Neeson (*Dietrich*); Joely Richardson (*Margrete*); John Gielgud (*Sunflower*); Sylvia Syms (*Linda's Mother*).

Rating: *

Total misfire plays like a Mel Brooks spoof of the WWII spy genre, especially Douglas's embarrassing performance as an American agent. Griffith is surprisingly game as a half-Irish, half-Jewish patriot who accompanies the hero on a secret mission. Confusing where it means to be complex, the narrative is a disaster. Loopholes in the plot ruin this as a thriller while a lack of chemistry between the stars kills it as romance. Laughably overwrought, over-the-top last-minute-rescue resembles a *Saturday Night Live* spoof.

SHIP AHOY (1942)

CREDITS:
Metro-Goldwyn-Mayer; Edward Buzzell, dir.; Matt Brooks, Bradford Ropes, Bert Kalmar, Harry Clork, Harry Kurnitz, scr.; Jack Cummings, pro.; George Bassman, George E. Stoll, mus.; Robert H. Planck, Leonard Smith (aka Arthur Miller), cin.; Blanche Sewell, ed.; B&W; 95 min.

CAST:
Eleanor Powell (*Tallulah Winters*); Red Skelton (*Merton K. Kibble*); Bert Lahr (*Skip Owens*); Virginia O'Brien (*Fran Evans*); William Post Jr. (*Bennet*); Stuart Crawford (*Higgins*); John Emery (*Dr. Farno*).

Rating: *** ½

Unlikely combination of *Anything Goes!* type shipboard-musical with ocean-bound thrills on the order of *Across the Pacific*. A Nazi spy (Emery) passes himself off as an American agent and convinces a hoofer (Powell) to take a magnetic mine on board a luxury liner bound for Puerto Rico. She meets/dates a hack novelist (Skelton) whose most recent work provided the Nazis with their plan! *I'll Take Manilla* was the working title. When the Japanese invaded the Philippines it was decided the cruise ship would head for someplace closer to home. A song, "I'll Take Manilla," was altered to "I'll Take Tallulah." Great singing and dancing: vocalists Connie Haines, Jo Stafford, Frank Sinatra perform; dance specialists Stump 'n' Stumpy out-Nicholas the Nicholas Bros.; Buddy Rich provides a drum solo.

SOFT BEDS, HARD BATTLES, aka *UNDERCOVERS HERO* (1974)

CREDITS:
Roy Boulting, dir.; Boulting, Leo Marx, scr.; Boulting, John Boulting, prod.; Martin Charles, ed.; Gilbert Taylor, cin.; Neil Rhoden, mus.; Rank; 107 min.; C; 1.85;1.

CAST:
Peter Sellers (*Gen. Latour/Maj. Robinson/Herr Schroeder/M. Le President des Forces Speciales/Adolf Hitler/Prince Kyoto*); Lila Kedrova (*Madame Grenier*); Curd Jurgens (*von Grotjahn*); Beatrice Romand (*Marie-Claude*); Gabriella Licudi (*Simone*).

Rating: NO STARS

The Boulting Bros. legendary comedy classics include *I'm All Right Jack* (1959), a memorable satire on the cynicism in post war England with an early lead for Peter Sellers. How could they (and he) sink so low? Here is a comedy about a resistance hero (one of Sellers' six roles, none memorable including his caricature of Hitler) in which not one gag works. The tone is that of a smirky lowbrow sex farce, though a *Benny Hill* TV show would seem sophisticated in comparison. A true disaster.

SPY SHIP (1942)

CREDITS:
Warner Bros.; B. Reeves Eason, dir.; George Dyer (novel), Robert E. Kent, scr.; Jack Warner, exec. pro.; William Lava, Max Steiner, mus.; Harry Neumann, cin.; James Gibbon, ed.; B&W; 1.37:1; 62 min.

CAST:
Craig Stevens (*Ward Prescott*); Irene Manning (*Pam*); Maris Wrixon (*Sue Mitchell*); Tod Andrews, aka Michael Ames (*Morrel*); Peter Whitney (*Zinner*); Keye Luke (*Haru*).

Rating: **

On the eve of Pearl Harbor, a gorgeous aviator (Manning) assumes an isolationist stance, using the radio to turn her fan base against a "warmongering" reporter (Stevens). In time, he unmasks her as a traitor, paid by fifth columnists to undermine America's fighting spirit. Obvious attempt to unmask the patriotic-sounding "America Above All" groups, depicting them as dangerous saboteurs. Initially intriguing plot becomes preposterous during the second half. Redeemed by strong waterfront shootout finale. Based on an earlier story, "The Five Fragments," concerning heroin smuggling. Filmed earlier as *Fog over Frisco* (1934).

SPY TRAIN (1943)

CREDITS:
Monogram; Harold Young, dir.; Scott Littlefield, Bart Lytton, Wallace Sullivan, Leslie Swabacker (as Schwabacker), scr.; Max King, pro.; Edward J. Kay, mus.; Mack Stengler, cin.; Martin G. Cohn, ed.; B&W; 1.37:1; 61 min.

CAST:
Richard Travis (*Bruce Grant*); Catherine Craig (*Jane Thornwall*); Chick Chandler (*Stewart*); Thelma White (*Millie*); Paul McVey (*Hugo*); Evelyn Brent (*Frieda*); Fred "Snowflake" Toones (*Porter*); Walter Hymer (*Krantz*).

Rating: NO STARS

A klutzy Nazi operative (Hymer) assigned to drop a suitcase containing a bomb leaves the contact information for German spies instead. His infuriated superior sends a top agent (McVey) to retrieve it. A US journalist (Grant) and his goofy photographer (Stewart) are on the train. With time off to romance a society deb (Craig) traveling with her maid (White), our hero foils the plan. Weak as entertainment even by the ultralow standards of Poverty Row studios. African American porters are depicted as mincing idiots; the movie opens with condescending jibe at women of color.

13 RUE MADELEINE (1947)

CREDITS:
20th Century Fox; Henry Hathaway, dir.; John Monks, Jr., Sy Bartlett, scr.; Louis De Rochemont, pro.; David Buttolph, mus.; Norbert Brodine, cin.; Harmon Jones, ed.; B&W; 1.37:1; 95 min.

CAST:
James Cagney (*Robert Emmett Sharkey*); Annabella (*Suzanne de Beaumont*); Richard Conte (*William O'Connell*); Frank Latimore (*Lassiter*); Walter Abel (*Gibson*); Sam Jaffe (*Galimard*); Karl Malden, Red Buttons (*Jump Masters*); E. G. Marshall (*Driver*); Reed Hadley (*Narrator/voice only*).

Rating: ****

Title refers to Gestapo headquarters in Le Havre, France. A Nazi agent tortures and interrogates a spy, hoping to break him and learn where and when D-Day will take place. Both are based on real people, the Nazi having infiltrated one of our first espionage groups (codename: 077, the inspiration for Ian Fleming's choice of James Bond's "number"), soon to be known as the OSS. In actuality, as in the film, Sharkey did know this supposed "patriot" was working for the enemy but, on orders from his superior Gibson, allowed him to remain so they could feed O'Connell false information about a mythical second front in Holland. Predecessor

DARK ALLEYS: James Cagney and Annabella inhabit a threatening (and notably unglamorized) shadow-world of spying in *13 Rue Madeleine.*

of the postwar docudrama style, seamlessly blends news footage with vivid on-location work, introducing audiences to the reasons for the creation of our country's intelligence community.

TWO-HEADED SPY, THE (1958)

CREDITS:
Columbia; André De Toth, dir.; Michael Wilson, scr.; Bill Kirby, pro.; Gerard Schurmann, mus.; Edward Scaife, cin.; Raymond Poulton, ed.; B&W; 1.37:1; 93 min.

CAST:
Jack Hawkins (*Schottland*); Gia Scala (*Lili*); Erik Schumann (*Reinisch*); Alexander Knox (*Müller*); Felix Aylmer (*Cornaz*); Laurence Naismith (*Hauser*); Michael Caine (*Gestapo Man*); Donald Pleasence (*Gen. Hardt*).

Rating: ****

Misleading title for this fine if historically controversial film. Hitler comes to believe he can fully trust only one top general—a half-German, half-English strategist who turned his back on Britain and returned to the fatherland. Other than service, Schottland's only interest is clocks— until he meets a gorgeous singer. A "sleeper spy," he's been planted by top Allied brass, offering what seems like excellent advice while undermining Germany's war effort. The film claims to be based on the case of one A. P. Scotland (1882–1965), though many critics call this a gross exaggeration. As drama, this offers endless surprises, large and small, all satisfying. One of the earliest movies to inform the public that a vast intelligence community had been formed and still existed. Accurate or not, low-key and convincing.

A MOST EXTRAORDINARY SECRET AGENT:
Jack Hawkins plays one of WWII's more unique
operatives in *The Two-Headed Spy*.

HARD DAYS FOR A 'DOG SOLDIER': As 'Ernie Pyle' in *The Story of G.I. Joe*, Burgess Meredith observes the hardships of the regular soldiers; in *Hell Is for Heroes*, a common man hero (Fess Parker) leads his squad into brutal combat.

Beginning of the End:
Assault On Northern Europe

ATTACK (1956)

CREDITS:
Associates and Aldrich; Robert Aldrich, dir.; Norman Brooks (play), James Poe, scr.; Aldrich, Walter Blake, pro.; Frank De Vol, mus.; Joseph F. Biroc, cin.; Michael Luciano, ed.; B&W; 1.37:1; 107 min.

CAST:
Jack Palance (*Lt. Joe Costa*); Eddie Albert (*Capt. Erskine Cooney*); Lee Marvin (*Col. Bartlett*); Robert Strauss (*Bernstein*); Richard Jaeckel (*Snowden*); Buddy Ebsen (*Tolliver*); Peter van Eyck (*SS Captain*).

Rating: *****

A cowardly officer is given command of an infantry company by an ambitious colonel (Marvin), the latter hoping to use this connection for political advantage once home. That hardly consoles Lt. Costa, whose men die when their superior officer fails to back them up. Unsparingly grim, Aldrich here establishes a first-rate track record that would reach fruition with *The Dirty Dozen*. Based on a play (*Fragile Fox*), effectively opened up for the movie medium. A top-notch cast delivers exceptional character studies. Albert, in his finest screen performance, should have won the Best Supporting Actor Oscar for his chilling yet pathetic lost soul. The mano-a-machino duel between Palance and a German tank remains one of the great set pieces in WWII films. The only false note is the upbeat

(Above and facing page) **CHRISTMAS IN THE ARDENNES, 1944:** Jack Palance, Buddy Ebsen, and Robert Strauss in the greatest of all Battle of the Bulge movies, *Attack!;* Telly Savalas starred in the worst, which took the great combat as its title; Van Johnson leads troops into combat in the Oscar winning *Battleground;* a frightened teenager becomes lost in the snow *in A Midnight Clear.*

ending, which might have been better left ambiguous, as in the play. This true Battle of the Bulge story would be retold by Spielberg as a segment of his *Band of Brothers* TV miniseries.

ATTACK ON THE IRON COAST (1968)

CREDITS:

Mirisch Films; Paul Wendkos, dir.; Herman Hoffman, scr.; John C. Champion, pro.; Gerard Schurmann, mus.; Paul Beeson, cin.; Ernest Hosler, ed.; C; 1.66:1; 89 min.

CAST:

Lloyd Bridges (*Maj. Jamie Wilson*); Andrew Keir (*Capt. Owen Franklin*); Sue Lloyd (*Sue Wilson*); Mark Eden (*Lt. Commander Kimberly*); Maurice Denham (*Admiral Grafton*).

Rating: *** 1/2

A Canadian commando leader who led a failed mission on the German-occupied French coast plans to try again with a new ploy: a worthless minesweeper will be loaded with explosives and rammed into the docks. Such a radical strategy is questioned by a stern Brit captain whose son was lost during the first ill-fated raid. Loosely based on an actual incident, this handsomely crafted film offers a strong portrayal of how military brass, after developing a plan and agreeing on it, suffer deep doubts. Failure too easily becomes a foregone conclusion when those in charge don't fully believe in the plan. If the supporting roles had been fleshed out, this might've been something special.

BATTLE OF THE BULGE (1965)

CREDITS:

Cinerama; Ken Annakin, dir.; Philip Yordan, Bernard Gordon, John Melson, Milton Sperling, Philip Yordan, scr.; Yordan, Sidney Harmon, Milton Sperling, Philip Yordan, Dino De Laurentiis, pro.; Benjamin Frankel, mus.; Jack Hildyard, cin.; Derek Parsons, Lester A. Sansom, ed.; C; 2.20:1; 167 min.

CAST:

Henry Fonda (*Col. Dan Kiley*); Robert Shaw (*Col. Hessler*); Robert Ryan (*Gen. Grey*); Dana Andrews (*Pritchard*); George Montgomery (*Duquesne*); Charles

Bronson (*Wolenski*); Hans Christian Blech (*Conrad*); James MacArthur (*Lt. Weaver*); Telly Savalas (*Sgt. Guffy*); William Conrad (*Narrator*).

Rating: *

A WWII movie so dreadfully, inconceivably bad that Eisenhower publicly denounced it for its embarrassing inaccuracies. Shooting in the cumbersome Cinerama process doomed this from the start. Breathtaking shots, rather than character and incident, became central. The script oversimplifies events from December 1944. The leads, all fictional, are too broadly drawn. While some snow is occasionally present, this was mostly shot in sunny Spain during the summer, leaving a naïve audience with the misconception that the battle took place in a desert rather than the white hell of a Belgian winter. The heart and soul of the Bulge, Bastogne, is glimpsed for a mere three minutes. Best sequence details the massacre at Malmedy. Otherwise: overblown, inept.

BATTLEGROUND (1949)

CREDITS:
Metro-Goldwyn-Mayer; William A. Wellman, dir.; Robert Pirosh, scr.; Dore Schary, pro.; Lennie Hayton, mus.; Paul Vogel, cin.; John D. Dunning, ed.; B&W; 1.37:1; 118 min.

CAST:
Van Johnson (*Holley*); John Hodiak (*Jarvess*); Ricardo Montalban (*Roderigues*); George Murphy (*Pop*); Marshall Thompson (*Layton*); Jerome Courtland (*Abner*); Don Taylor (*Standiferd*); James Whitmore (*Kinnie*); Douglas Fowley (*Kipp*); Denise Darcel (*Denise*); Richard Jaeckel (*Bettis*).

Rating: ****

Christmas, 1944: men of the 101st Airborne assume they'll soon head home, the war all but over. A massive offensive spearheaded by tanks leaves them isolated in the Ardennes. Sturdy depiction of the Battle of the

Bulge, peppered with excellent sequences: a soldier carrying fresh cracked eggs in his helmet, hoping to soon cook them, another buried in snow by buddies praying the Nazis won't find him. Admirable accuracy reveals frostbite was as dangerous as enemy gunfire. As in reality, the soldiers fighting to hold the town had no idea about the big picture all around them. Sadly diminished by MGM's insistence that much of the filming be done on the backlot. Several lighthearted scenes are awkwardly staged. Rah-rah dialogue left over from the war years is included, in contrast to the similar stories told in *A Walk in the Sun* and *The Story of GI Joe*.

BOMBER'S MOON (1943)

CREDITS:

20th Century Fox; Edward Ludwig, Harold D. Schuster, aka "Charles Fuhr," dir.; Kenneth Gamet, Leonard Lee, Aubrey Wisberg, scr.; Sol M. Wurtzel, pro.; David Buttolph, mus.; Lucien Ballard, cin.; Robert Fritch, ed.; B&W; 1.37:1; 67 min.

CAST:

George Montgomery (*Capt. Jeffrey Dakin*); Annabella (*Dr. Alexandra Zorich*); Kent Taylor (*Capt. von Block*); Martin Kosleck (*Von Streicher*); Walter Kingsford (*Mueller*).

Rating: ** 1/2

An English offensive against Germany is preceded by a bombing raid during which a captain is shot down. He's captured and tortured but escapes, taking information that could turn the tide in the Allies' favor. A gorgeous Russian doctor and a Czech Partisan help him overcome the nastiest of Nazis (Kosleck, satirizing the cartoonish Gestapo types he'd played earlier). A mishmash of WWII subgenres. None of the elements are executed memorably, and with the short running time, there is little narrative development. Akin to a condensed *Reader's Digest* version of a novel. A letdown for the usually dependable Fox!

BRIDGE AT REMAGEN (1969)

CREDITS:
Wolper Pictures; John Guillermin, dir.; Roger O. Hirson, Richard Yates, William Roberts, scr.; David L. Wolper, pro.; Elmer Bernstein, mus.; Stanley Cortez, cin.; William T. Cartwright, Harry V. Knapp, Marshall Neilan, Jr., ed.; C; 2.35:1; 115 min.

CAST:
George Segal (*Lt. Phil Hartman*); Robert Vaughn (*Maj. Paul Krüger*); Ben Gazzara (*Sgt. Angelo*); Bradford Dillman (*Maj. Barnes*); E. G. Marshall (*Gen. Shinner*); Peter van Eyck (*von Brock*).

Rating: *** 1/2

As Nazis leave Paris and retreat over the Rhine, only one bridge remains standing. German officers argue about whether it should be kept open to allow retreating troops an escape route or blown up to slow down the Allies. US commanders debate the same issue. On each side, dogface soldiers fight and die attempting first one and then the other tactic. Battle sequences are spectacularly visualized and accurately re-created. One wishes for a better script, however. At one point, the most beautiful Gallic blonde (Anne Gael) since Brigitte Bardot waltzes in, performs a topless scene, and then leaves without a word. A bitter sergeant threatens to gun down his lieutenant owing to a sarcastic comment and then beats up an aloof major without repercussions. Such contrived incidents diminish what could have been, with more believable drama, a worthy war movie.

BRIDGE TOO FAR, A (1977)

CREDITS:
Joseph E. Levine Productions; Richard Attenborough, dir.; Cornelius Ryan (book), William Goldman, scr.; Joseph E. Levine, Richard P. Levine, pro.; John Addison, mus.; Geoffrey Unsworth, cin.; Antony Gibbs, ed.; C; 2.35:1; 175 min.

THE RAID THAT DIDN'T WORK: The Allies lose a big one in Sir Richard Attenborough's enormous retro-epic *A Bridge Too Far.*

CAST:

Dirk Bogarde (*Gen. Browning*); James Caan (*Eddie Dohun*); Michael Caine (*Col. Vandeleur*); Sean Connery (*Gen. Urquhart*); Edward Fox (*Gen. Horrocks*); Elliott Gould (*Col. Stout*); Gene Hackman (*Gen. Sosabowski*); Anthony Hopkins (*Col. Frost*); Hardy Krüger (*Gen. Ludwig*); Ryan O'Neal (*Gen. Gavin*); Laurence Olivier (*Dr. Spaander*); Robert Redford (*Maj. Cook*); Maximilian Schell (*Gen. Bittrich*); Liv Ullmann (*Kate Ter Horst*).

Rating: ***

September 1944: Field Marshal Montgomery concocts a daring if overambitious strategy called Operation Market Garden. As Nazis retreat from Holland, Allies will secure the Rhine bridges via daylight parachute drops behind enemy lines. Expecting mild resistance from old men and untrained Hitler youth, they run into crack troops and a Panzer division. Like the mission, the film is gargantuan, lumbering, and ultimately ineffectual. The all-star epic's tone wavers between rah-rah patriotism and a post-Vietnam antiwar message. Many individual sequences are fine, but overall the film rates as less than the sum of its parts. During the final third, most viewers will find it impossible to keep straight which bridge any given outfit is fighting on and if they're winning or losing. Owing to fabulous battle action, this will be of more interest to WWII film buffs than mainstream audiences.

CASTLE KEEP (1969)

CREDITS:
Filmways/Columbia; Sydney Pollack, dir.; William Eastlake (novel), David Rayfiel, Daniel Taradash, scr.; Martin Ransohoff, John Calley, pro.; Michel Legrand, mus.; Henri Decaë, cin.; Malcolm Cooke, ed.; C; 2.20:1; 105 min.

CAST:
Burt Lancaster (*Maj. Abraham Falconer*); Patrick O'Neal (*Capt. Lionel Beckman*); Jean-Pierre Aumont (*Count of Maldorais*); Peter Falk (*Rossi*); Astrid Heeren (*Therese*); Scott Wilson (*Clearboy*); Tony Bill (*Amberjack*); Al Freeman, Jr. (*Benjamin*); Bruce Dern (*Bix*); Michael Conrad (*DeVaca*).

Rating: *

Just before the Battle of the Bulge, an eye-patched officer leads eight war-weary American soldiers into a remote art-filled castle called the Maldorais. What begins as a realistic study of their attempt to survive transforms, without rhyme or reason, into a surreal nightmare. This misguided project makes mincemeat of Eastlake's powerfully phantasmagoric 1965 novel. The issue of art versus life is better treated in *The Train*, with the same star. Falk somehow manages to come out smelling like roses as a philosophic sarge. Otherwise, a complete mess. Lancaster should have left the eye patch to John Wayne as Rooster Cogburn.

COMPANY OF HEROES (2013)

CREDITS:
Sony Pictures; Don Michael Paul, dir.; David Reed, Danny Bilson, Paul De Meo, scr.; Jeffery Beach, Philip J. Roth, pro.; Frederik Wiedmann, mus.; Martin Chichov, cin.; Cameron Hallenbeck, ed.; C; 1.78:1; 100 min.

CAST:
Tom Sizemore (*Dean Ranson*); Chad Michael Collins (*Nate*); Vinnie Jones (*Willoughby*); Neal McDonald (*Conti*); Jürgen Prochnow (*Gruenewald*).

Rating: *

A rifle squad patrolling Elsenborn in the Belgian Ardennes spots an immense tank force heading their way. As if that weren't enough, while returning to their post to report that the Battle of the Bulge has begun, they learn that the Nazis have an atomic bomb. Based on a videogame, this film is swiftly sunk by bottom-of-the-barrel CGI effects for action sequences, a musical score that bathes everything in melodramatic mush, a cast that doesn't seem to care, and German tanks that look nothing like the ones used near Bastogne.

DAY WILL DAWN, THE, aka AVENGERS, THE (1942)

CREDITS:
Paul Soskin Prods./Paramount; Harold French, dir.; Frank Owen, Terence Rattigan, Anatole de Grunwald, Patrick Kirwan, scr.; Paul Soskin, pro.; Richard Addinsell, mus.; Bernard Knowles, cin.; Michael C. Chorlton, ed.; B&W; 98 min. (UK); 87 min. (US).

CAST:
Hugh Williams (*Colin Metcalfe*); Griffith Jones (*Inspector Gunter*); Deborah Kerr (*Alstad*); Ralph Richardson (*Frank*); Francis L. Sullivan (*Kommandant Wettau*); Roland Culver (*Cmdr. Pittwaters*); Finlay Currie (*Alstad*).

Ratings: **** (UK)
*** 1/2 (US)

With U-boats threatening US and UK ships, military brass decide to strike at the heart of the problem. "Information received" reveals a major sub construction base in Norway. Before they can launch an all-out assault, specifics must be gathered by a secret agent. The only person who knows the geography well enough to do the job has a bad track record, but he pleads for a chance to redeem himself. Propagandistic piece plays well as wartime drama in the British theatrical cut, less so in the abbreviated American version. The great revelation is a young Kerr, lighting up the screen as a Norwegian girl who appears to have gone over to the enemy's side.

EIGHT IRON MEN (1952)

CREDITS:
Columbia; Edward Dmytryk, dir.; Harry Brown (play), scr.; Stanley Kramer, Edward Anhalt, pro.; Leith Stevens, mus.; J. Roy Hunt, cin.; Aaron Stell, ed.; B&W; 1.37:1; 80 min.

CAST:
Bonar Colleano (*Pvt. Collucci*); Lee Marvin (*Sgt. Joe Mooney*); Arthur Franz (*Carter*); Richard Kiley (*Coke*); Nick Dennis (*Sapiros*); James Griffith (*Ferguson*); Dickie Moore (*Muller*).

Rating: ** 1/2

A tough sergeant and six squad members hover in the ruins of a burned-out building while the eighth man lies outside in a huge mud puddle, Nazi snipers trying to kill him. The division is pulling out at dusk, and a debate rages about whether to try to save the trapped man. Based on a play, it's mostly talk, talk, talk, which alternates between good (sensible discussions about strategy) and horrible (comic-relief banter). At least the small-scale battle sequences are realistically staged. The project is diminished by cutaways (with suitably sleazy music) to the gorgeous cheese-cake girls the guys dream about. Marvin once again rises above his early so-so material.

EVERYMAN'S WAR (2010)

CREDITS:
One-Eighth Films/Koan Ent./Virgil Films; Thad (T.) Smith, dir.; Craig

Smith, scr.; Jay Lance, pro.; Chad Rehmann, mus.; Joel Stirnkorb, cin.; Alex Brown, ed.; C; 1.85:1; 104 min.

CAST:
Cole Carson (*Sgt. Don Smith*); Lauren Bair (*Dorrine*); Michael J. Prosser (*Sparks*); Sean McGrath (*Benedetto*); Brian Julian (*Heinrich*); Lee Selmyhr (*Elderly Smith*).

Rating: *** 1/2

January 1945, Nennig, Germany: while serving in the 94th Infantry Division during the Bulge, an ordinary yet singular sergeant from a small Oregon town relies on memories of home to make it through the fierce fighting and horrid weather. An admirable labor of love created by the actual soldier's sons as a tribute to him and all veterans of the Big One. Amateurish acting takes its toll, but the recognition of how much emotion can be elicited from a shoestring-budget film compensates for it. Bolstered by a sense of mission as firm as that of the troops. Winner of the Best Narrative Feature award at the GI Film Festival.

HELL IS FOR HEROES (1962)

CREDITS:
Paramount; Don Siegel, dir.; Richard Carr, Robert Pirosh, scr.; Henry Blanke, pro.; Leonard Rosenman, mus.; Harold Lipstein, cin.; Howard A. Smith, ed.; B&W; 1.85:1; 90 min.

CAST:
Steve McQueen (*Reese*); Bobby Darin (*Corby*); Fess Parker (*Pike*); Harry Guardino (*Larkin*); James Coburn (*Henshaw*); Mike Kellin (*Kolinsky*); L. Q. Jones (*Frazer*); Nick Adams (*Homer*); Bob Newhart (*Driscoll*).

Rating: ****

In 1944, several woefully outnumbered GIs are assigned to hold a strip of the Siegfried Line. Their assignment: convince Nazis that there are numerous Americans in place, delaying a full German attack until more Allied troops can arrive. Main focus is on three characters: a moody, mean-spirited rebel (McQueen), an easy-living con man (Darin), and a strong if sensitive sergeant (Parker). Admirable if not entirely successful attempt to create another *A Walk in the Sun*, though this has more in common with *The Bold and the Brave*: not a true classic but a memorable attempt to create something special. Based on an actual incident; spirited direction by cult favorite Siegel. Memorable scenes include communications man Newhart confusing the enemy over the radio, giving the comic a chance to perform one of his routines. At midpoint, the film loses its sense of direction, then picks up considerably with a strong final battle sequence. The last shot is striking.

IMITATION GENERAL (1958)

CREDITS:
Metro-Goldwyn-Mayer; George Marshall, dir.; William Bowers, William Chamberlain, scr.; William B. Hawks, pro.; George J. Folsey, cin.; Harold F. Kress, ed.; B&W; 2.35:1; 88 min.

A COMEDY SANS LAUGHS: Red Buttons, Glenn Ford in the would-be wartime spoof (The) *Imitation General.*

CAST:

Glenn Ford (*Murphy Savage*); Red Buttons (*Cpl. Chan Derby*); Taina Elg (*Simone*); Dean Jones (*Sellers*); Kent Smith (*Gen. Lane*); Tige Andrews (*Hutchmeyer*); John Wilder (*Clayton*).

Rating: **

August 1944, France: a dedicated general (Smith) believes his troops will be inspired by seeing a commanding officer up front. When that person is killed, a top sergeant (Ford) impersonates the officer, aided by a wiseacre corporal (Buttons) and a French girl (Elg). Uncertain, unappealing brew of contrived comedy and conventional combat violence, bolstered by Ford's genial performance. Moves at a snail's pace and feels twice its actual length. The final duel between four tanks is well staged.

INTO THE WHITE (2012)

CREDITS:

Zentropa/Film Europe; Petter Næss, dir.; Næss, Ole Melgaard, Dave Mango, scr.; Peter Aalbæk Jensen, Valerie Saunders, pro.; Nils Petter Molvaer, mus.; Daniel Voldheim, cin.; Frida Eggum Michaelsen, ed.; C; 2.35:1; 104 min.

CAST:

Florian Lukas (*Horst Schopis*); David Kross (*Josef Schwartz*); Stig Henrik Hoff (*Wolfgang Strunk*); Rupert Grint (*Robert Smith*); Kim Haugen (*Gustavsen*).

Rating: ***

During a sky battle over Norway, an English plane and a German one shoot each other down. Five survivors meet at an isolated cabin in the frozen terrain and pool their resources to survive. Most effective element is the vivid portrait of the white hell of a Norwegian winter, underscored by Molvaer's minimalist (almost nonexistent) score; the weakest: what transpires in the cabin. For a sparse chamber drama like this to work, the writer must supply fascinating dialogue that gradually reveals the unique characters, but here they remain stereotypes. There also needs to be a ticking-clock sense of suspense as time (and food and fuel) runs out; this, too, is missing. Too many unanswered questions: Why try to hike to safety through a storm rather than wait for the weather to clear? Solid, fact-based premise leads to mediocre results.

KINGS GO FORTH (1958)

CREDITS:
Frank Ross-Eton Productions; Delmer Daves, dir.; Joe David Brown (novel), Merle Miller, scr.; Frank Ross, Dick Ross, pro.; Elmer Bernstein, mus.; Daniel L. Fapp, cin.; William B. Murphy, ed.; B&W; 1.85:1; 109 min.

CAST:
Frank Sinatra (*Lt. Sam Loggins*); Tony Curtis (*Cpl. Britt Harris*); Natalie Wood (*Monique Blair*); Leora Dana (*Mrs. Blair*); Karl Swenson (*Col. Loggins*).

Rating: ***

Following the Allied invasion, a homely, decent New Yorker (Sinatra) finds himself in competition with a playboy (Curtis) for the affections of a young woman (Wood). The situation becomes complicated when they learn she is half black. Fascinating, ahead-of-its-time theme dared merge the then-controversial issue of interracial marriage with the WWII genre. Sadly, the results are undercut by the fatal miscasting of the male leads— the charismatic Sinatra as a loser, the ethnic Curtis as a blue-blooded WASP. Well-staged climactic battle determines which guy will ultimately win out; the final moment seems too schmaltzy.

LAST BLITZKRIEG, THE, aka THE BIG BLITZ (1959)

CREDITS:
Clover/Columbia; Arthur Dreifuss, dir.; Lou Morheim, scr.; Sam Katzman,

pro.; Hope de Groot, mus.; Edward Scaife, cin.; Lien d' Oliveyra, ed.; B&W; 1.85:1; 84 min.

CAST:
Van Johnson (*Sgt. Hans Von Kroner/Sgt. Leonard Richardson*); Kerwin Mathews (*Wilitz*); Dick York (*Sgt. Ludwig*); Larry Storch (*Ennis*); Lisa Bourdin (*Monique*).

Rating: **

To confuse Allies in Bastogne, German paratroopers, wearing US uniforms and well versed in idiomatic US English, land behind the lines. Their leader is played by Van Johnson, who is unbelievable as the kind of cold killer Robert Mitchum might have better projected. This lightweight actor can't convey the mixed emotions of a loner beginning to doubt Hitler. Minor-league item from the Katzman B unit at Columbia, one more of their program pictures lacking serious ambition. That might be acceptable if there were more action, but this is overly talky, none of it very interesting.

LAST DROP, THE (2006)

CREDITS:

Carnaby/Media Pro; Colin Teague, dir.; Teague, Gary Young, scr.; Hamish Skeggs, pro.; David Julyan, mus.; Maxime Alexandre, cin.; Michael Ellis, ed.; C/B&W; 2.35:1; 103 min.

CAST:
Billy Zane (*Lt. Robert Oates*); Laurence Fox (*SS Maj. Klaus Kessler*); Coral Reed (Saskia); Michael Madsen (*Col. Colt*); Lucy Gaskell (*Benitta*); Jack Dee (*Warren*).

Rating: **

Operation Market Garden (September 17–25, 1944) served as the basis for *A Bridge Too Far*. This British–Romanian film uses that attack as the backdrop for a *Kelly's Heroes*–type tale. Americans gone rogue, high-ranking Nazis, two self-serving women from the Dutch Resistance, and a Pattonesque commander (Madsen) dart about, hoping to be the first to locate European art stolen by the Germans. Sounds far better than it plays. The range of acting styles—from over-the-top cartoonish to ultrarealistic—fails to jell. Dialogue is, to be kind, uninspired. We've seen it all before; more importantly, we've seen it done far better. Contemporary rock music further muddies the waters.

LONGEST DAY, THE (1962)

CREDITS:
20th Century Fox; Darryl F. Zanuck, Ken Annakin, Andrew Marton, Bernhard Wicki, Gerd Oswald, dir.; Cornelius Ryan (book), Zanuck (uncredited), Romain Gary, James Jones, David Pursall, Jack Seddon, scr.; Zanuck, pro.; Maurice Jarre, mus.; Jean Bourgoin, Walter Wottitz, cin.; Samuel E. Beetley, ed.; B&W; 2.20:1 (70 mm); 2.35:1; 178 min.

CREDITS:
Robert Mitchum (*Brig. Gen. Norman Cota*); John Wayne (*Lt. Col. Benjamin Vandervoort*); Henry Fonda (*Gen. Theodore Roosevelt, Jr.*); Richard Beymer (*Pvt. Dutch Schultz*); Richard Burton (*David Campbell*); Wolfgang Büttner (*Dr. Hans Speidel*); Arletty (*Madame Barrault*); Red Buttons (*Pvt. John Steele*); Gert Fröbe (*Sgt. Kaffekanne*); Curd Jürgens (*Gen. Gunther Blumentritt*); Christian Marquand (*Kieffer*); Jeff(rey) Hunter (*Lt. Fuller*); Hans Christian Blech (*Maj. Werner Pluskat*); Bourvil (*Colleville Mayor*); Werner Hinz (*Erwin Rommel*); Richard Todd (*John Howell*); Eddie Albert (*Col. Thompson*); Roddy McDowell (*Pvt. Morris*); Sean Connery (*Pvt. Flannigan*); Henry Grace (*Gen. Dwight Eisenhower*); many others.

Rating: *****

The story of D-Day, told from numerous perspectives as an epic docudrama: the Allies and the Axis, officers and dog soldiers, sea-to-land assaults and parachute jumps, women and men, military and civilians. This was Zanuck's final superproduction and it's a masterpiece. For once,

(Above and facing page) **THE ULTIMATE EPIC**: In *The Longest Day*, Henry Fonda portrays Gen. Theodore Roosevelt Jr.; soldiers wade ashore only to face heavy enemy resistance: tanks, 'the cavalry of WWII,' play their part in this decisive battle.

an all-star cast clicks, absolutely necessary to keep all the characters straight in the viewer's mind. The casting of then-current rock 'n' rollers (Tommy Sands, Fabian, Paul Anka) appealed to the teen audience. Meticulous accuracy in the details of strategy comes from Ryan's book. Authentic uniforms and firearms were re-created based on years of research. Many indelible images; the shot of Red Buttons hanging from a church steeple by his tangled parachute is unforgettable. Jarre's score is patriotic without being hokey. The fighting at Pointe du Hoc contains one of the longest (and artistically impressive) moving-camera images in film history. The Rupert paradummies threaten to steal the show. Marvelous final bit involving Burton, Beymer, and a deceased Nazi was an inspired way to end this immense project on an intimate human note. From Ryan's 1959 book.

MALEDETTO TRENO BLINDATO, QUEL, aka INGLORIOUS BASTARDS, THE (1978)

CREDITS:
Film Concorde; Enzo G. Castellari, dir.; Sandro Continenza, Sergio Grieco, Romano Migliorini, Laura Toscano, Alberto Piferi, Franco Marotta, Fred Williamson, scr.; Roberto Sbarigia, pro.; Francesco De Masi, mus.; Giovanni Bergamini, cin.; Gianfranco Amicucci, ed.; C; 1.85:1; 104 min.

CAST:
Bo Svenson (*Lt. Robert Yeager*); Peter Hooten (*Tony*); Fred Williamson (*Fred Canfield*); Michael Pergolani (*Nick*); Jackie Basehart (*Berle*); Michael Constantin (*Veronique*); Debra Berger (*Nicole*).

Rating: ★★★★

France, 1944: a lieutenant (Svenson) who refused to slaughter civilians is on his way to a camp for execution, along with a deserter (Basehart), a thief (Pergolani), an assassin (Williamson), and a mutineer (Hooten). During a sudden air raid, the frightful five escape, Allies and Axis alike in pursuit. Among the numerous WWII films churned out in Italy (most failing to find an international audience), this is the best, explaining why it received global distribution. Well directed, boasting production values above those of most macaroni combat movies. Big plus is a smart script that provides endless turns, twists, and reversals. One limitation: a lackluster cast. Only Williamson is perfect for his role, and he plays it perfectly. With top character actors, this might've been a classic. A Tarantino favorite.

MIDNIGHT CLEAR, A (1992)

CREDITS:
A&M Films/Beacon; Keith Gordon, dir.; William Wharton (novel), Gordon, scr.; Bill Borden, Dale Pollock, pro.; Mark Isham, mus.; Tom Richmond, cin.; Don Brochu, ed.; C; 1.85:1; 108 min.

CAST:

Peter Berg (*Bud Miller*); Kevin Dillon (*Cpl. Mel Avakian*); Arye Gross (*Stan Shutzer*); Ethan Hawke (*Sgt. Knott*); Gary Sinise (*Wilkins*); Frank Whaley (*Mundy*).

Rating: ****

Mid-to-late December 1944: as snow blankets the Ardennes, Nazis secretly advance on foot and by tank to attack Bastogne. Six GIs—survivors of a decimated recon squad—hide out in an abandoned chateau. As Christmas Eve nears, both sides see the wisdom of calling a brief truce, meeting halfway between their positions to communicate as humans. An inspirational film based on an actual event. Touching little miniepic brushes up against broad sentiment without getting sidetracked. Actor-turned-director Gordon draws fine performances from his cast. A little rough around the edges with hints of fantasy that don't quite pay off. Ironic ending.

ON THE DOUBLE (1961)

CREDITS:

Dena Prods./Paramount; Melville Shavelson, dir.; Shavelson, Jack Rose, scr.; Rose, pro.; Leith Stevens, mus.; Harry Stradling (Sr.), cin.; Frank Bracht, ed.; C; 2.35:1; 92 min.

CAST:

Danny Kaye (*Pfc. Ernie Williams*); Dana Wynter (*Margaret MacKenzie-Smith*); Wilfrid Hyde-White (*Somerset*); Margaret Rutherford (*Lady Vivian*); Diana Dors (*Sgt. Stanhope*).

Rating: ****

If any GI appears hopeless, it's fearful Ernie Williams, who can't do KP much less fight. Then, officers note that Ernie resembles a British colonel. If the soldier agrees to take the ranking officer's place, the actual colonel can secretly head off to help plan the D-Day invasion. What our beloved sap did not count on: sharing "quality time" with the Brit's breathtaking wife and also becoming embroiled with a peroxide blonde. Loosely based on actual incidents that involved doubles employed to confuse the Germans about the whereabouts of Churchill and Montgomery. Memorable moments include a roaring out of the cinematic closet sequence with Kaye wildly vamping Marlene Dietrich.

ON THE FIDDLE, aka OPERATION SNAFU (1961)

CREDITS:
Coronado/American International; Cyril Frank, dir.; R. F. Delderfield (novel), Harold Buchman, scr.; Benjamin Fisz, pro.; Malcolm Arnold, mus.; Edward Scaife, cin.; Peter (R.) Hunt, ed.; B&W; 1.66:1; 89 min.

CAST:
Alfred Lynch (*Horace Pope*); Sean Connery (*Pedlar Pascoe*); Victor Maddern (*Airman*); Harry Locke (*Huxtable*); John Le Mesurier (*Hixon*); Eric Barker (*Doctor*); Edna Morris (*Lil*).

Rating: *** 1/2

A lovable lug can't wait to sign up and do his duty for crown and country. He teams up with a little fellow who is his precise opposite: desperate to keep out of combat. As members of the RAF, they constantly request transfers from one post to another, which interferes with being shipped out. Nice teaming of two then-in-embryo Brit stars. Wry and dry, nothing spectacular, but agreeable in all regards as a minor English comedy. Easy to take.

OVERLORD (1975)

CREDITS:
Joswend; Stuart Cooper, dir.; Cooper, Christopher Hudson, scr.; James Quinn, pro.; Paul Glass, mus.; John Alcott, cin.; Jonathan Gili, ed.; B&W;

1.75:1; 83 min.

CAST:
Brian Stirner (*Tom*); Davyd Harries (*Jack*); Nicholas Ball (*Arthur*); Julie Neesam (*The Girl*); Sam Sewell (*A Soldier*); John Franklyn-Robbins (*Dad*); Stella Tanner (*Mom*).

Rating: ****

Operation Overlord was England's moniker for what the US refers to as D-Day. Even as the eventful June 6, 1944, event begins, a youthful soldier experiences a premonition of death. From that moment on, as he moves in formation with the others, he becomes obsessed with the meanings of war, death, life, and patriotism, trying to decide where he stands on such issues. Without studio backing, filmmaker Cooper planned a documentary composed of stock footage. Along the way, he decided to cowrite and direct new scenes about an ordinary everyman, interspersing these with old material. Indie English filmmaker brought inspiration and considerable talent to the mix, resulting in an edgy arthouse item. Winner of the Silver Bear—Special Jury Prize at the Berlin Film Festival.

PARIS BRULE T-IL?, aka IS PARIS BURNING? (1966)

CREDITS:
Marianne Prods./Paramount; René Clément, dir.; Larry Collins (book), Dominique Lapierre (book), Gore Vidal, Francis Ford Coppola, Marcel Moussy, Beate von Molo, scr.; Paul Graetz, pro.; Maurice Jarre, cin.; Marcel Grignon, cin.; Robert Lawrence, ed.; B&W; 2.20:1; 175 min. (director's cut), 173 min. (US theatrical).

CAST:
Kirk Douglas (*Gen. George Patton*) Jean-Paul Belmondo (*Yvon Morandat*); Charles Boyer (*Dr. Monod*); Leslie Caron (*Labé*); Glenn Ford (*Gen. Omar Bradley*); Alain Delon (*Jacques Chaban-Delmas*); Gert Fröbe (*Gen. von*

Choltitz); Anthony Perkins (*Sgt. Warren*); Simone Signoret (*Café Owner*); Jean-Louis Trintignant (*Serge*); Orson Welles (*Raoul Nordling*); Billy Frick (Hitler).

Rating: **

Between August 19 and August 25, 1944, Allied forces close in on Paris for the grand liberation. Hitler, in his final stages of madness, has ordered the general in command to, before abandoning the City of Lights, reduce Paris to ashes. Does von Choltitz possess a hint of human compassion that may cause him to disobey? Among ultralengthy all-star WWII docudramas, this unsatisfying, unfocused piece is one of the worst. The storyline is impossible to follow, even for those who read the 1966 book. Clément, a talented director of small films, proved a poor choice. Attempts to depict arguments between Gaullists and Communists in the resistance weigh the film down in dull talk. An immense failure.

RED BALL EXPRESS (1952)

CREDITS:
Universal International; Budd Boetticher, dir.; William Grady, Jr., Marcy Klauber, John Michael Hayes, scr.; Aaron Rosenberg, pro.; Milton Rosen, Frank Skinner, mus.; Maury Gertsman, cin.; Edward Curtiss, ed.; 83 min.; B&W; 1.37:1; 83 min.

CAST:
Jeff Chandler (*Lt. Chick Campbell*); Alex Nicol (*Kallek*); Judith Braun (*Joyce McClellan*); Sidney Poitier (*Cpl. Robertson*); Bubber Johnson (*Taffy Smith*); Hugh O'Brian (*Wilson*).

Rating: ***

During late summer 1944, Patton's furious push to reach Paris in record time leaves his Third Army cut off from supplies. A group of misfits is assembled to create a high-speed trucking convoy that travels north over terrible roads at dangerous speeds, dodging minefields and enemy

THEY ALSO SERVE . . . : 'Negro' (as African Americans were politely referred to at the time) soldiers, not assigned to fight on the front lines, do their work for the war cause by transporting needed supplies in *The Red Ball Express.*

snipers. Racial turmoil threatens to destroy everything; this is one of the army's first integrated outfits. A great chapter in military history, reduced to a routine if adequate program picture, bogged down by expected WWII clichés (e.g., pretty WAC nurses and a gorgeous French girl). More interesting is the commander's need to redeem himself from a long-ago *Lord Jim*–like act of cowardice. Poitier reveals his talent in an early role. Still, the material could and should have made for a far more ambitious epic than this B movie.

SAINTS AND SOLDIERS (2003)

CREDITS:
Go Films; Ryan Little, dir.; Geoffrey Panos, Matt Whitaker, scr.; Little, Adam Abel, pro.; J. Bateman, Bart Hendrickson, mus.; Little, cin.; Wynn Hougaard, ed.; C; 90 min.

CAST:
Corbin Allred (*Cpl. Nathan "Deacon" Greer*); Alexander Polinsky (*Medic Steven Gould*); Kirby Heyborne (*Sgt. Oberon Winley*); Larry Bagby (*Kendrick*); Peter Holden (*Gunderson*).

Rating: ★★★★

December 1944: four survivors of the Malmedy massacre team up with a stranded Brit flyer in an attempt to bring secret Nazi plans back to headquarters. Focus is on a sharpshooter (Allred) from the heartlands who lost his ability to pull the trigger. An impressive example of what talented indie filmmakers can achieve with a less-than-a-million budget. Each character is a unique individual rather than a generalized type, including the young mother with whom the makeshift squad becomes stranded. A deeply humanistic film and, by implication, a powerful religious statement as well.

SAVING PRIVATE RYAN (1998)

CREDITS:
DreamWorks SKG/Amblin/Paramount; Steven Spielberg, dir.; Robert Rodat, scr.; Spielberg, Gary Levinsohn, Mark Gordon, Ian Bryce, pro.; John Williams, mus.; Janusz Kaminski, cin.; Michael Kahn, ed.; C; 1.85:1; 169 min.

CAST:
Tom Hanks (*Capt. Miller*); Matt Damon (*Pvt. Ryan*); Vin Diesel (*Pvt. Caparzo*); Tom Sizemore (*Sgt. Horvath*); Edward Burns (*Reiben*); Barry Pepper (*Jackson*); Adam Goldberg (*Mellish*); Giovanni Ribisi (*Wade*); Paul Giamatti (*Hill*); Harve Presnell (*Gen. Marshall*); Amanda Boxer (*Mrs. Ryan*).

Rating: ★★★★★

Spielberg's mighty epic begins with the Normandy invasion, far more intense, brutal, and honest regarding the horrific Allied losses than *The Longest Day*. Once Omaha Beach has been taken, an everyman captain

AN AMERICAN EVERYMAN: Like Henry Fonda, Gary Cooper, and James Stewart during the golden age of the Hollywood studios, Tom Hanks has become the modern screen embodiment of everything that is best in our national character; *Saving Private Ryan.*

is assigned to locate a missing private whose three brothers have all been killed. Spielberg drew on *The Sullivans* and that historic incident while filtering this through his recurring theme of a mother's devotion to her children. A squad of ordinary men attempts an extraordinary task, similar to but in no way an imitation of *A Walk in the Sun.* The final third, after locating Ryan, owes much to John Wayne's *The Alamo* (1960). Likewise, the final conversation between Hanks and Damon is informed by the finale of Howard Hawks's *Red River* (1948). Spielberg integrates these (and numerous other) references into the film's grander tapestry. He received his second Best Director Oscar. The apotheosis of not only virtually every great WWII film but also action movies in general, while totally original in conception. The uber-WWII movie.

SCREAMING EAGLES (1956)

CREDITS:
Allied Artists; Charles F. Haas, dir.; Virginia Kellogg (story), David Lang, Robert Presnell, Jr., scr.; Samuel Bischoff, David Diamond, pro.; Harry Sukman, mus.; Harry Neumann, cin.; Robert S. Eisen, ed.; B&W; 1.37:1; 79 min.

CAST:
Tom Tryon (*Pvt. Mason*); Jan Merlin (*Lt. Pauling*); Pat Conway (*Sgt. Forrest*); Jacqueline Beer (*Marianne*); Robert Blake (*Hernandez*); Martin Milner (*Dixie*).

Rating: *** 1/2

On the eve of the Normandy invasion, members of the 101st Airborne parachute into occupied territory. The 502nd has orders to seize and secure the Douve river bridge, but they find themselves twenty miles away. Fact-based incidents concerning "Dog Company" flesh out a story told later in *The Longest Day*. Tryon, who plays a pleasant officer in that large-scale film, is miscast here as a nasty soldier unable to get over a Dear John letter. Beer is a French woman whose ability to speak German aids them after the lieutenant is blinded. Impressive, considering the tight budget.

TESTA DI SBARCO PER OTTO IMPLACABILI, aka *HELL IN NORMANDY* (1968)

CREDITS:
Alcinter/Rhodes International; Alfonso Brescia, aka Al Bradley, dir.; Maurice De Vries, Lorenzo Gicca Palli, scr.; Giorgio Fabor, Italo Fischetti, mus.; Fausto Rossi, cin.; Renato Cinquini, ed.; C; 2.35:1; 90 min.

CAST:
Guy Madison (*Capt. Jack Murphy*); Peter Lee Lawrence (*Lt. Strobel*); Erika Blanc (*Denise*); Philippe Hersent (*Prof. Aubernet*); Massimo Carocci

(*Ryan*); Pierre Richard (*Doss*).

Rating: *** 1/2

The Germans create a nefarious device to trap the oncoming liberators: a massive machine will allow them to pour oil onto the waters at Omaha Beach, incinerating landing crafts. As spies have informed Ike and Montgomery, the commanders send in a tough-as-nails squad to destroy that mechanism, known as Operation Gambit. A beautiful Partisan (Blanc) creates sparks between the heroes. Dialogue is deplorable, especially in the dubbed prints. Yet, the three action sequences are strong enough to make this one of the better "spaghetti WWII flicks." French–Italian coproduction, filmed with an eye on the international market, especially the US, which explains the presence of nominal American star Madison. Despite hints that this is a docudrama, the incident is entirely fictitious.

36 HOURS (1965)

CREDITS:
Metro-Goldwyn-Mayer; George Seaton, dir.; Roald Dahl (story), Seaton, Carl K. Hittleman, Luis H. Vance, scr.; William Perlberg, pro.; Dimitri Tiomkin, mus.; Philip H. Lathrop, cin.; Adrienne Fazan, ed.; B&W; 2.35:1; 115 min.

CAST:
James Garner (*Maj. Jefferson F. Pike*); Eva Marie Saint (*Anna Hedler*); Rod Taylor (*Maj. Walter Gerber*); Werner Peters (*Otto Schack*); John Banner (*Ernst*).

Rating: ***

Initially intriguing, ultimately disappointing suspense film. A German intelligence officer (Taylor) comes up with a bizarre plan to learn where the D-Day Invasion will take place: capture an American officer (Garner), dye his hair white, and wrinkle his face. When he's revived, he'll believe that decades have passed while he's been in a coma and will talk freely about

A SOMETHING LESS THAN GREAT ESCAPE: In *36 Hours*, a fictional tale, James Garner and Eva Marie Saint make good their getaway.

"the old days." The manner in which the hero grasps what's really going on is so loudly telegraphed that practically all viewers will see it coming. Garner comes off as dull, devoid of not only a past but also a personality. The motivations of a nurse (Saint) are absurd. Seaton's stolid direction doesn't help. Taylor is strangely sympathetic as the supposed heavy. The film's final third, a routine escape/chase once the plot has been foiled, is listless.

UP FROM THE BEACH (1965)

CREDITS:
20th Century Fox; Robert Parrish, dir.; George Barr (novel), Claude Brulé, Howard Clewes, Stanley Mann, scr.; Christian Ferry, pro.; Edgar Cosma, mus.; Walter Wottitz, cin.; Samuel E. Beetley, ed.; B&W; 2.35:1; 99 min.

CAST:
Cliff Robertson (*Sgt. Ed Baxter*); Red Buttons (*Pfc. Harry Devine*); Irina Demick (*Lili*); Marius Goring (*German*); Slim Pickens (*Artillery Colonel*); James Robertson Justice (*Beachmaster*); Broderick Crawford (*MP*).

Rating: ** 1/2

Minor miniepic, and not bad, but certainly disappointing for audiences who bought tickets thinking it would be a full-scale follow-up to *The Longest Day* (it was originally to have been titled *The Next Day*). Based on a 1959 book, *Epitaph for an Enemy*, about a rugged American who, while pushing his squad inland, comes to respect a German officer (Goring) who stands in his way. Buttons and Demick, both in *The Longest Day*, play different roles here. Acceptable.

VALIANT (2005)

CREDITS:
Vanguard/Ealing Studios/Buena Vista (Disney); Gary Chapman, dir.; George Webster, George Melrod, Jordan Katz, scr.; John H. Williams, pro.; George Fenton, mus.; John Fenner, cin.; Tiffany L. Kurtz, aka Hillkurtz, Jim Stewart, ed.; C; 1.85; 76 min.

THE DISNEY VERSION: World War II was revived for contemporary family audiences in the animated *Valiant*.

CAST (voices only):

Ewan McGregor (*Valiant*); Ricky Gervais (*Bugsy*); Tim Curry (*Von Talon*); Jim Broadbent (*Sergeant*); Hugh Laurie (*Gutsy*); John Cleese (*Mercury*); John Hurt (*Felix*); Olivia Williams (*Victoria*).

Rating: ****

CGI animated film concerns carrier pigeons, essential to the D-Day invasion. Key messages must be picked up in occupied France, where the Resistance plans to do its part, and then relayed back to London so strategies can be coordinated. Valiant is a variation on the recurring Disney hero: the small one everyone thinks will falter but emerges as the greatest hero of all. Familiar plot devices soar owing to a British sense of satire, courtesy of Ealing. The marvelous choices for voice artists complement an appealingly unique approach to colorful visuals. As the adorable French mouse Charles da Girl might put it, *tres charmant.*

WHAT'S NEXT, CORPORAL HARGROVE? (1945)

CREDITS:

Metro-Goldwyn-Mayer; Richard Thorpe, dir.; Harry Kurnitz, scr.; George Haight, pro.; David Snell, mus.; Henry Sharp, cin.; Albert Akst, ed.; B&W; 1.37:1; 95 min.

CAST:

Robert Walker, Sr. (*Marion Hargrove*); Keenan Wynn (*Thomas Mulvehill*); Jean Porter (*Jeanne*); Chill Wills (*Sgt. Cramp*); Hugo Haas (*Mayor*); William Phillips (*Burk*); Cameron Mitchell (*Joe Lupot*).

Rating: ** 1/2

The army marches toward Paris aiming to liberate the city. For Hargrove (now a corporal, though he regularly gets busted), what follows has little in common with what most GIs experienced. Instead, the boys are free to chase pretty Frenchwomen. A dim shadow of the first film, with Walker appearing to no longer enjoy his connection with the role, giving as little as possible. Thrown together by MGM after *See Here, Private Hargrove* became a hit.

WHERE EAGLES DARE (1968)

CREDITS:
Metro-Goldwyn-Mayer; Brian G. Hutton, dir.; Alistair MacLean, scr.; Elliott Kastner, pro.; Ron Goodwin, mus.; Arthur Ibbetson, cin.; John Jympson, ed.; C; 2.35:1; 158 min.

CAST:
Richard Burton (*Maj. Jonathan Smith*); Clint Eastwood (*Lt. Morris Schaffer*); Mary Ure (*Mary Ellison*); Patrick Wymark (*Turner*); Michael Hordern (*Rolland*); Donald Houston (*Christiansen*); Ingrid Pitt (*Heidi*); Anton Diffring (*Kramer*).

Rating: *

From a 1967 novel by the author of *Guns of Navarone* comes this clunker that imitates the plot of the previous classic while missing its greatness. A special task force is assembled, led by an Englishman and an American. The mission: enter (and if possible destroy) an isolated castle while rescuing an Allied officer about to be interrogated by the SS. There's a traitor (maybe more than one) in the ranks. Half the fun of *Guns* was trying to figure out who that would be. Here, each commando is a mere cipher, interchangeable with the others, so who cares. Plot twists come *so* quickly (agents turn out to be double agents, then triple agents, then...) that silliness takes over. Little real action until the final fight atop a cable car, this undercut by already outmoded rear projection. Trick ending is contrived enough to anger viewers who have silently suffered through the paint-by-numbers adventures preceding it.

YOUNG LIONS, THE (1958)

CREDITS:
20th Century Fox; Edward Dmytryk, dir.; Irwin Shaw (novel), Edward Anhalt; Al Lichtman, pro.; Hugo Friedhofer, mus.; Joseph MacDonald, cin.; Dorothy Spencer, ed.; B&W; 2.35:1; 167 min.

CAST:
Marlon Brando (*Lt. Christian Diestl*); Montgomery Clift (*Noah Ackerman*); Dean Martin (*Michael Whiteacre*); Hope Lange (*Hope Plowman*); Barbara Rush (*Margaret*); May Britt (*Gretchen*); Maximilian Schell (*Capt. Hardenberg*); Lee Van Cleef (*Rickett*); Liliane Montevecchi (*Françoise*).

Rating: ***

An American playboy and his Jewish sidekick ship out for combat, unaware they have a date with destiny in the form of a Nazi tied to them through a woman. Perfectly cast version of Shaw's impressive novel never realizes

THE OTHER SIDE OF THE BATTLEGROUND: Maximilian Schell, Marlon Brando as diehard Nazis in *The Young Lions*.

the book's full potential. Many individual scenes are fine, though they never mesh into a cohesive vision. Brando ruined everything by insisting his character be transformed from Shaw's cold-blooded killing machine into an antiwar Christ figure. An inane happy ending destroys the full-blown modern tragedy aspect of Shaw's 1948 novel. Schell is excellent in his first Nazi role; he was in fact a Swiss Jew. A real pity! Considering the book's quality, this could've been as great as *From Here to Eternity*.

LONELY ARE THE BRAVE: The greatest actor of his generation, Montgomery Clift vividly portrayed the confusion of G.I.s as they face the incomprehensible in *The Search, The Big Lift, From Here to Eternity*, and (seen here) *The Young Lions*.

SOCIAL RELEVANCE: In films such as *Amen*, arthouse filmmaker Costa-Gavras proved himself to be the world's conscience when it comes to filmmakers.

Hell On Earth: The Holocaust

AMEN (2002)

CREDITS:
Canal+; Costa-Gavras, dir.; Rolf Hochhuth (play), Costa-Gavras, Jean-Claude Grumberg, scr.; Michèle Ray-Gavras, pro.; Armand Amar, mus.; Patrick Blossier, cin.; Yannick Kergoat, ed.; C; 1.85:1; 132 min.

CAST:
Ulrich Tukur (*Kurt Gerstein*); Mathieu Kassovitz (*Riccardo Fontana*); Ulrich Mühe (*Doctor*); Michel Duchaussoy (*The Cardinal*); Ion Caramitru (*Count Fontana*); Marcel Iures (*Pope Pius XII*).

Rating: **** 1/2

During the Holocaust's initial stages, a German doctor becomes aware of the still-secret Final Solution: Jews are not being exported but executed. Outraged, he tries to spread the word. He finds no outlet until a Jesuit priest contacts the Pope, only to find that the Vatican is mainly concerned with its own survival. This political art film had to be produced in Romania after Catholic officials refused to permit shooting on location. Influenced by *Shoah*, Costa-Gavras excludes the expected images of Holocaust horrors, focusing instead on the insanity of everyday life as growing evidence of evil is tacitly ignored. Based on a play but fully cinematic; one of the only Holocaust films to explain the process by which German people slipped into total denial. Just misses greatness by virtue of the less-than-satisfying finale.

AUSCHWITZ (2011)

CREDITS:
Boll World Sales; Uwe Boll, dir.; Boll, scr.; Boll, pro.; Jessica de Rooij, mus.; Mathias Neumann, cin.; Charles Ladmiral, ed.; C; 1.78:1; 73 min.

CAST:
Steffan Mennekes (*Guard*); Arved Birnbaum (*SS Commander*); Uwe Boll (*Guard*); Nik Goldman (*Prisoner*); Maximilian Gärtner (*Boy*); Friedhelm Gärtner (*The Boy's Father*).

Rating: NO STARS

Indie filmmaker Boll, concerned that many young Germans were unaware of the Holocaust, created this film to inform them about the atrocities. Rarely have good intentions gone so wrong. Shot in a bland building that looks nothing like a concentration camp, Boll concentrates his camera on horrid depictions of abuse that, without sufficient drama before and after, exist as torture chic: a turn-on for demented audiences. Shot on the set of the commercial exploitation item *BloodRayne*, which Boll also oversaw. Truly despicable.

BENT (1997)

CREDITS:
Channel Four Films; Sean Mathias, dir.; Martin Sherman (play), scr.; Dixie Linder, Michael Solinger, pro.; Philip Glass, mus.; Giorgos Arvanitis, cin.; Isabelle Lorente, ed.; C; 1.85:1; 105 min.

CAST:
Clive Owen (*Max*); Brian Webber (*Rudy*); Mick Jagger (*Greta*); Nikolaj (Coster-)Waldau (*Wolf*); Jude Law (*Stormtrooper*); Ian McKellan (Uncle Freddie); Gresby Nash (*Waiter*).

Rating: **** 1/2

Following the murder of SA leader Ernst Röhm, homosexual lovers Max and Rudy are sent to a concentration camp. Rudy dies en route as a result of beatings. In Dachau, Max realizes that Jewish prisoners are identified by yellow patches while gays are forced to wear pink. No matter how vicious toward Jews, the guards reserve their most horrific acts for Aryan homosexuals. To survive, Max develops a desperate plan to convince the guards he's a Jew. A new lover helps Max realize that accepting one's birth-determined identity is more important than day-to-day survival. Mathias effectively transfers the stage play to the screen. If there's a flaw, it's that Owen isn't nearly as spectacular as Ian McKellan (here relegated to a supporting role) was as Max in the original stage production. Truly depressing yet uplifting. A British–Japanese coproduction.

BLOODRAYNE: THE THIRD REICH (2001)

CREDITS:
Boll Kino/Brightlight Pictures; Uwe Boll, dir.; Michael (C.) Nachoff, scr.; Boll, Dan Clarke, pro.; Jessica de Rooij, mus.; Mathias Neumann, cin.; Charles Ladmiral, ed.; C; 2.35:1; 79 min.

CAST:
Natassia Maltha (*Rayne*); Brendan Fletcher (*Gregor*); Michael Pate (*Commandment*); William Belli (*Tishenko*); Annett Culp (*Magda*); Clint Howard (*Dr. Mangler*); Michael Paré (*Brand*).

Rating: 1/2 star

A succubus with a remarkable figure, which she proudly displays in a black leather-and-lace costume, sets out to help anti-Nazi guerillas free prisoners from a concentration camp. She makes the mistake of turning a bloodthirsty officer into a fellow vampire with her bite, even as a mad doctor plans to inject Rayne's blood into Hitler to render him immortal. Much graphic torture and lesbian lovemaking scenes for the franchise's target audience. Avoid as you would the bubonic plague.

BOY IN THE STRIPED PYJAMAS, THE (2008)

CREDITS:
Miramax/BBC Films/Heyday; Mark Herman, dir.; John Boyne (novel), Herman, scr.; Herman, David Heyman, pro.; James Horner, mus.; Benoit Delhomme, cin.; Michael Ellis, ed.; C; 1.85:1; 94 min.

CAST:
Zac Mattoon O'Brien (*Leon*); Domonkos Németh (*Martin*); Henry Kingsmill (*Karl*); Vera Farmiga (*Mother*); Cara Horgan (*Maria*); Amber Beattie (*Gretel*); László Áron (*Lars*).

Rating: ★★★★

A couple leaves Berlin when the husband is transferred to a new job location "in the country." Their boy searches for someone his age (eight) to play with. He finds such a child squatting behind barbed wire, wearing what appear to be striped pajamas. He's an Auschwitz prisoner; the other boy is the son of the camp's commander. Based on Boyne's 2006 novel for

FOCUSING ON CHIDREN: The fate of young prisoners served as the central narrative heart and thematic soul of the sadly overlooked film *The Boy in Striped (aka Stryped) Pajamas.*

young readers, this high-minded feature introduces teens and preteens to absorbing fiction that conveys ideas, notably the purity of children until their innocence is corrupted by adults. Several critics objected, calling it a Disney version of the Holocaust. Others argued that the willingness of mainstream moviemakers to try and remind today's youth about this dark chapter from the past sufficed. Truly touching.

CHI SCRIVERA LA NOSTRA STORIA (2018)

CREDITS:
Kalhadin Prods.; Roberta Grossman, dir.; Grossman, scr., Samuel Kassow (novel); Grossman, pro.; Todd Boekelheide, mus.; Dyanna Taylor, cin.; Chris Callister, Ondine Rarey, ed.; C; 95 min.

CAST:
Jowita Budnik (*Rachela Auerbach*); Piotr Glowwacki (*Emanuel Ringelblum*); Piotr Jankowski (*Hersz Wasser*); Wojciech Zielinski (*Abraham Lewin*); Karolina Gruska (*Judta Ringelblum*); Bartlomiej Kotschedoff (*Leib Goldin*).

Rating: **** ½

While most of the Polish Jews who were herded into Poland's Warsaw Ghetto focused on surviving along with their families, a handful of historians determined to create an accurate record of what occurred there so that, in the future, their story would be told not by outsiders but by themselves. In the form of diaries, poems, and journalistic descriptions not only of the everyday horrors but also interpersonal relationships, as well as visual records in the form of photographs, sketches, and paintings they amassed a human epic worthy of Homer and buried these deep under the ground. Though Kassow wanted to revive their heroic tale he did so (as was the case with the *Schindler's List* book) in the form of a novel rather than a volume of history. Auteur Grossman has created a one-of-a-kind film version, including old newsreel footage as well as staged/theatrical readings of key manuscripts and dramatic/cinematic performances of key scenes with unknown actors all but 'becoming' the characters. A notable, important achievement; had Grossman been able to amass a larger budget than the $1,500,000 she was able to raise, her work might have contained even more of these precious records.

COUNTERFEITERS, THE (2007)

CREDITS:
Magnolia/Beta Cinema; Stefan Ruzowitzky, dir.; Adolf Burger (book), Stefan Ruzowitzky, scr.; Josef Aichholzer, Nina Bohlmann, Babette Schröder, pro.; Marius Ruhland, mus.; Benedict Neuenfels, cin.; Britta Nahler, ed.; C; 1.85:1; 98 min.

CAST:
Karl Markovics (*Sorowitsch*); August Diehl (*Burger*); David Striesow (*Sturmbannführer Herzog*); Martin Brambach (*Holst*); August Zirner (*Dr. Klinger*); Veit Stübner (*Atze*); Sebastian Urzendowsky (*Kolya*).

Rating: **** 1/2

From Austria and Germany, a fictionalized account of Operation Bernhard, a plan to ruin the US and UK economies by flooding both countries with faux money. To facilitate this, the High Command employs an expert Jewish counterfeiter, offering him a less grim life in Linz's Mauthausen camp. Complications ensue when this self-serving person finds himself teamed with another Jew who insists they should sabotage the plan, sacrificing not only their newfound comfort but also their lives for the greater good. The merging of fiction and history results in a strong moviegoing experience for not only WWII buffs but anyone who enjoys an edge-of-your-seat thriller. Moral issues are subordinated to the immediate aim of providing entertainment. Adapted from a memoir, *The Devil's Workshop*, by the more idealistic of the two. Won the 2007 Oscar for Best Foreign Language Film. Effective use of tango and opera.

DALEKA CESTA, aka DISTANT JOURNEY (1949)

CREDITS:
Ceskolovensky Statni Film; Alfréd Radok, dir.; Radok, Mojmir Drvota, Erik Kolár, scr.; Jiri Sternwald, mus.; Josef Strecha, cin.; Jirina Lukesová, ed.; B&W; 1.37:1; 108 min. (director's cut); 78 min. (US theatrical print).

CAST:
Blanka Waleská (*Hana*); Otomar Krejca (*Antonin*); Viktor Ocásek (*Kaufmann*); Zdenka Baldová (*Hedvika*); Eduard Kohout (*Prof. Reiter*); J. O. Martin (*Karel*); Josef Chvalina (*Pepa*).

Ratings: **** 1/2 (director's cut)
*** 1/2 (US theatrical print)

Nothing would be the same after WWII, including movies. Gifted filmmakers experimented wildly, with psychological themes dominating, Freudian imagery a perfect visual projection of such concepts. In Hollywood, Hitchcock was among the first to do so with *Spellbound* (1945). In postwar Czechoslovakia, Radok combined narrative fiction, documentary footage, and ultraradical moviemaking tropes introduced by the avant-garde in the 1920s. He sensed that the mainstream—following the horrors of the Holocaust and the atomic bombing of Hiroshima—was ready for anything. A Jewish woman is happily married to a gentile until the Final Solution begins. The director alternates historic images with dramatized sequences. At times, they appear on-screen together, fiction presented as a smaller frame within the larger one containing documentary footage. Odd camera angles, designed to add an allegorical element, make clear this film is about more than one couple's personal struggle. Initially banned in Radok's native land by Stalin.

DAY THE CLOWN CRIED, THE (1972)

CREDITS:

Wachsberger Prods.; Jerry Lewis, dir.; Lewis, Joan O'Brien, Charles Denton, scr.; Rune Ericson, cin.; C; 2.20:1; 90 min.

CAST:

Jerry Lewis (*Helmut Doork*); Peter Ahlm (*Prisoner*); Harriet Anderson (*Ada*); Jones Bergstrom (*Franz*); Carl Billquist (*Gestapo Officer*); Tomas Bolme (*Adolf*); Anton Diffring (*Runkel*).

Rating: NO STARS

A Jewish German circus performer is arrested by the SS. Grasping that he's headed for a concentration camp, he decides to keep the innocent Jewish children smiling for as long as he can. From a well-intentioned script by actress-turned-writer O'Brien, rewritten by Lewis as a "sad clown" vehicle for himself. Distributors were unwilling to release it for fear that what had been intended as a pro-Jewish film might actually be (mis)interpreted as anti-Semitic. If *Life Is Beautiful* were created by incompetents, it might have turned out like this.

EICHMANN (2007)

CREDITS:

Entertainment Motion Pictures; Robert Young, dir.; Snoo Wilson, scr.; Karl Richards, pro.; Richard Harvey, mus.; Michael Connor, cin.; Saska Simpson, ed.; C/B&W; 1.85:1; 96 min.

CAST:

Thomas Kretschmann (*Adolf Eichmann*); Troy Garity (*Avner Less*); Franka Potente (*Versa*); Stephen Fry (*Minister*); Delaine Yates (*Miriam Fröhlich*); Tereza Srbová (*Ingrid von Ihama*).

Rating: ***

The trial of Nazi SS-*Obergruppenführer* Eichmann (1906–1962), following his capture on May 11, 1960, began April 11, 1961, in Israel, concluding on August 14, 1961. He was found guilty of having overseen the deportation of Jews to death camps. This version is far too reimagined to be considered a biopic. Such liberties, expansions, and creative license would be acceptable if they worked better than they do here. Essentially, a two-character chamber drama (the verbal combatant being prosecutor Less) in which the historical interview is performed while the characters are expanded in fictional ways. Sadly, they remain talking heads, good against evil, until the film turns terribly shrill.

ESCAPE (1940)

CREDITS:
Metro-Goldwyn-Mayer; Mervyn LeRoy, dir.; Grace Zaring Stone, aka Ethel Vance (novel), Arch Oboler, Marguerite Roberts; LeRoy, Lawrence Weingarten, pro.; Franz Waxman, mus.; Robert H. Planck, cin.; George Boemler, ed.; B&W; 1.37:1; 98 min.

CAST:
Norma Shearer (*Countess von Treck*); Robert Taylor (*Mark Preysing*); Conrad Veidt (*Gen. von Kolb*); (Alla) Nazimova (*Emmy Ritter*); Felix Bressart (*Keller*); Albert Bassermann (*Dr. Henning*); Philip Dorn (*Commandant*).

Rating: **** 1/2

A well-regarded stage actress (Nazimova) is confined to a camp. A glimmer of hope shines: the commandant (Philip Dorn), who has adored her from afar, wishes he could help. Her son (Taylor) arrives in Germany, desperate to free his mother. He meets a beautiful American-born German countess (Shearer) whom he persuades to help as romance develops between them. Florid and melodramatic, a soap opera with a social consciousness, this film (like the 1939 book it was based on) conveyed propaganda in favor of America joining the war. Top-shelf entertainment with a then-timely message.

FANNY'S JOURNEY (2016)

CREDITS:
Lola Doillon, dir.; Doillon, Anne Peyregne, scr., Fanny Ben-Ami (novel); Saga Blanchard, Marie de Lassigny, prods.; Pierre Cottereau, cin.; Valerie Deseine, ed.; Gisele Gerardtolini, mus.; Origami Films; C; 2.35:1; 94 min.

CAST:
Leonie Souchaud *(Fanny)*; Fantine Harduin *(Erika)*; Juliane Lepoureau *(Georgette)*; Ryan Brodie *(Victor)*; Anais Meiringer *(Diane)*; Lou Lambrecht *(Rachel)*; Igor van Dessel *(Maurice)*; Cecile De France *(Madame Forman)*; Stephane De Groodt *(Farmer)*.

Rating: ****

In 1943, an Underground network of caring Christian adults slips Jewish children from safe-houses in France Italy, then on to neutral Switzerland. Eventually the Nazis close in, forcing girls and boys to make the final lap of the journey on their own. Years later, one among them turned the story into a fact-based novel; the film version rates as a unique coming of age tale, as an unprepared 13-year-old Fanny suddenly finds herself appointed leader and, if with difficulty, rises to the occasion. An excellent cast of child-actors, most notably the lead, supported by strong writing allows them to emerge as complex characters. Raises the issue of ethnic identity among the young while dramatizing their unique point-of-view on the presence of evil in superficially beautiful world around them. Occasionally lapses into the clichés and conventions of a Hallmark Channel inspirational/sentimental TV movie.

GENOCIDE (1982)

CREDITS:
Moriah Films; Arnold Schwartzman, dir.; Schwartzman, Martin Gilbert, Marvin Hier, scr.; Schwartzman, pro.; Elmer Bernstein, mus.; Peter Shillingford, cin.; Bob Jenkis, ed.; B&W/C; 2.35:1; 90 min.

THE FINAL SOLUTION: A Jewish youth awaits his execution in *Genocide*.

CAST:
Simon Wiesenthal (*Himself*); Orson Welles (*Narrator*); Elizabeth Taylor (*various female voices*).

Rating: **** 1/2

Simon Wiesenthal visits the remains of Mauthausen, directly addressing the camera. This film traces the history of Jews in Europe, from early experiences of anti-Semitism to the rise of Hitler. Primary focus: the Führer's casting of Jewish scholars and professors, artists and scientists, as "the enemy" of his race. The film neither downplays atrocities nor emphasizes them for great impact. Impressively evenhanded at revealing the Christians who failed to stand up to evil and those who found the courage to challenge genocide. Schwartzman mixes disturbing photo relics with modern multimedia visions. Welles and Taylor project with their voices the required sensitivity. Bernstein's score quietly and effectively underlines the visuals. *Genocide* rates second only to *Shoah* among Holocaust documentaries. Only flaw: owing to the brief running time, not every element of the gargantuan tragedy is as fully explained and explored as in that much longer film.

GOOD (2008)

CREDITS:
Miromar; Vicente Amorim, dir.; C. P. Taylor (play), John Wrathall, scr.; Sarah Boote, Billy Dietrich, Miriam Segal, pro.; Simon Lacey, mus.; Andrew Dunn, cin.; John Wilson, ed.; C; 2.35:1; 96 min.

CAST:
Viggo Mortensen (*John Halder*); Jason Isaacs (*Maurice Israel Glückstein*); Jodie Whittaker (*Anne*); Steven Mackintosh (*Freddie*); Mark Strong (*Bouhler*); Steven Elder (*Eichmann*); Adrian Schiller (*Goebbels*).

Rating: *** 1/2

A liberal professor with an ill, depressed, senile mother pens a novel favoring mercy killing. To his surprise, the Nazi regime heartily approves, offering him a prestigious position. Too late does he realize his work is being misinterpreted to justify the Holocaust. Among the victims will be his best friend, a Jew. Here, Taylor's acclaimed play is opened up to numerous locales while the dialogue is streamlined, a process that diminishes the original's impact. So many similar works have come out since the play's premiere twenty-five years before this film that what once seemed fresh has become familiar. Still, the impact of the Night of Broken Glass proves as searing as ever.

GREY ZONE, THE (2001)

CREDITS:
Goatsingers/Killer Films; Tim Blake Nelson, dir.; Nelson (play), Miklós Nyiszli (memoir), scr.; Nelson, Pamela Koffler, Avi Lerner, Danny Lerner, Christine Vachon, pro.; Russell Lee Fine, cin.; Nelson, Michelle Botticelli, ed.; C; 1.85:1; 108 min.

CAST:
Harvey Keitel (*Dr. Eric Mußfeldt*); David Arquette (*Hoffman*); David Chandler (*Rosenthal*); Michael Stuhlbarg (*Cohen*); Steve Buscemi (*Abramowics*); Mira Sorvino (*Dina*).

Rating: **

In one of the most disturbing memoirs ever written—*Auschwitz: A Doctor's Eyewitness Account* (2011)—Miklos Nyiszli describes the *Sonderkommando*: Jews who lured other Jews into the gas chambers in exchange for better food and lodging. Hungarians who accepted such a role out of self-interest existed in a moral "gray zone." Director Nelson's modus operandi is to make this the most gruesome mainstream work about the Holocaust, focusing on mayhem and murder. Of course, *Schindler's List* contains horrific moments, but they are always subordinate to the human drama. But here, artistic honesty gives way to unintentional exploitation, a freak show that exists to disgust via images of depravity.

IN DARKNESS (2011)

CREDITS:
Schmidtz-Katz Films; Agnieszka Holland, dir.; Robert Marshall (book), David F. Shamoon, scr.; Leander Carell, Eric Jordan, Patrick Knippel, Juliusz Machulski, Steffen Reuter, Paul Stephens, pro.; Antoni Lazarkiewicz, mus.; Jolanta Dylewska, cin.; Michal Czarnecki, ed.; C; 1.85:1; 145 min.

CAST:
Robert Wieckiewicz (*Leopold Socha*); Benno Fürmann (*Mundek Margulies*); Agnieszka Grochowska (*Klara Keller*); Maria Schrader (*Paulina Chiger*); Herbert Knaup (*Ignacy*).

Rating: **** 1/2

A sewer worker in the Polish city of Lwów, aware that the occupying Nazis are relocating Jews to camps, comes up with the idea of saving as many as possible by spiriting them away through the complicated underground system. Far from a simple hero figure, Socha had been previously prosecuted for burglary. Still, like the better-known Schindler, this man rises to the occasion. The filmmakers were intent on remaining true to the complexity of the event, never watering it down. This edge-of-your-seat thriller ranks alongside the best of Hitchcock and Lang, allowing us to shudder at the evil happening all around while finding optimism in the courage of rare non-Jews risking their lives for humanity. Among the most acclaimed of all Polish films.

JACOB THE LIAR (1975)

CREDITS:
VEB-DEFA Studio; Frank Beyer, dir.; Jurek Becker (novel), Beyer, scr.; Joachim Werzlau, mus.; Günter Marczinkowsky, cin.; Rita Hiller, ed.; C; 1.66:1; 100 min.

CAST:
Vlastimil Brodsky (*Jakob Heym*); Erwin Geschonneck (*Kowalski*); Henry Hübchen (*Mischa*); Blanche Kommerell (*Rosa*); Manuela Simon (*Lina*); Dezsö Garas (*Frankfurter*); Friedrich Richter (*Dr. Kirschbaum*).

Rating: **** 1/2

A storyteller and mythmaker, Jacob Heym is unique among the many people surviving in a Jewish ghetto in occupied Poland. Questioned at Gestapo headquarters, he overhears a radio report that the tide of the war has turned against Germany. Back with friends and family, Jacob does more than simply share the good news. Expanding on the story, he transforms a rumor into a legend that inspires optimism, creating hope where previously there was only despair. This theme, explored in Renoir's WWI classic *Grand Illusion* (1937), is also included in several other darkly comic Holocaust films: the disastrous *The Day the Clown Cried* and the dazzling *Life Is Beautiful*. If Frank Capra had made a movie about Jewish survival, it might have turned out very much like this. A seemingly sentimental premise is handled so sensitively that the result never turns corny.

TWO TAKES ON A TALE: Vlastimil Brodsky in the successful 1974 version *Jacob the Liar*; Robin Williams in the considerably less well-received 1999 film *Jakob the Liar.*

JAKOB THE LIAR (1999)

CREDITS:
Columbia; Peter Kassovitz, dir.; Jurek Becker (novel), Kassovitz, Didier Decoin, scr.; Steven Haft, Marsha Garces Williams, pro.; Ed Shearmur, mus.; Elemér Ragályi, C; 1.85:1; 120 min.

CAST:
Robin Williams (*Jakob*); Hannah Taylor Gordon (*Lina*); Éva Igó (*Lina's Mother*); István Bálint (*Lina's Father*); Bob Balaban (*Kowalsky*); Alan Arkin (*Frankfurter*); Michael Jeter (*Avron*).

Rating: *

Few contemporary remakes of true classics miss the mark so completely as this Hollywoodization of the 1975 East German original. Kassovitz's version is devoid of everything that made the initial telling of the tale so irresistible. Arch and overplayed, preachy where it should have subtly conveyed ideas, featuring Williams in a gross caricature of the part, here's proof of an old adage: bigger is not necessarily better.

KAPÒ (1960)

CREDITS:
Cineriz/Zebra; Gillo Pontecorvo, dir.; Pontecorvo, Franco Solinas, scr.; Franco Cristaldi, Moris Ergas, pro.; Carlo Rustichelli, mus.; Aleksandar Sekulovic, cin.; Roberto Cinquini, Anhela Michelli, ed.; B&W; 1.66:1; 116 min. (US theatrical print), 118 min. (director's cut).

CAST:
Susan Strasberg (*Edith/Nicole*); Laurent Terzieff (*Sascha*); Emmanuelle Riva (*Terese*); Didi Prego (*Sofia*); Gianni Garko (*Karl*); Annabella Besi, Graziella Galvani (*Prisoners*).

Rating: *** 1/2

Through odd but believable circumstances, a fourteen-year-old Parisian captured by Nazis is interned in a camp for criminals and political dissidents, masking her Jewishness. Having to choose between dignity through ethnic identity (and likely death) and survival, she picks the latter, turning against her female inmates by becoming a *kapo*—a prisoner who guards other prisoners. The film's opening hour—the first dramatic movie ever made that takes place inside a concentration camp—is superb: ultrarealistic and harrowing. At midmovie, things fall apart. The docudrama approach dissipates. In its place emerges a chick flick: she regains her goodness the moment she meets and falls in love with a handsome Soviet POW. Their forbidden kisses by the barbed wire fence are ludicrous. This one starts out fine but degenerates into a Holocaust-set soap opera.

LAST DAYS, THE (1998)

CREDITS:
Ken Lipper/June Beallor Prods./The Shoah Foundation; James Moll, dir.; June Beallor, Ken Lipper, pro.; Hans Zimmer, mus.; Harris Done, cin.; Moll, ed.; C/B&W; 1.85:1; 105 min.

CAST:
Irene Zisblatt, Bill Basch, Randolph Braham, Alice Lok Cahana, Rene Firestone, Tom Lantos (*Themselves/Holocaust Survivors*); Warren Dunn, Katsugo Miho, Paul Parks (*Themselves, US Army, Dachau*); Hans Münch (*Nazi Doctor, Auschwitz*); many others.

Rating: **** 1/2

The Hungarian Holocaust situation was not precisely the same as that experienced in other places. Here, the Final Solution (i.e., extermination in death camps) did not begin until March 1944. Rare survivors offer vivid, telling, and gut-wrenching memories. Also interviewed are Nazi doctors from the camp, a Nazi commandant, and other eyewitnesses, including several American soldiers involved in the massive liberation. The uniqueness of so many of the stories told here helps qualify this as one of the several runners-up to *Shoah* for finest Holocaust documentary. Spielberg served as executive producer; this project provides an unofficial follow-up to *Schindler's List*, filling in information that, owing to time limitations, wasn't included there. Won the Oscar for Best Documentary Feature.

THE COMEDY OF TERRORS: Jerry Lewis attempted (and failed) to do so with *The Day the Clown Cried*; Roberto Benigni won an Oscar for *Life is Beautiful*.

LIFE IS BEAUTIFUL (1997)

CREDITS:
Checchi Gon/Tiger/Melampo/Mirimax; Roberto Benigni, dir.; Benigni, Vincenzo Cerami, scr.; Gianluigi Braschi, Elda Ferri, pro.; Nicola Piovani, mus.; Tonino Delli Colli, cin.; Simona Paggi, ed.; C; 1.85:1; 116 min.

CAST:
Roberto Benigni (*Guido*); Nicoletta Braschi (*Dora*); Giorgio Cantarini (*Joshua*); Giustino Durano (*Uncle Eliseo*); Sergio Bini Bustric (*Ferruccio*); Horst Buchholz (*Dr. Lessing*).

Rating: *****

Tragicomedy correctly describes this unique film. Benigni, a director/writer/actor in the tradition of Charles Chaplin, brings to life the unlikely yet believable tale of a Jewish Italian bookstore owner who, along with his son, is sent to a concentration camp. Guido formulates a unique strategy to maintain his son's purity, convincing him that this is an immense joke, an ongoing game they play—and, as such, nothing to fear. The audience waits to learn if—as acts of evil grow larger and more intense—this ruse can continue. Benigni avoids the conventions (some might say clichés) of many other Holocaust movies to offer a fresh view of a vast lingering horror. The premise sustains itself from the first moment to the final heartbreaking image. Oscars include Best Actor, Best Original Dramatic Score (Music), and Best Foreign Language Film.

NIGHT AND FOG (1955)

CREDITS:
Argos; Alain Resnais, dir.; Jean Cayrol, Chris Marker, scr.; Anatole Dauman, Samy Halfon, Philippe Lifchitz, pro.; Hanns Eisler, mus.; Ghislain Cloquet, Sacha Vierny, cin.; Resnais, ed.; C/B&W; 1.37:1; 32 min.

CAST:
Michel Bouquet (*Narrator*); Adolf Hitler, Julius Streicher, Heinrich

Himmler, Reinhard Heydrich (*historical figures, documentary footage, themselves*).

Rating: *****

Ten years after the closing of all Nazi concentration camps, aspiring young French filmmaker Resnais revisited the areas. His cinematographers captured stark images, often in color, bringing long-abandoned camps into the present tense. Viewers were forced to deal with the reality of skeletal buildings from a past most people wanted to forget. Such modern shots are set, through Resnais's editing/montage decisions, against grim archival footage. Several key narrative elements were written by Resnais's first choice for the screenplay, Cayrol (a survivor of Mauthausen-Gusen). These create a verbal bridge between contrasting visuals aspects, as does Eisler's score. The French government tried to censor certain sequences dealing with Gallic collaborators. Innovations in documentary technique influenced such future works as *Shoah*, revealing that the nonfiction film is much more than a string of realistic moments, objectively presented. This is the Resnais/Cayrol perspective on the Holocaust, presented as they perceived it to the public at large.

PATY JEZDEC JE STRACH, ...A, aka ... THE FIFTH HORSEMAN IS FEAR (1965)

CREDITS:
Filmove Studio Barrandov; Zbynek Brynych, dir.; Milan Nejedly, Ota Koval, Ester Krumbachova, scr.; Jiri Sternwald, mus.; Jan Kalis, cin.; Miroslav Hajek, ed.; B&W; 2.35:1; 100 min.

CAST:
Miroslav Machácek (*Dr. Braun*); Olga Scheinpflugová (*Music Teacher*); Zdenka Procházková (*Mrs. Vesely*); Jiri Adamira (*Mr. Veseley*); Josef Vinklár (*Fanta*).

Rating: **** 1/2

An elderly Jewish doctor passively accepts Germany's occupation of Czechoslovakia, scoffing at younger people who oppose the Nazis. His one desire: remain as low key as possible so he's less likely to be dragged off. Unable to practice medicine, which he loved, his spirit has settled into hard, cold stone. A radical anti-Nazi has been wounded while attempting escape; no one but this former doctor can operate. Will he do it? The experience shocks the old man into recognizing once deeply held values. He not only does an excellent job with the medical chores but also volunteers to search for morphine to ease the patient's pain—even though this will expose him to threats. A redemption tale of the first order, banned for years in its land of origin by Communist influences. Sadly, many current prints lack the all-important brothel scene.

PIANIST, THE (2002)

CREDITS:
Heritage Films/StudioCanal; Roman Polanski, dir.; Wladyslaw Szpilman (book), Ronald Harwood, scr.; Polanski, Robert Benmussa, Alain Sarde, pro.; Wojciech Kilar, mus.; Pawel Edelman, cin.; Hervé de Luze, ed.; C/B&W; 1.85:1; 150 min.

CAST:
Adrien Brody (*Wladyslaw Szpilman*); Emilia Fox (*Dorota*); Michael Zebrowski (*Jurek*); Ed Stoppard (*Henryk*); Maureen Lipman (*Mother*); Frank Finlay (*Father*); Jessica Kate Meyer (*Halina*).

Rating: *****

In late fall 1939, Poland is overwhelmed by German troops who insist that Jewish citizens wear yellow Star of David armbands. One victim is a musician who, with his family, is trapped in the overpopulated Warsaw ghetto, where children die of starvation and adults are shot dead by the SS. If this seems like hell on earth, things get worse at the Treblinka camp, designed for the Final Solution. Szpilman may save his own life while sacrificing his soul when a Nazi officer agrees to hide him provided he can hear the maestro play. Polanski's profound pessimism causes him to draw on his own darkest

COMMUNITY LOYALTY VS. INDIVIDUAL SURVIVAL: A brilliant Jewish musician (Adrien Brody) suffers at the sight of the Holocaust yet chooses to go on living by forging a deal with the devil in *The Pianist*.

memories (he had escaped from Krakow as a child). A depressing work, but a deeply rewarding one. Winner of three Academy Awards, including Best Screenplay, Best Actor, and Best Director; also nominated for Best Picture. Arguably, the best dramatic film ever made about the Holocaust.

RAFLE, LA (2010)

CREDITS:

Rose Bosch, dir.; Bosch, scr.; Alain Goldman, pro.; Aurelien Dupont, Yann Malcor, eds.; David Ungaro, cin.; Christian Henson, mus.; Legende Films/Gaumont; C; 2.35:1; 115 (theatrical cut), 124 (extended edition).

CAST

Jean Reno *(David Sheinbaum)*; Melanie Laurent *(Annette Monod)*; Gad Elmaleh *(Weismann)*; Raphaelle Agogue *(Sura Weismann)*; Hugo Leverdez *(Jo)*; Mathieu Di Concerto *(Nono)*; Roland Cope *(Petain)*; Rebecca Marder *(Rachel)*; Udo Schenk *(Hitler)*.

Rating: *** ½

Though the Jews of Paris must wear the despised yellow cloth patches with the Star of David, they are spared deportation until the summer of 1942. At that point, the Nazi High command in Berlin orders Petain and the Vichy government to institute a program of "denaturalization" in which Gallic police join the S.S. in a plan to round up nearly 25,000 French Hebrews. Women, children, and men are held in Veldrome d'Hiver until trains carry them east to "relocation" camps. The film is at its most effective when presenting large sequences involving crowds of victims and their brutal perpetrators, though Bosch tends to be a bit ham-fisted in intimate sequences involving personal human drama. The agenda appears to be a defense of France's non-Jews, often portrayed as universally anti-Semitic and pleased by the coming Holocaust. Here the focus is mostly on those who risked their lives to hide Jewish neighbors. An ever deepening relationship between a Protestant nurse (Laurent) and a Jewish doctor (Reno) is more vividly developed than most of the other relationships, drawn in broad strokes.

READER, THE (2008)

CREDITS:

The Weinstein Company/Mirage/Studio Babelsberg; Stephen Daldry, dir.; Bernhard Schlink (novel), David Hare, scr.; Donna Gigliotti, Anthony

Minghella, Redmond Morris, Sydney Pollack, pro.; Nico Muhly, mus.; Roger Deakins, Chris Menges, cin.; Claire Simpson, ed.; C; 1.85:1; 124 min.

CAST:
Kate Winslet (*Hanna Schmitz*); Ralph Fiennes (*Michael Berg*); David Kross (*Young Michael*); Lina Olin (*The Survivor*); Jeanette Hain (*Brigitte*); Hannah Herzsprung (*Julia*); Moritz Grove (*Holger*); Kirsten Block (*Judge*).

Rating: **** 1/2

In 1958, a fifteen-year-old German boy becomes involved with a thirty-six-year-old illiterate woman. Intense bouts of sex are followed by sweet sessions in which he reads classic books to her. Then, she disappears without a trace. In 1996, a lawyer visits a Holocaust survivor to learn about a horrific incident in which an SS guard burned down a church filled with helpless Jews. The boy and man are one and the same; the guard in charge was the woman he once loved. The most divisive mainstream movie ever made about Shoah. Every aesthetic element is brilliant, from the screenplay to the cinematography to the performances (Winslet won a Best Actress Oscar). Yet, the theme—ordinary Germans were as victimized as Jews, and we should feel some empathy, if not sympathy, for the female lead—led to incendiary attacks, insisting this supported "Holocaust negationists" (which was not the filmmakers' intent). Mesmerizing and infuriating.

ROSENTRASSE (2003)

CREDITS:
Studio Hamburg Letterbox Filmproduktion; Margarethe von Trotta, dir.; von Trotta, Pamela Katz, scr.; Henrik Meyer, Richard Schöps, Sabine Schild, Markus Zimmmer, pro.; Loek Dikker, mus.; Franz Rath, cin.; Corina Dietz, ed.; C; 2.35:1; 136 min.

CAST:
Katja Riemann (*Lena Fischer, age 35*); Doris Schade (*Lena, age 90*); Svea Lohde (*Ruth Weinstein, age 8*); Jutta Lampe (*Ruth, age 60*); Maria Schrader (*Hannah Weinstein*); Jürgen Vogel (*Arthur*).

Rating: *** 1/2

Late February 1943: Nazis prepare to remove the final Jewish residents from Berlin. Many are married to Aryan women, who use their bodies to create a roadblock in the title street, hoping to negotiate having their men moved to work squads rather than death camps. These events are stirringly, if not always accurately, re-created in a film designed to create a sense of hopeful inspiration in the present. By telling the tale from the point of view of a contemporary young woman who sets out to learn the truth—in a *Citizen Kane*–type approach of interviewing survivors to achieve a wider perspective—von Trotta creates an awkward narrative that actually makes the primary event even more difficult to comprehend. Emotionally involving, though the intellectual pretensions are not fully realized.

SAMSON (1961)

CREDITS:
Zespol Filmowy; Andrzej Wajda, dir.; Kazimierz Brandys (novel), Wajda, scr.; Tadeusz Baird, mus.; Jerzy Wójcik, cin.; Janina Niedzwiecka, ed.; B&W; 2.35:1; 117 min.

CAST:
Serge Merlin (*Jakub Gold*); Alina Janowska (*Lucyna*); Elzbieta Kepinska (*Kazia*); Jan Ciecierski (*Józef Malina*); Tadeusz Bartosik (*Pankrat*); Wladyslaw Kowalski (*Fialka*).

Rating: *** 1/2

Hoping a more enlightened Europe will emerge during the twentieth century, a well-to-do, well-intentioned Jewish mother (Netto) sends her son Jakub to an expensive private school. There, the child is taunted by other boys—a prelude to, during the Nazi occupation, a hovel in a filthy ghetto. He survives by believing in the possibility of escape via a deep personal connection with the Old Testament's Samson: strong in body, spirit, and mind. This guiding force aids the youth in his journey toward freedom. Wajda here opts for dark humor and self-conscious stylings that purposefully draw attention to themselves. In truth, he's less a master of such art-house cinema than the raw narratives he remains associated with, this film proving less successful than other ventures. Worthwhile mostly for its noble intentions.

SARAH'S KEY (2010)

CREDITS:
Hugo/Studio 37; Gilles Paquet-Brenner, dir.; Tatiana De Rosnay (novel), Paquet-Brenner, Serge Joncour, scr.; Stephane Marsil, pro.; Pascal Ridao, cin.; Hervé Schneid, ed.; Max Richter, mus.; C; 2.35:1; 111 min.

CAST:
Kristin Scott Thomas (*Julia Jarmond*); Mélusine Mayance (*Sarah*); Niels Arestrup (*Jules Dufaure*); Frédéric Pierrot (*Bertrand Tezac*); Michel Duchaussoy (*Édouard Tezac*).

Rating: **** 1/2

Paris, 1942: as a Jewish family is dragged from their home, the daughter desperately locks her little brother in a closet to try and save him. In modern-day France in 2009, a journalist researching French participation in the Final Solution tries to track down the details, no matter how painful, about Sarah. The present-/past-time trope predates that of *Rosentrasse*, and here it works more effectively. We care as much about the modern people as the lost souls who haunt them. Convincing, disturbing, deeply satisfying to the end, which may strike some as curt and pat in a way that is unlike anything else in this unique film.

SCHINDLER'S LIST (1993)

CREDITS:
Amblin/Universal; Steven Spielberg, dir.; Thomas Keneally (novel), Steven Zaillian, scr.; Spielberg, Branko Lustig, Gerald R. Molen, pro.; John Williams, mus.; Janusz Kaminski, cin.; Michael Kahn, ed.; B&W/C; 1.85:1; 195 min.

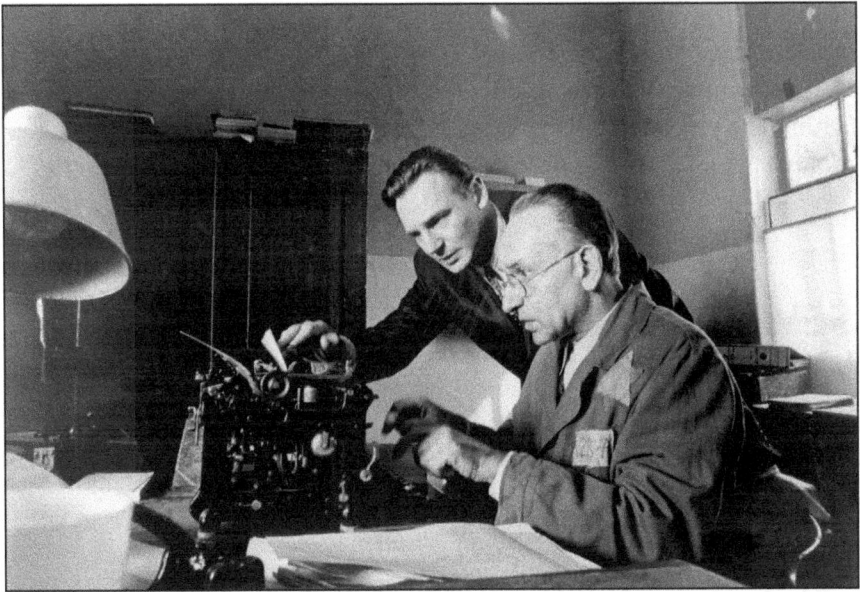

A RAY OF HOPE: Oskar Schindler (Liam Neeson), Emile Schindler (Caoline Goodall), and Itzhak Stern (Ben Kingsley) develop a plan to save Jewish lives by creating 'the list.'

CAST:

Liam Neeson (*Oskar Schindler*); Ben Kingsley (*Itzhak Stern*); Ralph Fiennes (*Amon Goeth*); Caroline Goodall (*Emile*); Jonathan Sagall

(*Poldek Pfefferberg*); Embeth Davidtz (*Helen Hirsch*); Shmuel Levy (*Chilowicz*).

Rating: **** 1/2

Initially hoping to increase his wealth, Schindler bribes Nazi officials to have Jews from Krakow's ghetto work in his factory, with a Jewish businessman/black marketeer as chief assistant. A brutal roundup of Jews, which Schindler witnesses firsthand, causes him to arc and become a champion of the oppressed. He fakes a friendship with a Nazi officer to rescue captives on his "list." The film has an abundance of riches, from subtle acting to vivid period re-creation to the work's overall sincerity. Keneally's 1982 book is *not* a historical document but a novel. The film further fictionalizes material to present the ongoing Steven Spielberg narrative: a man in a hat— who cannot relate on a mature level to women owing to his fear of raising children—becomes a whole human, a mensch, by rescuing the children of diverse women from monsters. Shot in black and white to capture the look of a documentary, the film uses color for the red dress of a doomed child. Brilliant in many regards. If only we came away with a stronger sense of Schindler's personality—what existed inside him that would allow a key moment to so affect him—this movie might well have gone to the limit.

SEVEN BEAUTIES (1975)

CREDITS:
Medusa/Cinema 5; Lina Wertmuller, dir.; Wertmuller, scr.; Wertmuller, Arrigo Colombo, pro.; Enzo Jannacci, mus.; Tonino Delli Colli, cin.; Franco Fraticelli, ed.; C; 1.66:1; 115 min.

CAST:
Giancarlo Giannini (*Pasqualino Frafuso*); Fernando Rey (*Pedro*); Shirley Stoler (*Prison Camp Commandant*); Elena Fiore (*Concettina*); Piero Di Iorio (*Francesco*).

Rating: ****

The title is ironic: Pasqualino has seven of the ugliest women in all of Italy for his sisters. He will do more or less anything to get away from them, whether it happens to be committing murder, going to jail, hiding in an insane asylum, or, finally, volunteering to fight for the Axis. When he deserts and is caught by the Germans, he is sent to a concentration camp where the commandant (Stoler) is derived from the actual Ilsa of the SS. A decidedly unpleasant film in which the communist Wertmuller offers her vision of the extent to which a middle-class man will degrade himself to survive. Not for the faint of heart. Nominated for five Oscars, including Best Foreign Language Film, but won none, perhaps because, artistry aside, this may be the most pessimistic film ever made.

SHOAH (1985)

CREDITS:
Historia/New Yorker Films; Claude Lanzmann, dir.; Lanzmann, scr.; Dominique Chapuis, Jimmy Glasberg, Phil Gries, William Lubtchansky, cin.; Ziva Postec, Anna Ruiz, ed.; C; 1.37:1; 566 min.

CAST:
Simon Srebnik, Michael Podchlebnik, Motke Zaidl, Hanna Zaidl, Jan Piwonski, Itzhak Dugin, Richard Glazer, Paula Biren, Pana Pietyra, Pan Filipowicz, Abraham Bomba, Rudolf Vrba, Franz Schalling, Raul Hilberg (*Themselves*); Lanzmann (*Interviewer*).

Rating: *****

At a length of more than nine hours, this definitive study of the Holocaust doesn't include black-and-white footage, which gradually came to seem essential for any documentary on the subject. Instead, Lanzmann interviewed diverse people, ranging from camp survivors to Nazi interrogators and guards. The color imagery—which captures the natural beauty of the countryside surrounding ghostlike, dull-brown extermination areas—is the essence of this piece's genius: How can anyone gazing on these contemporary images while hearing voices from the past speak eloquently (and often calmly!) about the evil that occurred there comprehend that "humans" did such things? The unthinkability of it, set against open admissions, renders this far more immediate than old, overly familiar newsreels. The verbal and visual elements, both presented realistically, become foils that produce a surrealistic impact. Sometimes criticized for failing to mention that there were many Poles who hid, and in other ways helped, their country's Jews.

SHOP ON HIGH STREET, THE (1965)

CREDITS:
Filmove Studio/Filmoteka; Ján Kadár, Elmar Klos, dir.; Kadár, Klos, Ladislav Grossman, scr.; Jordan Balurov, Milos Broz, Jaromír Lukás, pro.; Zdenek Liska, mus.; Vladimír Novotný, cin.; Diana Heringova, Jaromír Janácek, ed.; B&W; 1.37:1; 128 min.

CAST:
Ida Kaminska (*Rozalia Lautmannová*); Jozef Kroner (*Antonin Brtko*); Hana Slivková (*Evelyna*); Martin Hollý (*Imro*); Frantisek Zvarík (*Kolkocký*); Mikulas Ladizinsky (*Marian*).

Rating: *****

In 1942, a small Czech town deals with an "Aryanization" program as Jews lose control of stores and businesses. Antonin, a lazy "Arisator," assumes control of a tailor shop belonging to an elderly widow who mistakes him for a new employee. As Nazis grow ever less tolerant, this fellow arcs, drawn to her innate goodness. Without fully realizing it, he becomes her protector, committing to something other than himself for the first time in his life. An odd-couple tragedy, not without a sly, subtle sense of humor, rendered in the simple, vivid, poignant black-and-white imagery that distinguished the Czech New Wave. Kaminska received a Best Actor Oscar nomination for her world-class performance. The movie won the Oscar for Best Foreign Language Film. The definitive screen treatment of the Jewish removal program known as the pogrom. Many prints are retitled *The Shop on Main Street*.

SON OF SAUL, aka *SAUL FRIA* (2015)

CREDITS:
Laokoon/Hungarian National Fil;m; Laszlo Nemes, aka Nemes Lsazlo, dir.; Nemes, Clara Royer, scr.; Gabor Rajna, Gabor Sipos, prods.; Laszlo Melis, mus.; Matyas Erdely, cin.; Matthieu Taponier, ed.; 107 min.; C; 1/37;1.

CAST:
Geza Rohrig (*Saul Auslander*); Levente Molnar (*Abraham Warszawski*); Urs Rechn (*Obeerkapo Biederman*); Todd Charmont *(Bearded Prisoner*); Jerzy Walczak (*Rabbi Frankel*; Gergo Farkas (*Saul's 'Son'*); Sandor Zeoter (*Dr. Nyiszli*).

Rating: **** ½

A doomed member (Rohrig) of those Auschwitz prisoners assigned to dispose of dead Hebrew bodies in the Crematorium steps away from fellow Sonderkommanda members busily planning to rebel and escape. Highly individualistic, he chooses to save his soul rather than his life by insuring that the body of one young prisoner, whom Saul has come to think of as a son, is properly buried with a rabbi present. To achieve a sense of immediacy rather than scripted drama, outdoor shooting was achieved with natural lighting, the camera always hand-held. The result: a tale that apparently takes place within Saul's tortured mind as we watch his subjective reaction to events. For total reality, dialogue is kept as minimalist as it would have been in such a harrowing situation. Rohrig was not an actor but a poet chosen owing to his physical rightness for the role. Holocaust survivor and Nobel prize-winner Eli Weisel commented before his passing that this was among the most effective of fictional movies on this subject. One complaint: How much more accessible this would have been for general audiences if if the prologue fully explained why and how specific Jewish men were assigned to the Sonderkommandos unit (their plight also the subject of *The Grey Zone*). The only Hungarian film to ever win both the Golden Globe and the Academy Award for Best Foreign Language Film.

SOPHIE'S CHOICE (1982)

CREDITS:

Incorporated Television Production; Alan J. Pakula, dir.; William Styron (novel), Pakula, scr.; Pakula, Keith Barish, pro.; Marvin Hamlisch, mus.; Néstor Almendros, cin.; Evan A. Lottman, ed.; C; 1.85:1; 157 min.

ACADEMY AWARD PERFORMANCE: Meryl Streep won one of her many Oscars for portraying the title character, a Christian woman interred in a concentration camp owing to her marriage to a Jewish man in *Sophie's Choice*.

CAST:

Meryl Streep (*Sophie*); Kevin Kline (*Nathan Landau*); Peter MacNicol (*Stingo*); Rita Karin (*Yetta*); Stephen D. Newman (*Landau*); Greta Turken (*Leslie*); Josh Mostel (*Morris*); Josef Sommer (*Narrator*).

Rating: ****

A young Southerner relocates to New York. His neighbors include a brilliant schizophrenic and a deeply depressed Polish woman who, though not Jewish, was imprisoned in a camp. Bit by bit, the would-be writer finds himself drawn into their delicately bizarre relationship. In time, he learns a terrible secret: under pressure from Nazis and desperate to save her son's life, Sophie surrendered her daughter to the SS. The material is potent; the film might have been truly great but only intermittently reaches such heights. A formidable producer, Pakula was at best a fair director, here unable to re-create the full intensity of the novel. Alternately lethargic and languorous. Marvin Hamlisch's unsubtle score smothers rather than supports Styron's 1979 storyline. Streep rightly won an Oscar for her brittle, convincing performance as an emotionally scarred person suffering from survivor guilt.

SORSTALANSAG, aka *FATELESS* (2005)

CREDITS:

Hungarian Motion Picture Ltd./Magic Media Inc.; Lajos Koltai, dir.; Imre Kertész (novel), scr.; Péter Barbalics, Andras Hamori, Ildiko Kemeny, pro.; Ennio Morricone, mus.; Gyula Pados, cin.; Hajnal Sellő, ed.; C; 2.35:1; 140 min.

CAST:

Marcell Nagy (*Köves Gyuri*); Béla Dóra (*Smoker*); Bálint Péntek (*Prettyboy*); Áron Dimény (*Citrom Bandi*); Péter Fancsikai (*Older Kollmann boy*).

Rating: **** 1/2

Nobel Prize winner Kertész's book combines novel and memoir, drawing on his childhood for the plot while liberally altering events for a sense of narrative organization. One of the most costly films ever shot in Hungary (the budget equal to $12 million USD) and the first Hungarian film in Panavision. Concentration camps at Auschwitz, Buchenwald, and Zeitz are among the hellholes where this youth is, one after the other, interned. Part of the power is that each is vividly established as a particular place rather than another generic Movieland camp. Is life a series of meaningless incidents that just happen, or is it, the bad as well as the good, part of a grander scheme? The boyish hero tries to decide for himself. Despite a necessary reliance on the character's inner self, the novel has been strikingly transformed into a visual experience. Star Daniel Craig appears in a cameo as a US sergeant.

SUNSHINE (1999)

CREDITS:
Alliance/Atlantis; István Szabó, dir.; Szabó, Israel Horovitz, scr.; Andras Hamori, Robert Lantos, pro.; Maurice Jarre, mus.; Lajos Koltai, cin.; Michel Arcand, ed.; Michel Arcand, Dominique Fortin, ed.; C/B&W; 1.85:1; 181 min.

CAST:
Ralph Fiennes (*Ignatz Sonnenschein/Adam Sors*); Rosemary Harris (*Valerie Sors*); Rachel Weisz (*Greta*); Deborah Kara Unger (*Maj. Kovács*); Jennifer Ehle (*V. Sonnenschein*).

Rating: **** 1/2

This remarkable epic begins before the turn of the century, covering more than sixty years in Europe as seen through the eyes of one family over three generations. An impressive balance is achieved here between portraying the social backdrop and eliciting the viewer's feelings for the people. In Hungary, family members must in succession deal with the old monarchy, fascism, and communism, eventually learning a hard truth: most political systems have their own reasons for prejudice against Jews. Fiennes effectively plays three equally flawed, equally sympathetic men. By situating the Holocaust sequences at midmovie, Szabó (best known for

Mephisto) offers a clear perspective that no other movie provides. Only flaw: some of the domestic scenes come across as more melodramatic than tragic.

TRIUMPH OF THE SPIRIT (1989)

CREDITS:
Metro-Goldwyn-Mayer; Robert M. Young, dir.; Zion Haen, Andrzej Krakowski, Laurence Heath, scr.; Shimon Arama, Sonja Karon, Arnold Kopelson, pro.; Cliff Eidelman, mus.; Curtis Clark, cin.; Norman Buckley, Arthur Coburn, ed.; C; 1.85:1; 120 min.

CAST:
Willem Dafoe (*Salamo Arouch*); Edward James Olmos (*Gypsy*); Robert Loggia (*Papa*); Wendy Gazelle (*Allegra*); Kelly Wolf (*Elena*); Costas Mandylor (*Avram*); Kario Salem (*Jackson*).

Rating: **** 1/2

This fact-based story about a Jewish Greek boxer held with his family in Auschwitz is harrowing to watch and haunting afterward. The athlete realizes other inmates work for the Nazis to earn extra food. His moral dilemma: Fight in the ring for the amusement of the vicious officers to keep his loved ones from starving or idealistically defy the evil power structure? On-location shooting in the dead of winter allows for an almost unbearable authenticity owing to Young's previous work in documentary filmmaking. Effectively shot in subdued colors, which makes the viewing experience feel more immediate than, say, the distancing B&W of *Schindler's List*. The implied theme is that our choices determine our character; the more monstrous the circumstances, the more significant each choice becomes. With more fully developed characters, this might've been among the all-time classics.

*

WALKING WITH THE ENEMY (2103)

Mark Schmidt, dir.; Kenny Golde, Richard Lasser, Jack Snyder, scrs.; Mark, Schaun, Brian Schmidt, many others, prods.; Eric L. Beason, Richard Nord, ed.; Dean Cundey, cin.; Tim Williams, mus.; Dean Cundey, cin.; Castel Film Romania/Liberty Studios; 124 min.; B&W/C; 2.35:1.

WHERE THERE'S HOPE, THERE'S LFE: Ben Kingsley as Itzhak Stern, the stalwart assistant to the title character in *Schindler's List*.

CAST:
Jonas Armstrong (*Elek Cohen*); Flora Spencer-Longhurst (*Rachel Schoen*); Jeffrey C. Hawkins *(Andras)*; Simon Kunz (*Greenberg);* Charles Hubbell (*Eichmann*); Charles De'Ath (*Krieger*); Richard Albrecht (*Rabbi Cohen*); Ben Kingsley (*Miklos Hortny).*

Rating: *** ½

In spring 1944, Regent Hortny attempts to free Hungary of its bond with Germany and forge a treaty with oncoming Soviets. At once, Hitler dispatches Eichmann to seize control, murdering Hungary's Jews more a priority than setting up defenses on the Eastern front. One youth, called 'Elek Cohen' here but based on the real-life "Schindler of Hungary" Pinchas Rosenbaum (1923-1980), dresses in an S.S. uniform as a means of freeing thousands on their way to the death camps. The film's greatest asset is Cundey's powerful visualization of ever-increasing horror among citizens, Jewish and Christian. While the actors do well enough under the circumstances, they are hampered by the worst dialogue to appear so far in a serious movie of the 21st century, ranging from floridly melodramatic to inanely flat. Bolstered by a realistic depiction of 'The Glass House,' that Swiss embassy in which many Jewish-Hungarians hid away.

THE ROUND-UP: Nazi thugs arrest and the interrogate innocent people in *Walking With the Enemy.*

AIR FORCE: In Howard Hawks' masterpiece, a hot shot maverick (John Garfield, with dog) is mentored by an old-timer (Harry Carey, Sr.) to set individualism aside and join 'the group'; that community of men make ready for take-off.

Wild Blue Yonder: Soldiers of the Sky

AIR FORCE (1943)

CREDITS:

Warner Bros.; Howard Hawks, dir.; Dudley Nichols, William Faulkner, Leah Baird, scr.; Hal B. Wallis, pro.; Franz Waxman, mus.; James Wong Howe, cin.; George Amy, ed.; B&W; 1.37:1; 124 min.

CAST:

John Ridgley (*Pilot*); Gig Young (*Co-Pilot*); Arthur Kennedy (*Bombardier*); Charles Drake (*Navigator*); Harry Carey (Sr.) (*Crew Chief*); Ward Bond (*Radio Operator*); George Tobias (*Assistant Crew Chief*); John Garfield (*Aerial Gunner*).

Rating: *****

On the morning of Sunday, December 7, 1941, the crew of the B-17D *Mary Ann* realizes, while in midair, that Pearl Harbor (their destination) has been demolished. The reactions of diverse men form the nexus of this understated epic about the role of flying fortresses in the war. The most ruggedly individualistic among them (Garfield) arcs from being a rebel/ loner to functioning as part of a larger community. Such sentiments, offered and taken at face value in 1943, caused such films to be scrutinized during the postwar McCarthy era of red-baiting for possible Communist intent. An ensemble approach (no actor receives star billing) adds to the emphasis on group effort, as does the identification of characters less by name than by professional function. Hawks's "invisible" style makes this perfectly crafted piece appear effortless. Not above some propagandistic meddling with the facts, notably a depiction of Japanese Americans sabotaging war materials in Hawaii, which did not happen.

ANGEL OF THE SKIES (2013)

CREDITS:

DS Films; Christopher-Lee dos Santos, dir.; dos Santos, scr.; Carmel Nayanah, pro.; Geo Höhn, mus.; Christopher Grant Harvey, cin.; Kgotso Pedi, ed.; C; 2.35:1; 98 min.

CAST:

Nicholas Van Der Bijl (*Capt. Earl Kirk*); Brad Backhouse (*Flight Officer Ed O'Donnel*); Andre Frauenstein (*Lt. Raymond Hawkins*); Ryan Dittmann (*Flight Sgt. McEvoy*).

Rating: ** 1/2

This South African–lensed indie, shot on a budget equal to $35,000 USD, provides a tribute to volunteers from that country who served in the RAF. The plot features incidents that recall scripts from the war years: their craft damaged during a mission, a flight crew bails out and tries to make their way back to Blitz-menaced England, each man coming to know himself better owing to the ordeal. But the characterizations don't offer enough depth and complexity to make this old approach work, nor do the actors salvage that situation. So-so CGI for the combat scenes. The more the viewer considers the budget limitations, the better this may seem.

CAPTAINS OF THE CLOUDS (1942)

CREDITS:

Warner Bros.; Michael Curtiz, dir.; Arthur T. Homan, Richard Macaulay, Norman Reilly Raine, Roland Gillett, scr.; Hal B. Wallis, William Cagney, pro.; Max Steiner, mus.; Wilfred M. Cline, cin.; George Amy, ed.; C; 1.37:1; 114 min.

CAST:

James Cagney (*Brian MacLean*); Brenda Marshall (*Emily Foster*); Dennis Morgan (*Johnny Dutton*); Alan Hale (*Tiny*); George Tobias (*Blimp*);

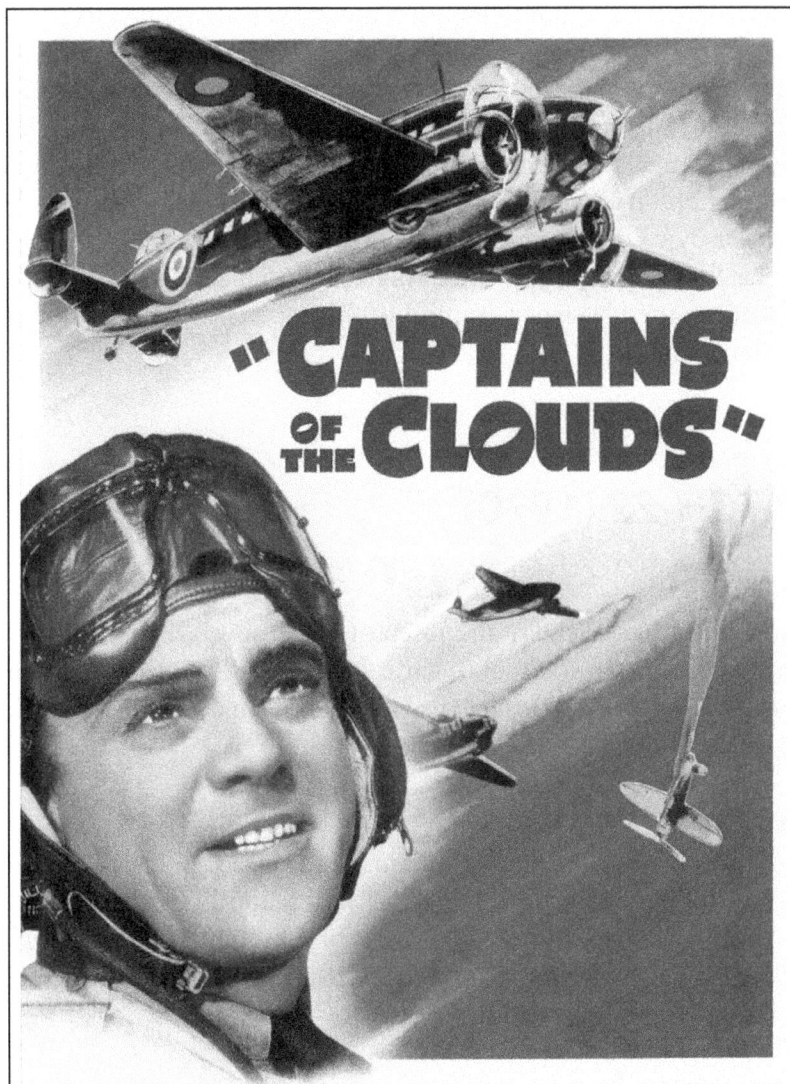

KNIGHTS OF THE SKY: Hollywood films (and their vivid poster art) glamorized the lives of fliers and their role in our Crusade in Europe.

Reginald Gardiner (*Harris*); Air Marshal W. A. Bishop (*Himself*).

Rating: **** 1/2

A tough-talking, skirt-chasing loner joins the Royal Canadian Air Force before the US officially enters the fray. In training, he competes with a milder man for the prettiest girl near the base. That plot was overfamiliar by the time this film was made. So why was it a box-office bonanza at the time, not to mention the aerial training flick everybody remembers today? Simple: it all works, from Cagney's boisterous yet lovable screen image to the superb supporting cast made up of the Warner stock company. Also excellent is the craftsmanship with which an underappreciated director brought the mix together. As the topping on the sundae, it employs color photography, never before used for such a project. Nice depiction of Canada's "bush pilots" making ready for war. Later sequences show the boys in skyborne action, all such flying sequences superbly staged. Typical of this type of film yet far superior to other examples.

CATCH-22 (1970)

CREDITS:
Paramount; Mike Nichols, dir.; Joseph Heller (novel), Buck Henry, scr.; John Calley, Martin Ransohoff, Clive Reed, pro.; Richard Strauss, mus. (from *Also sprach Zarathustra*); David Watkin, cin.; Sam O'Steen, ed.; C; 2.35:1; 122 min.

CAST:
Alan Arkin (*Yossarian*); Martin Balsam (*Col. Cathcart*); Richard Benjamin (*Maj. Danby*); Art Garfunkel (*Nately*); Jack Gilford (*Doc*); Buck Henry (*Col. Korn*); Bob Newhart (*Maj. Major*); Anthony Perkins (*Chaplain Tappman*); Paula Prentiss (*Nurse Duckett*); Martin Sheen (*Dobbs*); Jon Voight (*Milo Minderbinder*); Orson Welles (*Gen. Dreedle*).

Rating: ***

A SENSE OF THE ABSURD: 'Yossarian' (Alan Arkin) surrenders to the madness of 'the system' in Mike Nichols' film version of Joseph Heller's black comedy novel *Catch-22*.

Heller's 1961 novel became an underground favorite with hip antiwar readers of the time. With the birth of the New American Cinema at decade's end, such darkly comic visions could finally be mounted as commercial movies. Yossarian, a woebegone bombardier, is stuck in the title's lose-lose situation: every time a flyer comes close to reaching the number of missions required to go home, the limit is raised again. Nichols assembled a once-in-a-lifetime cast and did not cop out on the graphic violence, sex, or Heller's theme: war is not only hell but absurd. Still, his classical filmmaking approach feels wrong for such edgy material, especially compared to the improvisational approach Robert Altman simultaneously employed for *MASH*. Fine moments but, overall, bloated and bombastic.

CHAIN LIGHTNING (1950)

CREDITS:
Warner Bros.; Stuart Heisler, dir.; Lester Cole, aka J. Redmond Prior, Liam O'Brien, Vincent B. Evans, scr.; Anthony Veiller, pro.; David Buttolph, mus.; Ernest Haller, cin.; Thomas Reilly, ed.; B&W; 1.37:1; 94 min.

CAST:
Humphrey Bogart (*Col. Matt Brennan*); Eleanor Parker (*Joan Holloway*); Raymond Massey (*Leland Willis*); Richard Whorf (*Carl Troxell*); James Brown (*Hinkle*); Roy Roberts (*Hewitt*).

Rating: ** 1/2

On his twenty-fifth and final bombing mission, an American pilot spots the Nazis' first experiments with jet aircraft. Back home, he serves as test flyer for America's own embryonic jets, working with an overbearing raw-capitalist manufacturer as well as a gifted inventor. Dull and unengaging; one of the few clunkers among Bogie's WWII WB vehicles. One jet flight over the North Pole, depicted through the use of embarrassing special effects, seems laughable compared to the use of newsreel footage in earlier sequences. Of interest only as an American counterpart to England's far superior *Breaking (Through) the Sound Barrier* (1952).

COMMAND DECISION (1948)

CREDITS:
Metro-Goldwyn-Mayer; Sam Wood, dir.; William Winter Haines (play), George Froeschel, William R. Laidlaw, scr.; Sidney Franklin, pro.; Miklós Rózsa, mus.; Harold Rosson, cin.; Harold F. Kress, ed.; B&W; 1.37:1; 112 min.

CAST:
Clark Gable (*Brig. Gen. K. C. Dennis*); Walter Pidgeon (*Maj. Gen. Roland Kane*); Van Johnson (*Evans*); Brian Donlevy (*Gen. Gamet*); Charles Bickford (*Elmer Brockhurst*); John Hodiak (*Col. Martin*); Edward Arnold (*Malcolm*); Cameron Mitchell (*Goldberg*).

A NEW MATURITY: Films released following war's end, including *Command Decision*, played down propaganda to concentrate on complex relationships between differing personalities in conflict.

Rating: **** 1/2

A seasoned war correspondent (Bickford) is assigned to cover the inner workings of an English Air Force base where officers send flyers out to perform strategic bombings of Germany. Losses of crews and craft cause some civilians (including politicians) to wonder if such tactics are worth the price. Dennis, the no-nonsense general, lets stuffy senator Malcolm know why they must and will continue. Like many films produced during the years immediately after the war, this piece scales back the propaganda, jingoistic dialogue, and patriotic sentiment to focus on flawed men doing the best they can under inconceivable pressure. It also focuses on the psychological (this was the era when Freudianism entered popular filmmaking) and physical toll on those who served. Similar (and equal) to Fox's *Twelve O'Clock High*, released the same year, with a shared focus on decision-making processes rather than airborne adventure.

DAM BUSTERS, THE (1955)

CREDITS:
Associated British Picture Corp.; Michael Anderson, dir.; Paul Brickhill (book), Guy Gibson (book), R. C. Sherriff, scr.; Gordon Scott, W. A. Whittaker, pro.; Leighton Lucas, mus.; Erwin Hillier, cin.; Richard Best, ed.; B&W; 1.37:1; 124 min. (UK), 104 min. (US).

CAST:
Michael Redgrave (*Doc. B. N. Wallis*); Ursula Jeans (*Mrs. Wallis*); Richard Todd (*Wing Commander Guy Gibson*); Basil Sydney (*Arthur Harris*); Derek Farr (*Capt. Whitworth*).

Ratings: ***** (original UK cut)
**** 1/2(shortened US release print)

THEY FLY WHERE NO ONE EVER FLEW BEFORE... THEY FIGHT LIKE MEN FROM ANOTHER WORLD!

For the first time on the screen! The whole amazing story of the incredible "bombs that had to bounce" and the top-secret squadron that flew an impossible course to hurl them against Europe's toughest targets!

WARNER BROS. PRESENT

"THE DAM BUSTERS"

AMAZING AERIAL PHOTOGRAPHY! YOU'LL FLY AT BREAKNECK SPEEDS CLOSE ENOUGH TO THE EARTH TO TOUCH IT!

STARRING RICHARD TODD • MICHAEL REDGRAVE with URSULA JEANS · BASIL SYDNEY · Patrick Barr · Ernest Clark · Derek Farr Screenplay by R. C. SHERRIFF · Directed by MICHAEL ANDERSON · Presented by WARNER BROS.

The girl in the spotlight showed them the way!

ENGLAND'S GREATEST RAID: *The Dam Busters* allows British filmmakers to immortalize their greatest single moment in the air following The Blitz.

Spring 1942: eccentric genius Wallis devises a unique plan to shorten the war. Instead of detaching planes to bomb German industrial plants, go directly to the source: bomb the dams on the Ruhr river, knocking out the energy source and bringing production to a standstill. He must develop a new bomb—the skimmer—while dedicated wing commander Gibson trains men for low flying by night. Marvelous matter-of-fact tone taken toward a seminal historical mission. The movie relies on an unobtrusively impactful musical score rather than a high-style histrionic one and dares dramatize the least exciting aspects, including stubborn bureaucratic resistance to new ideas. Redgrave, fussy and funny, and Todd, eager for action, complement each other. The special effects were state of the art at the time.

DARK BLUE WORLD (2001)

CREDITS:
Eurimages/Portobello; Jan Sverák, dir.; Zdenek Sverák, scr.; Jan Sverák, Eric Abraham, pro.; Ondrej Soukup, mus.; Vladimír Smutný, cin.; Alois Fisárek, ed.; C; 2.35:1; 112 min.

CAST:
Ondrej Vetchý (*Frantisek Sláma*); Krystof Hádek (*Karel Vojtisek*); Tara Fitzgerald (*Susan Whitmore*); Charles Dance (*Bentley*); Oldrich Kaiser (*Machatý*); Linda Rybová (*Hanicka*).

Rating: ****

In 1939, following the occupation of Czechoslovakia, two pilots—teenager Karel and mentor Fran—escape to England and join the RAF. Things go well until both fall for the same woman. An unabashed romantic-triangle tearjerker, this will feel familiar to those who have seen *D-Day the Sixth of June*. The fine cast play their roles with such conviction it's impossible not to care about them. The film reaches its heights in its vivid imagery: grounded Spitfires awaiting the arrival of flyers in a fog-filled glen; Brit planes tackling Messerschmitts, as set against the big sky that lends the film its title. The glory days of WWII, depicted as a golden age, are alternated with scenes of the imprisonment of Czech heroes after the war.

They were arrested by invading Russians who feared that, having once fought for freedom, they might do so again against the Reds.

DIVE BOMBER (1941)

CREDITS:
Warner Bros.; Michael Curtiz, dir.; Frank Wead, Robert Buckner, scr.; Robert Lord, pro.; Max Steiner, mus.; Bert Glennon, Winton C. Hoch, cin.; George Amy, ed.; C; 1.37:1; 133 min.

CAST:
Errol Flynn (*Lt. Doug S. Lee*); Fred MacMurray (*Lt. Cmdr. Joe Blake*); Ralph Bellamy (*Lance Rogers*); Alexis Smith (*Linda Fisher*); Robert Armstrong (*Art Lyons*); Regis Toomey (*Tim Griffin*); Allen Jenkins (*Lucky*).

Rating: ****

As the Blitz rages over England, American flight surgeon Lee tries to convince skeptical squadron leader Blake that a scientific approach might solve the problem of pilot blackout during descents from high altitudes. One of the few films to focus less on men of action than on dedicated fellows serving behind the scenes. Excellent use of color (San Diego Naval Base) adds to the impact. The many long, slow takes of various aircraft in flight—too familiar today but impressive back then—should be understood as necessary at the time: a Frank "Spig" Wead script always meant accuracy in an aviation film. Long, burdened by an underdeveloped love triangle and overplayed lowbrow comedy relief. Intriguing: a notably casual attitude toward divorce for a 1940s film.

FIGHTER SQUADRON (1948)

CREDITS:
Warner Bros.; Raoul Walsh, dir.; Seton I. Miller, Martin Rackin, scr.; Miller, pro.; Max Steiner, mus.; Wilfred M. Cline, Sidney Hickox, cin.; Christian Nyby, ed.; C; 1.37:1; 96 min.

CAST:

Edmond O'Brien (*Maj. Ed Hardin*); Robert Stack (*Capt. Stu Hamilton*); John Rodney (*Col. Brickley*); Tom D'Andrea (*Dolan*); Henry Hull (*Gen. McCready*); Walter Reed (*Duke*): Sheppard Strudwick (*Gen. Gilbert*).

Rating: *** 1/2

During 1943–1944, American fighter pilots in London accompany bombers on missions over Berlin. For once, no romantic triangle; lone-wolf commander Hardin dissuades best pal Hamilton, believing that single men focus more on the assignment. Action sequences consist of the first newsreel footage shot in color, a novelty in 1948. Walsh's winning way with straightforward tales of men in war carries this, despite paper-thin characters and an insipid comedic subplot about compulsive womanizer Dolan. All the expected elements—-from late-night crap games to skirt chasing—-are broadly played. Interesting aspect: conflict between a conservative general (Strudwick), who believes men should take minimal risks and win the war slowly, and another (Hull) who approves of wild hotshots who get quicker results.

FLIGHT COMMAND (1940)

CREDITS:

Metro-Goldwyn-Mayer; Frank Borzage, dir.; John Sutherland, Wells Root, Comm. Harvey S. Haislip, scr.; Borzage, J. Walter Ruben, pro.; Franz Waxman, mus.; Harold Rosson, cin.; Robert J. Kern, ed.; B&W; 1.37:1; 116 min.

CAST:

Robert Taylor (*Alan Drake*); Ruth Hussey (*Lorna Gary*); Walter Pidgeon (*Squadron Cmdr. Gary*); Paul Kelly (*Rhodes*); Shepperd Strudwick (*Banning*); Red Skelton (*Mugger*).

Rating: **

A Pensacola cadet, overjoyed to learn he's been requested for the Navy Hellcats, is let down when he discovers they don't want him. He pursues the attractive older wife of his commanding officer as "a friend," unaware she's falling in love. Tedious pace, barely salvaged by a few fine flying sequences. Taylor is stiff, Pidgeon underused. Skelton appears to have wandered in from another film as a clown-in-residence. More soapsuds than action. Script might have worked better as a programmer than an overproduced A item.

FLYING FORTRESS (1942)

CREDITS:
Warner Bros.; Walter Forde, dir.; Edward Dryhurst, Gordon Wellesley, Brock Williams, scr.; Jack Beaver, mus.; Basil Emmott, cin.; Terence Fisher, dir.; B&W; 1.37:1; 68 min.

CAST:
Richard Greene (*James Spence Jr.*); Carla Lehmann (*Sydney Kelly*); Betty Stockfeld (*Debbie*); Donald Stewart (*Sky*); Bail Radford (*Capt. Wilkinson*); Sydney King (*Squeak*).

Rating: *

In 1938, Boeing initiated work on the B-17, a four-engine "heavy" bomber for daylight strategic flights. As the RAF did not yet have such planes, English pilots flew the Flying Fortress on early missions. Airborne imagery provides the only reason to watch this stinker, rushed into production without a decent script. The plot, involving a handsome hero, a regular girl, and an aristocratic lady, is worthless. An impressive level of professionalism usually on display even in lesser films from this studio is missing.

FLYING LEATHERNECKS (1951)

CREDITS:
RKO; Nicholas Ray, dir.; James Edward Grant, Beirne Lay, Jr., Kenneth Gamet, scr.; Edmund Grainger, pro.; Roy Webb, mus.; William E. Snyder, cin.; Sherman Todd, ed.; C; 1.37:1; 102 min.

CAST:
John Wayne (*Maj. Daniel Xavier Kirby*); Robert Ryan (*Capt. Carl Griffin*); Don Taylor (*Lt. Vern "Cowboy" Blithe*); Janis Carter (*Joan Kirby*); Jay C. Flippen (*MSgt. Clancy*).

Rating: ***

In 1942, as the battle for Guadalcanal rages on, US flyers realize their contribution may well make the difference between victory and defeat. New commander Kirby is strict, so the men prefer easygoing Griffin. It's the unpleasant fellow who has the outfit's best interests at heart, wanting to toughen them up so they'll survive. Wayne's characterization is a rehash of his *Sands of Iwo Jima* sergeant. None of Ray's usual directorial flourishes are on view. Best element: color newsreel footage edited in; some of it is actually from Korean War missions. Wayne's character is based on an actual hero, John L. Smith (1914–1972), who won the Medal of Honor for his "Cactus Air Force" (VMF-223) exploits.

FORTRESS (2012)

CREDITS:
Bayou Pictures; Mike Phillips, dir.; Adam Klein, scr.; Jerry Buteyn, Jason McKinley, Julian Moss, Brian Thompson, pro.; Christopher Ward, mus.; Jason Newfield, cin.; Paul Kavadias, ed.; C; 2.35:1; 93 min.

CAST:
Bug Hall (*Michael*); Donnie Jeffcoat (*Wally*); Sean McGowan (*Archie*); Chris Owen (*Burt*); Edward Finlay (*Philly*); Manu Intiraymi (*Charlie*); John Laughlin (*Base Commander*).

Rating: *

A Boeing B-17 Flying Fortress, the *Lucky Lass*, departs from Africa on a mission over Italy. An all-Irish veteran crew, sullen over the deaths of team members, is standoffish toward fresh replacements. The action in the air is sub-state-of-the-art CGI, affordable for the indie filmmakers behind this *Memphis Belle* wannabe. The unknown actors do give each sequence everything they've got. Might have been more successful if, instead of drama that occasionally incites laughs, they'd aimed for an *Airplane!*–type spoof.

GUY NAMED JOE, A (1943)

CREDITS:
Metro-Goldwyn-Mayer; Victor Fleming, dir.; Chandler Sprague, David Boehm, Frederick Hazlitt Brennan, Dalton Trumbo, scr.; Everett Riskin, pro.; Herbert Stothart, Alberto Colombo, mus.; George J. Folsey, Karl Freund, cin.; Frank Sullivan, ed.; B&W; 1.37:1; 120 min.

CAST:
Spencer Tracy (*Pete Sandidge*); Irene Dunne (*Dorinda*); Van Johnson (*Ted Randall*); Ward Bond (*Al*); James Gleason (*Nails*); Lionel Barrymore (*Sky Commander*); Barry Nelson (*Rumney*); Esther Williams (*Ellen*).

Rating: ****

None of the guys on view is named Joe; English children refer to any American by that nickname. One such regular fella, hotshot pilot Pete, dies in aerial combat. He's "shipped" back to earth as a guardian angel to mentor his replacement, young officer Randall. Things get complicated when the youth falls for Amelia Earhart–type aviator Dorinda, the older man's former love interest. Appealingly hokey fantasy will delight all but the most cynical. Also depicts several ultrarealistic combat missions. Such sentiment could only work in the unique context of WWII, as Spielberg learned the hard way when he attempted to update it in *Always* (1989).

PHANTASMAGORIC PATRIOTISM: The ghost (Spencer Tracy) of a dedicated flyer mentors a youth (Van Johnson) on a mission through the medium of a woman (Irene Dunne) both love.

INTERNATIONAL SQUADRON (1941)

CREDITS:

Warner Bros.; Lothar Mendes, Lewis Seiler, dir.; Frank Wead (play), Kenneth Gamet, Barry Trivers, scr.; Jack L. Warner, pro.; William Lava, mus.; Ted D. McCord, James Van Trees, cin.; Frank Magee, ed.; B&W; 1.37:1; 85 min.

CAST:

Ronald Reagan (*Jimmy Grant*); Olympe Bradna (*Jeanette*); James Stephenson (*Wyatt*); William Lundigan (*Lt. Wilkins*); Joan Perry (*Connie*); Reginald Denny (*Wing Commander Severn*); Cliff Edwards (*Omaha*).

Rating: *** 1/2

Antifascist flyers from across the globe volunteer for the RAF. US citizens do so by traveling north to Canada and then crossing the Atlantic. Among them is first-rate pilot Grant, who needs to be taken down a peg by a no-

nonsense flight instructor and a dedicated-to-the-cause girl. Sequences dealing with flying are better than what happens on the ground in this routine, derivative drama from a play by former flyer Frank "Spig" Wead. Reagan, at his best playing stalwart heroes, is miscast as a James Cagney type. Warner rushed this into production via his B-movie unit so his studio would be the first to offer a film on the subject.

ISLAND IN THE SKY (1953)

CREDITS:
Warner Bros.; William A. Wellman, dir.; Ernest K. Gann (novel), scr.; John Wayne, Robert Fellows, pro.; Emil Newman, Hugo Friedhofer, mus.; Archie Stout, cin.; Ralph Dawson, ed.; B&W; 1.37:1; 109 min.

CAST:
John Wayne (*Capt. Dooley*); Lloyd Nolan (*Capt. Stutz*); Walter Abel (*Fuller*); James Arness (*McMullen*); Andy Devine (*Moon*); Harry Carey, Jr. (*Hunt*); Sean McClory (*Lovatt*); Fess Parker (*Co-Pilot*).

LAST HOPE: John Wayne (left) and his stranded crew wave to potential rescuers in *Island in the Sky*.

Rating: **** 1/2

Midway through the war, a Douglas C-47 Skytrain makes a forced landing in below-freezing, uncharted forests along the Quebec-Labrador border. Seasoned captain Dooley tries to keep his panicky crew alive without supplies. A considerable distance away, dedicated captain Stutz vows to rescue them despite inclement weather. Familiar with such operations, novelist and screenwriter Gann accurately presents every aspect of each person's responsibilities (Gann also wrote *The High and the Mighty* and *Fate Is the Hunter*). Few directors could have brought as much vitality to this tale as Wellman, whose excellent aviation films include the first-ever Best Picture Oscar winner, *Wings* (1927). Not a single stereotype among the characters, who are convincing as living, breathing human beings in a tight spot.

KAZE TACHINU, aka THE WIND RISES (2013)

CREDITS:
Hayo Miyazaki, dir.; Miyazaki, scr.; Toshio Suzuki, pro.; Takeshi Seyama, ed.; Atsushi Okui, cin.; J. Hiaishi, mus.; Studio Ghibli; 126 min; C; 1.85:1.

CAST (Voices Only):
Original Version:
Hideaki Anno (Jiro Horikoshi); Hidetoshi Nishijima (Honjo); Miori Takimoto (Naoko); Mansai Nomura (G.B. Caproni).

U.S. Release Print:
Joseph Gordon-Levitt (*Jiro*); John Krasinski (*Honjo*); Emily Blunt (*Nahoko*); Stanley Tucci (*Caproni*).

Rating: **** ½

For his final masterpiece before retiring, legendary Manga artist Miyazaki brought one of his Asian graphic novels to the screen. Here is an epic about a Japanese boy who yearns to be a pilot but cannot qualify owing to poor eyesight. Instead, he becomes an aeronautical engineer, designing the Zero fighter employed by his nation during the war. Miyazaki's film deftly illustrates its central irony in alternating soft pastel hues and harsh primal colors: the moral near-sightedness of a true artist who can see only the beauty of his creations, unawares or uncaring about its deadly consequences. *Kaze c*aptures the rapturous love of flying as fully as films on that subject by Walt Disney and Steven Spielberg. The lead character is based on two people, J.H.(1903-1982) and Tatsuo Hori (1904-1953), their lives re-imagined as a national epic that includes such key events as the Kanto earthquake (1923), economic downturns, and the deadly tuberculosis outbreak. Lyrical and melancholic.

MAP OF THE HUMAN HEART (1992)

CREDITS:
Australian Film/Les Films Ariane/Working Title; Vincent Ward, dir.; Ward, Louis Nowra, scr.; Ward, Tim Began, pro.; Gabriel Yared, mus.; Eduardo Serra, cin.; John Scott, Frans Vandenburg, ed.; C; 2.35:1; 109 min.

CAST:
Jason Scott Lee (*Avik*); Robert Joamie (*Young Avik*); Anne Parillaud (*Albertine*); Annie Galipeau (*Young Albertine*); Patrick Bergin (*Russell*); Clotilde Courau (*Rainee*); John Cusack (*The Mapmaker*); Jeanne Moreau (*Sister Banville*).

Rating: **** 1/2

Boy meets girl, boy gets girl, boy loses girl. A variation (and reversal) of that old Hollywood formula finds new life in this underappreciated epic of the heart, mind, soul, and body. Star-crossed lovers worthy of Shakespeare: Avik, a half-Anglo, half-Inuit boy, and Albertine, a half-Indian, half-French girl. They meet while young and then spend their lives trying to find each other again. On-screen imagery transitions from realistic depictions of the raging war surrounding them to metaphysical levels that recall Native American states of being. New Zealand–born filmmaker Ward presents his hapless hero, an ace flyer involved in the firebombing of Dresden, while serving aboard a Lancaster bomber. Diverse cultures, Québécois among them, are handled in a noncliChéd manner. Cusack plays a sympathetic listener through whom we grasp Avik's remarkable tale. A reversal at the end is to die for. Rating applies *solely* to the complete director's cut.

MATTER OF LIFE AND DEATH, A, aka STAIRWAY TO HEAVEN (1946)

CREDITS:
The Archers/Eagle-Lion; Michael Powell, Emeric Pressburger, dir.; Powell, Pressburger, scr.; Powell, Pressburger, pro.; Allan Gray, mus.; Jack Cardiff, cin.; Reginald Mills, ed.; C/B&W; 1.37:1; 104 min.

CAST:
David Niven (*Peter Carter*); Kim Hunter (*June*); Robert Coote (*Bob*); Kathleen Byron (*Angel*); Richard Attenborough (*English Pilot*); Bonar Colleano (*American Pilot*); Raymond Massey (*Farlan*); Abraham Sofaer (*The Judge*).

Rating: *****

The real world of courageous flyers and the women who love them is presented in garish color, the alternative domain of a death dream in somber black and white. This aesthetic is oppositional to *The Wizard of Oz* (1939), though here, too, is a fairytale (for adults) about physical flight that transcends all boundaries, becoming an allegory. RAF squadron leader Carter attempts to bring his burning Lancaster back to London. His crew has bailed out, but he can't: his parachute is ripped. He speaks over the radio with US volunteer June, who's acutely aware these are his final moments, lost in a twilight zone between the quick and the dead. "Nothing is stronger than love," this guardedly optimistic film insists, fantasy and reality combined in appealing ways no one previously imagined possible. Often cited as the greatest British film ever made.

MCHALE'S NAVY JOINS THE AIR FORCE (1965)

CREDITS:
Universal; Edward Montagne, dir.; William J. Lederer, John Fenton Murray, scr.; Montagne, pro.; Jerry Fielding, mus.; Lionel Lindon, cin.; Sam E. Waxman, ed.; C; 1.78:1; 90 min.

CAST:
Joe Flynn (*Capt. Wallace B. Binghamton*); Tim Conway (*Ensign Charles Parker*); Bob Hastings (*Lt. Elroy Carpenter*); Gary Vinson (*George Christopher*); Susan Silo ("*Smitty*" *Smith*).

Rating: * 1/2

This second spin-off of the hit TV series floundered at the box office. With star Ernest Borgnine off shooting an A picture (*Flight of the Phoenix*), the plot focuses on the second (Flynn) and third (Conway) leads. Mistaken identity has the latter forced to impersonate an ace pilot, drawing the rest of the gang into aerial action. With a threadbare script, this unambitious exploitation flick is elevated a notch whenever Conway, a gifted comic, provides sight gags.

MEMPHIS BELLE (1990)

CREDITS:
Enigma Prods./Warner Bros.; Michael Caton-Jones, dir.; Monte Merrick, scr.; David Puttnam, Catherine Wyler, pro.; George Fenton, mus.; David Watkin, cin.; Jim Clark, ed.; C/B&W; 1.66:1; 107 min.

CAST:
Matthew Modine (*Capt. Dennis Dearborn*); Eric Stoltz (*Sgt. Danny Daly*); D. B. Sweeney (*Lowenthal*); Billy Zane (*Kozlowski*); Sean Astin (*Rascal*); Harry Connick, Jr. (*Busby*); John Lithgow (*Lt. Col. Derringer*).

THE PLANE THAT BECAME A LEGEND: The Memphis Belle earned its reputation as a special aircraft with a one of a kind crew of heroes.

Rating: ****

May 1943: the crew of a Boeing B-17 Flying Fortress readies its beloved *Memphis Belle* for its twenty-fifth and final bombing mission. If the members survive, they'll head home—that's a very big "if"! No contemporary revisionism here. This film looks, feels, and even plays like a rehash of several similar movies made during the war years, only with a fresh-faced cast and state-of-the-art special effects for the spectacular action sequences. Also, a smart-ass tone that recalls *Top Gun* (1986). Speaking of that film, *Memphis Belle* might have benefited from a star with Tom Cruise–like charisma in the lead. Highly entertaining in the rat-a-tat-tat style of contemporary action-oriented movies. Unfortunately, that leaves little time for serious character development.

MISSION OF HONOR, aka *HURRICANE* (2018)

CREDITS:
Head Gear Films/Pixoloid; David Blair, dir.; Robert Ryan, Alastar Galbraith, scrs.; , prod.; Krystian Kozlowski, Matthew Whyte, prods.; Laura Rossi, mus.; Plotr Sliskowski, cin.; Sean Barton, ed.; C; 107 min.

CAST:
Iwan Rheon (*Donald Zumbach*); Milo Gibson (*John Kentowski*); Stefanie Martini (*Phyllis*   Raphael Desprez (*Favier*); Rosie Gray (*Georgina*); Emily Wyatt (*Kate*).

Rating: **

Refugees from countries conquered early-on by the Nazis pour into England, many of the young men volunteering for the R.A.F. Former flyers from Poland's brief-lived air force joined the 'Hurricane Squadron,' serving with great distinction. This belated film about their service duty is undercut by a script that fails to expand any of the main characters beyond a two-dimensional level, special effects that fail to live up to what today's audience expects, and fictionalized flirtations with Brit girls that dramatically ring as too conventional. The most intriguing element: hostility between the Polish 'guests' and their English 'hosts,' though some historians insist this is overplayed in the film. Those few surviving WWII aces insist that the sky battles, though exciting, are less than accurate.

MOSQUITO SQUADRON (1969)

CREDITS:
Oakmont Productions; Boris Sagal, dir.; Joyce Perry, Donald S. Sanford, scr.; Lewis J. Rachmil, pro.; Frank Cordell, mus.; Paul Beeson, cin.; John S. Smith, ed.; C; 1.66:1; 90 min.

CAST:
David McCallum (*Quint Munroe*); Suzanne Neve (*Beth Scott*); Charles Gray (*Air Commodore Hufford*); David Buck (*Scotty*).

Rating: *** 1/2

Following the apparent death of his best friend in an aerial raid, Mosquito pilot Munroe tries to comfort the man's widow, falling in love. But is it morally right to put her through the same trepidations twice? He's assigned to employ new "rolling bombs" and knock out an installation where Nazis create the superweapon. Sluggish and plodding for the first half, this minor movie perks up with a surprising but believable turnabout at its midpoint. The romance is reminiscent of the superior, earlier *D-Day the Sixth of June*. Suspenseful resolution, dimmed by too-obvious overuse of stock footage.

ONE OF OUR AIRCRAFT IS MISSING (1942)

CREDITS:
British National Films/The Archers; Michael Powell, Emeric Pressburger, dir.; Powell, Pressburger, scr.; Powell, Pressburger, John Corfield, pro.; Ronald Neame, cin.; David Lean, ed.; B&W; 1.37:1; 106 min., 102 min., 82 min.

CAST:
Godfrey Tearle (*Sir George Corbett*); Eric Portman (*Tom Earnshaw*); Hugh Williams (*Shelley*); Bernard Miles (*Geoff*); Hugh Burden (*Haggard*); Emrys Jones (*Ashley*); Pamela Brown (*Els Meertens*); Peter Ustinov (*Priest*).

Ratings: ***** (116 min. cut); **** 1/2 (102 min. cut); **** (82 min. cut)

Another British bombing crew sets out on one more mission, across the Zuiderzee to hit Nazis in the Netherlands. Their Vickers Wellington (nicknamed "Bertie") is hit and goes down. The legendary Powell and

Pressburger team sets aside their stylized approach to let this simple story of courage tell itself in the understated manner such heroes deserve. A tribute to Dutch indomitability, focusing on one bold woman more than willing to risk her life at the hands of Germans to get the boys home. Wonderfully absurd scenes—such as disguised Englishmen riding bicycles past a sports match—present little-known but factual aspects of wartime escape. Their sojourn with a lady (Googie Withers) who's smarter than she seems crystalizes the sophisticated, understated form of British stiff-upper-lip puckishness. Humor and suspense comingle with vivid character studies and a propagandistic theme that, compared to most wartime films, doesn't drown the piece in jingoistic speeches.

PILOT #5 (1943)

CREDITS:
Metro-Goldwyn-Mayer; George Sidney, dir.; David Hertz, Robert Hardy Andrews, scr.; B. P. Fineman, pro.; Lennie Hayton, Johnny Green, mus.; Paul Vogel, cin.; George White, Albert Akst, ed.; B&W; 1.37:1; 71 min.

CAST:
Franchot Tone (*George Collins*); Marsha Hunt (*Freddie Andrews*); Gene Kelly (*Vito Alessandro*); Van Johnson (*Everett*); Peter Lawford (*Brit Soldier*).

Rating: *** 1/2

On war-torn Java in March 1942, a Dutch officer must choose from among five pilots for a suicide mission. Once Collins volunteers, the officer asks the others to explain his devotion, which they do via flashbacks, *Citizen Kane* style. His peacetime problems included romantic difficulties, professional conflicts, and political corruption. Intriguing combination of 1930s populist-liberal message movies with rah-rah 1940s wartime propaganda. Notable: a protofeminist vision of a woman who is intelligent and has absolute integrity. The hero's redemption via sacrifice in combat concludes this economically shot project.

Q PLANES, aka CLOUDS OVER EUROPE (1939)

CREDITS:
Columbia; Tim Whelan, Arthur B. Woods, dir.; Brock Williams, Jack Whittingham, Arthur Wimperis, Ian Dalyrmple, scr.; Irving Asher, Alexander Korda, pro.; Harry Stradling, Sr., cin.; Hugh Stewart, ed.; B&W; 1.37:1; 82 min.

CAST:
Laurence Olivier (*Tony McVane*); Ralph Richardson (*Maj. Charles Hammond*); Valerie Hobson (*Kay*); Gus McNaughton (*The Butler*); George Curzon (*Jenkins*); Sandra Storme (*Daphne*); Hay Petrie (*Doorkeeper*); Ian Fleming (*Air Ministry Officer*).

Rating: ****

By 1938, everyone who was anyone in British intelligence, politics, or the military knew war with Germany was inevitable. As this tongue-in-cheek romantic adventure would have it, the hope was to bide time so a fleet of superplanes could be developed for England's eventual defense. One after another Q Plane disappears from sight while airborne. Two superagents—handsome hero McVane and bookworm Hammond—set out to learn what's going on. Olivier receives top billing, but the film belongs to Richardson, proving that the character role can be more fascinating than a conventional lead. Uproariously funny at times and yet suspenseful all the same. Fleming, who plays a small role (think "M" in the James Bond films), apparently was greatly influenced by this movie's tone when creating the 007 franchise.

RED TAILS (2012)

CREDITS:
20th Century Fox; Anthony Hemingway, dir.; John B. Holway (book), John Ridgley, Aaron McGruder, scr.; Charles Floyd Johnson, pro.;

RED TAILS: George Lucas prepared a tribute to the African-American flyers who made their flying force an icon of courage and effectiveness.

Terence Blanchard, mus.; John B. Aronson, cin.; Ben Burtt; ed.; C; 2.35:1; 125 min.

CAST:

Terrence Howard (*Col. A. J. Bullard*); Cuba Gooding, Jr. (*Maj. Emanuelle Stance*); Nate Parker (*Marty "Easy" Julian*); David Oyelowo ("*Lightning*" *Little*); Tristan Wilds ("*Junior" Gannon*); Ne-Yo ("*Smokey" Salem*); Bryan Cranston (*Col. Mortamus*).

Rating: *** 1/2

The Tuskegee Airmen, America's first unit of African American flyers, had been a pet project for Lucas since 1988. Officially listed as executive producer, he was deeply involved in producing, writing, and codirecting this labor of love. Not surprisingly, it's a Lucas film, having far more in common with *Star Wars* (the aerial battles recall those in that trilogy) than contemporary films that depict WWII with heightened realism. The characters are fictional; issues of racial prejudice are addressed but take a back seat to fun and action aimed at teen audiences. Critics complained that the film trivializes a great event. The story of the 332nd Fighter Group was told with more integrity (if on a smaller budget) in the 1995 HBO film *Tuskegee Airmen*.

633 SQUADRON (1964)

CREDITS:

Mirisch Corporation; Walter Grauman, dir.; Frederick E. Smith (novel), James Clavell, Howard Koch, scr.; Cecil F. Ford, pro.; Ron Goodwin, mus.; Edward Scaife, cin.; Bert Bates, ed.; C; 2.35:1; 102 min.

CAST:

Cliff Robertson (*Wing Cmdr. Roy Grant*); George Chakiris (*Lt. Erik Bergman*); Maria Perschy (*Hilde*); Harry Andrews (*Air Vice Marshal Davis*); Donald Houston (*Capt. Barrett*).

Rating: *** 1/2

Norwegian Resistance leader Bergman heads for England with information about a secret plant developing fuel for a new Nazi superrocket. This idealist befriends cynical RAF commander Grant, assigned to lead a Mosquito raid using "earthquake bombs" that can level the mountaintop factory. The pilot warms up when he meets his colleague's gorgeous sister Hilde. Nothing new here storywise, though the game cast gives it their best. The best element for WWII buffs is the aerial photography—Mosquitoes zipping through fjords and then up and over towering cliffs.

TASK FORCE (1949)

CREDITS:
Warner Bros; Delmer Daves, dir.; Daves, scr.; Jerry Wald, pro.; Franz Waxman, mus.; Robert Burks, Wilfred M. Cline, cin.; Alan Crosland, Jr., ed.; C/B&W; 1.37:1; 116 min.

CAST:
Gary Cooper (*Jonathan L. Scott*); Jane Wyatt (*Mary Morgan*); Wayne Morris (*McKinney*); Walter Brennan (*Pete*); Julie London (*Barbara*); Bruce Bennett (*McCluskey*); Jack Holt (*Reeves*).

Rating: ****

After WWI, aviation expanded from a minor element in combat to a potentially primary undertaking. One man senses that planes can be uniquely employed at sea and, over two decades, carries on a single-minded crusade to convince navy brass about the need for large-scale carriers. Stirring tale about what naval personnel refer to as "flattops." News footage rounds things out nicely, with Wyatt quietly effective as a wife who stands by her man. Most memorable: a depiction of carrier-launched planes attacking Okinawa and the *Missouri*'s integral role in that action.

THOUSAND PLANE RAID, THE (1969)

CREDITS:
Oakmont Prods./United Artists; Boris Sagal, dir.; Ralph Barker (novel), Donald S. Sanford, Robert Vincent Wright, scr.; Lewis J. Rachmil, pro.; Jimmie Haskell, mus.; William W. Spencer, cin.; Henry Batista, Jodie Copelan, ed.; C; 1.85:1; 93 min.

CAST:
Christopher George (*Col. Greg Brandon*); Laraine Stephens (*Gabrielle*); J. D. Cannon (*Gen. Palmer*); Gary Marshall (*Taffy Howard*); Michael Evans (*Group Commander*); Gavin Macleod (*Sgt. Kruger*).

Rating: **

A maverick colonel begs his superiors to let him forego the usual cover of night and pull off a massive daylight bombing. The patchwork-quilt script begs, borrows, and steals characters and plot elements from every previous WWII airborne movie. Battle sequences, though impressive, are lifted from earlier movies and colorized black-and-white stock footage. Another film the British detest for attributing English victories to American servicemen. The first thousand plane raid was not carried out by members of the 8th (US) Air Force in 1943 but by the RAF, attacking Cologne, Germany, in May 1942.

THUNDER BIRDS (1942)

CREDITS:
20th Century Fox; William A. Wellman, dir.; Lamarr Trotti, Darryl F. Zanuck, Laurence Stallings, scr.; Trotti, pro.; David Buttolph, mus.; Ernest Palmer, cin.; Walter Thompson, ed.; C; 1.37:1; 78 min.

CAST:
Gene Tierney (*Kay Saunders*); Preston Foster (*Steve Britt*); John Sutton (*Peter Stackhouse*); Jack Holt (*Col. MacDonald*); Dame May Whitty (*Lady Jane*); Richard Haydn (*Lockwood*).

Rating: *** 1/2

At an Arizona US Army Air Force base, roguish old-timer Britt competes with young, insecure would-be flyer Peter for the loveliest girl around. Another romantic triangle, the writing for this one no better or worse than most. This short, sweet film occasionally soars thanks to the elegant female star as well as Wellman's expertise at fashioning films about our airborne military. Color allows for miraculous moments above the clouds. Also impressive: a rich verisimilitude of the era, including swing music and dancing styles. Captures a time now steeped in nostalgia.

TWELVE O'CLOCK HIGH (1949)

CREDITS:
20th Century Fox; Henry King, dir.; Beirne Lay, Jr. (book), Sy Bartlett, scr.; Darryl F. Zanuck, pro.; Alfred Newman, mus.; Leon Shamroy, cin.; Barbara McLean, ed.; B&W; 1.37:1; 132 min.

CAST:
Gregory Peck (*Gen. Frank Savage*); Hugh Marlowe (*Lt. Col. Ben Gately*); Gary Merrill (*Col. Davenport*); Millard Mitchell (*Gen. Pritchard*); Dean Jagger (*Maj. Stovall*).

Rating: **** 1/2

In 1942, the undermanned American 918th group is assigned to experiment with the new concept of daylight precision bombing, which proves effective but takes a terrible toll. Even those who survive suffer from airborne-combat fatigue. When sympathetic commander Davenport is replaced by hard-edged Savage, the men rebel, not realizing he's under more mental stress than they are. Like other fine films from the years immediately following the war, this depicts leaders not as near-perfect heroes but conflicted and vulnerable humans. Producer Zanuck, determined to educate the public about the emotional as well as physical horrors of war, hired the team behind the 1948 book to write an authentic screenplay. The final raid over Germany, assembled from Allied and

WEIGHT OF COMMAND: No flyer has to deal with as many moral and political issues as the leader: Clark Gable in *Command Decision*, Gregory Peck in *Twelve O' Clock High*.

Luftwaffe combat footage, is stunning. Longish film might have benefited from more on-screen action. Peck is excellent, his character based on Col. Frank Armstrong (1902-1969).

VICTORY THROUGH AIR POWER (1943)

CREDITS:
Walt Disney Company/United Artists; James Algar, Clyde Geronimi, Jack Kinney, dir. (animation); H. C. Potter, dir. (live action); Alexander de Seversky (book), Perce Pearce, T. Hee, Vernon Stallings, William Cottrell, scr.; Walt Disney, pro.; Edward H. Plumb, Paul J. Smith, Oliver Wallace, mus.; Ray Rennahan, cin.; Jack Dennis, ed.; C; 1.37:1; 70 min.

CAST:
Alexander de Seversky (*Himself*); Art Baker (*Narrator*); Billy Mitchell (*Himself, archival footage*).

Rating: **** 1/2

ANIMATION WITH A MESSAGE: The Disney Studio focused its artistry on the war cause as a proponent of contemporary combat in the air with *Victory through Air Power.*

Uncle Walt, a devotee of flying, began work on a film about the history of aviation before America entered the war. Once we were "in," he reimagined the completed footage as the first half of a propaganda piece arguing in favor of ideas first articulated by Gen. Billy Mitchell, restated by Seversky: if the Allies were to win, they must move beyond employing airborne bombs to eliminate enemy tanks in favor of specialized targets. Such targets would include munitions plants and railroad centers, even though this would cause more civilian deaths. This film turned Roosevelt around on the issue, leading to modern airborne warfare. Dazzling if, in retrospect, hard to deal with (at least for some). Art director Richard Irvine created a specific look that recalls earlier Disney animation but, under the unique circumstances, adjusted the visuals for more adult tastes. As remarkable as it is controversial.

WAR LOVER, THE (1962)

CREDITS:
Columbia; Philip Leacock, dir.; John Hersey (novel), Howard Koch, scr.; Arthur Hornblow, Jr., pro.; Richard Addinsell, mus.; Robert Huke, cin.; Gordon Hales, ed.; B&W; 1.85:1; 105 min.

CAST:
Steve McQueen (*Capt. Buzz Rickson*); Robert Wagner (*Lt. Ed Bolland*); Shirley Anne Field (*Daphne Caldwell*); Gary Cockrell (*Marty Lynch*); Michael Crawford (*Sgt. Sailen*).

Rating: * 1/2

Hersey's rightly well-received 1959 novel allows readers to enter the mind of a flying ace who, somewhere along the line, turned into a cold-blooded killer. Koch's shallow screenplay provides no such insight. We watch an unpleasant character (McQueen, in a one-note performance) treat all around him shabbily. Wagner is lifeless as an agent-of-the-norm fellow flyer. Tedious direction by Leacock slows the proceedings to a snail's pace. Accurate planes and models.

WILD BLUE YONDER, THE (1951)

CREDITS:
Republic; Allan Dwan, dir.; Richard Tregaskis, scr.; John H. Auer, pro.; Victor Young, mus.; Reggie Lanning, cin.; Richard L. Van Enger, ed.; B&W; 1.37:1; 98 min.

CAST:
Wendell Corey (*Capt. Harold Calvert*); Vera Ralston (*Lt. Helen Landers*); Forrest Tucker (*Maj. West*); Phil Harris (*Hank*); Walter Brennan (*Maj. Gen. Wolfe*); William Ching (*Cranshaw*).

Rating: ***

During the early 1940s, one type of WWII film subgenre focused on certain military innovations and the men trained to use them. Here, the Boeing B-29 "Superfortress" (built to fly faster and higher than any previous bomber) belatedly receives such treatment. Perhaps the financially troubled Republic brass yanked out an old, as-yet-unfilmed script to have something to produce. Not bad, though Corey never clicked as a leading man. Vera Ralston (wife of studio boss Hebert Yates) leaves much to be desired. Dwan provides effective images of the B-29 (which dropped the A-bomb on Hiroshima) amid cloud-filled skies.

ANGERING OUR ALLIES: Christopher George, best known as the star of TV's *Rat Patrol* WWWII series, here portrays a flying ace in *The Thousand Plane Raid*; British viewers were aghast that Americans took credit for this and other key projects they had initiated to swiftly end the war.

This Is Your Life: Real/Reel Heroes

ABOVE AND BEYOND (1951)

CREDITS:
Metro-Goldwyn-Mayer; Melvin Frank, Norman Panama, dir.; Frank, Panama, Beirne Lay, Jr., scr.; Frank, Panama, pro.; Hugo Friedhofer, mus.; Ray June, cin.; Cotton Warburton, ed.; B&W; 1.37:1; 122 min.

Robert Taylor (*Lt. Col. Paul W. Tibbets*); Eleanor Parker (*Lucey*); James Whitmore (*Maj. William Uanna*); Larry Keating (*Maj. Gen. Vernon C. Brent*); Larry Gates (*Parsons*).

Rating: **** 1/2

More than midway through the war, Lt. Col. Paul Tibbets (1915–2007) is recalled from aerial combat and offered a dubious distinction: fly a B-29 over Japan and drop the now-completed atomic bomb. Unable to confide to his wife, he suffers from time pressure and the moral consequences of his upcoming action as his happy marriage falls to pieces. Effectively understated. The final third offers a moment-by-moment re-creation of the August 1945 event, literally putting the viewer in the cockpit. Fine performances from Taylor (his best) and Parker (always underrated) add much. Thankfully, there is no sentimentalizing of Tibbets's tough, hard personality. At the time of its release, the film reaffirmed the necessity of America's development of the superweapon for concerned Cold War audiences.

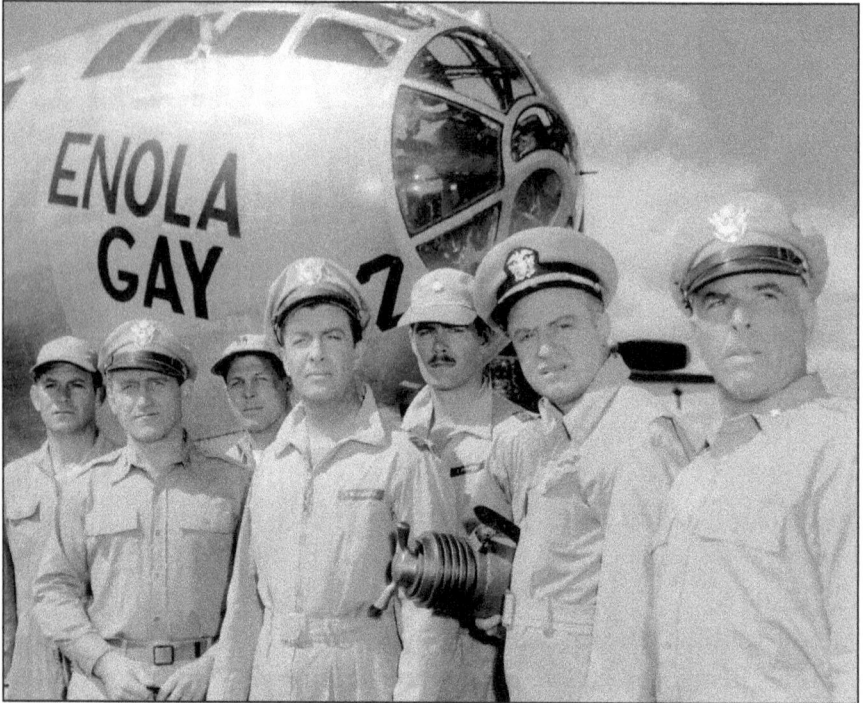

THE MAN AND THE MISSION THAT CHANGED THE WORLD: Robert Taylor (fourth from left) as Paul Tibbets in *Above and Beyond*.

AS FAR AS MY FEET WILL CARRY ME (2001)

CREDITS:

B & C Producktion/GmbH; Hardy Martins, dir.; Josef Martin Bauer (book), Martins, Bastian Clevé, Bernd Schwamm, scr.; Martins, Jimmy C. Gerum, pro.; Eduard Artemev, mus.; Pavel Lebeshev, cin.; Andreas Marschall, ed.; C; 2.35:1; 158 min.

CAST:

Bernhard Bettermann (*Clemens Forell*); Iris Böhm (*Kathrin*); Anatoliy Kotenyov (*Oberleutnant Kamenev*); Michael Mendl (*Dr. Stauffer*); Irina Pantaeva (*Irina*); Hans-Uwe Bauer (*Leibrecht*).

Rating: *** 1/2

Cornelius Rost (1919–1983), a German soldier sent in 1945 to a Siberian prison camp for war crimes he claimed not to have committed, insisted upon his return to Germany a decade later that he had escaped, traveling 14,000 kilometers across Asia to rejoin his family. Rost related his story, which skeptics believe was enhanced, to author Bauer, who retold the adventure in a 1955 novel. That led to a 1959 German TV miniseries and this would-be epic film. Almost all the large-scale set pieces— from a fierce battle with forest wolves to a happy meeting with native peoples—are convincing. But the essential drama does not click: not the hero's pursuit by an obsessed Soviet officer (a caricature of both Javert from *Les Mis* and Lt. Gerard from *The Fugitive*), and not the prologue and epilogue featuring an ever-vigilant, deeply religious, utterly generic family, which might've worked better in a faith-oriented TV movie. The overdone score—so much schmaltzy aural gravy—smothers an intended cinematic feast.

CARVE HER NAME WITH PRIDE (1958)

CREDITS:
Rank Films; Lewis Gilbert, dir.; R. J. Minney (biography), Gilbert, Vernon Harris, scr.; Daniel M. Angel, pro.; William Alwyn, mus.; John Wilcox, cin.; John Shirley, ed.; B&W; 1.66:7; 119 min.

CAST:
Virginia McKenna (*Violette Szabo*); Paul Scofield (*Tony Fraser*); Jack Warner (*Mr. Bushell*); Denise Grey (*Mrs. Bushell*); Alain Saury (*Etienne*); Sydney Tafler (*Potter*); Billie Whitelaw (*Winnie*).

Rating: **** 1/2

After meeting a handsome Frenchman in Blitz-devastated London, Violette (1921–1945) marries him, has his daughter, learns that he has been killed in combat, and is then recruited by the British spy network. She parachutes into occupied France, joining an underground clique in Rouen. Her first assignment is to help blow up a Nazi supply train. In addition to compelling storytelling, much of it staying close to the facts (though Szabo was a radiant brunette, not a blonde), the film is admirable for its willingness to depict the minute details that go into the planning and execution of any Partisan strike, not just the action. McKenna's performance is praiseworthy, to say the least.

CAST A GIANT SHADOW (1966)

CREDITS:
United Artists; Melville Shavelson, dir.; Shavelson, scr., Ted Berkman (book), Shavelson, John Wayne, Kirk Douglas, prod.; Elmer Bernstein, mus.; Aldo Tonti, cin.; Bert Bates, Gene Ruggiero, ed.; C/B&W; 2.35:1.; 146 min. (original release); 138 min. (shortened version).

CAST:
Kirk Douglas (*Col. David 'Mickey' Marcus*); Senta Berger (*Magda Simon*); Angie Dickinson (*Emma Marcus*); James Donald (*Maj. Safir*); Stathis Giallelis (*Ram*); Luther Adler (*Zion*); Topol (*Abou*); Frank Sinatra (*Vince Talmadge*); Yul Brynner (*Asher Gonen*); John Wayne (*The General*).

Rating: ** ½

Arguably Hollywood's original Christian-Zionist, The Duke convinced the man he considered 'the Jewish John Wayne,' Kirk Douglas, to star in a Batjac production about "the first true Israeli general since Joshua." Sadly, this lavish, lumbering biopic fails to capture the greatness of an American Jew who served with Patton in WWII and returned to N.Y. to practice law. Mickey Marcus (1901-1948) was then persuaded by Israel's emerging government to journey and join them in Canaan. There, he combined varied fighting forces into a single army. Such stars as Sinatra, Brynner, and Wayne appear in cameos hoping to bolster the box-office appeal. Adler plays a David Ben Gurion type. While production values are high, the script reduces a remarkable life to the most conventional of films. Most offensive is a totally fictional roman between M.M. and a too-beautiful-to-believed Kibbutz defender (Berger). A worthy opportunity squandered resulting in a mediocre action-romance.

CHETNIKS! aka THE FIGHTING GUERILLAS (1943)

CREDITS:
20th Century Fox; Louis King, dir.; Jack Andrews, Edward E. Paramore, Jr., scr.; Bryan Foy, Sol M. Wurtzel, pro.; Hugo (W.) Friedhofer, mus.; Glen MacWilliams, cin.; Alfred Day, ed.; B&W; 1.37:1; 73 min.

CAST:
Philip Dorn (*Gen. Draja Mihailovitch*); Anna Sten (*Lubitca*); Shepperd Strudwick (*Petrovic*); Virginia Gilmore (*Natalia*); Martin Kosleck (*Brockner*); Felix Basch (*Gen. von Bauer*).

Rating: ****

Fact-based story, a forerunner of the postwar docudrama style, about a Yugoslav commander (1893–1946) who dared confront Hitler's advancing troops. The usual clichés are avoided, including any type of contrived romance. It offers a generally honest (if tinged with war-era propaganda) account of Chetnik resistance against Axis forces, which, after the bombing of Belgrade on April 6, 1941, devastated the countryside. Though made by a major studio, it does not feel like a Hollywoodization. Mihailovitch (sometimes spelled Mihailović) is presented as a selfless idealist, helping explain why Fox pulled this popular item from distribution several years later when the general was tried for war crimes, found guilty, and executed.

CHURCHILL (2017)

CREDITS:
Jonathan Teplitzky, dir.; Alex von Tunzelmann, scr.; Claudia Bluemhuber, Nick Tausing, many others, prods.; Chris Gill, ed.; David Higgs, cin.; Lorne Balfe, mus.; Salon Pictures/ Tempo Prods.; C; 105 min.

CAST:
Brian Cox (*Churchill*); Miranda Richardson (*Clementine*); John Slattery (*Dwight D. Eisenhower*); Julian Wadham *(Montgomery);* Richard Durden (*Jan Smuts*); Ella Purnell (*Helen Garrett);* Danny Webb (*Alan Brooke*); James Purefoy (*King George VI).*

Rating: ★★★★

Less than a week before Operation Overlord (aka D-Day) is set to commence, the British Prime Minister surprises Eisenhower, Montgomery, even his King by raising doubts as to whether the risk (in terms of human lives) is worth the possible if far from clear victory. But are his concerns as altruistic as the great man believes, or might he be threatened that others are now assuming center-stage? A speculative drama about a moment in history. Ferociously criticized by some for offering a fictionalized chamber-drama about what may have transpired rather than a dramatized documentary. That attitude could be employed to dismiss the quasi-historical plays of Shakespeare. Judged objectively this is a strong work burdened by overly obvious expository dialogue. A warts and all approach to the title character (temperamental, self-pitying, prone to drink), as such a sobering alternative to the more heroic/iconic vision of him in *Darkest Hours.* The give and take between Churchill and his wife 'Clemmie' proves memorable, if highly influenced by modern feminist attitudes. Cox is powerful.

COUNTERFEIT TRAITOR, THE (1962)

CREDITS:
Perlsea/Paramount; George Seaton, dir.; Alexander Klein (book), Seaton, scr.; Seaton, William Perlberg, pro.; Alfred Newman, mus.; Jean Bourgoin, cin.; Alma Macrorie, ed.; C; 1.85:1; 140 min.

CAST:
William Holden (*Eric Erickson*); Lilli Palmer (*Frau Möllendorf*); Hugh Griffith (*Collins*); Carl Raddatz (*Holtz*); Ernst Schröder (*von Oldenburg*); Charles Regnier (*Kortner*).

Rating: ****

Erickson (1890–1983), an American of Swedish descent, had become well-to-do through oil deals. Allied agent Collins asks him to become a spy, his Aryan appearance allowing him to convince the Germans he's a diehard Nazi. Unable to reveal his secret, his anti-Nazi family becomes stressed. For the first time, the "good guys" are drawn in shades of gray: Erickson is threatened that his business will be destroyed if he refuses to comply. Slow to start, but fascinating details are well rendered by Seaton, a get-the-job-done director who tells the factual tale simply and directly. Might have been better titled *The Reluctant Spy* owing to its revelation of America's cynical use of blackmail on citizens. One memorable moment has him faking virulent anti-Semitism in front of a Jewish pal.

DARKEST HOUR (2017)

CREDITS:
Joe Wright, dir.; Anthony McCarten, scr.; McCarten, Tim Bevan, Eric Fellner, Dougla Urbanski, pros.; Valeria Bonelli, ed.; Bruno Delbonnel, cin.; Dario Marianelli, mus.; Perfect World Pictures; 125 min.; C/B&W; 1.85:1.

CAST:
Gary Oldman (*Winston Churchill*); Kristin Scott Thomas (*Clemmie*); Ben Mendelsohn (*King George VI*); Lily James (*Elizabeth Layton*); Ronald Pickup (*Neville Chamberlain*); Stephen Dilane (*Halifax*); Samuel West (*Anthony Eden*).

Rating: ****

In Spring, 1940, with most of England's army pinned down on the beaches of Normandy, a desperate British government all but begs the elderly warhorse Winston Churchill to accept the Prime Minister post. Gary Oldman deftly (in truth, brilliantly) embodies the popular image/mythic vision of 'Winnie' as larger than life charming curmudgeon, without ever digging under the surface to uncover anything more complex than his beliefs in patriotism and democracy. Though the film focuses on only one all-important issue--whether the U.K. ought to enter into "peace negotiations" (Chamberlain-like appeasement of Hitler) or assume a Thermopolae Pass-like "never surrender" stance--the entertainment element ranks high owing to a smart sense of humor not unlike Churchill's own. A failure to fully develop the central character's relationships with two highly intriguing women—his wife and a young secretary—assures that *D.H.* will never be considered a truly great film. It does rate as a good, solid one containing a great performance.

DEN 12. MANN (2017)

CREDITS:
Nordisk Film; Harold Zwat, dir.; Peter Skavia, scr.; Aage Aaberge, pro.; Christophe Beck, music; Geir Hartly Andreassen, cin.; Jens Christian Fodstad, ed.; C; 125 min.

CAST:
Thomas Gullestad (*Jan Baalsrud*); Jonathan Rhys Meyers (*Kurt Stage*); Marie Blokhus (*Gudrun*); Mads S. Pettersen (*Marius*); Vegar Hoel (*Sigurd*); Hakon Nielsen (*Reichelt*); Daniel Frikstad (*Salvesen*); Alexander Zwart (*Trovag*).

Rating: ****

When the Germans occupied Norway, patriot Jan Baalsrud (1917-1988) fled to England where he and fellow countrymen were trained as a special team that would return to their homeland by boat (disguised as civilian fisherman), then wreak havoc in the form of sabotage. When a Nazi craft fired on them, all died at sea excepting only Jan. He determined to make his way to neutral Switzerland, despite German patrols in hot pursuit, the craggy mountainous landscape, and inclement weather. After succeeding, Baalsrud always insisted that he was not in any way a hero; the term ought to rather be applied to those people of Norway who, risking their own lives, supported him step by step through the freezing snow that necessitated Baalsrud's cutting off his own frostbitten toes. Simply and effectively filmed tale of courage and persistence as to an undying dream of freedom.

DESERT FOX: THE STORY OF ROMMEL, THE (1951)

CREDITS:

20th Century Fox; Henry Hathaway, dir.; Desmond Young (biography), Nunnally Johnson, scr.; Nunnally Johnson, pro.; Daniele Amfitheatrof, mus.; Norbert Brodine, cin.; James B. Clark, ed.; B&W; 1.37:1; 88 min.

FROM VILLAIN TO HERO: In comparison to Erich von Stroheim's portrait of Field Marshal Rommel as a nasty Nazi in *Five Graves to Cairo*, James Mson re-imagined him in the postwar years as a sensitive anti-Hitler activist in *The Desert Fox*.

CAST:

James Mason (*Erwin Johannes E. Rommel*); Cedric Hardwicke (*Dr. Karl Strolin*); Jessica Tandy (*Lucie Marie*); Luther Adler (*Hitler*); Everett Sloane (*Burgdorf*); Leo G. Carroll (*von Rundstedt*); Richard Boone (*Aldinger*); George Macready (*Bayerlein*); Michael Rennie (*Narrator*).

Rating: *** 1/2

Supposed biopic of Field Marshal Rommel (1891–1944) begins with a well-mounted but bogus depiction of an Allied raid to "take out" the brilliant officer. Considering that this film about a truly remarkable personality runs less than ninety minutes, the lengthy teaser seems a waste of time. Likewise, the second half depicts the Hitler assassination attempt portrayed in *Valkyrie*, though Rommel had no involvement. We do not see Rommel's brilliant employment of the Afrika Corps, merely hinted at here. Sequences involving Rommel's family are well played by Mason and Tandy, and it's a hoot to watch Jewish actors Adler and Sloane caricaturing Nazis. Disappointing overall, though Mason is excellent.

ELSER, aka *13 MINUTES* (2015)

CREDITS:

Lucky Bird Pictures/Delphi; Oliver Hirschbiegel, dir.; Leonie- Claire and Fred Breinersdorfer, dir.; Boris Ausserer, Oliver Schundler, prod.; David Holmes, mus.; Judith Kaufmann, cin.; Alexander Dittner, ed.; C; 2.35:1; 114 min.

CAST:

Christian Friedel (*Georg Elser*); Katharina Schuttler *(Elsa);* Burghart KlauBner (*Arthur Nebe*); Johan von Bulow *(Muller);* Felix Eitner (*Eberle*); David Simerschied *(Schurr);* Rudiger Klink *(Erich);* Simon Licht (*SS Obergruppenfuhrer*).

Rating: ****

This ambitious, admirable biopic of Georg Elser (1903-1945) opens with the November, 1939 incident in which a low-key, self-serving, non-political carpenter and aspiring musician (Friedel) attempted to kill Hitler early-on by bombing the Munich beer-hall in which the Fuhrer was scheduled to speak. From that point on, the film effectively focuses the gradual build-up of frustration, bitterness, hunger, and anger that led the German people to accept a nightmare-scenario solution to their tragic post-World War I situation. Vivid, at times dazzling recreations of that unique moment in time do not compensate for an inability to help us fully grasp what made a seemingly ordinary, in truth unique man transform into a one-person Resistance movement. Worthwhile, to be sure, but never achieves the heights of this director's earlier *Downfall.*

FIRST OF THE FEW, aka *SPITFIRE* (1942)

CREDITS:
General Film Distribution/British Aviation Films; Leslie Howard, dir.; Henry C. James, Katherine Strueby, Miles Malleson, Anatole de Grunwald, scr.; Howard, George King, John Stafford, pro.; William Walton, mus.; Georges Périnal, scr.; Douglas Myers, ed.; 1.37:1; B&W; 118 min. (original cut), 90 min. (US print).

CAST:
Leslie Howard (*Reginald J. Mitchell*); David Niven (*Geoffrey Crisp*); Rosamund John (*Diana*); Roland Culver (*Bride*); Anne Firth (*Miss Harper*); David Horne (*Higgins*); J. H. Roberts (*McLean*).

Ratings: **** (original print)
*** 1/2 (US release)

Between battles with German planes, squadron leader Crisp tells Spitfire pilots the story of his best friend Reg (1895–1937), an aircraft designer who revolutionized flight in the early 1920s when he alone thought planes should be more closely modeled after birds. With the Battle of Britain, Mitchell threw himself into building a Spitfire (lightweight, high speed, easily maneuverable) at great cost to his health as he fought with

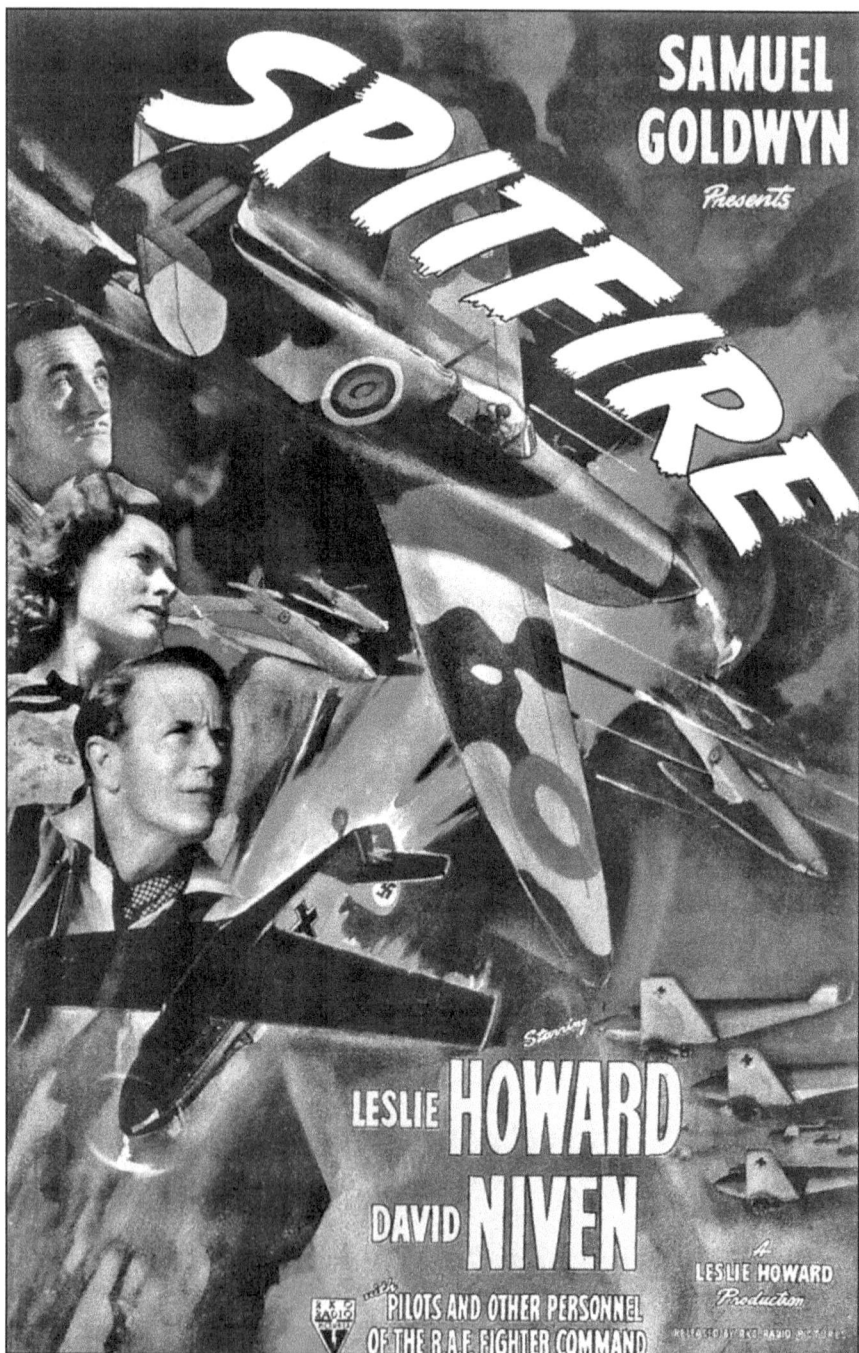

TRIBUTE TO AN INNOVATOR: Though the poster featured that remarkable plane in action, *Spitfire* focused on the gentle man who perfected this craft, R.J. Mitchell (Leslie Howard).

the brass, with their inside-the-box thinking regarding aircraft theory. Largely accurate, though Mitchell comes off as a plaster saint, forgivable considering the film's patriotic ambitions. Niven's skirt-chasing antics, added for comic relief, grow tiresome and repetitive. RAF members play themselves in the framing device, shot on-location at Ibsley field. Star/producer/director Howard died shortly after in a plane crash. Cut to ninety minutes for US release, retitled *Spitfire*.

FOUR JILLS IN A JEEP (1944)

CREDITS:
20th Century Fox; William A. Seiter, dir.; Carole Landis (story), Robert Ellis, Helen Logan, Fred Niblo, Jr., Froma Sand, Snag Werris, scr.; Irving Starr, pro.; J. Peverell Marley (as Peverell), cin.; Ray Curtiss, ed.; B&W; 1.37:1; 89 min.

CAST:
Kay Francis, Carole Landis, Martha Raye, Mitzi Mayfair, Jimmy Dorsey and His Orchestra, Betty Grable, Carmen Miranda, Alice Faye, George Jessel (*Themselves*); John Harvey (*Ted Warren*); Phil Silvers (*Eddie*); Dick Haymes (*Lt. Ryan*).

Rating: *** 1/2

Fox's craftsmanship at visualizing air-and-land action uplifts this slight, splashy, sentimental tribute to four medium-level Hollywood stars touring overseas. Based (loosely!) on Landis's (1919–1948) memoir. In the film, she meets and marries officer "Ted Warren" (in actuality Capt. Tom Wallace). Despite a contemporary fairytale aura, they were getting divorced when this was released. During the girls' extended stay in London, so little actually *happens* that "their story" becomes a framing device to showcase various performing acts, the Jimmy Dorsey orchestra included. Endearing moments appear when stars sing over the radio and the on-screen image cuts to GIs at the front, listening lovingly. Portrayed as giddy and easygoing, the deeply disturbed Landis took her own life four years later.

THE REAL DEAL, PART ONE: Movie/radio stars Kay Francis, Carole Landis, Martha Raye, and Mitzi Mayfair recreate their days of entertaining the troops in *Four Jills in a Jeep.*

GALLANT HOURS, THE (1960)

CREDITS:

United Artists; Robert Montgomery, dir.; Frank D. Gilroy, Beirne Lay, Jr., scr.; Montgomery, James Cagney, pro.; Roger Wagner, mus.; Joseph MacDonald, cin.; Fredrick Y. Smith, ed.; B&W; 1.66:1; 111 min.

CAST:

James Cagney (*Adm. Halsey*); Dennis Weaver (*Andy Lowe*); Ward Costello (*Capt. Black*); Vaughn Taylor (*Pulaski*); Richard Jaeckel (*Webb*); James Goto (*Adm. Yamamoto*); Art Gilmore, Robert Montgomery (*Narrators*).

Rating: ***

In 1942, "Bull" Halsey (1882–1959) achieves top command of US naval operations in the South Pacific. Immediately, he turns his attention to

A MAN OF DISTINCTION: James Cagney as Fleet Admiral William Frederick "Bull" Halsey, Jr. in *The Gallant Hours*.

Guadalcanal. He refuses to surrender, pull out, or cede victory, winning through the strategic use of sea support for the beleaguered marines. Well-intentioned attempt to create an intimate epic about the man and his chess-game-like intellectual duel with Yamamoto is hampered by a modest budget. No action scenes. Much heavenly choral music that drowns everything in bathos, and an incessant voice-over narration that never ceases introducing new characters. Cagney is in fine form, but the film's approach doesn't allow for the development of this historical figure.

GLENN MILLER STORY, THE (1953)

CREDITS:
Universal; Anthony Mann, dir.; Valentine Davies, Oscar Brodney, scr.; Aaron Rosenberg, pro.; William H. Daniels, cin.; Russell F. Schoengarth, ed.; C; 1.37:1; 115 min.

CAST:
James Stewart (*Glenn Miller*); June Allyson (*Helen Berger Miller*); Harry/ Henry Morgan (*Chummy MacGregor*); Charles Drake (*Don Haynes*); George Tobias (*Si Schribman*); Louis Armstrong, Gene Krupa, Frances Langford (*Themselves*).

Rating: ****

Sentimental, simplistic, utterly endearing biopic of the bandleader (1904– 1944) who created the musical landscape for the war years. Initial focus is on the formation of a group with a unique sound, achieved by combining a clarinet with four trombones in a pleasing, if in its time radical, way. Later scenes include the founding of the Army Air Force Band, which brought a cool, contemporary swing sound to what had been traditional military parades. A montage of American boys in action, accompanied by Miller's own hit parade, vividly communicates the degree to which he all but "scored" the war until a plane crash claimed his life.

GOD IS MY CO-PILOT (1945)

CREDITS:
Warner Bros.; Robert Florey, dir.; Robert Lee Scott, Jr. (book), William Faulkner, Abem Finkel, Peter Milne, scr.; Robert Buckner, pro.; Franz

Waxman, mus.; Sid Hickox, cin.; Folmer Blangsted, ed.; 1.37:1; B&W; 90 min.

CAST:
Dennis Morgan (*Col. Robert Lee Scott*); Dane Clark (*Johnny*); Raymond Massey (*Gen. Claire L. Chennault*); Alan Hale (*Big Mike*); Andrea King (*Catherine Scott*); John Ridgely (*Tex*).

Rating: ****

Odd, uneven, appealing biopic from the autobiography of Scott (1908–2006). His lifelong obsession with flying began during his childhood in Macon, GA. Morgan is energetic as the potential ace who lacks nothing except faith in a higher being, slowly learning to believe. Gung-ho types who, at age thirty-four, were considered too old for the Fighting Tigers fought a private war to win combat positions. A bit melodramatic, though the superb team of filmmakers had the craft to make this click. The dialogue is even more dated than in most films of the era. The dogfight sequences are among the best ever. Most intriguing: the hero's one-on-one duels with deadly "Tokyo Joe" (Richard Loo). Truman was integrating the armed forces at the time, so emphasis is placed on the strong roles of African American servicemen.

HACKSAW RIDGE (2016)

CREDITS:
Lionsgate/Cross Creek/Pandemonium; Mel Gibson, dir.; Robert Schenkkan, Andrew Knight, scr.; William D. Johnson, Paul Currie, Bruce Davey, pros.; Rupert Gregson-Williams, mus.; Simon Duggan, cin.; John Gilbert, ed.; 2.35:1; C; 139 min.

CAST:
Andrew Garfield (*Desmond Doss*); Hugo Weaving (*Tom Doss*); Rachel Griffiths (*Bertha*); Teresa Palmer (*Dorothy Schutte*); Luke Pegler (*Zane*); Ben Mingay (*Nolan*); Vince Vaughn (*Sgt. Howell*); Sam Worthington (*Capt. Glover*); Sean Lynch (*Popeye*).

Rating: ****

The fact-based story of Desmond Doss (1919-2006), a deeply committed Seventh Day Adventist who announced himself as a pacifist when war broke out but was determined to serve in a non-combatant role. At Okinawa, he became a hero-medic by rescuing one after another wounded member of the 77th Infantry Division, lowering each man from a besieged cliff. Garfield shines as the complex central character in an Oscar-nominated role; unfortunately, all others on view, including Desmond's parents (Weaving, Griffiths), are underdeveloped. Several (including Vaughn's tough sergeant) and Doss' all-American girlfriend (Palmer) are clichéd re-workings of overly familiar figures from films produced during the early 1940s. Gibson's staging of battle sequences offers a spectacular vision of men at war; his attempt to provide an inspirational movie-going experience proves successful enough on the simplistic storytelling level with which the director feels comfortable.

HANNAH'S WAR (1988)

CREDITS:
Golan-Globus Prods.; Menahem Golan, dir.; Golan, Stanley Mann, scr.; Golan, Yoram Globus, pro.; Dov Seltzer, mus.; Elemér Ragályi, cin.; Alain Jakubowicz, Dory Lubliner, ed.; C; 2.35:1; 148 min.

CAST:
Maruschka Detmers (*Hanna*); Ellen Burstyn (*Katalin*); Anthony Andrews (*McCormack*); Donald Pleasence (*Capt. Rosza*); David Warner (*Simon*); Vincent Riotta (*Yoel*); Ingrid Pitt (*Margit*).

Rating: *

Hannah Senesh (1921–1944), nicknamed the Jewish Joan of Arc, traveled from Palestine to Yugoslavia, freeing Jewish captives in occupied Hungary. Caught, she was tortured by Nazis and killed. This movie (far too free and easy with the facts) was produced by Golan-Globus, known for cheap junk movies. A great actor, Helena Bonham Carter, and a great director,

Peter Weir, had signed on to do the project. They dropped out once they realized that exploitation elements were to be added. A great opportunity missed.

HELL TO ETERNITY (1960)

CREDITS:
Allied Artists; Phil Karlson, dir.; Ted Sherdeman, Walter Roeber Schmidt, Gil Doud, scr.; Irving H. Levin, pro.; Leith Stevens, pro.; Burnett Guffey, cin.; Roy V. Livingston, George White, ed.; B&W; 1.85:1; 131 min.

CAST:
Jeffrey Hunter (*Guy Gabaldon*); David Janssen (*Bill*); Vic Damone (*Pete*); Patricia Owens (*Sheila Lincoln*); Richard Eyer (*Young Guy*); Miiko Taka (*Ester*); Michi Kobi (*Sono*); George Takei/Takai (*George*); Sessue Hayakawa (*Matsui*).

Rating: **** 1/2

Excellent epic about Guy Gabaldon (1926–2006), whose unique life experiences caused him to be nicknamed the Pied Piper of Saipan. Orphaned at an early age, young Guy was adopted by a Japanese family. When war broke out, he joined the marines, his bilingual abilities allowing him to act as an interpreter. Gabaldon saved American and Japanese lives by persuading Asians, military and civilian, to surrender. The underappreciated Hunter is excellent. Karlson, known for no-nonsense action, brings an authentic brutality to the battles, setting the pace for *Beach Red* and others to follow. No movie up to this point had portrayed the strategic approaches of American marines and their Japanese opponents with such understanding of the way elite fighting forces operate on the front lines. Gabaldon appears, in context, to be an Anglo American; he was in fact Latino.

HIDING PLACE, THE (1975)

CREDITS:

World Wide; James F. Collier, dir.; Corrie ten Boom (book), John Sherrill (book), Elizabeth Sherrill (book), Allan Sloane, Lawrence Holben, scr.; William F. Brown, Frank R. Jacobson, pro.; Tedd Smith, mus.; Michael Reed, cin.; Ann Chegwidden, ed.; C; 1.85:1; 150 min.

CAST:

Julie Harris (*Betsie ten Boom*); Jeannette Clift (*Corrie ten Boom*); Arthur O'Connell (*Papa*); Eileen Heckart (*Katje*); Robert Rietty (*Willem*); Pamela Sholto (*Tine*); Nigel Hawthorne (*Pastor*).

Rating: ****

Simple, sincere, slow-moving, ultimately winning drama about the ten Boom sisters, Betsie (1885–1944) and Corrie (1892–1983), Dutch women who worked in a watch shop until the Nazi invasion turned them into activists. The film's first half covers their creation of the title refuge for Jews; the second, their internment in a concentration camp. The film was produced by an indie company created by Billy Graham to make mainstream movies with Christian themes for a vast potential audience that did not respond to the New American Cinema of the 1970s. This movie marks the first on-screen depiction of what is now called the Judeo-Christian coalition, countering previous Christian anti-Semitism.

I WAS AN AMERICAN SPY (1951)

CREDITS:

Allied Artists; Lesley Selander, dir.; Claire Phillips (novel), Myron B. Goldsmith (magazine article), Sam(uel) Roeca, scr.; David Diamond, pro.; Edward J. Kay, mus.; Harry Neumann, cin.; Philip Cahn, ed.; B&W; 1.37:1; 85 min.

CAST:

Ann Dvorak (*Claire Phillips*); Gene Evans (*Cpl. John Boone*); Douglas Kennedy (*Sgt. John Phillips*); Richard Loo (*Col. Masamato*); Leon Lontoc

(*Pacio*); Philip Ahn (*Capt. Arito*).

Rating: *** 1/2

After witnessing her husband's murder during the death march following Corregidor's fall, a chanteuse vows revenge. Claire (1907–1960) joins the fight by establishing a high-style cabaret in Manila, pretending to be apolitical and hosting high-ranking Japanese officers. Over drinks, they gab about upcoming operations. Secret agent "Highpockets" transmits this info to the Allies. Derived from Phillips's *Manilla Espionage* (1947), but note that the book is a novel, not a memoir. Hampered by modest production values. Convincing; especially the deglamorized Dvorak. Phillips was the first woman awarded the Presidential Medal of Freedom.

I WAS MONTY'S DOUBLE (1958)

CREDITS:
Associated British Picture; John Guillermin, dir.; M. E. Clifton James (book), Bryan Forbes, scr.; Maxwell Setton, pro.; John Addison, mus.; Basil Emmott, cin.; Max Benedict, ed.; B&W; 1.85:1; 101 min.

CAST:
M. E. Clifton James (*Himself*); John Mills (*Maj. Harvey*); Cecil Parker (*Col. Logan*); Patrick Allen (*Mathers*); Patrick Holt (*Dawson*); Leslie Phillips (*Maj. Tennant*); Michael Hordern (*Governor of Gibraltar*); Marius Goring (*Nielson*).

Rating: *** 1/2

An unknown actor (James, 1898–1963) makes a surprise appearance at a London music hall where he impersonates Monty. In the audience sits a British agent who is inspired to pull off a ruse: encourage this man to play Monty on a grand scale, appearing in Gibraltar, misleading Nazis as to where D-Day will commence. Sequences dealing with the insecure fellow's training to enact one the most confident of officers—drawn from James's autobiography (1954)—are stirring. Forbes beefs up the action in this fictionalized, commercial version with a nonhistorical spectacle finale. Turning Mills into a prototype of James Bond, with endless womanizing, detracts from the believability.

IMITATION GAME, THE (2014)

CREDITS:
Black Bear/Bristol/Weinstein; Morten Tyldum, dir.; Graham Moore, scr.; Nora Grossman, Ido Ostrowsky, Teddy Schwarzman, pro.; Alexandre Desplat, mus.; Oscar Faura, cin.; William Goldenberg, ed.; C/B&W; 2.35:1; 114 min.

CAST:
Benedict Cumberbatch (*Alan Turing*); Keira Knightley (*Joan Clarke*); Matthew Goode (*Hugh Alexander*); Rory Kinnear (*Nock*); Allen Leech (*Cairncross*); Matthew Beard (*Hilton*); Charles Dance (*Denniston*).

Rating: *****

Adapted from Andrew Hodges's book *Alan Turing: The Enigma* (1983), this unique cinematic achievement draws on many genres (biopic, spy thriller, docudrama, social-message movie) without being limited to any particular one. Cutting across time and space, the film presents Turing (1912–1954) as a sad child in the 1930s who realizes he is homosexual. A WWII codebreaker, head of a crack team of crossword puzzle buffs, he breaks Germany's Enigma. During the 1950s, he becomes a forgotten hero whose teaching career is destroyed when he's prosecuted for being gay. The man Churchill said did more than any other single person to win the war, while inventing the computer, is superbly played by Cumberbatch. Knightly also fine as a straight woman who realizes she can love a gay man. The subtly powerful plea for gay rights is implied through the drama without didacticism. Smart, funny, highly entertaining.

OF COMMONORS AND KINGS: Benedict Cumberbatch as Alan Turing in *The Imitation Game*; Colin Firth as King George VI in *The King's Speech.*

INN OF THE SIXTH HAPPINESS, THE (1958)

CREDITS:

20th Century Fox; Mark Robson, dir.; Alan Burgess (book), Isobel Lennart, scr.; Buddy Adler, pro.; Malcolm Arnold, mus.; Freddie Young, cin.; Ernest Walter, ed.; C; 2.35:1; 158 min.

CAST:

Ingrid Bergman (*Gladys Aylward*); Curd Jürgens (*Capt. Lin Nan*); Robert Donat (*Mandarin of Yang Cheng*); Michael David (*Hok-A*); Ronald Squire (*Sir Francis*); Burt Kwouk (*Li*).

Rating: ****

Longish but never long-winded intimate epic about an English working-class woman (1902–1970) who hopes to dedicate her life to missionary work. When she's rejected, she travels alone to China, helping run a home for poverty-stricken people in a remote province. When the Japanese invade, she guides 100 orphans to safety over mountains and through enemy-held territory. Beautifully played by a nevertheless miscast Bergman. The movie contains admirably nonstereotypical portraits of Chinese people. Combat footage in the second half is brief but intense. Avoids hokyness.

JOHN RABE, aka CITY OF WAR (2009)

CREDITS:

Florian Gallenberger, dir.; Galleberger, scr.; Jan Mojto, Mischa Hoffman, many others, prod.; Hanjorg WeiBbrich, ed.; Jurgen Jurges, cin.; Annete Focks, Laurent Petigirard, mus.; Majestic Filmproduktion; C; 2.35:1; 134 min.

CAST:

Ulrich Tukur (*John Rabe*); Daniel Bruhl (*Dr. Georg Rosen*); Steve Buscemi (*Dr. Robert Wilson*); Anne Consigny (*Valerie Dupres);* Dagmar Manzel

(Dora Rabe); Jingchu Zhang *(Langshu);* Teruyuki Kagawa *(Prince Asaka Yashuhiko).*

Rating: *** ½

This ambitious German-French-Chinese coproduction relates the story of John Heinrich Detlef Rabe (1882-1950), a diehard Nazi party member who spent much of his adult life overseeing the construction of a factory in China. When the Japanese invaded Nanking on Dec. 12, 1937, he risked his life to escort the 200,000 workers who had become an extended family to safety. Gallenberger proves a more gifted director than screenwriter; the epic imagery impresses in a way the awkward story-telling does not. Many historians railed against the inclusion of a fictional Frenchwoman, 'Valerie Dupres,' in place of many actual heroic people who receive short shrift here. Intriguing to watch back to back with *City of Life and Death.* Not shown in Japanese theatres, despite an attempt to humanize one of the island nation's characters. From a book by Erwin Wickert.

KING'S SPEECH, THE (2010)

CREDITS:
See-Saw Films/Bedlam Prods.; Tom Hooper, dir.; David Seidler, scr.; Iain Canning, Emile Sherman, Gareth Unwin, pro.; Alexandre Desplat, mus.; Danny Cohen, cin.; Tariq Anwar, ed.; 1.78:1; C; 118 min.

CAST:
Colin Firth *(King George VI)*; Helena Bonham Carter *(Queen Elizabeth)*; Geoffrey Rush *(Lionel Logue)*; Derek Jacobi *(Archbishop Cosmo Lang)*; Calum Gittins *(Laurie Logue)*; Michael Gambon *(King George V)*; Guy Pearce *(King Edward VIII)*.

Rating: **** ½

As war clouds gather, the Duke of York cannot properly perform on radio owing to a pronounced stammer. His wife seeks out the services of a failed actor (Rush) who has taken up a new profession as speech therapist, if with an iconoclastic self-conceived approach. As the years pass, the king (Gambon) dies and Bertie's older brother abdicates for love of married American Mrs. Simpson. England's unexpected king realizes such therapy is more important than ever when Hitler refuses to withdraw from Poland and George VI must make the most important speech of his life: Announcing that Britain is once again at war. An intimate chamber drama between two fascinating if deeply flawed men in a unique relationship develops into an implied epic about a key moment in history. Worthy winner of the Oscars for Best Picture, Director, Writer and Actor (Firth) though the finest performances are by Rush as one of 'the little men' suddenly saddled with a huge responsibility and Bonham Carter as the proverbial great woman who quietly but powerfully stands behind a great man.

LION OF THE DESERT (1981)

CREDITS:
Falcon International; Moustapha Akkad, dir.; H. A. L. Craig, Paul Thompson, David Butler, scr.; Akkad, pro.; Maurice Jarre, mus.; Jack Hildyard, cin.; John Shirley, ed.; C; 2.35:1; 173 min.

CAST:
Anthony Quinn (*Omar Mukhtar*); Oliver Reed (*Gen. Rodolfo Graziani*); Irene Pappas (*Mabrouka*); Raf Vallone (*Col. Diodiece*); Rod Steiger (*Mussolini*); John Gielgud (*Sharif El Gariani*).

Rating: *** 1/2

M. Gaddafi poured money into this Libyan-based film (causing controversy in the West), shot by an Arabic filmmaker with cast and crew members from the US, UK, and Italy. In 1929, Omar Mukhtar (1858–1931) rallied the Bedouin tribes to stand against Italy's forces led by the cruel general Graziani, who considered the conquest of the desert a necessary first step toward world domination. Action sequences are large and well staged; the human drama is conventionally written with routine dialogue. The

ENEMIES TO THE END: The "rock" of Oliver Reed (left) smashes against "the hard place" of Anthony Quinn as desert warrior-activist Omar Mukhtar in *Lion of the Desert.*

casting of an aging Hollywood superstar in the lead proves effective while adding a commercial aspect, surprising for such a regional project. Major liability: Steiger's buffoonish Mussolini.

MACARTHUR (1977)

CREDITS:
Universal; Joseph Sargent, dir.; Hal Barwood, Matthew Robbins, scr.; Frank McCarthy, pro.; Jerry Goldsmith, mus.; Mario Tosi, cin.; George Jay Nicholson, ed.; C; 1.85:1; 130 min.

CAST:

Gregory Peck (*Gen. Douglas MacArthur*); Ivan Bonar (*Lt. Gen. Richard K. Sutherland*); Ward Costello (*Gen. George Marshall*); Nicolas Coster (Col. Huff); Marj Dusay (*Jean*); Ed Flanders (*Pres. Truman*).

Rating: *** 1/2

"Duty, Honor, Country!" Many men have said such words; Gen. MacArthur (1880–1964) lived by them. This biopic focuses on the period between 1942 and 1952, covering his success in retaking the South Pacific ("I will return!") and moving on to his problematic command in Korea, where he was eventually forced to stand down by Truman. Produced in large part owing to the success of *Patton*, though hardly in the same league. Peck, who might have made for a perfect Gen. George Marshall, is miscast in a role that begs for Charlton Heston. TV veteran Sargent shot this theatrical film as if it were intended for the small screen. Disappointing script boasts none of the perceptiveness that made *Patton* click. Routine.

MAX MANUS: MAN OF WAR (2008)

CREDITS:

B&T Films/Nordic Films; Joachim Rønning, Espen Sandberg, dir.; Thomas Nordseth-Tiller, scr.; Sveinung Golimo, John M. Jacobsen, pro.; Trond Bjerknes, mus.; Anders Refn, ed.; C; 2.35:1; 118 min.

CAST:

Aksel Henie (*Max*); Agnes Kittelsen (*Ida Lindebraekke*); Nicolai Cleve Broch (*Gram*); Ken Duken (*Fehmer*); Christian Rubeck (*Lauring*); Knut Joner (*Sønsteby*); Viktoria Winge (*Solveig*).

Rating: **** 1/2

This Norwegian epic presents the fact-based exploits of Manus (1914–1996), who represents for Norway what Audie Murphy does for America: the single greatest figure among those who fought. Here, the focus is on Partisan combat, though Manus was involved in the Winter War against the Soviets. He led a rebellion against Germany, surviving despite his notoriety and Hitler's fervent belief that Max was the Resistance leader most necessary to eliminate. The screenplay is listed as original; Manus's books served as references, along with other key historical writings. This is not a revisionist film that, like France's *Flamen and Citroen*, takes a long, hard look at past legends. Rather, it's a Norwegian equivalent of John Wayne's *The Alamo* (1960), which it recalls. A fitting flag-waving salute to the Oslo Gang.

NO MAN IS AN ISLAND (1962)

CREDITS:
Gold Cast Productions; Richard Goldstone, John Monks, Jr., dir.; Goldstone, Monks, scr.; Goldstone, Monks, pro.; Restie Umali, mus.; Carl Kayser, cin.; Basil Wrangell, ed.; C; 1.85:1; 114 min.

CAST:
Jeffrey Hunter (*George R. Tweed*); Marshall Thompson (*Jonn Sonnenberg*); Barbara Perez (*Jo Cruz*); Ronald Remy (*Chico Torres*); Paul Edwards, Jr. (*Turney*).

Rating: *** 1/2

During the Japanese occupation of Guam, sailor George R. Tweed (1902–1989) managed to avoid being taken prisoner. He waged a virtual one-man guerilla war, abetted by anti-Japanese natives. Intriguing screenplay dares to balance action with ideas as Tweed wonders if he was spared for some greater cause. Rough around the edges owing to a tight budget, resulting in a B-picture look. Hunter's performance has the same sincerity and strength he brought to so many WWII films. The material is unique enough to overcome any limitations in the production. "Tweed's Cave," his home for eighteen months, can still be visited on Guam today.

ODETTE (1950)

CREDITS:
British Lion/Lopert; Herbert Wilcox, dir.; Jerrard Tickell (book), Warren Chetham Strode, scr.; Wilcox, pro.; Anthony Collins, mus.; Mutz Greenbaum, aka Max Greene, cin.; Bill Lewthwaite, ed.; B&W; 1.37:1; 124 min. (UK), 105 min. (US).

CAST:
Anna Neagle (*Odette Sanson*); Trevor Howard (*Capt. Peter Churchill*); Marius Goring (*Henri*); Bernard Lee (*Jack*); Peter Ustinov (*Rabinovich*); Maurice Buckmaster (*Narrator*).

Rating: **** 1/2 (UK original print)
**** (US edited version)

Shortly after hostilities begin, a self-described "ordinary woman" (1912–1995) and French-born mother of three joins England's Special Operations Executive unit. By 1942, "codename: Lise" found herself in occupied France, working as an agent out of Cannes. The US version shows her involvements with nervous Jewish colleague Rabinovich and Mozart-loving German Henri. Wilcox chose a deliberately paced, matter-of-fact approach, avoiding the clichés of spy cinema. Precise location filming enhances the realism. Sequences involving her capture by the Gestapo and torture at Ravensbruck are harrowing without turning exploitive. One of those quietly dazzling works the English so aptly create. Though the credits list her name as "Sanson," some historical sources insist the proper spelling is "Sansom."

ONE THAT GOT AWAY, THE (1957)

CREDITS:
Rank Organization; Roy Ward Baker, dir.; Kendal Burt (book), James Leasor (book), Howard Clewes, scr.; Julian Wintle, pro.; Hubert Clifford, mus.; Eric Cross, cin.; Sidney Hayers, ed.; B&W; 1.66:1; 111 min. (UK), 106 min. (US).

CAST:
Hardy Krüger (*Franz von Werra*); Colin Gordon, Terence Alexander, Michael Goodliffe (*Interrogators*); Jack Gwillim, Andrew Faulds (*Grizedale Staff*); Alec McCowen (*Officer*).

Ratings: **** (UK print)
*** 1/2(US print)

During the Blitz, an *Oberleutnant* is shot down and sent to a camp. Franz von Werra (1914–1941) escaped, achieving fame as the only Nazi to do so. His eccentric attempts, many of them difficult to believe, are all fact-based. In addition to offering solid entertainment of 'The Great Escape' variety, this film proved significant in its time as the first British production to depict a Nazi positively, helping reopen communication between the two countries. Begrudging admiration for the man's bravery was bolstered by the knowledge that once back in Germany, he actively campaigned for better treatment of Allied POWs based on the humane conditions he himself experienced.

OUTSIDER, THE (1961)

CREDITS:
Universal; Delbert Mann, dir.; William Bradford Huie, Stewart Stern, scr.; Sy Bartlett, pro.; Leonard Rosenman, mus.; Joseph LaShelle, cin.; Marjorie Fowler, ed.; B&W; 1.66:1; 108 min.

Rating: **** 1/2

CAST:
Tony Curtis (*Ira Hamilton Hayes*); James Franciscus (*Pvt. James B. Sorenson*); Gregory Walcott (*Sgt. Kiley*); Bruce Bennett (*Gen. Bridges*); Vivian Nathan (*Nancy Hayes*).

This sturdy biopic faithfully relates the story of Hayes (1923–1955), from his youth on a destitute reservation to marine boot camp, to Iwo Jima (at midmovie), and finally to the shameless exploitation of his heroic stature, leading to an early death from alcoholism. The film is critical of our government's callous approach to those whose celebrity might be exploited, as well as America's widespread racism. It's fiercely defensive of the Corps as the single institution in which our country's code of individual worth, proven through action, applies. Also on view: the homoeroticism of the military experience, explicit in the deeply felt relationship between Hayes and buddy Sorensen. Minor complaints: the legendary battle appears too briefly for viewers to get a full, proper sense of it. Curtis is acceptable in a part Charles Bronson was born to play.

PASSWORD IS COURAGE, THE (1962)

CREDITS:
Metro-Goldwyn-Mayer; Andrew L. Stone, dir.; John Castle, aka Charles Coward (memoir), Stone, scr.; Andrew Stone and Virginia L. Stone, pro.; Virginia Stone, Christopher L. Stone, Derek New, Tommy Reilly, mus.; David Boulton, cin.; Noreen Ackland, ed.; B&W; 2.00:1; 116 min.

CAST:
Dirk Bogarde (*Sgt. Maj. Charles Coward*); Maria Perschy (*Irena*); Alfred Lynch (*Cpl. Bill Pope*); Nigel Stock (*Cole*); Reginald Beckwith (*Unterofficer*); Richard Marner (*Schmidt*).

Rating: *** 1/2

England's Charles Coward (1905–1976) was loved for madcap attempts at escape from Nazi POW camps, chronicled in this Stone family film. They were an indie outfit committed to high-quality, modestly budgeted work. On release, the movie was criticized for its lighthearted comedy bits, critics failing to recall that the classic *Stalag 17* included such gags in a POW picture. Innovative in presenting the camps as cleaner and less hostile than in other films—the way Coward honestly recalled them. What's included is fine, but problems arise from what's left out. Coward snuck *into* Auschwitz and rescued Jewish prisoners—his crowning achievement. By not including it (the filmmakers thought this was too serious considering the earlier light tone), a true hero is reduced to a puckish jokester.

PATTON (1970)

CREDITS:
20th Century Fox; Franklin J. Schaffner, dir.; Omar N. Bradley (book), Ladislas Farago (book), Francis Ford Coppola, Edmund H. North, scr.; Frank McCarthy, pro.; Jerry Goldsmith, mus.; Fred J. Koenekamp, cin.; Hugh S. Fowler, ed.; C; 2.20:1, 2.35:1 (35 mm); 172 min.

CAST:
George C. Scott (*George S. Patton Jr.*); Karl Malden (*Omar N. Bradley*); Stephen Young (*Capt. Hansen*); Michael Strong (*Gen.* Carver); Karl Michael Vogler (*Rommel*); James Edwards (*Sgt. Meeks*); Michael Bates (*Montgomery*).

Rating: **** 1/2

The WWII career of Patton (1885–1945). Scott (Oscar winner for Best Actor) allowed audiences to grasp why this maverick was the most damned and/or praised American officer since Custer. Possibly, Patton's famous cowboy-style pistols were part of a conscious effort to imitate that earlier arrogant, flamboyant, often glorious figure. The film doesn't avoid controversy, including the infamous moment when Patton slapped a soldier (Tim Considine) suffering from shell-shock. The WWII film that changed everything: a well-rounded portrait that does not reduce Patton to a plaster saint, showing the good, bad, and ugly aspects of a complex warrior. An iconic image of Patton dwarfed by an American flag set the pace for something different during the Vietnam era. Oscar winner for Best Picture. Liability: Schaffner's journeyman direction. Had Coppola helmed the project, it might've been *The Godfather* of WWII films.

THE GUYS AT THE TOP: Gregory Peck as General Douglas MacArthur; George C. Scott as General George Patton.

PRIDE OF THE MARINES (1945)

CREDITS:
Warner Bros.; Delmer Daves, dir.; Roger Butterfield (book), Daves, Marvin Borowsky, Albert Maltz, scr.; Jerry Wald, Jack L. Warner, pro.; Franz Waxman, mus.; J. Peverell Marley, cin.; Owen Marks, ed.; B&W; 1.37:1; 119 min.

CAST:
John Garfield (*Al Schmid*); Eleanor Parker (*Ruth Hartley*); Dane Clark (*Lee Diamond*); John Ridgely (*Jim*); Rosemary DeCamp (*Virginia*); Ann Doran (*Ella Mae*); Truman Bradley (*voice, radio announcer*).

Rating: **** 1/2

Al Schmid (1920–1982) grew up as a cocky blue-collar worker in Philadelphia. He joined the marines after Pearl Harbor and, at Guadalcanal, became a hero, single-handedly manning a machine gun after his buddies were killed. Blinded, on his return home Schmid feared his wife's reaction. Filmed during the war's closing hours, this is refreshingly free of sentimental jargon, serving as a transitional piece from *Wake Island* to *A Walk in the Sun*. Maltz's script reflects the fears of many wounded vets that they've been forgotten. Admirable attention to ethnic minorities in noncliin nonclichéd roles, qualifying this as a precursor to postwar civil rights cinema. Most memorable: a surreal dream sequence.

PT 109 (1963)

CREDITS:
Warner Bros.; Leslie H. Martinson, dir.; Robert J. Donovan (book), Richard L. Breen, Vincent Flaherty, Howard Sheehan, scr.; Bryan Foy, pro.; David Buttolph, Howard Jackson, William Lava, mus.; Robert Surtees, cin.; Folmar Blangsted, ed.; C; 2.35:1; 140 min.

SAD REMEMBRANCE: Cliff Robertson as John Fitzgerald Kennedy in *P.T. 109*; the film was released a few months previous to the president's assassination.

CAST:

Cliff Robertson (*Lt. John F. Kennedy*); Ty Hardin (*Ens. Thom*); James Gregory (*Cmdr. Ritchie*); Robert Culp (*Ens. Ross*); Grant Williams (*Lt. Cluster*); Robert Blake (*Bucky*); Andrew Duggan (*Narrator*).

Rating: * 1/2

Lifeless and listless, this overlong, overwrought telling of President Kennedy's (1917–1963) wartime experiences was a huge disappointment for audiences six months before the assassination. A genius like John Ford (originally set to direct) might have been able to make an American epic out of this tale of JFK's adventures at sea and the rescue operation for his men after their boat went down. Martinson was best known for helming Warner's TV westerns and junk movies (*Hot Rod Rumble* (1957)). Robertson is wrong for the lead, which he received only after JFK picked him over Warner's first choice: Warren Beatty. Crisp cinematography by Surtees helps. Culp mimics Jack Lemmon in *Mr. Roberts*.

REACH FOR THE SKY (1956)

CREDITS:
Rank/Angel Prods.; Lewis Gilbert, dir.; Paul Brickhill (book), Gilbert, Vernon Harris, scr.; Daniel M. Angel, pro.; John Addison, mus.; Jack Asher, cin.; John Shirley, ed.; B&W; 1.37:1; 135 min. (UK), 123 min. (US).

CAST:
Kenneth More (*Douglas Bader*); Muriel Pavlow (*Thelma Bader*); Lyndon Brook (*John Sanderson*); Lee Patterson (*Turner*); Dorothy Alison (*Nurse Brace*); Alexander Knox (*Mr. Joyce*).

Ratings: **** 1/2(UK)
**** (US)

Largely accurate depiction of Bader (1910–1982), a British aviator/maverick who, in 1930 while part of an aeronautics show, disobeyed orders, opting for low-level flying, banned by military brass as needlessly reckless. A crash resulted in Bader losing both legs, after which he dropped out of the service. As the Blitz began, Bader rejoined the RAF. As commander of a Canadian squadron, and later wing commander, he flew missions, bailed out over Europe, and was imprisoned in Colditz Castle. This tribute to England's most dubious WWII hero doesn't conceal his controversial nature but makes it part of his appeal. Stirring, solid. Richard Burton (the original choice) might have been far more scintillating. At the time of the film's release, Bader's image had been undercut by several nasty racist remarks.

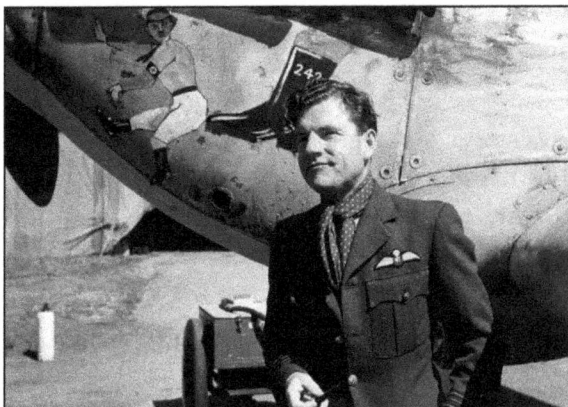

A CONTROVERSIAL HERO: Kenneth More offers a solid, stoic performance as Baden, one of the war's most debatable heroes.

RENGOU KANTAI SHIREI CHOUKAN: YAMAMOTO ISOKORU – TAIHEIYOU SENSOU NANAJUUNENME NO SHIMJITSU, aka *ISOROKO YAMAMOTO, THE COMMANDER-IN-CHIEF OF THE COMBINED FLEET* (2011)

CREDITS:

Bandei Visual/Toei Co.; Izuru Narushima, dir.; Yasuo Hasegawa, Kenzaburô Iida, scr.; Shohei Kotaki, pro.; Tarô Iwashiro, mus.; Takahide Shibanushi, cin.; Hirohide Abe, ed.; C; 140 min.

CAST:

Kôji Yakusho (*Isoroku Yamamoto*); Hiroshi Abe (*Yamaguchi tamon*); Shûichi Azumaya (*Yoshimasa Yamamoto*); Mitsugorô Bandô (*Hori*); Mieko Harada (*Yamamoto's wife*); Masatô Ibu (*Nagano*).

Rating: **** 1/2

"Sue for peace." So says Admiral Yamamoto (1884–1943) after Japan's unexpected loss at Midway and the fierce fighting for Guadalcanal. This film, created to commemorate the seventieth anniversary of "a day that will live in infamy," assumes a revisionist approach. The sneak attack cannot be justified, but it is more intelligible once the audience understands the decision derived from extreme economic unrest and an "any enemy of my enemy is my friend" mentality. Germany opposed the USSR, which Japan saw as their major threat. The irony: Yamamoto, the navy's most articulate voice opposing war with America, would be assigned the duty to win the South Pacific. Effectively shows how Japan's media intentionally misled the public for patriotic purposes rather than providing information that might've turned most against the coming disaster. Effective use of ordinary people gathering at a rice-bowl restaurant as an Asian equivalent of the Greek chorus. Of far more interest to history buffs than general audiences.

SOPHIE SCHOLL: THE FINAL DAYS (2005)

CREDITS:
Broth Film/Goldkind; Marc Rothemund, dir.; Fred Breinersdorfer, scr.; Breinersdorfer, Sven Burgemeister, pro.; Reinhold Heil, Johnny Klimek, mus.; Martin Langer, cin.; C; 1.85:1; 120 min.

CAST:
Julia Jentsch (*Sophie Magdalena Scholl*); Alexander Held (*Robert Mohr*); Fabian Hinrichs (*Hans Scholl*); Johanna Gastdorf (*Else Gebel*); Andre Hennicke (*Dr. Freisler*); Florian Stetter (*Probst*); Lilli Jung (*Gisela*).

Rating: **** 1/2

A twenty-one-year-old woman (1921–1943) was tried from February 17, 1943 to February 22, 1943, and then executed (by guillotine) for crimes against the Nazi state. A member of the White Rose, a Munich-

A WOMAN OF COURAGE: Julia Jentsch portrays the social activist and Holocaust victim in *Sophie Scholl: The Final Days*.

based resistance movement that opposed Hitler, she and her brother dared to exercise free speech by distributing mimeographed copies of an antifascist pamphlet. The film follows their arrest and incarceration in Stadelheim Prison. The trial is meticulously re-created. However dark and pessimistic this all sounds, Sophie's final words are pure optimism: "The sun still shines." Historians have noted minor departures from the record, but the film is mostly as faithful to history as it is powerful as human drama. An unsparing study of the horrors of the Hitler era, Sophie emerges as a fully realized character rather than a simple martyr.

SOTTO DRECI BANDIERE, aka *UNDER TEN FLAGS* (1960)

CREDITS:
Duilo Coletti, dir.; Coletti, many others, scr.; Dino De Laurentiis, pro.; Jerry Webb, ed.; Aldo Tonti, cin.; Nino Rota, mus.; Paramount; B&W; 1.37:1; 88 min.

CAST:
Van Heflin (*Capt. Bernhard Rogge*); Charles Laughton (*Admiral Russell*); Mylene Demongeot *(Zizi)*; John Ericson *(Kruger)*; Alex Nicol *(Knoche)*; Eleanora Rossi Drago (*Elsa*); Cecil Parker (*Howard*); Liam Redmond (Windsor); Gian Maria Volonte (*Sam*).

When 21 crafts are sunk during 1940-1941, the Brit admiral (Laughton) assumes a wolf park is responsible. In truth, the culprit ship is not a sub but a Surface Raider. Capt. Bernhard Rogge (1899-1982) created theatrical camouflage for the war at sea by having the *Atlantis* 'costumed' as a harmless merchant ship, his men as international sailors. In this manner they came close enough to blow English ships out of the water before revealing their true colors. Freely adapted from Rogge's diaries about his (in)famous Killer Ship. Superb production values and performances but whittled down in the editing suite from a mighty epic to a minor actioner. A long lost film!

SOUND OF MUSIC, THE (1965)

CREDITS:
20th Century Fox; Robert Wise, dir.; Howard Lindsay (play), Russel Crouse (play), Maria von Trapp (book), Ernest Lehman, George Hurdalek, scr.; Wise, Darryl F. Zanuck, pro.; Irwin Kostal, mus.; Ted D. McCord, cin.; William Reynolds, ed.; C; 2.35:1; 174 min.

CAST:
Julie Andrews (*Maria*); Christopher Plummer (*Capt. Von Trapp*); Eleanor Parker (*The Baroness*); Richard Haydn (*Max Detweiler*); Peggy Wood (*Mother Abbess*); Charmian Carr, Heather Menzies, Nicholas Hammond, Duane Chase, Angela Cartwright, Debbie Turner, Kym Karath (*The Children*); Daniel Truhitte (*Rolfe*).

Rating: *****

THE MOUNTAIN'S HIGH . . .: Christopher Plummer as Captain Van Trapp leads his family to safety in *The Sound of Music*.

Dedicated to serving God by helping humanity, Maria Von Trapp of Salzburg (1905–1987) decides not to take her final vows. She accepts a job as governess to the seven children of a seemingly coldhearted retired naval officer (1880–1947). After they marry, Austria embraces fascism. Opposed to the order, they must leave, climbing every mountain to freedom. The 1958 Rodgers and Hammerstein musical was enhanced with several additional Rodgers songs, necessary for a successful reimagining of the piece as a motion picture. Wise skillfully uses his camera to transform a theater piece into a true film. Won multiple Oscars and is still a beloved classic.

STERN VON AFRIKA, DER, aka *STAR OF AFRICA* (1957)

CREDITS:
Neue Emelka; Alfred Weidenmann, dir.; Herbert Reinecker, Udo Wolter, scr.; Rüdiger von Hirschberg, pro.; Hans-Martin Majewski, mus.; Helmut Ashley, Francisco Sempere, Jost von Hardenberg, cin.; C.O. Barning, J.A. Rojo, ed.; B&W; 2.37:1; 99 min.

CAST:
Joachim Hansen (*Hans-Joachim Marseille*); Marianne Koch (*Brigitte*); Hansjörg Felmy (*Franke*); Horst Frank (*Droste*); Peter Schmidt (*Sommer*); Carl Lange (Krusenberg).

Rating: ***

The Red Baron of WWII, Hans-Joachim Marseille (1919–1942), Luftwaffe pilot, shot down fifty Allied planes. A show-off, this maverick elicited both praise and contempt. Active in the Battle of Britain, he boldly, recklessly served in North Africa. The film captures a fair amount of that, though the portrait of a fascinating if controversial man remains superficial. The script suggests he was anti-Hitler to make Marseille more sympathetic. His on-screen plane is a HA-1109, made in Spain, sitting in for his Messerschmitt Bf 109.

SULLIVANS, THE aka FIGHTING SULLIVANS, THE (1944)

CREDITS:
20th Century Fox; Lloyd Bacon, dir.; Jules Schemer, Mary C. McCall, Jr., Edward Doherty, scr.; Sam Jaffe, pro.; Cyril J. Mockridge, mus.; Lucien N. Andriot, cin.; Louis R. Loeffler, ed.; B&W; 1.37:1; 112 min.

CAST:
Thomas Mitchell (*Pop Sullivan*); Anne Baxter (*Katherine*); Selena Royle (*Ma*); Ed Ryan (*Al*); Trudy Marshall (*Genevieve*); John Campbell (*Frank*); James Cardwell (*George*); John Alvin (*Matt*); George Offerman, Jr. (*Joe*); Ward Bond (*Lt. Cmdr. Robinson*).

Rating: **** 1/2

AN AMERICAN FAMILY/AN AMERICAN TRAGEDY: Thomas Mitchell as the father who loses all his sons in a single naval battle in *The Sullivans*, aka *The Fighting Sullivans*.

On November 13, 1942, the light cruiser USS *Juneau* sank near Guadalcanal. Among the dead: all five Sullivan brothers. The loss of this quintet of Irish Catholic youths caused our government to enact the Sullivan Law, prohibiting siblings from serving together. This film tribute, if mostly fiction, traces their relationships over the years, the brothers united by the saying, "We stick together." A sentimental tone hovers over the piece. The filmmakers managed to add what Spielberg (inspired by this story to create *Saving Private Ryan*) called "an up cry": a ray of hope as the Sullivans enter heaven together. Less a war film than a sprawling domestic drama laced with Irish humor. The point of view is the father's, ranging from his joy at each successive child's baptism to breaking the news to his wife. The boys' birthdates were as follows: George, 1914; Frank, 1916; Joseph, 1918; Matt, 1919, and Al, 1922.

THREE CAME HOME (1950)

CREDITS:
20th Century Fox; Jean Negulesco, dir.; Agnes Newton Keith (book), Nunnally Johnson, scr.; Johnson, pro.; Hugo Friedhofer, mus.; Milton R. Krasner, William H. Daniels, cin.; Dorothy Spencer, ed.; 1.37:1; B&W; 116 min.

CAST:
Claudette Colbert (*Agnes Newton Keith*); Patric Knowles (*Harry Keith*); Florence Desmond (*Betty Sommers*); Sessue Hayakawa (*Colonel Suga*); Sylvia Andrew (*Henrietta*).

Rating: **** 1/2

Heart-wrenching tale, vividly rendered via on-location filming in North Borneo, of an American author (1901–1982) living with her businessman husband and child at the war's outbreak. Chronicles her four-year internment in prison camps, including complex relationships with other women, Asian guards who are alternately brutal and kind, and an ever-evolving friendship with the officer in charge. Colbert projects nobility and class, most poignantly in a scene that depicts the lady risking her life to slip off and see (by implication, make love with) her less stalwart husband, located in a separate camp. A sequence showing the slaughter of a squad of playful Australians remains riveting today. The first postwar film to elicit compassion for some Japanese. Keith appears in a cameo as one of the British captives.

TO HELL AND BACK (1955)

CREDITS:
Universal; Jesse Hibbs, dir.; Audie Murphy (book), Gil Doud, scr.; Aaron Rosenberg, pro.; Irving Gertz, William Lava, Henry Mancini, Lou Maury, mus.; Maury Gertsman, cin.; Edward Curtiss, ed.; C; 2.55:1; 106 min.

CAST:
Audie (L.) Murphy (*Himself*); Marshall Thompson (*Johnson*); Charles Drake (*Brandon*); Jack Kelly (*Kerrigan*); Paul Picerni (*Valentino*); David Janssen (*Lt. Lee*); Susan Kohner (*Maria*); Mary Field (*Mrs. Murphy*); Gordon Gebert (*Audie as a child*); Gen. Walter B. Smith (*Himself*).

Rating: ****

That rarest of rarities—an autobiographical film, based on the memoir of WWII's most decorated hero. Murphy (1925–1971), while accepting the Congressional Medal of Honor, flashes back to his boyhood in rural Texas and then to the African and European battlefields. Murphy is perfect as himself: charming, humble, and dangerous in a baby-faced way. Most of the supporting actors are, in contrast, too clearly playing at being soldiers. Dialogue in scenes featuring average GIs is far too stereotypical. Still, stirring, with powerful battle scenes that, at Murphy's insistence, play down his heroism to showcase his fellow dogfaces. Big complaint from WWII veterans (Audie included!): the uniforms aren't as dirty as they would be in reality. A brief romance with an Italian girl is pleasant if contrived.

THE REAL DEAL, PART TWO: Audie Murphy as Audie Murphy in *To Hell and Back*, based on the hero's autobiography.

TRIPLE CROSS (1966)

CREDITS:
Cineurop; Terence Young, dir.; Frank Owen (book), René Hardy, William Marchant, scr.; Jacques Bertrand, Georges Cheyko, Fred Feldkamp, pro.; Georges Garvarentz, mus.; Henri Alekan, cin.; Roger Dwyre, ed.; C; 1.66:1; 144 min.

CAST:
Christopher Plummer (*Eddie Chapman*); Romy Schneider (*Countess*); Trevor Howard (*Freddie Young*); Gert Fröbe (*Col. Steinhager*); Claudine Auger (*Paulette*); Yul Brynner (*Baron von Grunen*).

Rating: *** 1/2

Fascinating if flawed movie attempts to tell the story of WWII triple agent Eddie Chapman (1914–1997) in the style of the recently popular 007 films. Helmed by the director of the best of the Bonds, *From Russia With Love. Goldfinger* villain Fröbe and *Thunderball* heroine Auger add to this aura, as do glossy color and lighthearted playing. Ian Fleming knew Chapman; some observers insist this was the template for that character. Slick cinematography and the casual tone of an escapist flick are countered by realistic depictions of the unique imbroglio Chapman found himself in. Brynner's over-the-top parody of Erich von Stroheim (monocle and all) as the "good" (i.e., anti-Hitler) German suggests that perhaps this was to have been a spoof.

UNBROKEN (2014)

CREDITS:
3 Arts. Ent.; Angelina Jolie, dir.; Joel Coen, Ethan Coen, Richard LaGravenese, William Nicholson, scr.; Jolie, Matthew Baer, Erwin Stoff, Clayton Townsend, pro.; Alexandre Desplat, mus.; Roger Deakins, cin.; William Goldenberg, ed.; C; 2.35:1; 137 min.

CAST:

Jack O'Connell (*Louis Zamperini*); Domhnall Gleeson (*Phil*); Garrett Hedlund (*Fitzgerald*); Takamasa Ishihara (*Watanabe*); Finn Wittrock (*Mac*); Jai Courtney (*Cup*); Maddalena Ischiale (*Louise*); C. J. Valleroy (*Young Louie*).

Rating: ****

Spectacular telling of the life of Louis Zamperini (1917–2014), from his youth as a bullied Italian American boy in California to his juvenile delinquency and transition to track star, including the Olympic games. During WWII, the bombardier and two others are adrift at sea in a life raft following their plane's crash. Next, internment in a POW camp, where a Japanese corporal singles out Zamperini for abuse. Jolie's directorial debut is impressive, with a grim approach that recalls *The Bridge on the River Kwai*. The impact is diminished in the first half by clichéd dialogue and in the second by a failure to fully explore the hero's complex personality. An overly inspirational tone likewise undercuts the film's power. Worthwhile for its vividness and accuracy. From a 2010 book by Laura Hillenbrand.

WINGS AND THE WOMAN (1942)

CREDITS:

Hebert Wilcox Prods./RKO; Herbert Wilcox, dir.; Viscount Castlerosse, Miles Malleson, scr.; Wilcox, Victor Hanbury, pro.; William Alwyn, Marr Mackie, mus.; Mutz Greenbaum, cin.; Geoffrey Foot, ed.; B&W; 1.37:1; 94 min. (US), 103 min. (UK).

CAST:

Anna Neagle (*Amy Johnson*); Robert Newton (*Jim Mollison*); Edward Chapman (*Mr. Johnson*); Nora Swinburne (*TA Commandant*); Martita Hunt (*Miss Bland*).

Rating: ****

Also known as *They Flew Alone*, still-stirring Brit biopic of the remarkable Amy Johnson (1903–1941). The story traces the career of England's first celebrity aviator—their own Amelia Earhart (with her own tragic end)—including her childhood obsession with flight and her daring, dangerous solo expeditions. Also covers her romance and failed marriage with an aviation pioneer and her volunteering to ferry planes for the newly formed twenty-five-member Women's Air Corps, concluding with her disappearance in thick fog. Effectively traces the early history of aviation and the slow, steady acceptance of the commercial and military uses of planes. Also impressive: a protofeminist approach to the boys-club attitude toward Johnson, as well as a tribute to nonconformity in either gender. The male secretary is played by James Bond creator Ian Fleming. The depicted aircraft are accurate for the time periods, Johnson piloting an Airspeed Oxford during her final flight.

ZOOKEEEPER'S WIFE, THE (2017)

CREDITS:
Niko Carol, dir.; Angela Workman, scr, Diane Ackerman (book); Diane Miller Levin, Kim Zubick, prods.; David Coulson, ed.; Andrij Parekh, cin.; Harry Gregson-Williams, mus.; Scion Films/Focus Features; 127 min.; C; 2.35:1.

CAST:
Jessica Chastain (*Antonina Zabinska*); Johan Heldenbergh (*Jan*); Daniel Bruhl (*Lutz Heck*); Timothy Radford (*Ryszard*); Efrat Dor (*Magda Gross*); Iddo Goldberg (*Maurycy Fraenkel*); Shira Haas (*Urszula*); Michael McElhatton *(Jerzyk)*.

Rating: ****

In the tradition of *The Hiding Place* and *Schindler's List,* this appealingly old-fashioned melodrama/biopic relates the story of Antonina (1908-1971) and Jan (1897-1974) Zabinski, owners of the Poland Zoo. In 1939, when the Nazis invaded, their animals were liquidated or displaced. They committed their resources (underground tunnels and cells, as well as the safety of

A DIFFERENT ORDER OF WAR HERO: *The Zookeeper's Wife* tells the fact-based tale of a courageous woman who hoped to save her beloved animals and then employ their living areas to hide away victims of the Nazis.

their lives and their young son's) to the Righteous Cause: helping remove imprisoned Jews from the Warsaw Ghetto, hiding them on their property. The low-key style effectively contrasts with films focusing on the interior of concentration camps; here is a rare work which reveals that for most people in an occupied city, life simply goes on . . . at least on the surface. The work's impact is diminished by a less than fully successful (and largely invented) attempt to create a love triangle involving a Nazi officer with vast power who dreams of seducing Antonina. Chastain delivers a nuanced performance that elevates her into the Meryl Streep league; Bruhl's German is rendered as a fascinatingly intricate individual.

The Big Picture: From Training To Victory

AERIAL GUNNER (1943)

CREDITS:
Medallion; William H. Pine, dir.; Jack F. Dailey, Maxwell Shane, scr.; Pine, William Thomas, pro.; Daniele Amfitheatrof, mus.; Fred Jackman, Jr., cin.; William H. Ziegler, ed.; B&W; 1.37:1; 78 min.

CAST:
Chester Morris (*Sgt. Foxy Pattis*); Richard Arlen (*Jon Davis*); Jimmy Lydon (*Pvt. Sandy Lunt*); Amelita Ward (*Peggy Lunt*); Robert Mitchum (*Benson*).

Rating: **

Pilot Davis returns to base from a bombing mission over Japan and explains why tail-gunner Foxy is missing. Lifelong enemies, they were thrown together at a Texas Army Air Force training center, where both fell in love with the sister of fellow trainee Sandy. Ordinary melodrama with shoddy production values. Any appeal derives from the documentary-like depiction of training near Brownsville, on the ground and in the air, and the use of ingenious devices for target practice. An effective depiction of the unique working relationship between the man at the wheel and the one covering the crew's backside during airborne combat.

AGE OF HEROES (2011)

CREDITS:

Content/Giant/Matador; Adrian Vitoria, dir.; Vitoria, Ed Scates, scr.; James Brown, Lex Lutzus, Nick O'Hagan, James Youngs, pro.; Michael Richard Plowman, mus.; Mark Hamilton, cin.; Chris Gill, Joe Parsons, ed.; C; 2.35:1; 90 min.

CAST:

Sean Bean (*Maj. Jack Jones*); Danny Dyer (*Cpl. Bob Rains*); Aksel Henie (*Lt. Steiner Mortensen*); Izabella Miko (*Jensen*); James D'Arcy (*Ian Fleming*).

Rating: *** 1/2

A *Dirty Dozen*–type adventure, loosely based on the real-life exploits of England's 30 Commando Unit, including author Ian Fleming. Corporal Rains bullies his way out of a prison for Brit troublemakers to join a new outfit that the ultraprofessional Maj. Jones is forming. We follow them through training in the Scottish highlands and on a parachute jump into occupied Norway. Their assignment: seize the Nazis' state-of-the-art radio technology and bring it back. The sequences are well staged, and several—including the massacre of a farming family by Germans—are riveting. How sad that few characters are fleshed out while relationships between individuals are left unexplored. Why introduce the convention of a beautiful Partisan but fail to use her as a catalyst for drama? What's on the screen is fine; what's missing leads to disappointment.

BATTLE CRY (1955)

CREDITS:

Warner Bros.; Raoul Walsh, dir.; Leon Uris (novel), scr.; Jack L. Warner, pro.; Max Steiner, mus.; Sidney Hickox, cin.; William H. Ziegler, ed.; C; 2.35:1; 149 min.

BATTLE CRY; James Whitmore and Van Heflin train young volunteers;
Aldo Ray eventually leads them into action.

CAST:

Van Heflin (*Maj. Sam Huxley*); Aldo Ray (*Pvt. Andy Hookens*); Mona Freeman (*Kathy*); Nancy Olson (*Mrs. Pat Rogers*); James Whitmore (*Sgt. Mac/Narrator*); Raymond Massey (*Gen. Snipes*); Tab Hunter (*Danny Forrester*); Dorothy Malone (*Elaine*); Anne Francis (*Rae*); Justus E. McQueen (*L. Q. Jones*); Perry Lopez (*Spanish Joe*); Fess Parker(*Speedy*).

Rating: ****

Another story following a fighting outfit from basic training to combat, here the 2nd Battalion, 6th Marine Regiment. Based on a blockbuster 1953 book, the film—popular at the box office—was savaged by critics. On-screen portrayals of gorgeous women resemble the lurid covers of pulp fiction bus station books. Sexual encounters between servicemen and numerous females take on a low-camp sensibility. But bloodthirsty combat footage was expertly shot by action expert Walsh. Ray and Hunter are horrible while Heflin, Whitmore, and Massey are excellent. The snappy theme song became a great jukebox and radio hit. Actor McQueen became so associated with his part that he legally changed his name to that of the character.

BIG RED ONE, THE (1980)

CREDITS:

Lorimar/United Artists; Samuel Fuller, dir.; Fuller, scr.; Gene Corman, pro.; Dana Kaproff, mus.; Adam Greenberg, cin.; Morton Tubor, ed.; C/B&W; 1.85:1; 162 min. (director's cut), 113 min. (original theatrical release).

CAST:

Lee Marvin (*The Sergeant*); Mark Hamill (*Pvt. Griff*); Robert Carradine (*Pvt. Zab*); Bobby Di Cicco (*Pvt. Vinci*); Kelly Ward (*Pvt. Johnson*); Stéphane Audran (*Walloon Fighter*).

Ratings: ***** (director's cut)
**** (original theatrical print)

The title refers to the 1st Infantry Division, their shoulder patch featuring an enormous "1" in blazing red. Fuller, a paperback writer who would become an acclaimed filmmaker, served with the outfit. This is the movie he dreamed of making for thirty-five years, hoping John Wayne would play the sergeant. Enormous, accurate, involving fictionalization of events Fuller witnessed follows a squad through North Africa and Sicily, and then on to Normandy (Omaha Beach) and the liberation of the Czechoslovakian camp at Falkenau. Before *Saving Private Ryan*, this was the most significant of all postmodern WWII movies. Drawing on elements of *A Walk in the Sun* and *The Story of GI Joe*, the film incorporates Hollywood's finest films on the subject into a vision that reveals the attitudes of its auteur. *T.B.R.O.* also reflects changes in the American consciousness regarding war over the intervening decades by putting contemporary values into the mix.

BREAKING (THROUGH) THE SOUND BARRIER (1952)

CREDITS:
London Films/British Lion; David Lean, dir.; Terence Rattigan, scr.; Lean, Norman Spencer, Alexander Korda, pro.; Malcolm Arnold, mus.; Jack Hildyard, cin.; Geoffrey Foot, ed.; B&W; 1.37:1; 118 min. (UK), 109 min. (US).

CAST:
Ralph Richardson (*John Ridgefield*); Ann Todd (*Sue Garthwaite*); Nigel Patrick (*Tony Garthwaite*); John Justin (*Philip*); Dinah Sheridan (*Peel*); Joseph Tomelty (*Will*).

Ratings: **** 1/2 (UK release print)
**** (US release print)

As the war draws to a close, farsighted Brits work on a futuristic jet (nicknamed "Prometheus," aka "Submarine Swift") that can pierce the sound barrier. Wartime flyer Garthwaite handles the dangerous testing, which is complicated by his marriage to the daughter of Ridgefield, the company's owner. Often regarded as an example of postwar docudrama: it re-creates historical events so accurately we almost believe we're seeing what actually happened. The irony: none of the characters are based on actual people, the storyline a work of fiction! One inspiration was Geoffrey de Havilland, Jr. (1910–1946), who died trying to fly faster than sound. The film offered something of a turnabout for the Brits, taking credit for an event that the US's Chuck Yeager managed on October 14, 1947.

BREAKTHROUGH (1950)

CREDITS:
Warner Bros.; Lewis Seiler, dir.; Joseph Breen, Bernard Girard, Ted Sherdeman, scr.; Bryan Foy, pro.; William Lava, mus.; Edwin B. DuPar, mus.; Folmar Blangsted, ed.; B&W; 1.37:1; 91 min.

CAST:
David Brian (*Capt. Tom Hale*); John Agar (*Lt. Joe Mallory*); Frank Lovejoy (*Sgt. Pete Bell*); William Campbell (*Dominick*); Paul Picerni (*Rojeck*); Greg McClure (*Finley*).

Rating: ** 1/2

Okay, if routine, B picture/time killer about the formation of a company and its rowdy adventures, from basic training through to the D-Day invasion. The rugged Wayne-like commanding officer Hale, his eager young assistant Mallory, and uncouth sergeant Bell shepherd men from raw recruits into experienced soldiers. Clichéd characterizations, recycled dialogue. Enough action scenes (lifted from earlier, better pictures) to qualify this as bearable for WWII completists. Script boasts a savvy sense of "taking ground" to a military mind.

CAPTAIN AMERICA: THE FIRST AVENGER (2011)

CREDITS:
Marvel Ent./Paramount; Joe Johnston, dir.; Joe Simon (comic), Jack Kirby (comic), Christopher Markus, Stephen McFeely, scr.; Kevin Feige, pro.; Alan Silvestri, mus.; Shelly Johnson, cin.; Robert Dalva, Jeffrey Ford, ed.; C; 2.35:1; 124 min.

CAST:
Chris Evans (*Steve Rogers/Captain America*); Hayley Atwell (*Peggy Carter*); Sebastian Stan (*James Barnes*); Tommy Lee Jones (*Col. Phillips*); Hugo Weaving (*Red Skull*); Samuel L. Jackson (*Nick Fury*).

Rating: ****

In 1942, scientists transform a 4-F from Brooklyn into a superhero. Initially employed to rally folks on the home front, Captain America heads for the front lines, where he faces off with Red Skull, once human, now a supervillain. Taking orders from a Pattonesque officer while falling for a top

REVIVING A SUPER-HERO: 'Captain America' (Chris Evans) proves as valuable in modern times as he was back during World War II.

British agent, he frees Allied prisoners and rallies them into a *Magnificent Seven/Dirty Dozen* team. Effective blend of fairly realistic WWII action and contemporary superhero fun. One explosive action sequence after another, well staged, and more than 1,600 F/X shots to satisfy the *Star Wars* crowd. Impressive re-creation of the early 1940s, steeped in gaudy nostalgia.

COCKLESHELL HEROES, THE (1955)

CREDITS:
Columbia/Warwick; José Ferrer, dir.; Bryan Forbes, George Kent, Richard Maibaum, scr.; Phil C. Samuel, pro.; John Addison, mus.; John Wilcox, cin.; Alan Osbiston, ed.; C; 2.35:1; 97 min.

CAST:
José Ferrer (*Maj. Stringer*); Trevor Howard (*Capt. Thompson*); Dora Bryan (*Myrtle*); Victor Maddern (*Craig*); Anthony Newley (*Clarke*); Percy Herbert (*Lomas*); Christopher Lee (*Sub Commander*).

Rating: ****

A fitting tribute to England's Royal Marines, set between March and August 1942. Their primary objective: halt German cargo ships slipping by Britain's blockade of Bordeaux. Maverick major Stringer and by-the-book captain Thompson train misfits for a suicide mission via two-man canoes. Fine first half sets the pace for *The Great Escape* while the second serves as a predecessor to *Dirty Dozen*. Star/director Ferrer combines nail-biting suspense, creatively staged action, and strong doses of droll comedy. The submarine voyage to their port of entry is particularly memorable. Based on a historical incident.

DARBY'S RANGERS (1958)

CREDITS:
Warner Bros.; William A. Wellman, dir.; James J. Altieri (book), Guy Trosper, scr.; Martin Rackin, pro.; Max Steiner, mus.; William H. Clothier,

A SPECIAL UNIT: James Garner as Gen. Darby witnesses a battlefield promotion in *Darby's Rangers*.

cin.; Owen Marks, ed.; B&W; 1.66:1; 121 min.

CAST:

James Garner (*William O. Darby*); Jack Warden (Sgt. *Saul Rosen*; *Narrator*); Etchika Choureau (*Angelina*); Edd Byrnes (*Lt. Arnold Dittman*); Venetia Stevenson (*Peggy*); Torin Thatcher (*McTavish*); Peter Brown (*Burns*).

Rating: *** 1/2

Inexperienced officer Darby (1902–1945) revives Rogers' Rangers from the French and Indian War. After training in Scotland, the elite group serves in North Africa and Italy. Originally to have been a major project starring Charlton Heston, who dropped out over disappointment with the script. WB then scaled down the scope and budget, recasting using popular TV actors, which forced Wellman to abandon his epic intentions. Many sequences were shot on studio sets. The soldiers' romances with impossibly beautiful women are ridiculous. Several strong moments hint at what Wellman had originally hoped for: an ambitious, uncompromising work on the order of *The Story of GI Joe*.

DEVIL'S BRIGADE, THE (1968)

CREDITS:
Wolper Pictures; Andrew V. McLaglen, dir.; Robert H. Adleman (book), Col. George Walton (book), William Roberts, scr.; Julian Ludwig, Theodore Strauss, David L. Wolper, pro.; Alex North, mus.; William H. Clothier, cin.; William T. Cartwright, ed.; C; 2.35:1; 130 min.

CAST:
William Holden (*Lt. Col. Robert T. Frederick*); Cliff Robertson (*Maj. Alan Crown*); Vince Edwards (*Maj. Bricker*); Andrew Prine (*Ransom*); Jeremy Slate (*O'Neill*); Claude Akins (*Rockman*); Richard Jaeckel (*Greco*); Richard Dawson (*MacDonald*); Harry Carey, Jr. (*Rose*); Michael Rennie (*Gen. Clark*); Carroll O'Connor (*Gen. Hunter*).

Rating: *** 1/2

Fact-based story of the First Special Service Force follows red berets through rigorous training and combat in Italy. Initially criticized as a carbon copy of *The Dirty Dozen*, this boasts an intriguing odd-couple situation: US misfits combined with an elite group of Canadian fighters. Holden looks exhausted and underacts while Edwards overacts and seems puffed up. Great performance from Robertson as a Dunkirk-seasoned vet. Big problem here is McLaglen's uninspired direction, especially his lackluster approach to the expected comic shenanigans. The final battle is well staged, especially a massive sequence involving a ferocious man-to-man fight on a dangerous incline. Routine, acceptable; worth watching once.

DIRTY DOZEN, THE (1967)

CREDITS:

Metro-Goldwyn-Mayer/Seven Arts; Robert Aldrich, dir.; E. M. Nathanson (novel), Lucas Heller, Nunnally Johnson, scr.; Kenneth Hyman, pro.; Frank De Vol, mus.; Edward Scaife, cin.; Michael Luciano, ed.; C; 1.75:1; 2.20:1 (70 mm); 150 min.

CAST:

Lee Marvin (*Maj. Reisman*); Ernest Borgnine (*Gen. Worden*); Charles Bronson (*Wladislaw*); Jim Brown (*Jefferson*); John Cassavetes (*Victor Franko*); Richard Jaeckel (*Bowren*); George Kennedy (*Maj. Armbruster*); Trini Lopez (*Jiminez*); Ralph Meeker (*Capt. Kinder*); Robert Ryan (*Col. Breed*); Telly Savalas (*Maggott*); Donald Sutherland (*Pinkley*); Clint Walker (*Posey*); Robert Webber (*Gen. Denton*).

Rating: *****

THE GRAND ADVENTURE: Lee Marvin and his team of misfits, maniacs, and miscreants attack a chateau in *The Dirty Dozen*.

As Allies prepare for D-Day, the title misfits, commanded by a maverick major, drop into Rennes near Brittany. In a suicide attack, they infiltrate a chateau and kill German officers. The film follows them through training, their mission, and desperate attempts to survive. A perfect adventure film with spot-on casting (several top-billed stars play officers, not members of the dozen). Bronson is particularly memorable in a sympathetic role. Broad comedy neatly balanced with bloodthirsty action by genre expert Aldrich. On its release, *New York Times* critic Bosley Crowther lambasted the film for extreme violence; the same summer, he attacked *Bonnie and Clyde* for identical reasons. In fact, these were a 1930s gangster film and 1940s WWII action flick revised for the youthful audience of the late sixties, when Vietnam and the Civil Rights Movement brought new levels of violence to everyday life via TV. Though fictional, the 1965 novel was inspired by a real-life outfit, the Filthy Thirteen.

FIGHTING SEABEES, THE (1944)

CREDITS:
Republic Pictures; Edward Ludwig, dir.; Borden Chase, Æneas MacKenzie, scr.; Albert J. Cohen, pro.; Walter Scharf, mus.; William Bradford, cin.; Richard L. Van Enger, ed.; B&W; 1.37:1; 100 min.

CAST:
John Wayne (*Lt. Cmdr. Wedge Donovan*); Susan Hayward (*Constance Chesley*); Dennis O'Keefe (*Lt. Cmdr. Robert Yarrow*); William Frawley (*Powers*); Leonid Kinskey (*Novasky*); J. M. Kerrigan (*Collins*); Grant Withers (*Spreckles*); Adele Mara (*Twinkles*).

Rating: *** 1/2

A fictionalized chronicle of the Navy's "Construction Battalions." This solved the problem of unarmed civilians bulldozing much-needed roads and airstrips on the Pacific Islands by incorporating the men into the military with a double duty: "We build, we fight." The Duke brings his ongoing cocky-hero image to the brawling leader, competing in a romantic triangle with naval officer Yarrow for the hand of spunky protofeminist

REEL WAR AND REAL WAR: In *The Fighting Seabees*, the title heroes employ tractors to destroy Nazi tanks in a Hollywood romanticization of combat; written and directed by Samuel Fuller, The Big Red One accurately portrayed the trials and tribulations of an outfit he had served wih.

journalist Chesley. Sadly, that unconvincing subplot takes up too much time, almost submerging the more significant historical story. Still, two battles (one at the midpoint, the other for the finale) are superb. Similar in style and tone to the studio's later *Sands of Iwo Jima*, though never on the level of that classic. You haven't lived until you've watched Wayne jitterbug with breathtaking Mara.

FIRST TO FIGHT (1967)

CREDITS:
Warner Bros.; Christian Nyby, dir.; Gene L. Coon, scr.; William Conrad, pro.; Fred Steiner, mus.; Harold E. Wellman, cin.; George R. Rohrs, ed.; C; 2.35:1; 92 min.

CAST:
Chad Everett (*Sgt./Lt. Jack Connell*); Marilyn Devin (*Peggy Sanford*); Dean Jagger (*Lt. Col. E. J. Baseman*); Bobby Troup (*Overman*); Claude Akins (*Mason*); Gene Hackman (*Tweed*); James Best (*Carnavan*).

Rating: ** 1/2

A marine proves his heroism at Guadalcanal, wins the Congressional Medal of Honor, returns stateside for a war bonds tour, falls in love with his guide, marries her, takes a job training volunteers, suffers from survivor guilt after an overseas friend is killed, and then heads back to the Pacific. This time, he appears cowardly. Not that he fears for his life—he's just concerned about the girl he left behind. The script is a patchwork quilt of earlier movies, the acting dull and stiff. Loosely based on the story of John "Manila" Basilone (1916–1945). Routine, unexceptional, conventional.

FROM HELL TO VICTORY (1979)

CREDITS:
Frade Prods.; Umberto Lenzi/Hank Milestone, dir.; Lenzi, Anthony Fritz,

José Luis Martínez Mollá, scr.; Edmondo Amati, pro.; Riz Ortolani, mus.; José Luis Alcaine, cin.; Vincenzo Tomassi, ed.; C; 2.35:1; 103 min.

CAST:
George Peppard (*Brett Rosson*); George Hamilton (*Maurice Bernard*); Horst Buchholz (*Dietrich*); Anny Duperey (*Fabienne*); Jean-Pierre Cassel (*Sanders*); Capucine (*Nicole*); Sam Wanamaker (*MacDonald*).

Rating: **

Paris, 1939: international friends pledge that whatever happens in the emerging conflict, they will join one another at this cafe should any remain alive afterwards. Sprawling, ineffectual saga follows each through combat, fighting on either side, learning to love and hate. Sounds far more intriguing than it is. One of Lenzi's many Italian-lensed WWII films (a remake of his earlier *The Greatest Battle*), and one of the few to make it to US screens. Arthouse ambitions are undermined by junk-movie execution.

GO FOR BROKE! (1951)

CREDITS:
Metro-Goldwyn-Mayer; Robert Pirosh, dir.; Pirosh, scr.; Dore Schary, pro.; Alberto Colombo, Leo Shuken, mus.; Paul Vogel, cin.; James E. Newcom, ed.; B&W; 1.37:1; 92 min.

CAST:
Van Johnson (*Lt. Michael Grayson*); Lane Nakano (*Sam*); George Miki (*Chick*); Akira Fukunaga (*Frank*); Ken K. Okamoto (*Kaz*); Henry Oyasato (*Ohhara*); Harry Hamada (*Masami*); Gianna Maria Canale (*Rosina*).

Rating: ****

Engrossing, episodic depiction of the 442nd Regiment, made up of Japanese American volunteers who left relocation camps to fight for the US. The point-of-view character is an Anglo lieutenant suffering from racial prejudices that, with difficulty, he overcomes—a solid approach for 1950s civil rights cinema. MGM made this movie when onetime allies, the Chinese, had become Cold War enemies. Mainstream Americans now needed to be "reed-ucated" about the Japanese, currently important allies. An ironic voice-over, noting discrepancies between military policy and the reality that GIs experience, adds a unique touch. One subplot concerning a doomed pig is a classic. Biggest liability: Johnson, inadequate in a role that begs for Robert Mitchum. The title refers to the slogan of an outfit referred to as the "Banzai Brigade."

GUNG HO!: THE STORY OF CARLSON'S MAKIN ISLAND RAIDERS (1943)

CREDITS:

Universal; Ray Enright, dir.; Lt. W. S. LeFrancois (USMC), Lucien Hubbard, Joseph Hoffman, scr.; Walter Wanger, pro.; Frank Skinner,

AN AMERICAN UNIT WITH A COMMUNIST SENSIBILITY: Randolph Scott (right) as a fictionalized version of the controversial officer in *Gung Ho! The Story of Carlson's Raiders.*

mus.; Milton (R.) Krasner, cin.; Milton Carruth, ed.; B&W; 1.37:1; 88 min.

CAST:
Randolph Scott (*Col. Thorwald*); Alan Curtis (*Haribson*); Noah Beery, Jr. (*Richter*); J. Carrol Naish (*Cristoforos*); Sam Levene (*Andreof*); Robert Mitchum (*Pig-Iron*); Chet Huntley (*Narrator*).

Rating: ★★★★

Lt. Col. Evans Carlson (1896–1947) conceived of a special-forces unit that would fight the Japanese in an unorthodox manner, hearkening back to the Native Americans of the colonial era. In a bloodthirsty battle on August 17, 1942, they conquered Makin Island, then went on to the "long patrol" behind enemy lines (November/December 1942). Clichéd characters keep this from rating as a classic. Early sequences are so realistic that for years the Marines used it for training purposes. The decision not to use Carlson's name had to do with his belief in Chinese-style Communism. There were no class distinctions in the raiders; officers ate with the men. "Gung ho" means working in perfect harmony.

HALLS OF MONTEZUMA (1950)

CREDITS:
20th Century Fox; Lewis Milestone, dir.; Michael Blankfort, scr.; Robert Bassler, pro.; Sol Kaplan, mus.; Winton C. Hoch, Harry Jackson, ed.; William Reynolds, ed.; C; 1.37:1; 113 min.

CAST:
Richard Widmark (*Lt. Carl Anderson*); Jack Palance (*Pigeon Lane*); Reginald Gardiner (*Sgt. Johnson*); Robert Wagner (*Coffman*); Karl Malden ("*Doc*"); Richard Boone (*Col. Gilfillan*); Skip Homeier ("*Pretty Boy*"); Jack Webb (*Dickerman*); Neville Brand (*Zelenko*).

Rating: ★★★★

Like Milestone's earlier *A Walk in the Sun*, this follows a platoon—led by an ordinary man who learns by doing—as they hit the beach (presumably at Leyte on October 12, 1944), then push inland. One of the first movies to include color news footage from the war's final days. Notable for several grim battle sequences, a fine cast, and a willingness to raise issues not previously dramatized, such as one man's drug addiction and another's secret joy in killing. The operation's commander announces the need to take prisoners, as information leads to victory. More focused on strategy than combat, though there's plenty of that. Flashbacks to peacetime, intended to round out the characters, are riddled with clichés.

HUMAN CONDITION, THE (1959–1961)

CREDITS:
Ninjin Club; Masaki Kobayashi, dir.; Jumpei Gomikawa (novel), Kobayashi, Zenzô Matsuyama, scr.; Shigeru Wakatsuki, Chûji Kinoshita, mus.; Yoshio Miyajima, cin.; Keiichi Uraoka, ed.; B&W; 2.35:1; 579 min.

CAST:
Tatsuya Nakadai (*Kaji*); Michiyo Aratama (*Michiko*); Chikage Awashima (*Tôfuku Kin*); Ineko Arima (*Shunran Yô*); Keiji Sada (*Kageyama*); Sô Yamamura (*Okishima*); Akira Ishihama (*Chin*); Kôji Nanbara (*Kô*).

Rating: *****

In this ambitious film (actually a series of interrelated movies), we follow Kaji, the least likely warrior ever, through the great conflict. *No Greater Love* (1959) has this Asian everyman sent to Manchuria to oversee Chinese POWs, but he is transferred owing to his "overly humane" approach. *Road to Eternity* (1959) depicts ugly experiences while serving with the Kwantung military group owing to his own leftist leanings. Finally, *A Soldier's Prayer* (1961) depicts the war's intense final battles. Throughout the saga, Kaji must balance his humanistic ideals with the brutal realities of everyday life. Virulently antiwar. Like the six novels on which it is based, this shows us the widest possible range of life during WWII from one thinking person's perspective. Nakadai, who had himself been drafted, managed a tricky juggling act between faithfulness to the literary source and cinematic self-expression. The viewer becomes totally immersed, experiencing Kaji's life alongside him rather than observing it from a distance. One of the great WWII films; one of the great Japanese films; one of the great films.

IN LOVE AND WAR (1957)

CREDITS:
20th Century Fox; Philip Dunne, dir.; Anton Myrer (novel), Edward Anhalt, scr.; Jerry Wald, pro.; Hugo Friedhofer, mus.; Leo Tover, cin.; William Reynolds, ed.; C; 2.35:1; 111 min.

CAST:
Robert Wagner (*Frankie O'Neill*); Dana Wynter (*Sue Trumbell*); Jeffrey Hunter (*Sgt. Nico Kantaylis*); Hope Lang (*Andrea Lenaine*); Bradford Dillman (*Alan Newcombe*); Sheree North (*Lorraine*); France Nuyen (*Kalai*); Mort Sahl (*Danny*).

Rating: *

A college-educated marine (Dillman), about to be shipped out for the final big push in the South Pacific, visits his favorite professor to discuss life and death, pacifism and patriotism. Everything to follow depends on what the older intellectual (Sebastian Cabot) says. Fearing that this sequence slowed the film down, Fox cut it. As a result, nothing in this big, bad movie makes any sense. The first half concerns three servicemen and the women they adore or lust after. These stories would be rejected by any self-respecting afternoon soap opera. The second half, dealing with combat, relies entirely on stock footage. Myrer's novel *The Big War* (1957) might not have been on par with *The Naked and the Dead*, but it deserved better treatment than this.

INDIGENES, aka DAYS OF GLORY (2006)

CREDITS:
Tessalit Prods.; Rachid Bouchareb, dir.; Rachid Bouchareb, Olivier Lorelle, scr.; Jean Bréhat, pro.; Armand Amar Khaled, mus.; Patrick Blossier, cin.; Yannick Kergoat, ed.; C; 2.35:1; 120 min. (US), 128 min. (France).

CAST:
Jamel Debbouze (*Saïd Otmari*); Samy Naceri (*Yassir*); Roschdy Zem (*Messaoud Souni*); Sami Bouajila (*Abdelkader*); Bernard Blancan (*Sgt. Roger Martinez*); Mathieu Simonet (*Leroux*); Mélanie Laurent (*Margueritte*).

Rating: ****

Algiers, 1943: young Africans join France's 7th Algerian Infantry, serving from Italy to the Vosges. The depiction of battle is unsparingly honest, leading to a memorable finale that recalls the Alamo-like conclusion

MEN OF HONOR: True Heroes come in all shapes, sizes, and ethnicities: the cast of *Indigenes*.

of *Saving Private Ryan*. These volunteers realize they are considered unequal to the Gallic forces they fight alongside, receiving inferior food and disrespectful treatment. The implication: the anti-French fervor that gripped Algeria and colonial Africa after WWII had its roots in such condescension during the war, survivors returning home bitter. By concentrating on ideology over character, *Indigenes* (*Days of Glory* in the US) often reduces its heroes to simplistic stick figures. The 128-minute French cut is superior to the US print.

INGLOURIOUS BASTERDS (2009)

CREDITS:
Universal/The Weinstein Co.; Quentin Tarantino, dir.; Tarantino, scr.; Lawrence Bender, pro.; mus.; Sally Menke, ed.; C; 2.35:1; 153 min.

CAST:
Brad Pitt (*Lt. Aldo Raine*); Mélanie Laurent (*Shosanna*); Eli Roth (*Sgt. Donowitz*); Christopher Waltz (*Col. Hans Landa*); Michael Fassbender (*Lt. Hicox*); Diane Kruger (*Bridget von Hammersmark*); Daniel Brühl (*Fredrick Zoller*); Til Schweiger (*Sgt. Stiglitz*); Martin Wuttke (*Hitler*).

Rating: *****

The opening sequence of Tarantino's operatic epic depicts the murder of a family in Nazi-occupied France by a cruel colonel and the way he inexplicably allows a Jewish refugee he'd been searching for to escape. "The Green Leaves of Summer" (from Wayne's *The Alamo* (1960)) appears on the soundtrack. This is the first hint this will be less a movie about WWII than one about the movies: how old images, ideas, dialogue, and music scramble in our collective unconscious, forming an imperfect, subjective memory pool. The film contains homages to the Italian actioner *Inglorious Bastards* as well as references to other movies (at one point becoming a remake of *The Dirty Dozen* with Jewish antiheroes). Also, it's a redux of female-agent films, involving Kruger as a femme fatale. Influenced by great moviemakers from Sergio Leone to Sam Peckinpah, Tarantino uses slow-motion violence, served up Soviet montage style. Another tale, concerning

ALTERNATIVE HISTORY: Quentin Tarantino rewrote the history of World War II with his tale of intrigue, action, and the assassination of Hitler in a movie theatre in *Inglorious Basterds.*

a German youth who becomes the Axis's Audie Murphy, has him starring in a film about his life (the film within the film directed by actor Roth), which premieres in the theater where Hitler's assassination will be carried out. Viewers are surprised when that action succeeds. This all occurs in an alternate reality (i.e., the movies) where anything is possible. A cinematic phantasmagoria that invokes previous WWIIs films.

ITALIANI BRAVA GENTE, aka *ATTACK AND RETREAT* (1964)

CREDITS:

Galatea/Mosfilm/Embassy; Giuseppe De Santis, dir.; De Santis, Gian Domenico Giagni, Augusto Frassinetti, Ennio De Concini, scr.; Lionello Santi, pro.; Armando Trovajoli, mus.; Antonio Secchi, cin.; Klavdiya Moskvina, Mario Serandrei, ed.; B&W; 1.85:1; 137 min.

CAST:
Zhanna Prokhorenko (*Katya*); Raffaele Pisu (*Gabrielli*); Tatyana Samoylova (*Sonya*); Andrea Checchi (*Sermonti*); Arthur Kennedy (*Ferro Ferri*); Peter Falk (*Medic*).

Rating: **** 1/2

An estimated 80,000 Italian soldiers were employed in the Nazi invasion of Eastern Europe. This epic, in many ways resembling *The Victors* of the previous year, follows a representative company into combat, allowing for a sense of the unique individuals. Here's a representative film of the mid-1960s, when attitudes toward war soured all over the world. Officers are no longer visionary but cynical and self-serving; the men are less heroes than pathetic souls scrambling to survive. The title of the version shown in the West refers to small gains followed by inevitable setbacks in a ritual that eventually seems insane to the uncomprehending grunts. Uneven but mostly successful shades-of-gray overview of material earlier depicted in black-and-white moral simplicities. Soviet–Italian coproduction agreement derived from the hope to make a movie that would not only be antiwar but pro-Communist. The inclusion of American stars, ironically, had to do with a desire to succeed at the US (i.e., capitalist) box office.

MAI WEI, aka *MY WAY* (2011)

CREDITS:
Directors/SK Planet/CJ Ent.; Je-kyu Kang, dir.; Kang, Byung-in Kam, scr.; Yong-hwa-Kim, Je-kyu Kang, pro.; Dong-jun Lee, mus.; Mo-gae Lee, cin.; Gok-ji Park, ed.; C; 2.35:1; 137 min.

CAST:
Dong-gun Jang (*Jun-shik Kim*); Joe Odagiri (*Tatsuo Hasegawa*); Bingbing Fan (*Shirai*); In-kwon Kim (*Lee Jong-dae*); Hee-won Kim (*Chun-Bok*); Tae-kyung Oh (*Kwang-Chun*); Kwak Jung Wook (*Min-Woo*).

Rating: **** 1/2

Among the most bizarre fact-based films ever, collapsing two men's lives into a single character. Yang Kyoungjong (1920–1992), a Korean soldier, was forced to fight for the Japanese against the Chinese, then for the Russians against the Germans, and finally for the Germans against the Allies (at Normandy). Sohn Kee-chung (1914–2002), a Korean athlete, ran for the Japanese team at the 1936 Berlin Olympics and won the marathon gold medal. Realistic details from each man's unique life are combined in a fable about the hybrid character's ongoing relationship with a Chinese competitor as hate turns to love, love to hate, enemies to friends. Unfortunately, incessantly rapid editing fragments the narrative. This might have been intended as an innovation, but it's more of a nuisance. Fine acting, dazzling battle sequences.

NOVECENTO, aka *1900* (1976)

CREDITS:
Produzioni Europee/Artemis; Bernardo Bertolucci, dir.; Bertolucci, Giuseppe Bertolucci, Franco Arcalli, scr.; Alberto Grimaldi, pro.; Ennio Morricone, mus.; Vittorio Storaro, cin.; Franco Arcalli, ed.; C; 1.66:1; 317 min. (director's cut).

CAST:
Robert De Niro (*Alfredo Berilnghieri*); Gerald Depardieu (*Olmo Dalcò*); Dominique Sanda (*Ada*); Sterling Hayden (*Leo Dalcò*); Alida Valli (*Signora Pioppi*); Burt Lancaster (*Alfredo the Elder*); Donald Sutherland (*Mellanchini*); Stefania Sandrelli (*Anita*).

Rating: *** 1/2

As the twentieth century opens, sons are born to a peasant (Hayden) and an aristocrat (Lancaster). The boys (Depardieu, De Niro) discover that contrasting class status does not keep their lives from crisscrossing, especially during the rise of Mussolini. Brilliant images of fields and villages of the Emilia area, captured by the great Storaro, magnificently abetted by a classical score from Morricone and a cast to die for. This should (and could) have been a magnificent movie. What begins as an

Italian twentieth-century *War and Peace* declines, step by step, when human relationships take a back seat to far-left propaganda. Sutherland's depiction of a monstrous Nazi is so over the top that it might better belong in a Mel Brooks spoof than a Bertolucci epic. Shrill, didactic, off-putting.

ONLY THE BRAVE (2006)

CREDITS:
Mission From Buddha Prods.; Lane Nishikawa, dir.; Nishikawa, scr.; Jay Koiwai, Lane Nishikawa, pro.; Kimo Cornwell, mus.; Michael G. Wojciechowski, ed.; Michael G. Wojciechowski, C; 99 min.

CAST:
Tamlyn Tomita (*Mary Takata*); Lane Nishikawa (*Sgt. Takata*); Greg Watanabe (*Pvt. Freddy Watada*); Mark Dacascos (*Sgt. Senzaki*); Kipp Shiotani (*Cpl. Nomu Nomura*); Jason Scott Lee (*Takase*).

Rating: ★★★

"The Purple Heart Battalion" (a nickname proffered owing to a willingness to be wounded) refers to the 100th/442nd. Composed of loyal Japanese American volunteers, they served (under Anglo officers) in North Africa, Italy, and France. The latter included the rescue of the Texas 36th Division, which had been trapped in the Vosges Mountains—WWII's "lost battalion" (October 30, 1944). The story had been previously told in *Go for Broke!*, which, according to Hollywood conventions, focused on the white commander. Here, a Japanese director tells the tale with the Nisei soldiers up front in a $3 million production—expensive by indie film standards. Combat scenes are strong; flashbacks intended to flesh out each soldier's life become intrusive. A fictional framing device is intended as a psychological mystery but plays like a standard soap-opera device.

PARATROOP COMMAND (1959)

CREDITS:
American International Pictures; William Witney, dir.; Stanley Shpetner, scr.; Shpetner, Samuel Z. Arkoff, James H. Nicholson, pro.; Ronald Stein, mus.; Gilbert Warrenton, cin.; Robert S. Eisen, ed.; B&W; 35 mm.; 71 min.

CAST:
Richard Bakalyan (*Charlie*); Ken Lynch (*Lt.*); Jack Hogan (*Ace Mason*); Jimmy Murphy (*Sgt.*); Jeff Morris (*Pigpen*); James Beck (*Cowboy*); Carolyn Hughes (*Gina*).

Rating: ** 1/2

Screw-up Charlie, sick of failing, joins the paratroops, hoping they'll transform him into a success. On his first mission in Africa, he accidentally kills a squad member, earning further animosity. They hit the silk over rural Sicily; he prays for a second chance. Ultra-low-budget item allows character actor Bakalyan, known for 1950s juvenile delinquent roles, his only lead. One risky moment has GIs ogling (from the back) an Italian beauty (Hughes) while she bathes. Lots of stock footage. Never boring.

PEARL HARBOR (2001)

CREDITS:
Touchstone Pictures; Michael Bay, dir.; Randall Wallace, scr.; Bay, Kenny Bates, Jerry Bruckheimer, pro.; Hans Zimmer, mus.; John Schwartzman, cin.; Roger Barton, Mark Goldblatt, Chris Lebenzon, Steven Rosenblum, ed.; C; 2.35:1; 183 min.

CAST:
Ben Affleck (*Capt. Rafe McCawley*); Josh Hartnett (*Capt. Danny Walker*); Kate Beckinsale (*Lt. Evelyn Johnson*); Cuba Gooding, Jr. (*Petty Officer Doris Miller*); Jon Voight (*Pres. Roosevelt*); Alec Baldwin (*Lt. Col. James Doolittle*); Dan Aykroyd (*Capt. Thurman*).

Rating: *** 1/2

Less focused on Pearl Harbor than the significance of aircraft in WWII. The friendship between two youths, both obsessed with flying, is tested when each falls for a nurse. The romantic triangle is trite, derivative, and tiresome. When the Japanese bomb Hawaii, both boys get their planes into the air. Surviving, they volunteer for the Doolittle raid against Tokyo. Too much time given over to annoying melodrama. Still, when combat sequences occur, they are spectacularly wrought via modern CGI effects. The deaths of soldiers and civilians are depicted using state-of-the-art techniques, rendering such moments horrifying.

SANDS OF IWO JIMA (1949)

CREDITS:
Republic Pictures; Allan Dwan, dir.; James Edward Grant, Harry Brown, scr.; Edmund Grainger, pro.; Victor Young, mus.; Reggie Lanning, cin.; Richard L. Van Enger, ed.; B&W; 1.37:1; 100 min.

CAST:
John Wayne (*Sgt. John M. Stryker*); John Agar (*Pfc. Peter Conway*); Adele Mara (*Allison*); Forrest Tucker (*Al Thomas*); Wally Cassell (*Regazzi*); James Brown (*Bass*); Julie Bishop (*Mary*); Richard Jaeckel (*Frank Flynn*); Arthur Franz (*Cpl. Dunne/Narrator*).

Rating: **** 1/2

An uber-patriotic flag-waver; the only major postwar film to surpass earlier combat movies in terms of rah-rah fervor. A tough sergeant oversees the training of young marines. His harsh approach (he does have a heart of gold, as well as his own demons: alcohol and a broken family) masks a desire to give the boys what they need to survive at Tarawa, and then during the deadly climb up Mt. Suribachi. Battle sequences combine combat footage, large-scale location work, and in-studio shooting with rear projection. The first film to collapse Wayne's earlier Western and WWII images: "Alright, marines, *saddle up*; let's get back into this war!"

MOMENT OF GLORY: Three marines (Forest Tucker, John Wayne, John Agar) witness the flag-waving; the actual event.

The three surviving marines who raised the flag—Rene A. Gagnon, Ira H. Hayes, John H. Bradley—portray themselves. Hardly an artistic masterpiece. Still, this big, broad, entertaining movie effectively leads to Stryker's classic last line: "This is the happiest day of my life."

STAND BY FOR ACTION (1942)

CREDITS:
Metro-Goldwyn-Mayer; Robert Z. Leonard, dir.; Laurence Kirk (story), Capt. Harvey S. Haislip, George Bruce, John L. Balderston, Herman J. Mankiewicz, scr.; Leonard, Orville O. Dull, pro.; Lennie Hayton, mus.; Charles Rosher, cin.; George Boemler, ed.; B&W; 1.37:1; 109 min.

CAST:
Robert Taylor (*Lt. Gregg Masterman*); Charles Laughton (*Rear Adm. Stephen Thomas*); Brian Donlevy (*Lt. Cmdr. Roberts*); Walter Brennan (*Chief Yeoman Johnson*); Marilyn Maxwell (*Audrey*).

Rating: **

Best sequence is the documentary/montage opening, beginning with Pearl Harbor, depicting our immediate call to arms. What follows is a long-winded, listless tale about a gruff admiral who teaches his cocky playboy assistant a lesson by assigning him to a reconstituted WWI destroyer, captained by a tough by-the-book type who worked his way up through the ranks. Dull drama in the first half, with an at best routine depiction of training at sea; unworkable comedy in the second, when women and children come on board. Final shootout with enemy battleship comes across as lackluster.

THIRTY SECONDS OVER TOKYO (1944)

CREDITS:
Metro-Goldwyn-Mayer; Mervyn LeRoy, dir.; Robert Considine (book), Ted. W. Lawson (book), Dalton Trumbo, scr.; Sam Zimbalist, pro.; Herbert

THE GREAT RAID: Van Johnson as one of the volunteers who spent "30 Seconds over Tokyo"; the moment of truth depicted.

Stothart, mus.; Harold Rossen, Robert Surtees, cin.; Frank Sullivan, ed.; B&W; 1.37:1; 138 min.

CAST:
Van Johnson (*Ted Lawson*); Robert Walker (*David Thatcher*); Phyllis Thaxter (*Ellen Lawson*); Spencer Tracy (*Lt. Col. James B. Doolittle*); Stephen McNally (*Doc*); Robert Mitchum (*Bob Gray*); Don DeFore (*McClure*).

Rating: **** 1/2

Four months after Pearl, Col. Doolittle (1896–1993) and his strike force, including Ted Lawson (1917–1992), carried out the retaliatory bombing mission followed by a perilous trek home for the survivors. The film meticulously re-creates the process, with realism regarding the training at Florida's Eglin Field and documentary footage for total accuracy. Stories of the men themselves, and the women who loved them, are handled with the sentimentality (all-American guys and girls are all wonderful folks) so characteristic of the era, at least as civilians experienced it in theaters. The lack of enough fuel for most of the B-25s to safely return home adds an aura of ticking-clock suspense. If only Mitchum, wasted in a small role, had played Lawson! Tracy is, not unexpectedly, perfect as the intrepid leader.

THUNDERBIRDS (1952)

CREDITS:
Republic; John H. Auer, dir.; Mary C. McCall, Jr., Kenneth Gamet, scr.; Herbert Yates, John H. Auer, pro.; Victor Young, mus.; Reggie Lanning, cin.; Richard L. Von Enger, ed.; B&W; 1.37:1; 98 min.

CREDITS:
John Derek (*Lt. Gil Hackett*); John Drew Barrymore, aka John Barrymore, Jr. (*Tom McCreery*); Mona Freeman (*Ellen Henderson*); Gene Evans (*Braggart*); Ward Bond (*McCreery*); Barton MacLane (*Durkee*); Ben Cooper (*Jones*).

Rating: *** 1/2

At the war's start, an Oklahoma National Guard unit is called to duty. Soon these men serve with the 45th Infantry Division. Among the heroes are Navajos acting as Native American code talkers. Though burdened by another traditional romantic triangle (best friends Derek and Barrymore romance the same girl), this tightly budgeted item has much going for it. The first screen salute to such unique heroes. However modest the action sequences may be, it's superior to the more recent *Windtalkers*. Indian characters, not some white officer overseeing them, are central in this spunky rendering of their exploits. Mostly focused on the Italian front— specifically, the Sicilian campaign. Proof that an economically produced if sincere work can be more impressive than an empty big-budget rendering.

VICTORS, THE (1963)

CREDITS:
Columbia; Carl Foreman, dir.; Alexander Baron (novel), Foreman, scr.; Foreman, Harold Buck, pro.; Sol Kaplan, mus.; Christopher Challis, cin.; Alan Osbiston, ed.; B&W; 2.35:1; 175 min.

CAST:
George Hamilton (*Trower*); George Peppard (*Chase*); Eli Wallach (*Sgt. Craig*); Melina Mercouri (*Magda*); Jeanne Moreau (*French Woman*); Vince Edwards (*Baker*); Michael Callan (*Eldridge*); Peter Fonda (*Weaver*); Jim Mitchum (*Grogan*); Rosanna Schiaffino (*Maria*); Romy Schneider (*Regine*); Elke Sommer (*Helga*); Albert Finney (*Russian Soldier*).

Rating: ***** (full director's cut)

This massive, masterful movie failed to find an audience, despite the then-young rising stars, male and female. Half an hour was cut out before a butchered print was shipped around the country, eliminating its brilliance and meaning. A great work was reduced to a series of action and romance episodes. Foreman had set out to reinvent the WWII film for a new decade. An infantry squad lands in Italy and moves northward, their later experiences occurring on the road to Berlin. Characters disappear without explanation, confusing to a mainstream moviegoer yet

DEATH OF A PACIFIST: The first Hollywood film to depict the execution of Pvt. Slovik was Carl Foreman's *The Victors*.

precisely how veterans recall the war. Episodes involve everything from homosexuality to the meaningless killing of a small dog. No rah-rah epic, though the director wrote the earlier *Guns of Navarone*. War's absurdity reaches an ironically illogical finale as a once innocent GI (Hamilton) and his Russian counterpart (Finney) meet, fail to communicate, and then kill each other, predicting the Cold War to come. Foreman intercuts grim incidents (including the execution of Pvt. Slovik) with newsreel footage. The cast is uniformly excellent. If the original is ever fully restored, this may finally be appreciated as one of the great WWII movies.

WAY AHEAD, THE, aka *IMMORTAL BATTALION, THE* (1944)

CREDITS:
Twin Cities Films/20th Century Fox; Carol Reed, dir.; Eric Ambler, Peter Ustinov, scr.; John Sutro, Herbert Smith, pro.; William Alwyn, mus.; Guy Green, cin.; Fergus McDonnel, Clive Donner, ed.; B&W; 115 min. (UK), 91 min. (US).

CAST:

David Niven (*Lt. Jim Perry*); Stanley Holloway (*Ted Brewer*); James Donald (*Evan Lloyd*); John Laurie (*Luke*); Leslie Dwyer (*Beck*); Leo Genn (*Edwards*); Tessie O'Shea (*Herself*); Peter Ustinov (*Rispoli*); Trevor Howard (*Officer*); Quentin Reynolds (*Presenter, American version only*).

Ratings: ***** (UK)
*** 1/2 (US)

One of those rare cases in which a film's evolution offers as great a story as the one related. In 1942, Reed, Ambler, and Ustinov donated their services to the British government/military kinematograph and were assigned to produce a training film. In 1943, "The New Lot" was completed; top brass felt it was too discouraging to be seen by recruits. Churchill, impressed by *In Which We Serve*, believed the "The New Lot" could provide the basis for a major film, achieving for the army what the earlier work had for the navy. The trio added Niven to the training sequences and then expanded the piece further as incompetent bunglers not only learn necessary skills but put them into practice at El Alamein. The relationship between a lieutenant and his top sergeant has never been more honestly portrayed. The concept of a democratic army composed of citizen soldiers receives its seminal treatment. Powerful study of the Brit class system in uniform rounds this one out nicely.

WHERE DO WE GO FROM HERE (1945)

CREDITS:

20th Century Fox; Gregory Ratoff, dir.; Morris Ryskind, Sig Herzig, scr.; William Perlberg, pro.; David Raksin, David Buttolph, mus.; Leon Shamroy, cin.; J. Watson Webb, Jr., ed.; C; 1.37:1; 74 min.

CAST:

Fred MacMurray (*Bill Morgan*); Joan Leslie (*Sally Smith*); June Haver (*Lucilla Powell*); Gene Sheldon (*Ali the Genie*); Anthony Quinn (*Chief*

Badger); Alan Mowbray (*George Washington*); Fortunio Bonanova (*Christopher Columbus*).

Rating: * 1/2

At a USO, sad-face Bill can't get a dance with the girls (Leslie, Haver) because he's been ranked 4-F. He brushes dust off an old lamp and a genie appears, whisking the confused hero into the past. This was supposed to be a musical pageant through our country's history, but something went terribly wrong. There's Washington at Valley Forge and at sea with Columbus (in a minioperetta with songs by Kurt Weill and Ira Gershwin) but not much else as one tall tale after another was edited out as too poorly executed to be included in the release. Only appeal is as an odd curio.

WHY WE FIGHT (1942–1945)

CREDITS:

The War Dept./Warner Bros.; Frank Capra, Anthony Veilleur, Anatole Litvak, others, dir.; Capra, Julius J. Epstein, Philip G. Epstein, many others, scr.; Capra, pro.; PHugo Friedhofer, Max Steiner, Dmitri Tiomkin, David Raksin, others, mus.; B&W; 1.31:1. Chapter running times: "Prelude to War," 52 min.; The Nazis Strike," 41 min.; "Divide and Conquer," 57 min.; "Battle of Britain, (The)," 54 min.; "Battle of Russia, (The)," 83 min.; "Battle of China, (The)," 65 min.; "War Comes to America," 70 min.

Rating: *****

As America entered the conflict, the War Department sought out the most patriotic of studios, WB (while also drawing on talents from other companies), to create a documentary/propaganda series. These films provided the public with an ongoing sense of what was at stake and why. They shaped raw material photographed in on-location situations so that the films—individually and as an evolving saga—would shape America's collective vision. Under the general guidance of Capra, this project created a progressive national vision that would carry over into the postwar years. The idea (which was Capra's) espoused cautious optimism: out of the evil

Hitler inflicted on the world, a greater good might arise if the emergent international community seized the day once the war ended and together created a more enlightened world. However much Capra detested the meaning and message of *Triumph of the Will*, he learned much from Riefenstahl's technical tricks for manipulating public responses. Adding to the series' sense of conviction were voice-overs delivered by great actors, Walter Huston among them. Capra's team worked directly with Chief of Staff Gen. George Marshall. Viewed piecemeal at the time, the individual installments offered in succession vivid pieces of an international jigsaw puzzle; these combine to form the biggest "big picture" of them all.

WINDTALKERS (2002)

CREDITS:
Metro-Goldwyn-Mayer; John Woo, dir.; John Rice, Joe Batteer, scr.; Woo, Terence Chang, Tracie Graham-Rice, Alison R. Rosenzweig, pro.; James Horner, mus.; Jeffrey L. Kimball, cin.; Jeff Gullo, Steven Kemper, Tom Rolf, ed.; C; 2.35:1; 134 min. (release print), 153 min. (director's cut).

CAST:
Nicolas Cage (*Sgt. Joe Enders*); Adam Beach (*Ben Yahzee*); Christian Slater ("*Ox*" *Anderson*); Peter Stormare (*Sgt. Hjelmstad*); Noah Emmerich (Chick); Mark Ruffalo (Pappas).

THE GREAT NATIVE AMERICAN CONTRIBUTION: Tribal codes allow the Allies to win victories in *Windtalkers*.

Rating: * 1/2

At Camp Pendleton, CA, Sgt. Enders trains Navajos to be code talkers, employing their unique language for communications that Japanese code busters couldn't crack. Though he cares for likeable windtalker Yahzee, secret orders dictate that under no circumstances can the code, or the man who knows it, fall into enemy hands on Sai Pan. A great subject for an epic results in a forgettable film. Misguided focus on Anglo rather than Native characters marries the project to an outdated mindset. Woo transfers the violent macho clichés of Asian action flicks to a serious piece that demanded an artistic treatment. Clever camera tricks include exhaustive use of dissolves that distances the audience. Brutal battles are overplayed. These alternate with quiet moments in which marines talk conventionally about "back home."

INSTITUTIONALIZED ANTI-SEMITISM: A vicious non-com picks out Jewish soldier 'Noah Ackerman' for prejudicial harassment; Lee Van Cleef and Dean Martin look on in *The Young Lions.*

SOME DREAMS NEVER DIE: The end of the war marked the beginning of a new chapter in the lives of those European civilians who had survived the bombings, only to discover that continuing to live during 'peace-time' would present as great a challenge; here, one woman attempts to make a life for herself in *Anonyma*.

Battle Cry: The Final Days

ANONYMA – EINE FRAU IN BERLIN, aka WOMAN OF BERLIN, aka FALL OF BERLIN, THE (2008)

CREDITS:
Max Farberbock, dir.; Catherina Schuchman, scr., Martha Hillers (book); Eva J. Liand, ed.; Benedict Neuenfels, cin.; Gunter Rohrback, pro.; Constantin Film/Tempus; 131 min., theatrical; 175 min. (director's cut); C; 2.35:1.

CAST:
Nina Hoss (*Anonyma*); Evgeniy Sidikhin (*Maj. Rybkin*); Irm Hermann (*Witwe*); Rudiger Vogler (*Eckhart*); Ulrike Krumbiegel (*Ilse*); Rolf Kanies (*Hotch*).

Rating: **** ½

Between April 29 and June 22, 1945, Russian troops besiege Berlin, occupy the city, shoot all male troublemakers, and rape the women. Horrified by the reoccurring assaults, an attractive frau decides take matters into her own hands, insistent on surviving while other/passive females submit and, in many cases, go mad. The unnamed heroine picks a Soviet major as her 'protector,' afterwards spared attacks by common soldiers, also eating and living decently amid the rubble. In time, this arrangement of mutual convenience transforms into if not love then certainly something very much like it. A former journalist, she (recently identified as Martha Hillers, 1911-2001) kept a diary, a decade later rewritten as a book. The literary piece met with disdain and was all but banned in Germany owing to its less than flattering if unsparingly honest portrait of what German women did to remain not only alive but well in body if not mind or spirit. This film, visualizing chaos as only motion picture can with Hoss' complex performance as its centerpiece, is indelible.

ASHES AND DIAMONDS (1958)

CREDITS:
Zespol Filmowy; Andrzej Wajda, dir.; Wajda, Jerzy Andrzejewski, scr.; Filip Nowak, mus.; Jerzy Wójcik, cin.; Halina Nawrocka, ed.; B&W; 1.66:1; 103 min.

A STUDY IN COURAGE: Young Czechs opposite fascism with what little they have in *Ashes and Diamonds*.

CAST:
Zbigniew Cybulski(*Maciek Chelmicki*); Ewa Krzyzewska (*Krystyna*); Waclaw Zastrzezynski (Szczuka); Adam Pawlikowski (*Andrzej*); Bogumil Kobiela (Drewnowski).

Rating: *****

Spring 1945: Polish guerillas realize their long fight against German invaders is coming to a close. Anyone hoping this will result in peace is in for a rude awakening. A young hero of the Home Army, his early idealism tempered by harsh reality, is assigned to assassinate a Communist previously considered an uneasy ally. Intense drama that moves beyond political considerations into profound moral issues. The title refers to Cyprian Norwid's nineteenth-century poem, which notes that diamonds, the most beautiful inanimate objects on earth, are created when ugly pieces of coal are subjected to great heat and pressure. This also holds true for the creation of heroes from ordinary citizens. Beyond complex characterizations and intricate ideology, rightly recognized as a masterpiece of black-and-white cinema aesthetics.

ATTACK FORCE Z (1982)

CREDITS:
Australian Film Commission/Argent Films; Tim Burstall, dir.; Roger Marshall, scr.; Lee Robinson, pro.; Eric Jupp, mus.; Hung-Chung Lin, cin.; David Stiven, ed.; C; 1.85:1; 93 min. (Australia), 84 min. (US).

CAST:
John Phillip Law (Lt. J. A. Veitch); Mel Gibson (*Capt. P. G. Kelly*); Sam Neill (*Sgt. D. J. Costello*); Chris Haywood (*Sparrer*); John Waters (*Kingo*); Chun Ku (*Rice Farmer*).

Ratings: ** 1/2 (Australian theatrical release)
** (US print)

The Australian Special Forces unit completed more than 280 missions. Most memorable: Project Opossum (April 9 to April 11, 1945). They attacked Singapore from the Krait in hopes of liberating Japan and then launched a suicide mission on Rimau. Unfortunately, this low-budget item inspired by those events is a work of fiction, paying little attention to historic detail. That might be acceptable if the made-up tale were interesting. Not so. The script was extensively rewritten and ruined when Burstall took over from original director Philip Noyce. Battle scenes, cheaply done, are unconvincing.

BATTLE STATIONS (1956)

CREDITS:
Columbia; Lewis Seiler, dir.; Ben Finney, Crane Wilbur, scr.; Bryan Foy, pro.; Burnett Guffey, Mischa Bakaleinikoff, mus.; cin.; Jerome Thoms, ed.; B&W; 1.37:1; 81 min.

CAST:
John Lund (*Father Joseph McIntyre*); Keefe Brasselle (*Chris Jordan*); Richard Boone (*The Captain*); William Leslie (*Kelly*); William Bendix (*Buck*); Jimmy Lydon (*Squawk*).

Rating: *** 1/2

In 1945, new chaplain McIntyre joins the crew of a refurbished aircraft carrier. As old-timer Buck introduces him to this craft, audiences learn about what occurs on a daily basis above board and below. Details of men's lives—duties, relaxation, etc.—are accurately chronicled. This is *the* film to see for anyone interested in the unique life aboard such a ship. On-location filmmaking adds to the realism as does the documentary footage of Pacific action. Still, the film becomes bogged down by clichéd characters: the martinet captain (Boone) with a heart of gold; a maverick (Leslie) who proves his value. Based on occurrences aboard the USS *Franklin* and USS *Bunker Hill* (though this was shot aboard the USS *Princeton*). The same story is told in *Task Force*.

BEACH RED (1967)

CREDITS:
United Artists; Cornel Wilde, dir.; Peter Bowman (novel), Wilde, Clint Johnston, Jefferson Pascal, Don Peters, scr.; Wilde, pro.; Antonino Buenaventura, mus.; Cecil R. Cooney, cin.; Frank P. Keller, ed.; C; 1.85:1; 105 min.

CAST:
Cornel Wilde (*Capt. MacDonald/Narrator*); Rip Torn (*Sgt. Ben Honeywell*); Burr DeBenning (*Egan*); Patrick Wolfe (*Joseph Cliff*); Jean Wallace (*Julie*); Jaime Sánchez (*Colombo*).

Rating: *** 1/2

Wilde's independently produced WWII epic predated *Bonnie and Clyde* and *The Wild Bunch* in creating public furor over graphic screen violence. During the invasion of the Pacific (apparently Leyte), a wounded soldier raises his arm and remains on the ground, spurting blood. Damned as irresponsible exploitation by some; others hailed it as a kind of bold new honesty, necessary for antiwar films during the Vietnam era. Without this groundbreaker, modern masterpieces like *Saving Private Ryan* and *The Thin Red Line* could not exist. Drawbacks: most of Wilde's costars are amateurish, the writing stilted, the flashbacks intrusive. Important, innovative, semisuccessful.

BEGINNING OR THE END, THE (1947)

CREDITS:
Metro-Goldwyn-Mayer; Norman Taurog, dir.; Robert Considine, Frank Wead, scr.; Samuel Marx, pro.; Daniele Amfitheatrof, mus.; Ray June, cin.; George Boemler, ed.; B&W; 1.37:1; 112 min.

CAST:
Brian Donlevy (*Maj. Gen. Leslie R. Groves*); Hume Cronyn (*Dr. J. Robert Oppenheimer*); Robert Walker (*Col. Jeff Nixon*); Tom Drake (*Matt Cochran*); Beverly Tyler (*Anne*); Audrey Totter (*Jean*); Hurd Hatfield (*Dr.

Wyatt); Barry Nelson (*Paul Tibbets Jr.*); Ludwig Stössel (*Albert Einstein*); Ward Baker (*Pres. Truman*).

Rating: *** 1/2

When this film about the development and use of the atomic bomb went into production, it was to have been a docudrama, sharing with a mass audience what had necessarily been kept secret before Hiroshima. Scripting problems involved striking a proper balance between portraying real high-profile people honestly while respecting their concerns about their popular image and maintaining a modicum of privacy. Then, the first stage of the Cold War developed. Rewrite after rewrite tried to bring this true tale from the early 1940s into focus with ever-increasing fears of nuclear holocaust, which explains the question posed in the title. Cronyn steals the show with a finicky portrait of the Manhattan Project's scientific genius. An invented romance is one of several pulled punches that keep this from clicking as intended.

BREAKTHROUGH (1979)

CREDITS:
Palladium/Rapid Film; Andrew V. McLaglen, dir.; Peter Berneis, Tony Williamson, scr.; Wolf C. Hartwig, Hubert Lukowski, pro.; Peter Thomas, mus.; Tony Imi, cin.; Helga Borsche, Raymond Poulton, Herbert Taschner, ed.; C; 2.35:1; 115 min. (US theatrical), 111 min. (German theatrical), 93 min. (international TV print).

CAST:
Richard Burton (*Sgt. Rolf Steiner*); Rod Steiger (*Gen. Webster*); Helmut Griem (*Maj. Von Stransky*); Horst Janson (*Berger*); Véronique Vendell (*Yvette*); Robert Mitchum (*Col. Rogers*); Curd Jürgens (*Gen. Hoffman*).

Rating: *

In-name-only sequel to Peckinpah's *Cross of Iron* with Burton and Griem in the Coburn and Schell roles. Somehow, both characters survived the first film's hopeless finale. With the Germans in full retreat, they must cover the rear. Owing to weak direction, the result is as much a shambles as the military situation depicted. Mitchum and Steiger appear as American generals who hope to convince noble Sgt. Steiner to assassinate Hitler. Violent but dull.

BRIDGE, THE (1959)

CREDITS:
Fono Film; Bernhard Wicki, dir.; Manfred Gregor, aka Gregor Dorfmeister (novel), Wicki, Karl-Wilhelm Vivier, Michael Mansfeld, scr.; Hermann Schwerin, pro.; Hans-Martin Majewski, mus.; Gerd von Bonin, cin.; Carl Otto Bartning, ed.; B&W; 1.37:1; 103 min.

CAST:
Folker Bohnet (*Hans Scholten*); Fritz Wepper (*Albert Mutz*); Michael Hinz (*Walter Forst*); Frank Glaubrecht (*Borchert*); Karl Michael Balzer (*Horber*); Gunther Hoffman (*Sigi*).

THE INNOCENT AND THE DAMNED: Young German boys are led to the slaughter in *The Bridge*.

Rating: *****

April 27, 1945: in Cham (Bulgaria), a handful of fifteen-year-old boys are assigned to hold the Florian-Geyer bridge at all costs. The officer class knows the war is lost, but since a surrender hasn't been arranged, their approach is business as usual. The boys have no notion of this. From childhood, they were indoctrinated into the Nazi youth; each believes he is striking a blow for the fatherland. This ugly irony underlies what may be the most intense coming-of-age story ever filmed. Each youth is particularized; the audience perceives them as real people rather than dramatic characters. As the bridge will eventually be blown up by the Germans—an absurdity the boys have not been informed about—the vision darkens further. Sans didactic statements, this rates as one of the great antiwar movies via its implications in a deceptively simple narrative. Mesmerizing, memorable.

BURMESE HARP, THE (1956)

CREDITS:
Nikkatsu; Kon Ichikawa, dir.; Michio Takeyama (novel), Natto Wada, scr.; Masayuki Takagi, pro.; Akira Ifukube, mus.; Minoru Yokoyama, cin.; Masanori Tsujii, ed.; B&W; 1.33:1; 116 min.

CAST:
Rentarô Mikuni (*Capt. Inouye*); Shôji Yasui (*Mizushima*); Jun Hamamura (*Ito*) Taketoshi Naitô (*Kobayashi*); Shunji Kasuga (*Maki*); Kô Nishimura (*Baba*); Keishichi Nakahara (*Takagi*).

Rating: **** 1/2

Yasui, a military messenger, or "harp," disguises himself as a monk and embarks on a personal odyssey to locate former comrades. Meanwhile, he comes to terms with what the great defeat means for him and his nation. Most of his hours are spent burying deceased soldiers, an eerie ritual for this deeply troubled everyman. Eventually, he emerges as a secular saint, dedicated to not only a nearly endless self-assumed task but also

END OF THE LINE: Young Japanese warriors, grasping that victory is impossible, prepare to die with dignity *in The Burmese Harp.*

spreading the antiwar doctrine that harsh experience has taught him. A meditation on the value of life and the insanity of war, as well as the unexpected manner in which people seek to obtain wisdom. Stark visuals involving nature recall Kurosawa.

EROICA (1958)

CREDITS:
ZRF "Kadr"/POLart; Andrzej Munk, dir.; Jerzy Stefan Stawinski, scr.; Jan Krenz, mus.; Jerzy Wójcik, cin.; Miroslawa Garlicka, Jadwiga Zajicek, ed.; B&W; 1.66:1; 87 min.

CAST:
"Scherzo alla Polacca": Edward Dziewonski (*Gorkiewicz*); Barbara Polomska (*Zosia*); Ignacy Machowski (*The Major*); Leon Niemczyk (*Lt.*

Kolya). "Ostinato Lugubre": Kazimierz Rudzki (*Lt. Turek*); Henryk Bak (*Lt. Krygier*); Mariusz Dmochowski (*Lt. Makowski*); Roman Klosowski (*Lt. Szpakowski*).

Rating: **** 1/2

This fine two-part work (originally, there was to have been third chapter) is an excellent example of how WWII movies impose on that conflict the tenor of the times in which they were made, as well as the attitudes of the country of origin. "Scherzo alla Polacca" offers irony galore. A Polish youth, who in combat avoids heroics to save his skin, inadvertently becomes a hero of the people. A POW adventure is presented in "Ostinato Lugubre." The lead (Rudzki) sneaks out, not owing to an idealistic desire to rejoin the fight but because of a realistic problem: his fellow prisoners annoy him. He, too, becomes a hero to his fellows. Comedies on the edge of tragedy; enlightening in terms of what the concept we call "heroism" really means.

FAT MAN AND LITTLE BOY, aka SHADOW MAKERS (1989)

CREDITS:
Paramount; Roland Joffe, dir.; Joffe, Bruce Robinson, scr.; Tony Garnett, pro.; Ennio Morricone, mus.; Vilmos Zsigmond, cin.; Francoise Bonnot, ed.; C; 2:35:1; 127 min.

CAST:
Paul Newman (*Gen. Leslie R. Groves*); Dwight Schultz (*J. Robert Oppenheimer*); John Cusack (*Michael Merriman*); Bonnie Bedelia (*Kitty*); John Cusack (*Michael Merriman*); Natasha Richardson (*Jean Tatlock*).

Rating: * 1/2

A secretive mission in New Mexico served as a cover for the creation of nuclear weapons. Everything was overseen by tough old General Groves and brilliant young scientist Oppenheimer. The title refers to the workers' nicknames for the bombs, soon to be dropped on Nagasaki and Hiroshima. One more Joffe project that, on the surface, looks like an important movie but lacks depth, effective storytelling, and well-developed characters. Newman, appearing tired, is dreadful in the kind of role John Wayne all but patented; Schultz has no charisma. Stupefyingly dull.

FIRES ON THE PLAIN (1959)

CREDITS:
Daiei Studios/Kadokawa Herald Pics.; Kon Ichikawa, dir.; Shohei Ooka (novel), Natto Wada, scr.; Masaichi Nagata, pro.; Yasushi Akutagawa, mus.; Setsuo Kobayashi, Setsuo Shibata, cin.; Tatsuji Nakashizu, ed.; B&W; 2.25:1; 108 min.

CAST:
Eiji Funakoshi (*Tamura*); Osamu Takizawa (*Yasuda*); Mickey Curtis (*Nagamatsu*); Mantarô Ushio (*Sergeant*); Kyû Sazanka (*Surgeon*); Yoshihiro Hamaguchi(*Officer*); Asao Sano, Masaya Tsukida (*Soldiers*).

Rating: *****

February 1945: for the surviving Japanese defenders of Leyte, defeat is an inevitable fate. They cannot be reinforced or resupplied by home bases owing to the Allied fleet. Sad-faced Pvt. Funakoshi has been abandoned by his own unit since his tuberculosis slows down the others. As he wanders, Funakoshi notices small fires burning in the distance in the evening. He wonders who might be lighting them and why. What he fails to grasp is that precise answers matter less than understanding the human need to create bright spots as darkness descends (symbolically as well as realistically) to maintain a small sense of hope. Bizarre black humor suffuses this almost nihilistic piece. It dares to acknowledge that cannibalism became an option for those who believed it more important to continue living at any cost than to die with dignity. Overpowering.

FIRST YANK INTO TOKYO (1945)

CREDITS:

RKO; Gordon Douglas, dir.; J. Robert Bren, Gladys Atwater, scr.; Bren, pro.; Leigh Harline, mus.; Harry J. Wild, cin.; Philip Martin, ed.; B&W; 1.37:1; 82 min.

CAST:

Tom Neal (*Maj. Steve Ross*); Barbara Hale (*Abby Drake*); Marc Cramer (*Lewis Jardine*); Richard Loo (*Okanura*); Key Luke (*Haan-Soo*); Leonard Strong (*Nogira*); Benson Fong (*Tanahe*).

Rating: ** 1/2

American patriot Ross makes an extreme sacrifice: he undergoes then-still-risky plastic surgery, having his face altered into that of an Asian. He then parachutes into Japan and finds work at a prison camp. There, he makes contact with an Ally who has key information that must be relayed back to the US government. Hale plays the love interest with a tendency to show up at the wrong place at the wrong time. Original, to say the least, and amusing in its exaggerated B-movie way. When the atomic bomb was dropped on Hiroshima, the film (ready for release) had to be returned to the studio, its ending reshot to adhere to, rather than conflict with, recent history. The first feature to acknowledge Hiroshima, even if the last-minute rewriting left much to be desired. The camp in question is Kamuri. A great favorite of Quentin Tarantino.

FLAGS OF OUR FATHERS (2006)

CREDITS:

DreamWorks/Amblin/Malpaso; Clint Eastwood, dir.; James Bradley (book), Ron Powers (book); William Broyles, Jr., Paul Haggis, scr.; Eastwood, Steven Spielberg, Robert Lorenz, pro.; Eastwood, mus.; Tom Stem, cin.; Joel Cox, ed.; C; 2.35:1; 135 min.

THE WORLD WAR II EPIC FILM LIVES ON: Director Clint Eastwood brings a classic form back to theatre screens in *Flags of our Fathers*.

CAST:

Ryan Phillippe (*John "Doc" Bradley*); Jesse Bradford (*Rene Gagnon*); Adam Beach (*Ira Hayes*); John Benjamin Hickey (*Keyes*); John Slattery (*Bud Gerber*); Barry Pepper (*Strank*).

Rating: *****

February 19, 1945: marines land on Iwo Jima as part of the final retaking of the Pacific. Despite three days of naval bombardment, Japanese defenders inflict heavy casualties during a sea-to-land assault via Higgins boats. Two days later, during the bloodthirsty battle for Mt. Suribachi, five members of the Second Platoon raise an American flag. Two soon die under heavy fire. A photograph of the flag-raising, supposedly caught on the fly, is circulated on the home front, a unifying symbol of American indomitability. Three survivors, including Native American Ira Hayes, return stateside to appear at bond rallies. Each knows that if the facts behind this supposedly "true" story were ever told, it would destroy this media-made myth. Eastwood–Spielberg collaboration offers a revisionist reply to such rah-rah films as *Sands of Iwo Jima*. The manner in which men of integrity are destroyed by an inability to speak the truth is presented here through interlocking if contradictory flashbacks. Absolutely stunning.

FLYING MISSILE, THE (1950)

CREDITS:
Columbia; Henry Levin, dir.; Richard English, James Gunn, H. Richard Nash, scr.; Jerry Bresler, pro.; George Duning, mus.; William E. Snyder, cin.; Viola Lawrence, ed.; B&W; 1.37:1; 91 min.

CAST:
Glenn Ford (*Cmdr. William A. Talbot*); Viveca Lindfors (*Karin Hansen*); Henry O'Neill (*Rear Adm. Thomas A. Scott*); Carl Benton Reid (*Gates*); Joe Sawyer (*Fuss Payne*).

Rating: * 1/2

After seeing the recently devised V-2 missile, a sub commander wonders if underwater crafts such as his USS *Bluefin* ("portrayed" by the USS *Cusk*) might be armed with it. The complex series of events by which subs were retooled to employ flying missiles is oversimplified such that the film has no historical value. Nor is the drama involving the hero and the gorgeous Lindfors convincing. Set in the later days of WWII, this film was fashioned at the height of the Cold War to remind audiences of the firepower in our possession which, if necessary, could be employed again, this time against the Reds.

FRANKENSTEIN'S ARMY (2013)

CREDITS:
MPI Media/Dark Sky; Richard Raaphorst, dir.; Raaphorst, Miguel Tejada-Flores, scr.; Raaphorst, Todd Brown, Nick Jongerius, Daniel Koefoed, Greg Newman, pro.; Reyn Ouwehand, mus.; Bart Beekman, cin.; Aaron Crozier, Jasper Verhorevoort, ed.; C; 1.78:1; 84 min.

CAST:
Robert Gwilym (*Novikov*); Hon Ping Tang (*Ivan*); Alexander Mercury (*Dimitri*); Luke Newberry (*Sacha*); Joshua Sasse (*Sergei*); Mark Stevenson (*Alexei*).

Rating: **

This Dutch-American-Czech collaboration concerns a squad of Soviet soldiers who set out to scout the Eastern front. They discover a Nazi using Dr. Frankenstein's theories to create a monster-zombie army of the undead. Clever idea is okay for half an hour but then has nowhere to go. Might have worked better as a ten-minute *Saturday Night Live* skit, especially since it's shot in the "found-footage" style popularized by *The Blair Witch Project* (1999)—so overdone by now that the shaky-camera style is a laughable cliché. Best element: effective creature special effects.

FURY (2014)

CREDITS:
Columbia; David Ayer, dir.; Ayer, scr.; Ayer, Bill Block, John Lesher, Ethan Smith, pro.; Steven Price, mus.; Roman Vasyanov, cin.; Jay Cassidy, Dody Dom, ed.; C; 2.35:1; 134 min.

A UNIQUE FORM OF WARFARE: Few films have brought the operations within a tank so vividly to life as *Fury* with Brad Pitt.

CAST:
Brad Pitt (*Don "Wardaddy" Collier*); Shia LaBeouf (*Boyd "Bible" Swan*); Logan Leman (*Norman Ellison*); Michael Peña (*Trini "Gordo" Garcia*); Jon Bernthal (*Grady "Coon-Ass"*).

Rating: *** 1/2

With the 66th Armored Regiment, 2nd Armored Division, tank commander Collier, his five battle-seasoned crewmembers, and new replacement Ellison head their M4A3E8 Sherman into the eye of the storm. Tension develops between the leader, planning to mercilessly kill the enemy, and the newcomer, who still hangs on to the values of society. The tank battles are among the greatest (perhaps *the* greatest) ever put on film by an American company, offering an in-your-face, unromanticized vision of combat. Ayer's wobbly script cannot match his excellent direction. Individuals aren't developed nor are the relationships fleshed out. Always believable. The cast is admirable, and the final last-stand sequence is memorable, but the reversal/twist ending doesn't make sense. Belton Y. Cooper's *Death Traps* (2003) provided the historic details.

HASTY HEART, THE (1949)

CREDITS:
Warner Bros.; Vincent Sherman, dir.; John Patrick (play), Ranald MacDougall, scr.; Robert Clark, pro.; Jack Beaver, mus.; Wilkie Cooper, cin.; Edward B. Jarvis, ed.; B&W; 1.37:1; 102 min.

CAST:
Richard Todd (*Cpl. Lachlan MacLachlan*); Patricia Neal (*Margaret Parker*); Ronald Reagan (*Yank*); Orlando Martins (*Blossom*); Anthony Nicholls (*Lt. Col. Dunn*).

Rating: **** 1/2

Allies rejoice that combat has ceased. For the wounded, forced to remain in an isolated Burma hospital, the horror is far from over. Bitter, overly self-reliant Scotsman MacLachlan moves into a bamboo house with five other patients. They, and nurse Parker, know what he does not: apparently recovered, he will die within weeks. Excellent melodrama drawn from Patrick's successful play of the same name. This analysis of the relationship between pity and friendship finds Reagan, as an easygoing American, in one of his best roles. Still-sturdy tearjerker has one limitation: a single set with the act and scene divisions all too obvious. It's hard to think of this as a true movie rather than canned theater.

HAUPTMAN, DER, aka CAPTAIN, THE (2017)

CREDITS:
Filmgalerie 451/Alfalma; Robert Schwentke, dir.; Schwentke, scr.; Frieder Schlaich, pro.; Martin Todsharow, mus.; Florian Ballhaus, cin.; Michal Czarnecki, ed.; 2.35:1; B&W/C; 118 min.

CAST:
Max Hubacher *(Willi Herold)*; Milan Peschel *(Freytag)*; Bernd Holscher *(Schutte)*; Frederick Lau *(Kipinski)*; Waldemar Kobus *(Hansen)*; Alexander Fehling *(Junker)*; Samuel Finzi *(Roger)*; Wolfram Koch *(Schneider)*; Eugenie Anselin *(Irmgard)*.

Rating: **** ½

During the war's final weeks, numerous German soldiers deserted in hopes of returning to civilian life and being spared by the encroaching Allies. One, Willi Herold (1925-1946), wrapped himself in a discarded Luftwaffe captain's jacket to avoid freezing. When a company of hardcore Nazis happened upon him, they assumed Herold to be what he appeared and put him in command. "Power corrupts," an old saying goes, "and absolute power corrupts absolutely." Crazed with sudden adulation he had never before known, Herold led the others on a mad killing spree that earned him the notorious nickname 'Executioner of Emsland.' A fascinating retelling of a fact-based tale, also a perceptive meditation on human personality, and the manner in which any man's 'identity' is shaped less by inner character than the perceptions of those around him. Highly effective use of black and white cinematography to recapture the feel of war-time documentaries. Hailed at the 2017 Toronto Film Festival.

HELL IN THE PACIFIC (1968)

CREDITS:
Selmur Productions; John Boorman, dir.; Alexander Jacobs, Eric Bercovici, scr.; Reuben Bercovitch, pro.; Lalo Schifrin, mus.; Conrad L. Hall, cin.; Thomas Stanford, ed.; C; 2.35:1; 103 min.

CAST:
Lee Marvin (*The American Pilot*); Toshirô Mifune (*Captain Tsuruhiko Kuroda*).

Rating: ****

A Japanese warrior, stranded on a remote island, hopes to be rescued. Then, an American washes ashore. Initially, they try to kill each other, gradually realizing they must cooperate to survive. Not, as the title might suggest, a big-scale action film. Rather, it's an intimate chamber drama about war's absurdity. A WWII film informed by Vietnam and the public's growing distaste for war. Brilliant visual storytelling nearly devoid of dialogue; ideas and emotions are conveyed through images by this superb filmmaker. *H.I.T.P.* might've been a towering classic. Sadly, an absurd apocalyptic ending was tacked on by the producers that negates everything Boorman's film had intended to say.

HEROES (1973)

CREDITS:
Antlantida Films; Duccio Tessari, dir.; René Havard, Albert Kantof (novel), Sergio Donati; José Luis Martínez; Luciano Vincenzoni, scr.;

THE ULTIMATE SAMURAI: Toshiro Mifune embodied the Japanese warrior in *Hell in the Pacific.*

Alfredo Bini, pro.; Riz Ortolani, mus.; Carlo Carlini, cin.; Mario Morra, ed.; 2.35:1; 105 min.

CAST:

Rod Taylor (*Bob Robson*); Rod Steiger (*Baron Guenther von Lutz*); Rosanna Schiaffino (*Katrin*); Claude Brasseur (*Raphael*); Aldo Giuffrè (*Spartaco*);

Terry-Thomas (*Cooper*).

Rating: **

Released under various titles (*Gli Eroi* among them), with different running times, not to mention multinational dubbings. This is one of those intriguing concepts that, with craft and care, might've resulted in a comic gem on the order of *Kelly's Heroes*. Taylor plays an Allied officer saddled with a captured German aristocrat (Steiger, overacting to the hilt), a bizarre English twit (Terry-Thomas), and a feisty Greek prostitute (Schiaffino). They steal treasure by disguising the loot in plasma boxes. The choice between personal profit and selfless duty, the theme of the substantial novel on which this was based, gets lost in a slipshod international production.

HITLER: THE LAST TEN DAYS (1973)

CREDITS:
Paramount/Tomorrow Ent.; Ennio De Concini, dir.; Gerhardt Boldt (book), De Concini, Maria Pia Fusco, Ivan Moffat, Wolfgang Reinhardt, scr.; Reinhardt, pro.; Mischa Spoliansky, mus.; Ennio Guarnieri, cin.; Kevin Connor, ed.; C; 1.77:1; 108 min.

CAST:
Alec Guinness (*Adolf Hitler*); Simon Ward (*Capt. Hoffman*); Adolfo Celi (*Gen. Krebs*); Diane Cilento (*Hanna Reitsch*); Gabriele Ferzetti (*Keitel*); Eric Porter (*Gen. von Greim*); Doris Kunstmann (*Eva Braun*).

Rating: ** 1/2

April 20, 1945: the Führer, celebrating his birthday in a Berlin bunker, decides not to evacuate as the Allies close in. Based on Boldt's reminiscences about the way Hitler alternately denied that the end was at hand and launched into out-of-control tirades when he saw the writing on the wall. This ambitious work falls victim to pedantic, methodical, by-the-book direction. The result is a mishmash that fails to live up to Sir

SIR ALEC'S TAKE ON ABJECT EVIL: Mr. Guinness in *Hitler: The Last Ten Days.*

Alec's nuanced, complex portrait. Obvious cross-cuts from the single set to historical footage results in overdone didacticism rather than the intended irony. The final conversation between Hitler and his mistress Eva Braun— the only interchange that's invented—is the weakest moment in the movie.

HOME OF THE BRAVE (1949)

CREDITS:

Stanley Kramer Prods.; Mark Robson, dir.; Arthur Laurents (play), Carl Foreman, scr.; Stanley Kramer, Robert Stillman, pro.; Dimitri Tiomkin, mus.; Robert De Grasse, cin.; Harry W. Gerstad, ed.; B&W; 1.37:1; 85 min.

CAST:

James Edwards (*Pvt. Peter Moss*); Douglas Dick (*Maj. Robinson*); Jeff Corey (*Medic*); Lloyd Bridges (*Finch*); Frank Lovejoy (*Sgt. Mingo*); Cliff Clark (*Col. Baker*).

Rating: **** 1/2

THE BIRTH OF CIVIL RIGHTS CINEMA: James Edwards portrays the first African-American soldier in a previously all-white company in the breakthrough film *Home of the Brave.*

Edwards (1918–1970) was the first African American to play lead roles in mainstream movies, reflecting changing attitudes toward race in postwar America. Here, he enacts a replacement who joins a combat unit following Truman's edict that the military must be integrated. Met by taunts and worse, he must force the squad to accept him through trial by combat. Grim, harrowing, convincing. An early important work by producer Kramer, who would define the message movie. The play on which this was based dealt with anti-Semitism; following the release of *Crossfire* and *Gentleman's Agreement* (1947), that subject seemed to have been covered. Small-scale production bolstered by breakthrough thematic daring and Robson's sure-handed direction of the cast.

HOTEL BERLIN (1945)

CREDITS:
Warner Bros.; Peter Godfrey, dir.; Vicki Baum (novel), Alvah Bessie, Jo Pagano, scr.; Louis F. Edelman, pro.; Franz Waxman, mus.; Carl E. Guthrie, cin.; Frederick Richards, ed.; B&W; 1.37:1; 98 min.

CAST:
Andrea King (*Lisa Dorn*); Helmut Dantine (*Martin Richter*); Faye Emerson (*Tillie Weiler*); Raymond Massey (*von Dahnwitz*); Peter Lorre (*Koenig*); Alan Hale (*Plottke*); George Coulouris (*Helm*); Henry Daniell (*Von Stetten*).

Rating: ****

Berlin 1945: anti-Nazi German Underground leader Richter escapes a concentration camp. He hides in a hotel where elegant guests continue their upscale lifestyle, in denial that Allied bombing raids will soon end their regime. He becomes the secret lover of beautiful actress Lisa, who is the mistress of high-ranking officer von Dahnwitz. A follow-up to author Baum's more famous *Grand Hotel*, proving once more what a master of intricate plotting this forgotten writer was. Fascinating film featuring an odd combination of A-movie production values and a B-level female lead. King is lovely as the femme fatale but lacks the acting chops of a Dietrich, Garbo, or Bergman. Notable as the first film to make explicit that many Nazis escaped, relocating somewhere in the Americas to create a Fourth Reich. Also, honest regarding how cruelly unsparing resistance members could be.

JOY DIVISION (2006)

CREDITS:
Reg Traviss, dir.; Traviss, Rosemary Mason, scr.; Kim Legatt, pro.; Peter Cartwright, ed.; Bryan Loftus, cin.; George Kallis, mus.; Dreamtool Ent.; 105 min.; C.

CAST:

Ed Stoppard *(Thomas, age 31)*; Tom Schilling *(Thomas, age 14)*; Bernadette Heerwagen *(Melanie)*; Bernard Hill *(Dennis)*; Lea Mornar *(Astrid)*; Michelle Gayle *(Yvonne)*; Sean Chapman *(Harris)*; Sybille Gebhardt *(Steph)*; Ricci Harnett *(Sgt.)*.

Rating: *** ½

The last bastions of Berlin crumble under Soviet attack in 1944; desperate, the German military rounds up children to fight. As in an earlier classic *The Bridge*, Joy Division depicts their courage despite such boys' lack of comprehension as to the hopelessness of the situation. Stunning cinematography brings the true terrors of Nazi-end-game to vivid life. Unfortunately, the strong action scenes are presented as flashbacks in a spy story set during the Beatles era of swingin' London. This aspect is confusing and appears incomplete, as if some moments were never filmed or, sadly, left on the cutting room floor.

KELLY'S HEROES (1970)

CREDITS:

Metro-Goldwyn-Mayer; Brian G. Hutton, dir.; Troy Kennedy-Martin, scr.; Sidney Beckerman, Gabriel Katzka, Harold Loeb, pro.; Lalo Schifrin, mus.; Gabriel Figueroa, cin.; John Jympson, ed.; C; 2.35:1; 144 min.

CAST:

Clint Eastwood *(Kelly)*; Telly Savalas *(Sgt. "Big" Joe)*; Don Rickles *(Crapgame)*; Carroll O'Connor *(Gen. Colt)*; Donald Sutherland *(Oddball)*; Gavin MacLeod *(Moriarty)*; Stuart Margolin *(Little Joe)*; Harry Dean Stanton *(Willard)*.

Rating: **** 1/2

The Dirty Dozen meets *The Good, the Bad, and the Ugly* for a unique WWII action-comedy. Demoted from lieutenant to private owing to other men's mistakes, Kelly grows cynical and self-serving. When he

A TURNABOUT IN VALUES: Soldiers who for years fought for altruistic reasons turn cynical and self-serving as the war approaches its end in *Kelly's Heroes* with Clint Eastwood.

learns that a stash of gold bars sit in a bank thirty miles behind enemy lines, Kelly assembles his scavengers, including tough Sgt. Joe, New York gambler Crapgame, and anachronistic hippie Oddball. Imitated many times, including the film *Three Kings* (1999). WWII as seen through the prism of Vietnam; now, all combat—even the crusade in Europe—could be cynically depicted. The absurdist image of a Sherman tank blithely mowing down not only Nazi soldiers but also French prisoners as "The Yellow Rose of Texas" blares provides the seminal sequence. Overuse of zoom lenses doesn't detract from the snappy pace (despite the inordinate length) and surefire ensemble playing. Eastwood, Savalas, and Sutherland facing down the Nazis spaghetti-western style is priceless.

LAST TEN DAYS, THE (1955)

CREDITS:

Cosmopol-Film/Columbia; Georg Wilhelm (G. W.) Pabst, dir.; Fritz Habeck (novel), Erich Maria Remarque, scr.; Carl Szokoll, pro.; Erwin Halletz, mus.; Gunther Andrews, cin.; Herbert Taschner, ed.; B&W; 1.37:1; 113 min.

CAST:

Albin Skoda (*Hitler*); Oskar Werner (*Hauptmann Wüst*), Lotte Tobisch (*Eva Braun*); Willy Krause (*Goebbels*); Erich Stuckmann (*Himmler*); Erland Erlandsen (*Speer*); Curt Eilers (*Bormann*).

Rating: ****

Inside the bunker, mad discussions of survival strategies alternate with outrageous orgies. Such events are presented to the postwar viewer through the eyes of an everyman figure: humble guard Hauptmann, who never wanted to be in uniform. This allows for an objective perspective, filtering surreal occurrences through the mind of an ordinary person who finds himself in the wrong place at the wrong time. Working on a tight budget, legendary director Pabst makes the most of each situation, penned by Germany's revered antifascist author Remarque. Historians will note several inaccuracies, minor in terms of the major scope of this forgotten film.

LETTERS FROM IWO JIMA (2006)

CREDITS:

DreamWorks; Clint Eastwood, dir.; Tadamichi Kuribayashi (book), Iris Yamashita, Paul Haggis, scr.; Clint Eastwood, Robert Lorenz, Steven Spielberg, pro.; Kyle Eastwood, Michael Stevens, mus.; Tom Stern, cin.; Joel Cox, Gary Roach, ed.; C; 2.35:1; 141 min.

CAST:

Ken Watanabe (*General Kuribayashi*); Kazunari Ninomiya (*Saigo*); Tsuyoshi Ihara (*Baron Nishi*); Ryo Kase (*Shimizu*); Shido Nakamura (*Ito*);

Hiroshi Watanabe (*Fujita*); Takumi Bando (*Tanida*).

Rating: *****

The battle of Iwo Jima is here related from the Japanese perspective. This allows American audiences to grasp that Suribachi represented to its defenders an Asian Alamo: men fighting on, knowing there would be no reinforcements, in desperate hope of keeping the enemy from conquering their homeland. Eastwood chose an epistolary approach derived from Gen. Kuribayashi's letters. The piece effectively humanizes and de-demonizes the Japanese without patronizing or sentimentalizing them. However much we sympathize with sensitive commanding general Kuribayashi or desperate-to-survive common man Saigo, we witness the vicious treatment of Japanese defenders by their officers, as well as the cold-blooded killing of a captured American, which is balanced by a later horrific turnaround. Battle sequences, shot in diffused color, harrowingly approximate black-and-white newsreels.

MARINE RAIDERS (1944)

CREDITS:
RKO; Harold D. Schuster, dir.; Warren Duff, Martin Rackin, scr.; Robert Fellows, pro.; Roy Webb, mus.; Nicholas Musuraca, cin.; Philip Martin, ed.; B&W; 1.37:1; 90 min.

CAST:
Pat O'Brien (*Maj. Steve Lockhart*); Robert Ryan (*Capt. Dan Craig*); Ruth Hussey (*Ellen Foster*); Frank McHugh (*Sgt. Leary*); Barton MacLane (*Maguire*); Martha Vickers (*Sally*).

Rating: ***

Two marines meet again at Camp Elliott, where each has been sent for retraining. Higher-ranking Lockhart ruined the love affair between subordinate Craig and an Australian girl while he recuperated from battle fatigue. Still, the 1st Marine Raider Battalion's volunteers must learn Leatherneck skills. Personal enmity aside, the two must get the job done. Shot on location, authentic drilling sequences bolster an otherwise lackluster film. The melodrama is familiar, contrived, unconvincing.

MAUDITS, LES, aka DAMNED, THE (1947)

CREDITS:

Speva; René Clément, dir.; Clément, Jacques Rémy, Jacques Companéez, Victor Alexandrov, Henri Jeanson, scr.; André Paulvé, Michel Safra, Paul Wagner, pro.; Yves Baudrier, mus.; Henri Alekan, cin.; Roger Dwyre, ed.; B&W; 1.37:1; 105 min.

CAST:

Marcel Dalio (*Larga*); Henry Vidal (*Dr. Guilbert*); Florence Marly (*Hilde Garosi*); Fosco Giachetti (*Garosi*); Paul Bernard (*Couturier*); Jo Dest (*Forster*); Michel Auclair (*Willy*).

Rating: ****

April 19, 1945: an odd assortment of Nazi collaborators and brass escape in a sub, headed for South America. Forced to join them: kidnapped doctor Guilbert, ordered to attend to medical needs. He provides a moral perspective on these despicable people as they use and verbally abuse one another, each desperate for individual survival. Symbolically, they are all dead already, merely going through the motions of daily life until, one by one, they descend into hell. Jean-Paul Sartre's similarly structured play *No Exit* (1944), sans the WWII setting, likely inspired this existential piece. Clément provides a ray of sunlight (in comparison to Sartre) via the innocent narrator, indicating that decent humans still exist. Suitably claustrophobic.

MOUNTAIN ROAD, THE (1960)

CREDITS:
William Goetz Productions; Daniel Mann, dir.; Theodore H. White (novel), Alfred Hayes, scr.; William Goetz, pro.; Jerome Moross, mus.; Burnett Guffey, cin.; Edward Curtiss, ed.; B&W; 1.85:1; 102 min.

CAST:
James Stewart (*Maj. Baldwin*); Lisa Lu (*Madame Sue-Mei Hung*); Glenn Corbett (*Collins*); Henry/Harry Morgan (*Michaelson*); Frank Silvera (*Col. Kwan*); James Best (*Niergaard*).

Rating: *** 1/2

In 1944, as Japanese troops pour into eastern China, refugees flee via the title route along with American engineers trying to slow down the enemy by blowing up a bridge. Talky, leisurely paced, directed in a matter-of-fact style. Fashioned from White's 1958 revisionist work, adjusted for a time when the two Asian nations had traded places in our view. Here, Chinese are so self-serving they inadvertently kill a nice American boy trying to feed them. The invading army is notably less monstrous than in 1940s films. The final battle is waged between Americans and the Reds. Thoughtful film delves into such themes as unconscious-but-potent racism, the corrupting influence of power, and the responsibility of command.

NEGRO SOLDIER, THE (1944)

CREDITS:
The War Department; Stuart Heisler, dir.; Carlton Moss, scr.; Frank Capra, pro.; Dmitri Tiomkin, Howard Jackson, Calvin Jackson, Earl Robinson, Albert Glasser, mus.; Allen Q. Thompson, Paul Vogel, Horace Woodard, cin.; B&W; 1.37:1; 43 min.

CAST:
William Broadus, Clarence Brooks, Norman Ford, Carlton Moss, Clyde Turner, Bertha Woolford, George Washington Carver, Jesse Owens (*Themselves*).

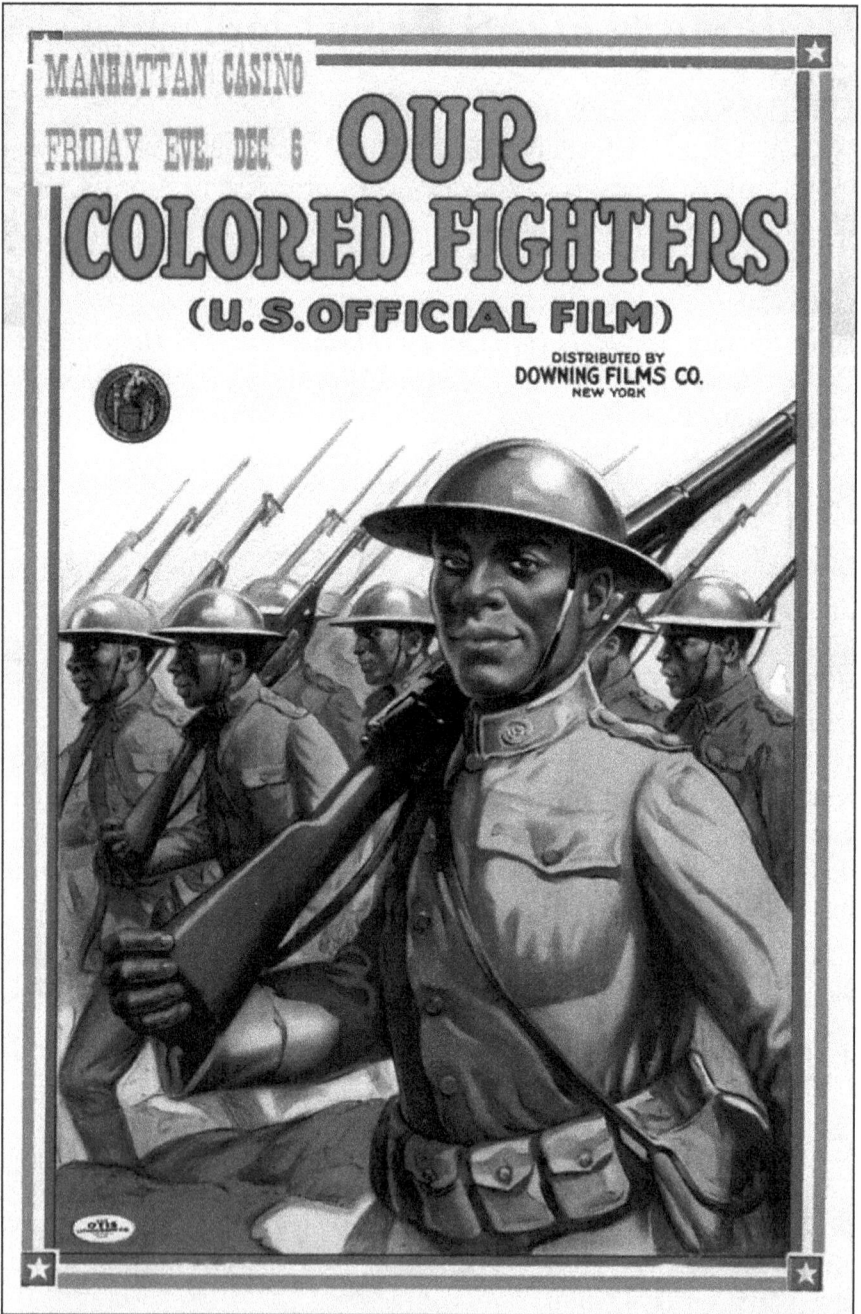

TOWARD AN INTEGRATED AMERICA: The end of segregation in the military led to the Civil Rights Movement in post-war America; that key moment in time was captured in a film known as *The Colored Soldier* and alternately *The Negro Soldier*.

Rating: ****

As early as the Great War, filmmakers supported African Americans in the armed services (*Negro Soldiers Fighting for Uncle Sam* (1918), *Heroic Negro Soldiers of the World War* (1919)). Such efforts increased when, during WWII, the military was integrated. The talents that had assembled the educational *Why We Fight* series were called upon to educate black Americans about the value of joining up, whites on the need to overcome prejudices. Created by the War Department, this film did play in theaters. Producer Capra, an officer, was the first filmmaker to tacitly avoid stereotypes in his on-screen portrayals of Negro soldiers. Employing stock footage from earlier Hollywood projects, the film includes tributes to black heroes dating back to the Boston Massacre. As a framing device, Capra chose a rural church to emphasize deep devotion on the part of his characters. Commercial moviemakers soon picked up the ball.

NIHON NO ICHIBAN NAGAIHI, aka *JAPAN'S LONGEST DAY* (1967)

CREDITS:
Toho Company; Kihachi Okamoto, dir.; Soichi Oya (book), Shinobu Hashimoto, scr.; Sanezumi Fujimoto, Tomoyuki Tanaka, pro.; Masaru Satô (mus.); Hiroshi Murai, cin.; Yoshitami Kuroiwa, ed.; B&W; 2.35:1; 157 min.

CAST:
Seiji Miyaguchi (*Shigenori Togo*); Rokkô Toura (*Shunichi Matsumoto*); Chishû Ryû (*Baron Kantaro Suzuki*); Sô Yamamura (*Adm. Mitsumasa Yonai*); Toshirô Mifune (*Gen. Korechika Anami*); Hakuô Matsumoto (*Hirohito*).

Rating: **** 1/2

Despite warnings from Truman in early August 1945 that Japan must surrender unconditionally or face the consequences, the emperor refused. Hiroshima (August 6, 1945) and Nagasaki (August 9, 1945) were hit with atomic bombs. On August 14/15, Hirohito announced a surrender, made official aboard the USS *Missouri* (September 2, 1945). This first-rate docudrama from Toho (the studio that gave the world Godzilla) offers a finely edited, accurate depiction of high-level meetings. The magnificent Mifune provides the focus as a general who represents Asian values not easily understood by the West. Admirable re-creations of details of the debate are balanced with a desire to give outsiders a better understanding of the unique Bushido mindset. Special kudos go to Iwao Akune's production design, vividly capturing the reality of the historical settings while adding a subtle sense of surrealism to emphasize increasing paranoia.

NONE BUT THE BRAVE (1965)

CREDITS:
Warner Bros.; Frank Sinatra, dir.; Kikumaru Okuda, John Twist, Katsuya Susaki, scr.; Sinatra, Okuda, William H. Daniels, Howard W. Koch, pro.; John(ny) Williams, mus.; Harold Lipstein, cin.; Sam O'Steen, ed.; C; 2.35:1; 106 min.

CAST:
Frank Sinatra (*Francis*); Clint Walker (*Capt. Bourke*); Tommy Sands (*Lt. Blair*); Brad Dexter (*Bleeker*); Rafer Johnson (*Johnson*); Tatsuya Mihashi (*Lt. Kuroki*); Takeshi Katô (*Sgt. Tamura*); Homare Suguro (*Hirano*); Kenji Sahara (*Fujimoto*).

Rating: **

As the war winds down, several Japanese soldiers have been all but forgotten on a strategically insignificant island. An American plane crashes. The surviving marines begin a war of attrition, which ends when the two groups realize they need each other to survive. Well intentioned though unconvincing and preachy, dragged down by Sands (then director/star Sinatra's son-in-law) as a cocky lieutenant. The decision to have the Japanese speak their language *without* subtitles proved disastrous. Sinatra's debut and swan song as a director; he plays an alcoholic medic.

OBA: THE LAST SAMURAI (2011)

CREDITS:
Chukyo/Dentsy/Toho Co.; Hideyuki Hirayama, dir.; Don Jones (book), Takuya Nishioka, Cellin Gluck, Gregory Marquette, scr.; Morio Amagi, Nobuyuki Iinuma, Toshio Tanaka, Takuya Itô, pro.; Takashi Kako, mus.; Kôzô Shibasaki, Garry Waller, cin.; Jim Munro, Chieko Suzaki, ed.; C; 2.35:1; 128 min.

CAST:
Yutaka Takenouchi (*Capt. Oba*); Marcus Waldow (*Soldier*); Sean McGowan (*Capt. Lewis*); Mao Inoue (*Chieko Aono*); Daniel Baldwin (*Col. Pollard*); Treat Williams (*Wessinger*); Toshiaki Karasawa (*Horiuchi*).

Rating: ****

Summer 1944: marines complete the process of retaking the South Pacific. One old-fashioned Japanese officer, Sakae Oba (1914–1992), refuses to admit defeat. He leads troops on a desperate Banzai attack, certain his faith in such traditional fighting will carry the day. Instead, he and his men are defeated, with terrible losses. Oba and the few survivors climb Mount Tapochau to fight guerilla style for as long as possible, even after Japan has surrendered. This impressive film portrays the man's complexity and his sense of honor, undercut by tragic naïveté. Americans depicted as menacing antagonists are not reduced to simple villains. Excellent combat re-creations appear brutally honest. Main limitation: dialogue that sounds derivative of numerous earlier WWII pictures.

OPERATION CROSSBOW, aka GREAT SPY MISSION, THE (1965)

CREDITS:
Metro-Goldwyn-Mayer; Michael Anderson, dir.; Duilio Coletti, Vittoriano Petrilli, Emeric Pressburger (aka Richard Imrie), Derry Quinn, Ray Rigby, scr.; Carlo Ponti, pro.; Ron Goodwin, mus.; Erwin Hillier, cin.; Ernest Walter, ed.; C; 2.35:1; 115 min.

CAST:

Sophia Loren (*Nora*); George Peppard (*Lt. John Curtis*); Trevor Howard (*Lindemann*); John Mills (*General Boyd*); Richard Johnson (*Duncan*); Tom Courtenay (*Henshaw*); Anthony Quayle (*Bamford*); Lilli Palmer (*Frieda*); Paul Henreid (*Ziemann*); Richard Todd (*Kendall*).

Rating: ***

Odd, unsuccessful attempt to combine *Guns of Navarone* with the then-new James Bond spy thrillers. Before time runs out for the Reich, Hitler's scientists hope to perfect superrockets and destroy London. Brit agent Duncan recruits a unique team, which then parachutes into Germany. Courtenay is topnotch as a dedicated if obsessive colleague. Several plot twists (those involving Quayle, from *Navarone*, as a duplicitous figure) are clever if not entirely believable. One reversal features Loren, wife of producer Ponti, in an interminable midmovie cameo. More suspense than action, though the final confrontation in an underground facility recalls the big blow-up at the end of *Dr. No*. Big scale but without much impact.

OPERATION MAD BALL (1957)

CREDITS:

Columbia; Richard Quine, dir.; Arthur Carter (play), Blake Edwards, scr.; Jed Harris, pro.; George Duning, mus.; Charles Lawton, Jr., cin.; Charles Nelson, ed.; B&W; 1.85:1; 105 min.

CAST:

Jack Lemmon (*Pvt. Hogan*); Ernie Kovacs (*Capt. Locke*); Kathryn Grant (*Betty*); Arthur O'Connell (*Col. Rousch*); Mickey Rooney (*Skibo*); Dick York (*Bohun*); James Darren (*Widow*).

Rating: * 1/2

France, 1945: enlisted man Hogan wants to date nurse Betty. Since she's an officer, he must arrange for an off-base party to avoid obnoxious captain

Locke. Run-of-the-mill service comedy lacks verve, style, charm, and clever gags. A good cast is wasted. Lemmon's Ensign Pulver "operator" routine wears thin without solid material to support it. Loud and inane. They didn't even have the common sense to film this in color to make use of the lovely Le Havre settings!

OVERLORD (2017)

CREDITS:
Bad Robot/Paramount; Julius Avery, dir.; Billy Ray, Mark L. Smith, scrs.; J.J. Abrams, Lindsey Weber, prod.; Lee Kurzel, mus.; Laurie Rose, Fabian Wagner, cin.; Matt Evans, ed.; 2.39:1; C; 110 min.

CAST:
Jovan Adepo (*Boyce*); Wyatt Russell (*Ford*); Mathilde Ollivier (*Chloe*); Pilou Asbaek *(Wafner)*; John Megaro (*Tibbet*); Ian De Caestecker (*Chase*); Jacob Anderson (*Dawson*); Hayley Charmichael (*Mrs. Lesser*).

Rating: ** ½

The Longest Day meets *Return to Castle Wolfenstein* in an ambitious if far from successful genre hybrid. The opening would appear to be setting up one more 'secret mission' adventure: a quintet of elite soldiers parachute behind enemy lines on the day before our D-Day invasion commences, knocking out the Nazi's communication center. Instead, they come face to face with a mad doctor and his monstrous creations as the tone veers none too convincingly from WWII realism to monster-movie fantasy. Lots of loud action (maybe too much), no character development at all for the paper-thin heroes constituting this 'lost patrol,' resulting in an aloof, distanced exercise in violent stylistics.

424 • *From Hell To Hollywood: Volume 2*

SKI TROOP ATTACK (1960)

CREDITS:
Filmgroup; Roger Corman, dir.; Charles B. Griffith, scr.; Corman, pro.; Fred Katz, mus.; Andrew (M.) Costikyan, cin.; Anthony Carras, ed.; B&W; 1.85:1; 63 min.

CAST:
Michael Forest (*Lt. Factor*); Frank Wolff (*Sgt. Potter*); Wally Campo (*Ciccola*); Richard Sinatra (*Grammelsbacher*); James Hoffman, Chan Biggs, David Mackie (*Germans*).

Rating: ** 1/2

During the brutal winter of 1945, an Allied special mission employs skis to slip behind enemy lines and destroy a vital bridge. Germans take to skis to stop them. Grizzled Sgt. Potter finds himself in conflict with their ninety-day-wonder Lt. Factor. Another ultra-low-budget WWII flick turned out by Corman's exploitation team in between rock 'n' roll flicks and drive-in monster movies. In part informed by the battle of Hurtgen Forest. Much stock footage. Swiftly paced but unmemorable.

TANKS ARE COMING, THE (1951)

CREDITS:
Warner Bros.; Lewis Seiler, dir.; Samuel Fuller (story), Robert Hardy Andrews, scr.; Bryan Foy, pro.; William Lava, mus.; Edwin B. DuPar, cin.; James Moore, ed.; B&W; 1.37:1; 90 min.

CAST:
Steve Cochran (*Sgt. Francis Sullivan*); Philip Carey (*Lt. Rawson*); Mari Aldon (*Patricia Kane*); Paul Picerni (*Kolowicz*); Harry Bellaver (*Lemchek*); James Dobson (*Ike*).

Rating: *** 1/2

As Allies hurry north toward the Siegfried Line, a wounded tank sergeant in the Third Armored is replaced by arrogant newcomer Sullivan: "Mine will be the first tank to reach Berlin!" Effectively shows how five men rely on one another to maintain their vehicle's usefulness in the larger theater of war. Based on a treatment by Fuller, who knew his stuff, including the problem of America's 75 mm equipped vehicles taking on superior 88s. Shows the unique problems of a German American serviceman attacking the city where his grandparents live. Produced on a larger scale than most such program pictures. For a female lead, the writers introduce a gorgeous female photographer from *Stars* magazine (Aldon). Supporting characters are superficially sketched in.

TOO LATE THE HERO (1970)

CREDITS:
ABC Films; Robert Aldrich, dir.; Aldrich, Lukas Heller, Robert Sherman, scr.; Aldrich, Walter Blake, pro.; Gerald Fried, mus.; Joseph F. Biroc, cin.; Michael Luciano, ed.; C; 1.85:1; 135 min.

CAST:
Michael Caine (*Pvt. Tosh Hearne*); Cliff Robertson (*Lt. Sam Lawson*); Ian Bannen (*Thornton*); Harry Andrews (*Thompson*); Ronald Fraser (*Campbell*); Denholm Elliott (*Hornsby*); Percy Herbert (*Johnstone*); Henry Fonda (*Nolan*).

Rating: ****

Owing to his ability to speak fluent Japanese, antiheroic American officer Lawson joins a British unit launching an attack on an enemy radio center. He grasps that the group commander Hornsby is unbalanced; others, especially cocky Cockney Hearne, are the lowest dregs and therefore expendable. Aldrich's follow-up to *The Dirty Dozen* was a box-office bust, in part because the film required a Steve McQueen–level star. Lacks the entertaining qualities of Aldrich's previous picture. Effectively includes an aura of profound pessimism, resulting in a virulent antiwar statement. A memorable genre piece, with exquisite work from the British cast, well-wrought characters in complex relationships, and an authentic feel for jungles. The final race back to the base is terrific.

UNTERGANG, DER, aka DOWNFALL (2004)

CREDITS:
Constantin Films; Oliver Hirschbiegel, dir.; Joachim Fest (book), Traudl Junge (book), Melissa Müller (book), Bernd Eichinger, scr.; Eichinger, pro.; Stephan Zacharias, mus.; Rainer Klausmann, cin.; Hans Funck, ed.; C; 1.85:1; 178 min. (director's cut), 156 min. (theatrical release print).

CAST:
Bruno Ganz (*Adolf Hitler*); Alexandra Maria Lara (*Traudl Junge*); Corinna Harfouch (*Magda Goebbels*); Ulrich Matthes (*Goebbels*); Juliane Köhler (*Eva Braun*); Heino Ferch (*Speer*); Christian Berkel (*Schenck*); Ulrich Noethen (*Himmler*).

THE FASCINATION OF WICKEDNESS: Many historians agree that the most incisive and accurate screen portrait of Hitler was delivered by Bruno Ganz in *Downfall*.

Rating: ***** (director's cut)
**** 1/2(theatrical release print)

Mid-to-late April 1945: the Russians close in on Berlin. Panicky citizens search for a safe place that does not exist. A twelve-year-old Nazi child sets out to destroy encroaching tanks with a bazooka bigger than he is. In the bunker, Hitler's mistress encourages friends to eat, drink, dance, and make merry. Loyal generals are shot for crimes of cowardice they didn't commit. Some soldiers kill themselves while others plan to fight to the final bullet. This scenario of insanity is viewed over the shoulder of Hitler's secretary Traudl, who coauthored the book *Bis Zur Letzten Stunde* (2002). Ganz provides the most riveting cinematic portrayal of Hitler to date in the definitive film on "the last ten days." Criticized in some quarters for refusing to assume an obvious moral stance, instead objectively presenting the story and "humanizing" the monsters. Such a reading is negated by stern words from Junge recited during the opening.

HIT THE SILK; In *Overlord*, Allied soldiers making ready to parachute down will find themselves fighting not only the real-life Nazis but fantasy creatures as well.

A SMALL HUMAN TRAGEDY AMID OUR GREAT NATIONAL VICTORY: As the years passed since war's end, independently produced small budget projects with large ambitions allowed the public at large to consider those innocents who fell through the cracks.

Aftermath: The Ghosts of War

AFTERMATH, THE (2019)

CREDITS:
Amusement Park Films/Fox Searchlight; James Kent, dir.; Joe Shrapnel, Anne Waterhouse, Rhodian Brook, scr., Brook (novel); Jack Arbuthnott, Malte Grunnert, Ridley Scott, prods.; Martin Phipps, mus.; Franz Lustig, cin.; Beverly Mills, ed.; 1.85;1; C; 108 min.

CAST:
Keira Knightley (*Rachael Morgan*); Jason Clarke (*Lewis Morgan*); Alexander Skarsgard (*Stephen Lubert*); Jack Laskey (*Wilkins*); Kate Phillips (*Susan*); Fionn O'Shea (*Barker*); Martin Compston (*Burnham*); Rosa Enskat (*Greta*).

Rating: *** ½

No sooner is the war over than the Allies attempt to physically rebuild and morally re-invent Germany. Brit army officer Clarke (Morgan) and his wife Rachael (Knightley) are billited in the home of an embittered German (Skarsgard), who finds himself at odds with the strident beauty. Until mutual anger transforms into another kind of emotion entirely... lavishly produced, vivid as to the long-gone world recreated for the camera, marvelously acted by all. But the initially unique plot becomes predictable as the film gradually loses its sense of serious social drama, slipping instead to the level of a handsomely costumed soap- opera. Recalls Three Handkerchief Weepies of the postwar era, without updating their sensibility for a postmodern audience.

ACT OF LOVE (1953)

CREDITS:
Anatole Litvak, dir.; Alfred Hayes (novel), Joseph Kessel, Irwin Shaw, scr.; Litvak, pro.; Michel Emer, Joe Hajos, Michel B. Rosenstein, mus.; Armand Thirard, cin.; William Hornbeck, ed.; Benagosse/U.A.; B&W; 108 min.

CAST:
Kirk Douglas (*Robert Teller*); Dany Robin (*Lise Gudayec*); Serge Reggiani (*Claude*); Barbara Laage (*Nina*); Fernand Ledoux (*Fernand*); Brigitte Bardot (*Mimi*); Robert Strauss (*Sgt. Blackwood*); George Matthews (*Commanding Officer*).

Rating: ****

The underappreciated novel *Girl on the Via Flaminia* became an underappreciated film: Several years after the war, a former G.I. (Douglas), haunted by memories of a girl (Robin) he met during the war, revisits the Riviera and their secret meeting place. By coincidence or fate, he runs into the commanding officer (George Mathews) who disapproved of the relationship set into motion a transfer to break them up. What could have degenerated into maudlin melodrama reaches a higher dramatic—tragic, even--level owing to the sense that these two lovely young people truly are, as Shakespeare put it, star-crossed. On-location shooting, which had just become a key element in post-war filming, adds to the sense of absolute conviction. Might have clicked better at the box office had charismatic Bardot, wasted in a small role, played the female lead.

BACK AT THE FRONT (1952)

CREDITS:
Universal; George Sherman, dir.; Bill Mauldin (book), Lou Breslow, Oscar Brodney, Don McGuire, scr.; Leonard Goldstein, pro.; Henry Mancini, Herman Stein, mus.; Clifford Stine, cin.; Paul Weatherwax, ed.; B&W; 1.37:1; 87 min.

CAST:
Tom Ewell (*Willie*); Harvey Lembeck (*Joe*); Mari Blanchard (*Nina*); Richard Long (*Rose*); Palmer Lee/Gregg Palmer (*Capt. White*).

Rating: * 1/2

Any similarity to Mauldin's glorious cartoons about a pair of pathetic GIs disappeared as Universal attempted to turn them into a franchise. Like many other dogfaces, the boys sign up for "inactive reserve" on return only to be called up for army-of-occupation duty in Japan. Silly stuff involving a dragon-lady-type femme fatale and black market smuggling are poorly developed. Such triteness wouldn't seem so bad were it not for warm memories of a WWII classic.

BEFORE WINTER COMES (1969)

CREDITS:
Windward/Columbia; J. Lee Thompson, dir.; Frederick L. Keefe (novel), Andrew Sinclair, scr.; Robert Emmett Ginna, pro.; Ron Grainer, mus.; Gilbert Taylor, cin.; Willy Kemplen, ed.; C; 1.85:1; 107 min. (UK), 103 min. (US).

CAST:
David Niven (*Maj. Burnside*); Topol (*Janovic*); Anna Karina (*Maria*); John Hurt (*Lt. Pilkington*); Anthony Quayle (*Brig. Bewley*).

Rating: *** 1/2

Victorious Allies gather refugees in an Austrian camp, the Brit commander assigned to their relocation. This stiff-upper-lip chap's desire to do the right thing is hindered by the language gap. A jokester/antihero worthy of myth appears, able to speak numerous languages and seemingly solve the problem. The script (from a delightful 1968 novel, *The Interpreter*) combines comedy and drama, neatly balancing the two. Niven and Topol are perfectly cast as the odd couple. Yet, this potentially classic comedy works only intermittently owing to the choice of director. Thompson, effective for action epics like *The Guns of Navarone*, did not possess the necessary light touch for such material. Some scenes work well; others do not.

BERLIN EXPRESS (1948)

CREDITS:
RKO Radio Pictures; Jacques Tourneur, scr.; Curt Siodmak, Harold Medford, scr.; Bert Granet, pro.; Frederick Hollander, mus.; Lucien Ballard, cin.; Sherman Todd, ed.; B&W; 1.37:1; 87 min.

CAST:
Merle Oberon (*Lucienne*); Robert Ryan (*Robert Lindley*); Charles Korvin (*Perrot*); Paul Lukas (*Dr. Bernhardt*); Robert Coote (*Sterling*); Robert Shaw (*Spy*).

Rating: ****

Documentary-style portrait of postwar Europe. American operative Lindley travels from Paris to Berlin on a train reserved for those involved in the reclamation of Germany. Among the first Neorealist movies from a US company with an on-location shoot that, in a thriller's guise, allowed audiences to grasp the grim devastation of a country. Tourneur, who cut his teeth on such low-budget classics as *Cat People*, brings a similar sense of ever-imminent danger to this tale of a peace-loving German (Lucas) targeted by a new underground run by fascists. Soviets are portrayed as unpleasant thugs. Oberon merely provides window dressing. The real stars are the hollow ruined buildings, ghosts of a once-elegant prewar Berlin.

POSTWAR NEOREALISM: Borrowing from the era's great Italian filmmakers, American directors adapted The New Realism for Hollywood-financed pictures: A sensitive American (Montgomery Clift) considers the plight of poor refuge children; he and his co-pilot drop food by plane in *The Big Lift*.

BIG LIFT, THE (1950)

CREDITS:
20th Century Fox; George Seaton, dir.; Seaton, scr.; William Perlberg, pro.; Alfred Newman, mus.; Charles G. Clarke, cin.; William Reynolds, Robert L. Simpson, ed.; B&W; 1.37:1; 120 min.

CAST:
Montgomery Clift (*Sgt. Danny MacCullough*); Paul Douglas (*Sgt. Henry "Hank" Kowalski*); Cornell Borchers (*Frederica Burkhardt*); Bruni Löbel (*Gerda*); O. E. Hasse (*Stieber*).

Rating: ****

The inner workings of the Berlin Airlift are explained both in principle and practice to journalists, allowing the viewer to grasp why we were there and what we hoped to accomplish. For entertainment purposes, romance is added: a sensitive serviceman (Clift) falls for a young German (Borchers), who is secretly married to an SS escapee. His cynical friend (Douglas) casually sleeps with an out-for-herself fraulein (Lobel). Seaton offers honest glimpses of the civilian population living in the abject squalor of postwar Berlin, along with an evenhanded attitude toward German people. Plays as an unofficial sequel to *Berlin Express*.

BOYS FROM BRAZIL, THE (1978)

CREDITS:
20th Century Fox; Franklin J. Schaffner, dir.; Ira Levin (novel) Heywood Gould, scr.; Stanley O'Toole, Martin Richards, Sir Lew Grade, pro.; Jerry Goldsmith, mus.; Henri Decaë, cin.; Robert E. Swink, ed.; C/B&W; 125 min.

CAST:
Gregory Peck (*Dr. Josef Mengele*); Laurence Olivier (*Ezra Lieberman*); James Mason (*Eduard Seibert*); Lilli Palmer (*Esther*); Uta Hagen (*Frieda Maloney*); Steve Guttenberg (Barry); John Rubinstein (*David*).

THE EVIL CONTINUES: Gregory Peck reverses his usual heroic image to play real-life villain Dr. Joseph Mengele in *The Boys from Brazil*.

Rating: ★★★★

An aged Nazi Hunter (Olivier) learns that former SS officers are converging in Paraguay to establish a Fourth Reich. The butcher Mengele (1911-1979) will consolidate his long-term plan to people the world with 14-year-old Hitlers in hopes one will assume leadership of their organization. Like most films inspired by Levin novels--*Rosemary's Baby*, *The Stepford Wives*--this opens in a realistic setting only to effectively reach into the worlds of nightmare-fantasy. It's intriguing to watch perennial good-guy Peck powerfully play a representation of evil even as Olivier, stunning in such a Nazi role in *Marathon Man*, incarnates a thinly disguised portrait of heroic Simon Weisenthal 1908-2005). A bit over the top at times, but that's what this genre is all about. The first film to effectively 'educate' audiences about the existence of cloning. Bloody good show.

BOY WITH GREEN HAIR, THE (1948)

CREDITS:

RKO Radio Pictures; Joseph Losey, dir.; Betsy Beaton (story), Ben Barzman, Alfred Lewis Levitt, scr.; Stephen Ames, Dore Schary, pro.; Leigh Harline, mus.; George Barnes, cin.; Frank Doyle, ed.; C; 82 min.

CAST:

Pat O'Brien (*Gramp*); Robert Ryan (*Dr. Evans*); Barbara Hale (*Miss Brand*); Dean Stockwell (*Peter Fry*); Richard Lyon (*Michael*).

Rating: *** 1/2

War orphan Peter wakes one day to discover his hair has turned green. He then runs away from the home he shares with a sweet grandfather to learn if there's some deeper meaning to this. Ryan is cast in a thankless role as the child's analyst, allowing the story to be revealed in flashbacks. Occasionally enchanting, thanks largely to Stockwell's natural performance. More often pedantic, so overtly didactic that director Losey has the child preach directly to the camera when he realizes he's been sent from beyond to pave the way for world peace. Allegorical elements appear terribly dated today. The theme song "Nature Boy," performed by Nat King Cole, became a pop classic.

BRASS TARGET (1978)

CREDITS:

Metro-Goldwyn-Mayer; John Hough, dir.; Frederick Nolan (novel), Alvin Boretz, scr.; Berle Adams, Arthur Lewis, pro.; Laurence Rosenthal, mus.; Tony Imi, cin.; David Lane, ed.; 2.35:1; 111 min.

CAST:

Sophia Loren (*Mara*); John Cassavetes (*Maj. Joe De Lucca*); George Kennedy (*Gen. George Patton*); Robert Vaughn (*Rogers*); Patrick McGoohan (*McCauley*); Max von Sydow (*Shelley/Webber*).

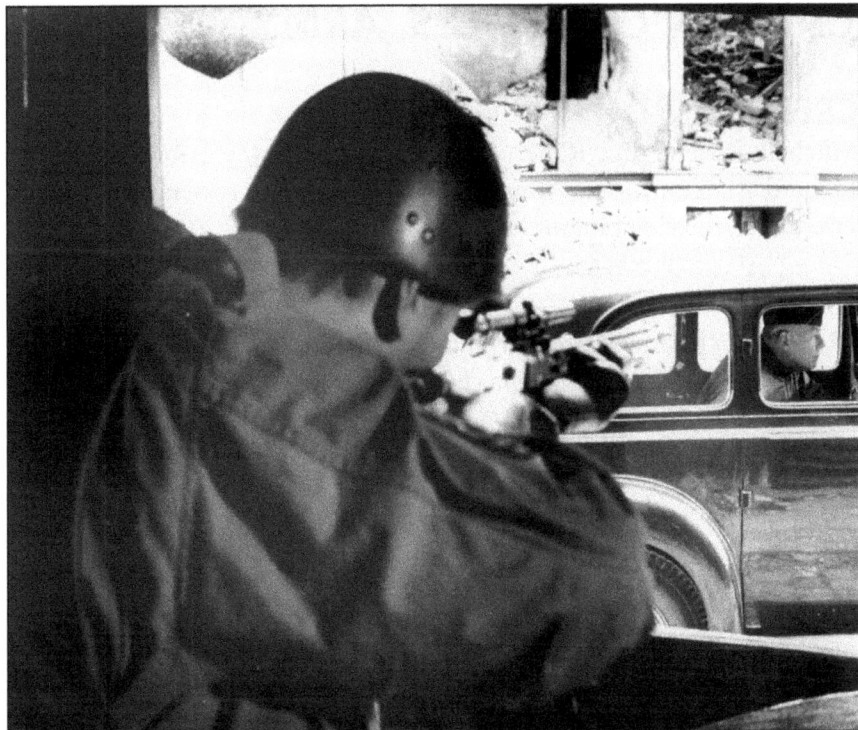

ACCIDENT OR MURDER?: *The Brass Target* suggests that the sudden death of Gen. Patton (George Kennedy) may have actually been an assassination.

Rating: ** 1/2

No sooner has the war ended than a train carrying a fortune in recaptured Nazi loot is attacked, all fifty-nine servicemen on board killed. Old Blood 'n' Guts, deeply upset that this happened on his watch, sets out to solve the crime. Since it was an inside job, corrupt officers hire a hitman to assassinate Patton while making it appear an accident. Intriguing premise, done in by a routine, predictable approach. There's no suspense since the audience, having recently seen *Patton*, knew the great man couldn't be saved. Worth noting as the first film to acknowledge that gangster Charles "Lucky" Luciano was instrumental in our successful invasion of Sicily.

CAPTAIN CAREY, U.S. ARMY (1950)

CREDITS:
Mitchell Leisen, dir.; Robert Thoeren, scr., Martha Albrand (novel); Richard Maibum, pro.; Alma Macrorie, ed.; John F. Seitz, cin.; Hugo Friedhofer, mus.; Paramount; 82 min.; B&W; 1.37:1.

CAST:
Alan Ladd *(Webster Carey)*; Wanda Hendrix *(Giulia de Greffi)*; Francis Lederer *(Rocco)*; Joseph Callelia *(Lunati)*; Celia Lovsky *(Francesca)*; Frank Puglia *(Luigi)*; Russ Tamblyn *(Pietro)*.

Rating: *** ½

Special agent Carey returns home even as his outfit (O.S.S.) transforms into a postwar spy network (C.I.A.). Unable to adjust to a peacetime mentality, he's haunted by a bloody operation that went south owing to a traitor in their midst. Compulsion/obsession with the villain's identity causes him to return to Italy, where a powerful baron may be his target or, for that matter, the baron's beautiful wife, our hero's one time lover. Intriguing idea, tepid treatment; Following a strong opening, the film bogs down in uninteresting soap-opera clichés, only to pick up steam with a surprisingly satisfying ending. Liesen was not a strong enough director to bring out the best points of lackadaisical actor Ladd. Best element is the period music, including a classic, "Mona Lisa."

CRY FOR HAPPY (1961)

CREDITS:
Columbia Pictures; George Marshall, dir.; George Campbell (novel), Irving Brecher, scr.; William Goetz, pro.; Chester W. Schaeffer, ed.; George Duning, mus.; Burnett Guffey, cin.; 2.35:1 C; 110 min.

CAST:
Glenn Ford *(CPO Andy Cyphers)*; Donald O'Connor *(Murray Prince)*; Miiko Taka *(Chiyoko)*; James Shigeta *(Suzuki)*; Miyoshi Umeki *(Harue)*;

Michi Kobi (*Hanakichi*); Howard St. John (*Adm. Bennett*).

Rating: *

A playboy photographer/Naval officer (Ford), stationed in post-war Japan, supposedly runs an orphanage while actually living in a geisha house. Sold on initial release as "the guy from *Teahouse of the August Moon* meets the *Sayonara* girls." Smarmy gags, forced humor, contrived situations, and a way-too-slow pace for a supposed comedy. Even the widescreen/color process doesn't help since, other than a few on-location bits with doubles standing in for Ford and sidekick O'Connor, most of this was shot on a studio sound stage. Unrewarding kitsch.

EMPEROR (2012)

CREDITS:
Lionsgate; Peter Webber, dir.; Shiro Okamoto (book), Vera Blasi, David Klass, scr.; Gary Foster, Russ Krasnoff, Yôko Narahashi, Eugene Nomura, pro.; Alex Heffes, mus.; Stuart Dryburgh, cin.; Chris Plummer, ed.; C; 2.35:1; 105 min.

CAST:
Matthew Fox (*Gen. Bonner Fellers*); Tommy Lee Jones (*Gen. Douglas MacArthur*); Eriko Hatsune (*Ava Shimada*); Toshiyuki Nishida (*Gen. Kajima*); Masayoshi Haneda (*Takahashi*).

Rating: *** 1/2

Gen. MacArthur and his command arrive in Japan to begin the complex task of occupation. He delegates responsibilities for specifics to members of his staff. Gen. Fellers must determine whether the emperor ought to be tried (and executed) as a war criminal. Fellers's dedication to his task shares screen time with his desire to locate Asian beauty Shimada, whom he once loved and lost. As the film cuts between present and past, that romance emerges as a series of superficial clichés, rendered in chick-flick fashion via prettified cinematography. The legal case is stark and strong. Opportunities were missed, notably, developing MacArthur's own emperor-like attitudes, similar to Hirohito's. Jones is well cast.

THE BIRTH OF MODERN ISRAEL: Jewish-American Col. Mickey Marcus (Kirk Douglas) and his mentor, a thinly disguised Gen. George Patton (John Wayne), face the realities of the Holocaust in *Cast a Giant Shadow*; Jewish refugees hope to travel by boat to Palestine in *Exodus*.

EXODUS (1960)

CREDITS:
United Artists; Otto Preminger, dir.; Leon Uris (novel), Dalton Trumbo, scr.; Preminger, pro.; Ernest Gold, mus.; Sam Leavitt, cin.; Louis R. Loeffler, ed.; C; 2.20:1; 208 min.

CAST:
Paul Newman (*Ari Ben Canaan*); Eva Marie Saint (*Kitty Fremont*); Ralph Richardson (*Gen. Sutherland*); Peter Lawford (*Maj. Caldwell*); Lee J. Cobb (*Barak Ben Canaan*); Sal Mineo (*Dov Landau*); John Derek (*Taha*); Jill Haworth (*Karen*).

Rating: **** 1/2

Impressive historical fiction about the birth of Israel told from the point of view of American widow Kitty. She takes an interest in Jewish child Karen and falls in love with freedom fighter Ari. When desperate Jewish refugees on Cypress arrange for a ship to take them to the near Middle East, English overseers find themselves in a no-win situation: stop them and there will be blood; let them go and violate the international agreement. Evenhandedly dramatized via two officers, one (Richardson) sympathetic to the Israeli cause, the other (Lawford) an anti-Semite. The birth of modern Israel is effectively chronicled as part of a rapidly changing postwar world.

FOREIGN AFFAIR, A (1948)

CREDITS:
Paramount; Billy Wilder, dir.; Wilder, Charles Brackett, Richard L. Breen, Robert Harari, David Shaw, scr.; Brackett, pro.; Friedrich Hollaender, mus.; Charles Lang, cin.; B&W; 1.37:1; 116 min.

CAST:
Jean Arthur (*Phoebe Frost*); Marlene Dietrich (*Erika Von Schluetow*); John Lund (*Capt. John Pringle*); Millard Mitchell (*Col. Plummer*); Peter von Zerneck (*Hans Birgel*).

Rating: *****

A planeload of politicians, including Congresswoman Phoebe, lands in Berlin to size up our occupying army's morale. The middle-American Iowa moralist is outraged to find that most of the boys "enjoy" the local frauleins, trading silk stockings for favors. Convinced she's found the last truly old-fashioned male among them after meeting Capt. Pringle, she's shocked to learn that he's the worst sinner of all. Wilder's black comedy about the black market (Dietrich croons a memorable ballad about it) ranks as a saucy satire, filled with sharp observations of our puritan values in conflict with European sophistication. The odd-couple casting of two classic female icons works, as they size one another up, each after the same man amid the truly grim rubble. As with other "serious comedies" by Wilder, this one constantly threatens to transform into tragedy. A time capsule about postwar internationalization.

FRÄULEIN (1958)

CREDITS:
20th Century Fox; Henry Koster, dir.; James McGivern (novel), Leo Townsend, scr.; Walter Reisch, pro.; Daniele Amfitheatrof, mus.; Leo Tover, cin.; Marjorie Fowler, ed.; C; 2.35:1; 95 min.

CAST:
Dana Wynter (*Erika Angermann*); Mel Ferrer (*Maj. Foster MacLain*); Dolores Michaels (*Lori*); Margaret Hayes (*Lt. Berdie Dubbin*); Theodore Bikel (*Col. Bucaron*).

Rating: *** 1/2

Fascinating if not entirely successful film tells us more about the year in which it was shot than the moment in time (a decade earlier) when it takes place. Title refers to a college professor's classy daughter, Erika, trying to survive in postwar Berlin. She falls for American major McLain, whom she once helped escape from the Nazis. German citizens are humanized in contrast to the cartoonish portraits from 1940s films. Russians, symbolized by crude officer Bucaron, are subhuman. In keeping with postwar civil rights cinema, a fair-minded African American soldier (James Edwards) saves the woman's reputation when events cause her to unfairly be branded a prostitute. Particularly interesting to watch back to back with the thematically antithetical *Verboten!*

GERMANY YEAR ZERO (1948)

CREDITS:
Tevere Film; Roberto Rossellini, dir.; Rossellini, Carlo Lizzani, Max Kolpe, scr.; Rossellini, pro.; Renzo Rossellini, mus.; Robert Juillard, cin.; Eraldo Da Roma, ed.; B&W; 1.37:1; 78 min.

CAST:
Edmund Moeschke (*Edmund*); Ernst Pittschau (*Padre*); Erich Guhne (*Maestro*); Ingetraud Hinze (Eva); Christl Merker (*Christl*); Heidi Blankner (*Frau Rademaker*); Jo Herbst (*Jo*).

Rating: **

Switching his focus from wartime Italy to postwar Germany, the father of Neorealism attempted to capture the pessimism that overtook Germany. Rossellini's goal was to make a movie about a boy (Moeschke) forced to provide for his family by scrounging the streets where black marketeers mix with child molesters. The film's first half, honest and grim, lives up to expectations. Everything turns upside down midmovie when the good boy decides that murder and suicide are the way to go. Progressively less believable; a huge disappointment.

GLASS WALL, THE (1953)

CREDITS:
Columbia; Maxwell Shane, dir.; Ivan Tors, Maxwell Shane, scrs.; Tors, Ben Coleman, prod.; Leith Stevens, mus.; Joseph F. Biroc, cin.; Stanley Frazen, Herbert L. Strock, ed.; B&W; 1.37: 82 min.

CAST:

Vittorio Gassman (*Peter Kaban*); Gloria Grahame (*Maggie Summers*); Jerry Paris *(Tom)*; Douglas Spencer *(Inspector Bailey);* Robin Raymond *(Tanya);* Joe Turkel (*Freddie*); Else Back (*Mrs. Zakoyla*): Michael Fox (*Toomey/Narrator).*

Rating: *** ½

A desperate Hungarian stowaway (Gassman) jumps ship, hoping to lose himself in New York's asphalt jungle; his only chance to avoid deportation is by finding a former G.I. (Paris) whose life he saved during the war. Intriguing premise unfortunately done in by ever less believable plotting. Grahame spectacular as a B girl who helps him. Best features: Biroc's strong, moody photography of the Times Square area; Bob Keene, Jack Teagarden, Jimmy Giuffre, Shelley Manne, and Shorty Rogers performing one of the greatest jazz riffs ever captured on film. Incidentally, the title refers to the U.N. Building.

GOOD GERMAN, THE (2006)

CREDITS:

Warner Bros.; Steven Soderbergh, dir.; Joseph Kanon (novel), Paul Attanasio, scr.; Ben Cosgrove, Gregory Jacobs, pro.; Thomas Newman, mus.; Peter Andrews (Soderbergh), cin.; Mary Ann Bernard (Soderbergh), ed.; B&W; 1.66:1; 107 min.

CAST:

George Clooney (*Jake Geismer*); Tobey Maguire (*Tully*); Cate Blanchett (*Lena Brandt*); Dominic Comperatore (*Levi*).

Rating: *

Summer 1945: a reporter arrives in Berlin to cover the Big Three Potsdam conference while reconnecting with his lost love. Shot on the WB lot, with self-consciously obvious back projection of European locales plus newsreel stock footage. This emerges as less a film about its ostensible subject and more an extended homage to postwar movies, with intentionally hokey dialogue, now with rough language and graphic sex. A paint-by-numbers "exercise in style." Precious and pointless; visually intriguing, intellectually empty.

GUILT OF JANET AMES, THE (1947)

CREDITS:
Columbia; Henry Levin, dir.; Lenore J. Coffee, Devery Freeman, Louella MacFarlane, Allen Rivkin, scr.; Helen Deutsch, Virginia Van Upp, pro.; George Duning, mus.; Joseph Walker, cin.; Charles Nelson, ed.; B&W; 1.37:1; 83 min.

CAST:
Rosalind Russell (*Janet Ames*); Melvyn Douglas (*Smitty Cobb*); Sid Caesar (*Sammy Weaver*); Betsy Blair (*Katie*); Nina Foch (*Susie Pearson*); Charles Cane (*Walker*).

Rating: ****

Not the crime noir the title suggests but an early earnest attempt to forge an emergent postwar psychological cinema augmented by surreal sets. The "guilt" is entirely mental: two years after the war, Janet still cannot accept that at Bastogne, her husband threw himself on a hand grenade to save five friends. Was this unselfish heroism, or had the marriage been so unsatisfying that he preferred to die rather than return? She obsessively tracks down the veterans who survived, hoping to learn the truth. Little-seen film adopts a proto-postmodernist vision: all reality exists in the human mind; we can only know a subjective, never objective, truth. Dated by today's standards; demands to be seen and appreciated in the unique context in which it was created.

HIROSHIMA MON AMOUR (1959)

CREDITS:
Argos Films/Daiei Studios; Alain Resnais, dir.; Marguerite Duras, scr.; Anatole Dauman, Samy Halfon, pro.; B&W; 1.37:1; 90 min.

CREDITS:
Emmanuelle Riva (*Elle*); Eiji Okada (*Lui*); Stella Dassas (*Mother*); Pierre Barbaud (*Father*); Bernard Fresson (*German Lover*).

Rating: *****

For thirty-six hours, a French actress and a Japanese architect, about to part after a brief love affair, try to break through the barriers—language and culture among them—that make it difficult for human intimacy (beyond the sexual) to occur. They constantly return to the issue of memory and its subjectivity. She speaks of her previous lover; he wants to talk about the bombing's lingering impact. In the early planning stages, this was to have been a straight documentary. Inspiration led its Gallic auteur to mix romantic fiction with hard cold facts, creating a new kind of film experience that would lead to the Nouvelle Vague. Instead of allowing flashbacks to play out as complete stories, Resnais innovatively fragments them, without explanation, as subliminal shots create a cinematic stream of consciousness. One of those rare films that changed the course of cinema while revealing that one person's human concerns can never be separated from those of the world at large.

HOUSE OF BAMBOO (1955)

CREDITS:
20th Century Fox; Samuel Fuller, dir.; Fuller, Harry Kleiner, scr.; Buddy Adler, pro.; Leigh Harline, mus.; Joseph MacDonald, cin.; James B. Clark, ed.; C; 2.55:1; 102 min.

CAST:
Robert Ryan (*Sandy Dawson*); Robert Stack (*Eddie Kenner*); Shirley

Yamaguchi (*Mariko*); Cameron Mitchell (*Griff*); Brad Dexter (*Capt. Hanson*); Sessue Hayakawa (*Kito*).

Rating: ****

During the robbery of a munitions train passing through Tokyo, an army-of-occupation soldier is killed. US authorities work with Japanese police to track down the responsible parties. Undercover agent Kenner infiltrates a mob composed of former soldiers, led by cynical gang lord Dawson, who hopes to establish his own Mafia in Asia. Suitably stylish exercise from Fuller, the man who brought the pulp fiction sensibility of bus-station books to the big screen. This typically flamboyant outing is bolstered by on-location photography and capped by a dazzling final chase through a crowded amusement park. Homoerotic competition between Kenner and Dawson's number-one gangster Griff is obvious today in a way it wasn't in 1955. The "romance" between Kenner and Japanese widow Mariko comes across as vivid and offbeat rather than conventional.

IDA (2013)

CREDITS:
Opus Film/Canal+ Polska; Pawel Pawlikowski, dir.; Pawlikowski, Rebecca Lenkiewicz, scr.; Eric Abraham, Piotr Dzieciol, Ewa Puszczynska, pro.; Kristian Eidnes Andersen, mus.; Lukasz Zal, Ryszard Lenczewski, cin.; Jaroslaw Kaminski, ed.; B&W; 1.33:1; 92 min.

CAST:
Agata Kulesza (*Wanda*); Agata Trzebuchowska (*Anna*); Dawid Ogrodnik (*Lis*); Jerzy Trela (*Szymon*); Adam Szyszkowski (*Feliks*); Halina Skoczynska (*Mother Superior*); Joanna Kulig (*Singer*).

Rating: **** 1/2

Novitiate Anna is surprised when her mother superior insists that before she takes her final vows, she must make a personal odyssey to visit her elderly aunt Wanda. That woman, an esteemed judge, shares with the youth a buried truth: she is Jewish, raised in a convent after her parents were killed during the German occupation. A onetime resistance fighter, the aunt is a Communist who used her position to eliminate non-Red former Partisan friends during the 1950s purge. The film raises an issue never before touched upon in a movie: some seemingly altruistic Poles who hid Jews during the Holocaust harbored dark motivations for doing what appeared idealistic. Shot in black and white to convey a proper glumness; Helena Wolińska-Brus (1919–2008) was the model for Aunt Wanda. Several reviewers used the term "austere" to describe the vividly sustained tone, mood, and atmosphere. Complaint: the final moments could have been less ambiguous. First Polish-made movie to win the Oscar for Best Foreign Language Film.

IKIMONO NO KIROKU, aka A LIVING MAN, aka I LIVE IN FEAR (1955)

CAST:
Toshro Mifune (*Kiichi Nakajima*); Takashi Shimura (*Dr. Harada*); Minoru Chiaki *(Jiro)*; Eiko Miyoshi *(Toyo)*; Kyoko Aoyama *(Sue)*; Haruko Togo (*Yoshi)*; Noriko Sengoku (*Kimie)*; Akemi Negishi (*Asako).*

CREDITS:
Akira Kurosawa, dir.; Kurosawa, Hideo Oguni, Fumio Hayasaka, Shinobu Hashimoto, scrs.; Sojiro Moloki, prod.; Asakazu Nakai, cin.; Masaro Sato, mus.; Toho Films; 1.37:1; B&W; 103 min.

Rating: **** 1/2

Ten years after the nuclear holocaust that knocked Japan out of the war, people have seemingly adjusted to The New Normal: going about everyday life, work, and family pursuits. Yet the newspapers and televised reports insist the horror is far from over. Poison exists in the air everyone breathes, the water they drink, the soil in which they plant. Least quiet among those 'in the know,' factory owner Kiichi plans to sell out and move his family to the Brazilian rainforest. When his family decides their patriarch is paranoid, they request civil servant Dr. Haraka to consign their father to an institution. Kurosawa employs this plot device to explore the lonely crowd sensibility of his nation at that moment in time and the unique relationships that exist only within the specific nature of a Japanese family structure; also such greater, more universal issues as the nature of insanity, the difficulties and responsibilities of rendering judgment and (as in *Roshomon* five years earlier) the subjectivity of what we call 'truth.'

JOE BUTTERFLY (1957)

CREDITS:
Universal International; Jesse Hibbs, dir.; Evan Wylie (play), Jack Ruge (play), Sy Gomberg, Marion Hargrove, Jack Sher, scr.; Aaron Rosenberg, pro.; Irving Gertz, Earl E. Lawrence, mus.; Irving Glassberg, cin.; Milton Carruth, ed.; C; 2.35:1; 90 min.

CAST:
Audie Murphy (*Pvt. Joe Woodley*); Burgess Meredith (*Joe Butterfly*); George Nader (*Sgt. Kennedy*); Keenan Wynn (*Harold Hathaway*); Kieko Shima (*Chieko*); Fred Clark (*Col. Fuller*).

Rating: *** 1/2

Minor-league *Teahouse of the August Moon*. Following Japan's surrender, a team of *Yank* magazine reporters enters Tokyo to comment on the situation. Sweet-spirited GI Woodley meets black marketeer Joe and breathtaking Asian girl Chieko. Today's political correctness would condemn the casting of a non-Asian star as the title character, though Meredith proves again that he was one of Hollywood's great character actors. Murphy is surprisingly adept at comedy. Cowriter Marion was the author and subject of the *Hargrove* films. Easygoing, mild, pleasant; unavailable for viewing.

JUDGMENT AT NUREMBERG (1961)

CREDITS:

Roxlom Films; Stanley Kramer, dir.; Abby Mann, scr.; Kramer, pro.; Ernest Gold, mus.; Ernest Laszlo, cin.; Frederic Knudtson, ed.; B&W; 1.75:1; 186 min.

THE RECKONING: Maximilian Schell (who in reality is a Swiss Jew) won a Best Actor Oscar as a defence attorney for Germany's Nazi war criminals; could anyone have embodied the fair-minded judge more effectively than Spencer Tracy?

CAST:
Spencer Tracy (*Chief Judge Dan Haywood*); Burt Lancaster (*Dr. Ernst Janning*); Richard Widmark (*Col. Tad Lawson*); Marlene Dietrich (*Mrs. Bertholt*); Maximilian Schell (*Hans Rolfe*); Judy Garland (*Irene Hoffman*); Montgomery Clift (*Rudolph Petersen*).

Rating: *****

In 1948, small-time American judge Haywood is tapped for the trials of "lower level" Nazis. Prosecutor Lawson demands life sentences; the defense (Schell, Oscar winner for Best Actor) argues that civilization itself is at fault. The film focuses on educated defendant Janning and the judge's inner search to grasp how this onetime humanitarian could possibly be guilty. America and Russia enter the Cold War, causing higher-ups to call for "expedient leniency" to keep the German people on our side. Mann's writing is dazzling; Kramer's direction more than adequate. Clift improvised much of his dialogue as a mentally challenged witness. Uncompromising, down to the final frightening title card.

KATYN (2007)

CREDITS:
Akson Studio/TVP; Andrzej Wajda, dir.; Wajda, Andrzej Mularczyk, Przemyslaw Nowakowski, Wladyslaw Pasikowski, scr.; Michal Kwiecinski, pro.; Krzystof Penderecki, mus.; Pawel Edelman, cin.; Milenia Fiedler, Rafal Listopad, ed.; C; 2.35:1; 122 min. (director's cut), 121 min. (US theatrical), 118 min. (international theatrical).

CAST:
Andrzej Chyra (*Lt. Jerzy*); Maja Ostaszewska (*Anna*); Arthur Zmijewski (*Andrzej*); Danuta Stenka (*Róza*); Jan Englert (*General*); Magdalena Cielecka (*Agnieszka*); Agnieszka Glinska (*Irena*).

Ratings: **** 1/2 (director's cut); **** (US theatrical); *** 1/2 (international theatrical)

Here is a film Wajda long wanted to make but was unable to while the Soviet Union controlled his country. Wajda's father was among those who surrendered in 1939 when Poland was invaded by Germans and Russians, before the dissolution of their pact. Soldiers were sent home, officers removed to a faraway location. A year later, 20,000 were massacred in Katyn forest. After the war, Russia insisted the bestial act had been committed by Nazis. Over the years, investigations revealed that the killings (including Wajda's parent) were committed by Soviets. This "truth will out" piece reveals all the facts, saving the horrific incident for the end. A jigsaw puzzle of a film, Wajda's work features no story in the conventional sense, presenting instead a cinematic tapestry that resembles real life more than narrative art.

LADRI DI BICICLETTE, aka *BICYCLE THIEVES*, aka *BICYCLE THIEF, THE* (1948)

CREDITS:
PDS/ENIC; Vittorio De Sica, dir.; Luigi Bartolini (novel), De Sica, Cesare Zavattini, scr.; De Sica, Giuseppe Amato, pro.; Alessandro Cicognini, mus.; Carlo Montuori, cin.; Eraldo Da Roma, ed.; B&W; 1.37:1; 93 min.

CAST:
Lamberto Maggiorani (*Antonio Ricci*); Enzo Staiola (*Bruno*); Lianella Carell (*Maria*); Gino Saltamerenda (*Baiocco*); Vittorio Antonucci (*The Thief*); Sergio Leone (*Seminarian*).

Rating: *****

In postwar Rome, the once-solid blue-collar working class has been reduced to poverty as there are few jobs. Face-in-the-crowd Antonio is fortunate enough to own a bicycle, allowing him to go to work. A youth steals this precious item; the common-man hero and his son Bruno set out on a doomed odyssey, desperately hoping to track down the bike. A first-time viewer will likely think this was improvised, the camera recording reality on the fly thanks to street shooting and a nonprofessional cast.

What we experience is the *illusion* of reality: every shot is artistically composed, each movement choreographed. De Sica's art is one that conceals its artistry. When released in the US, its impact revolutionized American film, leading to 1950s new street realism (i.e., *On the Waterfront* (1954)). Neorealism's crowning classic.

LAND OF MINE (2015)

CREDITS:
Nordisk Film/Majgaard; Martin Vandvliet, dir.; Vandvliet, scr.; Daniel Baur, Mikael Chr. Rieks, pro.; Sune Martin, mus.; Camilla Hjelm, cin.; Per Sandholt, Molly Marlene Stensgaard, ed.; 2.35:1; C; 100 min.

CAST:
Roland Moller (*Sgt. Carl Rasmussen*); Louis Hoffman (*Schumann*); Joel Basman (*Morbach*); Mikkel Boc Folsgaard (*Jensen*); Laura Bro (*Karin*); Zoe Zandvliet (*Elisabeth*); Mads Rusom (*Peter);* Oskar Bokelmann (*Haffke*); Emil Belton (*Ernst*).

Rating: **** 1/2

This film's title may offer the darkest double-entendre of all time. With the liberation of Denmark in Spring 1945 a bitter sergeant (Moller) is assigned to oversee the removal of mines buried along his nation's west coast by Nazis who (wrongly) anticipated the D-Day invasion to take place there. P.O.W.s must dig into the sand and attempt to remove the deadly objects; history records that half (most teenagers conscripted by Hitler toward the war's end) died while doing so. The initially unsympathetic sergeant (Moller offers a complex portrayal) gradually comes to realize that continuing to 'follow orders' may transform him into what he most hates: a moral fascist. Similar in conception to *Ten Seconds to Hell* if considerably more successful at conveying identical themes: the universality of human conscience, the destruction of a single soul, and the responsibility of all adults to naive youth. Among the most depressingly nihilistic movies ever made until a single ray of sunlight breaks through at the very end.

LISA (1962)

CREDITS:

Red Lion Films/20th Century Fox; Philip Dunne, dir.; Jan de Hartog (novel), Nelson Gidding, scr.; Mark Robson, pro.; Arthur Ibbetson, cin.; Ernest Walter, ed.; C; 2.35:1; 112 min.

CAST:

Stephen Boyd (*Peter Jongman*); Dolores Hart (*Lisa Held*); Leo McKern (*Brandt*); Hugh Griffith (*Van der Pink*); Donald Pleasence (*Wolters*); Harry Andrews (*Ayoob*); Robert Stephens (*Dickens*).

Rating: ****

Holland, 1946: a young woman is spirited out of the country by a mystery man, headed toward England. Both are followed by a Dutch inspector, aware that while the concentration camp survivor believes her supposed mentor will help find her a husband in America, the ex-Nazi is now a white slaver. Effective suspense-thriller plot is abetted by a notable psychological dimension: the inspector is less a simple White Knight than an inwardly tortured soul who might have saved his Jewish fiancée from the Holocaust but suffered a failure of courage. Hart, who left Hollywood shortly after to become a nun, might well have become the next Grace Kelly. The strange, subtle sense of an ever-ripening love between the two wounded leads is truly touching.

LITTLE BOY LOST (1953)

CREDITS:

Paramount; George Seaton, dir.; Seaton, Marghanita Laski, scr.; William Perlberg, pro.; Victor Young, mus.; George Barnes, cin.; Alma Macrorie, ed.; B&W; 1.37:1; 95 min.

CAST:

Bing Crosby (*Bill Wainwright*); Claude Dauphin (*Pierre Verdier*); Christian Fourcade (*Jean*); Gabrielle Dorziat (*Mother Superior*); Nicole Maurey (*Lisa Garrett*).

Rating: ****

Before the war, an American journalist covering stories in Paris fell in love with a Jewish woman. After marrying and conceiving a son, the family was shattered when the wife was dragged off to a camp, the child presumed dead. Home, but unable to adjust to his old life, the reporter receives word his son is alive and in an orphanage. However, it is not certain which of the boys is his biological offspring. Almost immediately, he bonds with one sad child (Fourcade, who is quite wonderful), hoping against hope this is his child, though the data suggest otherwise. Poignant and prescient; a worthy little movie that somehow slipped through the cracks and remains unknown today. Similar in theme to *The Search*, if never reaching the heights of that masterpiece.

MAN IN THE GLASS BOOTH, THE (1975)

CREDITS:
Arthur Hiller, dir.; Edward Anhalt, scr.; Ely A. Landau, pro.; David Bretherton, ed.; Sam Leavitt, cin.; American Film Theatre; 1.85:1; C; 117 min.

CAST:
Maximilian Schell (*Arthur Goldman*); Lois Nettleton (*Miriam Rosen*); Lawrence Pressman *(Charlie Cohn)*; Luther Adler *(Judge)*; Lloyd Bochner (*Churchill*); Robert H. Harris (*Dr. Weisburger)*; Henry Brown (*Jack).*

Rating: * ½

Actor/author Robert Shaw's 1968 play, adapted for the stage from his novel by himself and director Harold Pinter, dazzled the live-audience with its then shocking tale: a New York Jewish businessman (Donald Pleasence onstage) whisked, from his home by Israel agents,is tried in Israel as an Eichmann like war-criminal who adapted his current guise to survive. As the accused man howls that they are tragically mistaken the stern judge wonder if they may indeed have the wrong man. One of the era's great directors—-say, John Frankenheimer of *The Manchurian Candidate* (1963)--might have successfully brought this fusing of stark realism and Kafka-esque paranoia to the screen. Journeyman Hiller is, to be kind, way out of his league. Shaw insisted his name be removed from the credits.

MARATHON MAN (1976)

CREDITS:
John Schlesinger, dir.; William Goldman, Robert Towne, scr.; Robert Evans, Sidney Beckerman, prod.; Jim Clark, ed.; Conrad Hall, cin.; Paramount; 125 min.; C; 1.85:1.

CAST:
Dustin Hoffman *(Tom 'Babe' Levy)*; Laurence Olivier *(Szell);* Roy Scheider *(Doc)*; William Devane *(Janeway)*; Marthe Keller *(Elsa)*; Fritz Weaver *(Biesenthal)*; Richard Bright *(Karl).*

Rating: **** ½

A Jewish grad student at Columbia University studies the Holocaust for his thesis project. To escape such depressing research, he trains to run in an upcoming marathon. That proves serendipitous, as neo-Nazis operating in Manhattan pursue 'Babe' in order to keep his findings from being revealed to the public. Near-perfect realization of the bestseller, with Olivier dazzling as a variation on the real life Joseph Mengele. (What a great double feature this would make with *The Boys in Brazil!*) The unforgettable sequence involving torture by dentistry combines the best sequences in Alfred Hitchcock's *The Man Who Knew Too Much* (1934) and Roger Corman's *Little Shop of Horrors* (1960). Sadly, the beautiful though talentless Keller is unable to bring the mystery girl to life; Julie Christie had been everyone's original choice.

MARRIAGE OF MARIA BRAUN, THE aka *EHE DER MARIA BRAUN, DIE* (1979)

CREDITS:
Rainer Werner Fassbinder, dir.; Fassbinder, Rea Frohlich, Peter Marthesheimer, Kurt Raab, scr.; Wolf-Dietrich Brucker, Volker Canaris, Michael Fengler, prods.

CAST:
(*Oswald*); Gisela Uhlen (*Mother*); Elisabeth Trisenaar (*Betti*); Gottfried John (*Klenze*); Hark Bohn (*Senkenberg*); George Eagles (*Bill*); Claus Holm (*Doctor*); Gunter Lamprecht (*Hans.*)

Rating: **** ½

From Bavaria's visually dazzling, inwardly tortured, always controversial R.W. Fassbinder (1945-1982), a tale of one woman's attempt to not only survive but succeed in the Brave New World following Germany' defeat. Her singular story is meant to serve as an allegory for the entire country, faced with surrendering to total despair or crawling up and out of the desolated landscape by any (and every, including sexual) means. Married for a single day to a soldier who disappears during the final hours, Schygulla's persona here purposefully recalls Marlene Dietrich; the filmmaking style refences the histrionic, flamboyant, surrealistically colored Hollywood films of Douglas Sirk (*Written on the Wind*, 1956). R.W.F. 'borrowed' narrative elements from the Bertold Brecht play "Mother Courage and Her Children" (1938) and *Baby Face* (1933), an American melodrama starring Barbara Stanwyck. Critics debate whether the resultant film is profoundly pessimistic or superficially cynical; the shimmering surface qualifies this as one of the cinema's landmarks of cinematic eye candy.

MINIVER STORY, THE (1950)

CREDITS:
Metro-Goldwyn-Mayer; Henry C. Potter, dir.; Jan Struther (original characters), George Froeschel, Ronald Millar, scr.; Sidney Franklin, pro.;

Miklós Rózsa, Herbert Stothart, mus.; Joseph Ruttenberg, cin.; Frank Clarke, Harold F. Kress, ed.; B&W; 1.37:1; 104 min.

CAST:

Greer Garson (*Kay Miniver*); Walter Pidgeon (*Clem Miniver*); John Hodiak (*Spike Romway*); Leo Genn (*Steve Brunswick*); Cathy O'Donnell (*Judy Miniver*); Reginald Owen (*Foley*).

Rating: ** 1/2

Bland follow-up to the overrated original fails to achieve for this fictional British family what David Selznick's *The Best Years of Our Lives* did for postwar America. An honest attempt to depict shortages that Londoners had to live with following the war. Garson is again the English supermom, Pidgeon her loyal husband. The children have been reimagined; fans of the first film will wonder why those intriguing tots are not followed into the postwar era. Hodiak shows up in his all-pervasive if short-lived status as the American Soldier incarnate.

NIGHT PORTER, THE (1974)

CREDITS:

Ital-Noleggio; Liliana Cavani, dir.; Cavani, Barbara Alberti, scr.; Esa De Simone, Robert Gordon Edwards, pro.; Daniele Paris, mus.; Alfio Contini, cin.; Franco Arcalli, ed.; C; 1.85:1; 118 min.

CAST:

Dirk Bogarde (*Maximilian Theo Aldorfer*); Charlotte Rampling (*Lucia Atherton*); Philippe Leroy (*Klaus*); Gabriele Ferzetti (*Hans*); Giuseppe Addobbati (*Stumm*); Isa Miranda (*Countess Stein*).

Rating: *

Briefly, Cavani managed to pass herself off as another Lina Wertmuller. Her self-consciously ugly films are shallow, incompetent, and—irony of ironies—antifeminist by implication. Lucie, once interned by Nazis,

ROLE REVERSAL: In *The Night Porter*, Charlotte Rampling plays a Holocaust survivor who turns the tables on former predators.

realizes worker Max at her hotel is the vicious SS man who once tortured her. Missing the sadomasochistic relationship, she begs him to take it up again. A nasty, Nazisploitation-style film.

NOTORIOUS (1946)

CREDITS:

Vanguard Films/RKO; Alfred Hitchcock, dir.; John Taintor Foote (short story), Hitchcock, Ben Hecht, Clifford Odets, scr.; Hitchcock, pro.; Roy Webb, mus.; Ted Tetzlaff, cin.; Theron Warth, ed.; B&W; 1.37:1; 101 min.

CAST:

Cary Grant (*Devlin*); Ingrid Bergman (*Alicia Huberman*); Claude Rains (*Alexander Sebastian*); Leopoldine Konstantin (*Mme. Sebastian*); Louis Calhern (*Prescott*).

Rating: *****

Alicia, whose life was shattered when her father was unmasked as a German spy, is approached by American agent Devlin. He's willing to blackmail her, if necessary, into traveling to Brazil to marry escaped Nazi Sebastian and then spy on his fascist clique. Among the first films to capture the unexpected malaise that settled into postwar life. Technically superb, especially the editing of a virtually wordless sequence that has Grant, in a mansion's cellar, trying to find a bottle of wine that holds the MacGuffin: uranium ore. The oddest romantic triangle of all time, with a monstrous if sexy hero and a sweet, loving bad guy competing for a Hitchcock blonde. The new moral complexity (our *hero* is named Devlin) was introduced to viewers. Konstantin is magnificent as a deadly dowager.

ODESSA FILE, THE (1974)

CREDITS:
Ronald Neame, dir.; Frederick Forsyth (novel), Kenneth Ross, George Markstein, scr.; John R. Sloan, John Woolf, pro.; Ralph Kemplen, ed.; Oswald Morris, cin.; Andrew Lloyd Webber, mus.; Columbia; 130 min.; C/B&W; 2.35:1.

CAST:
Jon Voight (*Peter Miller*); Maximilian Schell (*Eduard Roschmann*); Maria Schell (*Frau Miller*); Mary Tamm (*Sigi*); Derek Jacobi (*Klaus Wenzer*); Peter Jeffrey (*David*); Kurt Meisel (*Oster*).

Rating: **

When an elderly Jewish concentration camp survivor takes his own life in Germany, 1963, a young journalist (Voight) reads the man's journal and becomes obsessed with tracking down the camp's evil S.S. captain (Schell, Maximilian), still at large. In the process he encounters a monolithic group of Nazis in the process of forming a Fourth Reich. Forsyth's memorable page-turner is reduced to a routine thriller with little suspense or emotional involvement. Neame's glossy but lack-

SHADOW-WORLD: Ingrid Bergman as an American spy infiltrating The Boys (And Girls) in Brazil in *Notorious*; Rod Steiger plays a bitter U.S. immigrant suffering from survivor guilt in *The Pawnbroker*.

lustre direction reduces an important expose to the level of an ordinary commercial enterprise. Beginning a movie so dominated by the most wicked ghosts of WWII with Perry Como singing a sweet Christmas song, apparently sans irony, was only the first of many miscalculations. legendary Nazi hunter Simon Wiesenthal, played here by lookalike Shmuel Rodensky, served as the film's historical advisor. Might have workd better as a TV mini-series.

OPERATION FINALE (2018)

CREDITS:
Automatik/MGM; Chris Weitz, dir.; Matthew Orton, scr.; Fred Berger, Oscar Isaac, prods.; Alexander Desplat, mus.; Javier Aguirresarobe, cin.; Pamela Mentin, ed.; 185; C; 123 min.

CAST:
Oscar Isaac (*Peter Malkin*); Ben Kingsley *(Adolph Eichmann);* Melanie Laurent (*Peter Ellen*); Lior Raz (*Isser Harel*); Nick Kroll (*Eitan*); Michael Aronov (*Abaroni); Ohad Knoller (Ilani);* Greg Hill (*Tabor*); Greta Scacchi (*Verna Eichmann).*

Rating: *** ½

In May 1960, members of the Mossad (an elite Israel attack force) responded to an unexpected tip and tracked down war criminal Adolph Eichmann (Kingsley) in Buenos Aires. This retelling of the events, augmented with a great deal of fictive elements, collapses such various forms as the purposefully slow-moving docudrama (for the cat-and-mouse search and discovery) and exciting spectacle of action scenes that might have been lifted from a DC/Marvel superhero epic. Also ,the screenplay attempts to explore the eerie seductiveness of evil, a la *The Silence of the Lambs* (1991), if without that masterwork's depth. Kingsley, who is in fact himself Jewish, proves masterful as the cunning fascist; Isaac effectively plays Malkin as a true movie hero rather than a flawed human being. Brief flashbacks to the Holocaust provide a frame for what occasionally appears to be transforming into a splashy *The Dirty Dozen* type entertainment.

PAWNBROKER, THE (1964)

CREDITS:
Allied Artists/Landau Prods.; Sidney Lumet, dir.; Edward Lewis Wallant (novel), Morton S. Fine, David Friedkin, scr.; Phillip Langner, Roger H. Lewis, pro.; Quincy Jones, mus.; Boris Kaufman, cin.; Ralph Rosenblum, ed.; B&W; 1.85:1; 116 min.

CAST:
Rod Steiger (Sol Nazerman); Geraldine Fitzgerald (*Marilyn Birchfield*); Brock Peters (*Rodriguez*); Jaime Sanchez (*Jesus*); Thelma Oliver (*Jesus's Girlfriend*); Marketa Kimbrell (*Tessie*); Juano Hernandez (*Smith*).

Rating: **** 1/2

Survivor guilt entered Holocaust cinema with this of-its-time daring depiction of an elderly New York City pawnshop owner who trudges through life, incapable of enjoyment. This stems from the loss of his wife and children during the Final Solution. He's incapable of grasping (initially) that the nasty way he treats African Americans on the mean streets outside his shop approximates the prejudice his own people suffered under Hitler. Painful events that restore him compose this mostly excellent film's grim narrative. The unrealized scream with which this concludes reveals how powerful silence can be in the context of a sound film. Still, an overemphasis on allegorical devices (Nazerman's name and that of a street youth; a Greek chorus in a contemporary setting) diminishes rather than adds to Lumet's realistic camera eye. For once, Steiger's overacting serves the piece well.

PLENTY (1985)

CREDITS:

RKO/20th Century Fox; Fred Schepisi, dir.; David Hare (play), scr.; Edward R. Pressman, Joseph Papp, pro.; Bruce Smeaton, mus.; Ian Baker, cin.; Peter Honess, ed.; C; 2.35:1; 121 min.

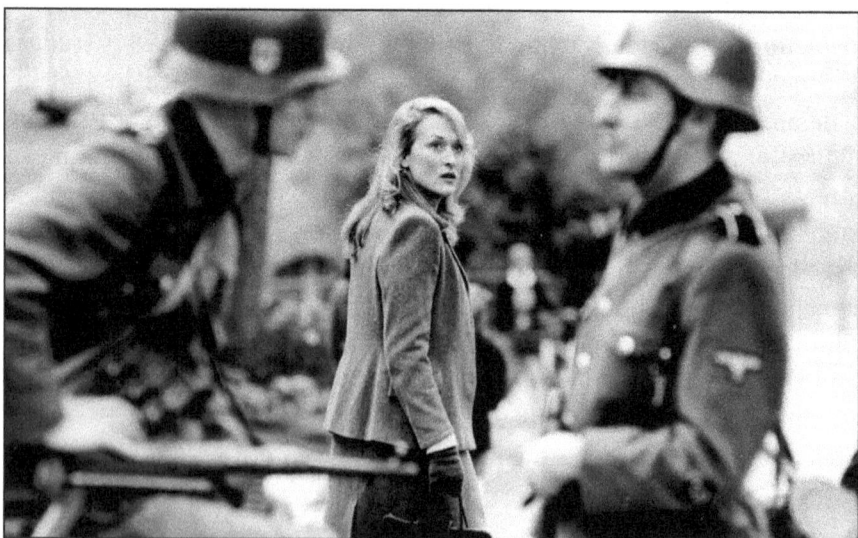

THE BIG THRILL: In *Plenty*, Meryl Streep plays a member of the French Resistance who risk her life daily; following the war, she cannot adjust to the boring aspects of daily existence.

CAST:
Meryl Streep (*Susan Traherne*); Charles Dance (*Raymond Brock*); Tracey Ullman (*Alice Park*); Sir John Gielgud (*Sir Leonard*); Sting (*Mick*); Ian McKellan (*Charleson*); Sam Neill (*Lazar*).

Rating: *

An Englishwoman fights for the French Resistance and enjoys a one-night stand with a British spy. After 1945, such heroes are supposed to enjoy a rebirth of "plenty." Instead, those days when she lived on the edge come to seem like a golden age in memory. What unfolds is an endless series of unpleasant scenes in which Susan takes her frustration out on family and friends. It's hard to grasp why anyone would think this person's rantings and ravings add up to serious drama. From an inexplicably popular play.

QUILLER MEMORANDUM, THE (1966)

CREDITS:
Michael Anderson, dir.; Harold Pinter, scr., Trevor Dudley Smith/'Adam Hall' (novel); Ivan Foxwell, pro.; Frederick Wilson, ed.; John Barry, mus.; Erwin Hillier, cin.; Frederick Wilson, ed; Rank/20th Century Fox; 104 min.; C/B&W; 2.35:1.

CAST:
George Segal (*Quiller*); Alec Guinness (*Pol*); Max von Sydow (*Oktober*); Senta Berger (*Inge Lindt)*; George Sanders (*Gibbs*); Robert Flemyng (*Rushington*); Peter Carsten (Hengel).

Rating: **

A top British spy (Guinness) learns Neo-Nazis are on the move in contemporary Berlin, his own agents all swiftly dispatched. A young American (Segal) poses as a journalist and comes face to face with the Old German (von Sydow) currently recruiting new 'werewolves.' Disappointing, despite the pedigree of a Pinter script. The film is alternately obvious and obscure, Segal's romance with a schoolteacher (Berger) patently absurd. Worse, the tone is flippant in the manner of a sixties Bond flick in one sequence, deadly serious on the order of a Harry Palmer the next. Segal's flat delivery of sardonic lines makes a viewer dream of Paul Newman. Strongest feature: Barry's bristling edge-of-your-seat *Ipress File*-like score.

RED DANUBE, THE (1949)

CREDITS:
Metro-Goldwyn-Mayer; George Sidney, dir.; Bruce Marshall (novel), Gina Kaus, Arthur Wimperis, scr.; Carey Wilson, pro.; Miklós Rózsa, mus.; Charles Rosher, cin.; James E. Newcom, ed.; B&W; 1.37:1; 119 min.

CAST:
Walter Pidgeon (*Col. Michael Nicobar*); Ethel Barrymore (*Mother Superior*); Peter Lawford (*Maj. McPhimister*); Angela Lansbury (*Audrey*); Janet Leigh (*Maria*); Louis Calhern (*Piniev*).

Rating: ** 1/2

Marshall's 1947 book *Vespers in Vienna* becomes an overobvious conversion tale about Col. Nicobar, who arcs from barely believing in God to becoming born again while overseeing operations in divided Vienna. A Russian-born ballerina is threatened by smug Soviet commander Piniev with "repatriation." Significant information about the postwar situation, especially the rapid turn of the Allies against our recent Russian comrades, is buried in hokey dialogue. Even Rózsa's score lacks the verve of his best work. Did our Brit friends really have to be reduced to nits and twits? One of Hollywood's first virulent anti-Soviet films.

REMEMBER (2015)

CREDITS:
Atom Egoyan, dir.; Benjamin August, scr.; Ari & Robert Lantos, prods.; Christopher Davidson, ed.; Paul Sarossy, cin.; Mychael Danna, mus.; Distant Horizons/A24 Films; C; 1.85:1; 94 min.

CAST:
Christopher Plummer (*Zev Guttman*); Amanda Sith (*Cele*); Martin Landau (*Max Rosenbaum*); Sean Francis (*Max's Aide*); Howard Jerome (*Rabbi*); Henry Czerny (*Gutman*).

Rating: **** ½

In a New York nursing home, elderly Zev mourns the loss of his wife. Friend Max reminds the confused Zev of a half-forgotten promise: Once alone, Zev would slip away and track down the now old *Blockfuhrer* who at Auschwitz executed each of these survivors' children. As Max is too feeble to accompany him, Zev sets out alone, purchases a Glock pistol, and methodically searches for the onetime Nazi, now integrated into American society. The two stars create unique characterizations for their equally bitter geriatrics; in addition to a Holocaust revenge tale, this edge-of-your-seat suspenser can be 'read' as a study of those afflicted with Alzheimer's, dementia, or both. The plot borrows heavily from Christopher Nolan's 2000 neo-noir *Memento* but with a social-justice issue not raised there. The twist ending, which few will see coming, is subtly prepared for. Only flaw: the plot occasionally strains credulity.

SAYONARA (1957)

CREDITS:
Joshua Logan, dir.; Paul Osborn, scr., James Michener (novel); William Goetz, pro.; Philip Anderson, Arthur Schmidt, ed.; Franz Waxman, mus.; Pennebaker/W.B.; 147 min.; C/ 2.35:1.

CAST:

Marlon Brando (Maj. Gruver); Patricia Owens (Eileen Webster); James Garner (Captail Bailey); Miko Taka (Hanna-Ogi); Red Buttons (Joe Kelly); Ricardo Montalban (Nakumura); Miyoshi Umeki (Katsumi).

Rating: ** ½

Time has not been kind to the reputation of director Logan (1908-1988) or his once lauded 'classics': *Picnic* (1955), *Bus Stop* (1956), and this tale of then-forbidden intermarriages between American military and Asian women in post-war Japan. Brando plays the bourbon-and-branch officer who discourages his men from such liaisons until he falls for a sensitive beauty (Taka). Buttons and Umeki are endearing as star-crossed lovers (each won a Best Supporting Actor Oscar); the finest performance is by Latin actor Montalban as a wise Japanese, unacceptable by current P.C. standards. The problem with the film, though, is far more basic: halfway between a serious study of an important issue and a maudlin romantic soap-opera *Sayonara* plays like an Asian *Peyton Place*: less colourful in the positive sense than glossy like an overly pretty postcard.

SCHRECKLICHE MADCHEN, DAS, aka *NASTY GIRL, THE* (1990)

CREDITS:

Michael Verhoeven, dir.; Verhoeven, scr. Verhoeven, Senta Berger, prod.; Barbara Hennings, ed.; Axel de Roche, cin.; Mike Herting, many others, mus.; Filmverlag de Autoren; B&W/C; 94 min.

CAST:

Lena Stolze *(Sonja)*; Hans-Reinhard Muler *(Juckenack)*; Monika Baumgartner *(Mother)*; Elisabeth Bertram *(Grandmother)*; Robert Giggenbach *(Martin)*; Michael Gahr *(Paul)*; Sandra White *(Iris)*; Richard SuBmeier *(Mayor)*; Christof Wackemagel *(Zopfel)*.

Rating: ** ½**

'Sonja' is one of the most popular girls among the teenagers living in a small German town that prides itself on courageous resistance to the Third Reich in general, the Holocaust in particular. Admiring of family and friends, she enters an essay contest: research their history, then accept accolades from the community. Facts that Sonja uncovers reveal everything she had learned is but a self-serving myth; townspeople were in the 1930s and 1940s as horrible to their Jewish neighbors as had been the case in Berlin; descendants of those people will do anything to keep the truth from coming out. This fact-based film (the actual girl was Anna Rosmus, 1960-) unspools like an update of Henrik Ibsen's realist play *An Enemy of the People* (1882). German director Verhoeven (no relation to the Danish director Paul) and his actress wife produced. Powerful.

SEARCH, THE (1948)

CREDITS:
Praesens-Film/Metro-Goldwyn-Mayer; Fred Zinnemann, dir.; Richard Schweizer, David Wechsler, Paul Jarrico, Peter Viertel, Betty Smith, scr.; Lazar Wechsler, pro.; Robert Blum, mus.; Emil Berna, cin.; Herman Haller, ed.; B&W; 1.37:1; 104 min.

CAST:
Montgomery Clift (*Ralph Stevenson*); Aline MacMahon (*Mrs. Murray*); Wendell Corey (*Jerry Fisher*); Jarmila Novotna (*Mrs. Malik*); Ivan Jandl (*Karel Malik*).

Rating: *****

Children whose parents were killed or displaced wandered through Europe in search of food and shelter. The cataclysmic problem was not well known in America until this striking film dramatized it. MacMahon plays a volunteer feeding and clothing lost boys and girls of the road while trying to determine whether any of their relatives have survived. Jandl, whose sad face is truly unforgettable, radiates as the focal child. Clift (in his initial movie role, though *Red River* was released first) lights up the screen as a singular soldier who vows to reunite him with his mother

(Novotna). Shot on location in Berlin and surrounding areas, this was among the first US–European coproductions. Zinnemann combines Italian Neorealism with England's recently developed docudrama, both forms collapsed into postwar Hollywood filmmaking at its finest. Heartbreaking and overpowering.

SECRET, UN, aka *SECRET, A* (2007)

CREDITS:
Canal+/Alfa Films; Claude Miller, dir.; Philippe Grimbert (novel), Miller, Natalie Carter, scr.; Yves Marmion, pro.; Zbigniew Preisner, mus.; Gérard de Battista, cin.; Véronique Lange, ed.; C/B&W; 1.85:1; 105 min.

CAST:
Cécile de France (*Tania Stirn/Grimbert*); Patrick Bruel (*Maxime/ Grimbert*); Ludivine Sagnier (*Hannah Stirn*); Julie Depardieu (*Louise*); Mathieu Amalric (*Francois*).

Rating: **** 1/2

Maxime and his wife have always been healthy and happy. Why is their son Francois sad, thin, and susceptible to illness? Nothing is quite what it seems concerning these Parisians. The truth will out, a process that begins when the troubled boy realizes an imaginary friend—an older brother—he relies on to get through the day does (or did, before the Holocaust) exist. One of the most atypical, and refreshing, dramas about the Final Solution. The film touches on a rarely addressed issue: the initial denial among some Jews that the Holocaust could touch them as long as they silently acquiesced. Unsparing about the manner in which France largely turned its collective back on ever-escalating horrors. One of those rare films in which the victims are not portrayed as the flawless innocents we meet in *Schindler's List* but diverse, in some cases unlikable, people.

SEQUESTRATI DI ALTONA, IL, aka CONDEMNED OF ALTONA, THE (1962)

CREDITS:
Titanus/20th Century Fox; Vittorio De Sica, dir.; Jean-Paul Sartre (play), Abby Mann, scr.; Carlo Ponti, pro.; Nino Rota, mus.; Roberto Gerardi, cin.; Manuel de Campo, Adriana Novell, ed.; B&W; 2.35:1; 114 min.

CAST:
Sophia Loren (*Johanna von Gerlach*); Maximilian Schell (*Franz von Gerlach*); Fredric March (*Albrecht von Gerlach*); Robert Wagner (*Werner*); Françoise Prévost (*Leni*).

Rating: *

Though the war is over, diehard Nazi von Gerlach, now mad, believes that combat continues. He's locked away in the family mansion by a devoted father and is an embarrassment for normal son Werner and his wife Johanna. Sartre's 1959 play is an existential masterpiece about the subjectivity of reality. Everything that could go wrong did with this adaptation (despite the pedigrees of the cast and director). The original's complexity is stripped away to make this an arty mainstream movie. The great De Sica's worst film. Saving grace: fine performance by Prévost.

SERGEANT, THE (1968)

CREDITS:
Warner Brothers; John Flynn, dir.; Dennis Murphy (novel), scr.; Richard Goldstone, pro.; Michel Magne, mus.; Henri Persin, cin.; Françoise Diot, ed.; C; 1.85:1; 108 min.

CAST:
Rod Steiger (*Sgt. Albert Callan*); John Phillip Law (*Pfc. Tom Swanson*); Ludmila Mikaël (*Solange*); Frank Latimore (*Capt. Loring*); Memphis Slim (*Himself*).

Rating: * 1/2

During the occupation, rugged Sgt. Callan develops an intense obsession for angelic-looking Pfc. Swanson. The film plays as a contemporary retelling of *Billy Budd*, in narrative if not quality. Here, the Claggart figure's motivation, wisely left unstated in Melville, is rendered painfully obvious: he's a repressed homosexual. The film is by implication antigay, if unintentionally, collapsing homosexuality with insanity and sadism. Steiger overacts; Law underacts. Scripting is ponderous and preposterous; the direction flat, uninspired. An ambitious disaster.

SITUATION HOEPELESS... BUT NOT SERIOUS (1962)

CREDITS:
Gottfried Reinhardt, dir.; Silvia Reinhardt, Jan Lustig, scr.; Reinhardts, Jose de Villaverde, prod.; Walter Boos, ed.; Kurt Hasse, cin.; Harold Byrne, mus.; Castle See/Paramount; B&W; 35 mm: 97 min.

CAST:
Alec Guinness (*Wilhelm Frick*); Mike Connors (*Sgt. Lucky Finder*); Robert Redford *(Capt. Hank Wilsonk)*; Anita Hofer *(Edeltraud)*; Mady Rahl *(Lissie)*; Paul Dahlke (*Herr Neusel);* Frank Wolff (*Quartermaster);* Carola Regnier *(Senta).*

Rating: **

A pair of Allied fliers bail out of their burning plane over Germany. A seemingly kindly old man promises to hide them from the S.S. in his cellar, though his intentions are selfish, even cryptic. Lonely, he hungers for company, keeping the two youths prisoner long after war's end. The 1959 novel by Robert Shaw (1927-1978), hailed for its effective combination of dark comedy and existential drama, had been successfully dramatized on TV's *Playhouse 90* (3/22/600 under its original title, *The Hiding Place.* The semi-talented Reinhardt's dropped the ball entirely by playing the piece as a broad mainstream fun film. Nothing works; Guinness, though, is always watchable.

SO WELL REMEMBERED (1947)

CREDITS:
RKO; Edward Dmytryk, dir.; James Hilton (novel), John Paxton, scr.; Adrian Scott, pro.; Hanns Eisler, mus.; Freddie Young, cin.; Harry W. Gerstad, ed.; B&W; 114 min.

CAST:
John Mills (*George Boswell*); Martha Scott (*Olivia*); Patricia Roc (*Julie*); Trevor Howard (Dr. *Whiteside*); Richard Carlson (*Charles*); Reginald Tate (*Mangin*); James Hilton (*Narrator*).

Rating: ****

Working-class people dance in the streets of the small Lancashire mill town "Bradley" (modeled after Macclesfield) when the war in Europe ends. Their soft-spoken mayor spends that moment alone, sensing that once such celebrations are over, a postwar letdown will commence. He reminisces about his family surviving the era and the tragedy of a young volunteer who returned physically and emotionally scarred. More concerned with complex labor relations than the war per se. This sturdy, underappreciated film projects the sense of oncoming gloom found in many late-1940s Hollywood movies.

STATEMENT, THE (2003)

CREDITS:
Serendipity Point Films/Odessa; Norman Jewison, dir. Ronald Harwood, scr., Brian Moore (book); Jewison, Robert Lantos, pro.; Normand Corbeil, mus.; Kevin Jewison, cin.; Andrew S. Eisner, ed.; B&W/C; 1.85:1; 120 min.

CAST:
Michael Caine (*Pierre Brossard*); Tilda Swinton (*Annemarie Livi*); Jeremy Northam (*Col. Roux*); Alan Bates (*Bertier);* Charlotte Rampling (*Nicole*); Matt Craven (*Mannenbaum*); John Neville (Old Man); Frank Finlay (*Vionnet*); Noam Jenkins (*Levy*); Malcolm Sinclair (*Cardinal).*

Rating: **** ½

The Malice was composed of Vichy French policemen who, during the war, executed Gallic Jews even before being ordered to by Nazi superiors. In 1945, most were tried as collaborators; one (Caine) got away. Nearly half a century later, a passionate judge (Swinton, superb as ever) and a rational army officer (Northam) set out to bring him to belated justice, only to discover he is protected by a right-wing sect within the Catholic Church and a prominent French politician. The film's purposefully slow pace allows for a realistic approximation of an actual 'procedural process' as compared to the slam-bang action approach of most modern movies. Making the villain three dimensional though never in the least empathetic adds to the impact. Director Jewison's best film since his Oscar-winner *In the Heat of the Night* (1967).

TEAHOUSE OF THE AUGUST MOON, THE (1956)

CREDITS:
Metro-Goldwyn-Mayer; Daniel Mann, dir.; Vernon J. Sneider (book), John Patrick (play), scr.; Jack Cummings, pro.; Saul Chaplin, mus.; John Alton, cin.; Harold F. Kress, ed.; C; 2.35:1; 123 min.

CAST:
Marlon Brando (*Sakini*); Glenn Ford (*Capt. Fisby*); Machiko Kyô (*Lotus Blossom*); Eddie Albert (*Capt. McLean*); Paul Ford (*Col. Wainwright Purdy III*); Jun Negami (*Seiko*).

Rating: ** 1/2

Hailed as an instant classic on Broadway, *Teahouse* is one of those popular/critical hits that quickly lost its luster. Likeable screw-up officer Fisby arrives in postwar Okinawa and, with the help of conniving translator Sakini, teaches a village about democratic capitalism, falling under the spell of their simple lifestyle. Brando is ripe, on a play-acting level, however offensive an Anglo playing an Asian might be today.

POLITICALLY INCORRECT? Despite the brilliance of Marlon Brando's performance, *Teahouse of the August Moon* is rarely revived today owing to the casting of an Anglo as an Asian.

Cross-cutting between on-location work and studio sets doesn't help. Badly dated.

TEN SECONDS TO HELL (1959)

CREDITS:

Seven Arts/Hammer; Robert Aldrich, dir.; Lawrence P. Bachmann (novel); Aldrich, Teddi Sherman, scr.; Michael Carreras, pro.; Kenneth V. Jones, mus.; Ernest Laszlo, cin.; Henry Richardson, ed.; B&W; 93 min.

CAST:

Jack Palance (*Erik Koertner*); Jeff Chandler (*Karl Wirtz*); Martine Carol (*Margot Hofer*); Robert Cornthwaite (*Franz Loeffler*); Virginia Baker (*Frau Bauer*); Richard Wattis (*Haven*).

Rating: *** 1/2

From Bachmann's *The Phoenix* (1958, a tale of Berlin trying to rise from the ashes. The English occupying force assigns six Germans, experts at bomb dismantlement, to dispose of explosives dropped from Allied airplanes, which failed to explode on contact. Assuming they'll die one by one, these lost souls create a lottery, the pot intended for the last man standing. This escalates tensions between poetic Koertner and mean-spirited individualist Wirtz. Hostilities are further aggravated by competition for world-weary woman Hofer. Bleak on-location shooting qualifies this as closer to Nietzschean nihilism than any other commercial film of its time. One of a kind, to say the least; memorable if less than satisfying.

THIRD MAN, THE (1949)

CREDITS:

London Film Prods.; (Sir) Carol Reed, dir.; Reed, Orson Welles, Alexander Korda, scr.; Graham Greene (novel); Reed, Korda, David O. Selznick, pro.; Anton Karas, mus.; Robert Krasker, cin.; Oswald Hafenrichter, ed.; B&W; 1.37:1; 104 min. (director's cut), 93 min. (US theatrical).

CAST:

Joseph Cotten (*Holly Martins*); (Alida) Valli (*Ana Schmidt*); Orson Welles (*Harry Lime*); Trevor Howard (*Maj. Calloway*); Bernard Lee (*Sgt. Paine*); Paul Hörbiger (*Karl*); Wilfrid Hyde-White (*Crabbin*).

Ratings: ***** (director's cut)
**** 1/2 (original US theatrical)

Alcoholic American pulp fiction author Holly arrives in divided postwar Vienna to visit old friend Harry. As he arrives, that man's funeral is in progress. Among those in attendance: a mystery woman and an unidentified third man. One of the few perfect movies, from stellar performances—including excellent actors in minor roles—to the use of a film noir atmosphere in a European-lensed movie. Reed's camera is often employed in an off-balance manner, suggesting the postwar world has been turned on its side. Classic moments include the Ferris wheel confrontation (Welles wrote his own dialogue), a polite literary festival that turns into chaos, the shadowy nature of an underground pursuit through the city's sewers, and what may be the greatest final shot in movie history. Zither music adds to the overall aura of originality. At once funny and tragic. An "essential."

THREE STRIPES IN THE SUN (1955)

CREDITS:

Columbia; Richard Murphy, dir.; E. J. Kahn, Jr. (magazine article), Murphy, Albert Duffy, scr.; Fred Kohlmar, pro.; George Duning, mus.; Burnett Guffey, cin.; Charles Nelson, ed.; B&W; 1.85:1; 93 min.

CAST:

Aldo Ray (*Sgt. Hugh O'Reilly*); Philip Carey (*The Colonel*); Dick York (*Cpl. Neeby Muhlendorf*); Chuck Connors (*Idaho*); Camille Janclaire (*Sister Genevieve*).

Rating: ***

A tough sergeant, haunted by memories of Pearl Harbor, resents serving as part of the occupying force. He arcs while caring for Osaka's hungry orphans and sets out to improve their lot, falling in love with his translator. Despite Ray's acting limits, here is a solid, sturdy little program picture. On-location shooting adds to the authenticity. A fact-based film that asked its audience to accept intermarriage with a member of a recent enemy nation while educating viewers about the objectives of our postwar mission.

TOWN WITHOUT PITY (1961)

CREDITS:
United Artists; Gottfried Reinhardt, dir.; Manfred Gregor (novel), George Hurdalek, Jan Lustig, Silvia Reinhardt, scr.; Reinhardt, Eberhard Meichsner, pro.; Dimitri Tiomkin, mus.; Kurt Hasse, cin.; B&W; 105 min.

CAST:
Kirk Douglas (*Maj. Steve Garrett*); Barbara Rütting (*Inge Koerner*); Christine Kaufmann *(Karin Steinhof)*; E.G. Marshall (*Col. Pakenham*); Robert Blake *(Jim Larkin)*; Richard Jaeckel (*Birdie*); Frank Sutton (*Snyder*).

Rating: NO STARS

After drunken G.I.s rape a German girl (Kaufmann), the American prosecuting attorney (Marshall) requests the death penalty. This creates a problem for the defense lawyer (Douglas) who believes one of the four (Blake) did not participate. To get that man off, he must save the others; the only way to accomplish that is to destroy the girl's reputation. Perhaps intended as an anti-capital punishment message movie, this rates as a disaster: dramatically dishonest, ugly without being enlightening and, by today's standards, sexist in suggesting that the life of an innocent man is worth far more than that of an equally innocent woman.

TWO WOMEN (1960)

CREDITS:

Compagnia Cinematografica/Titanus; Vittorio De Sica, dir.; Alberto Moravia (novel), De Sica, Cesare Zavattini, scr.; Carlo Ponti, pro.; Armando Trovajoli, mus.; Gábor Pogány, cin.; Adriana Novelli, ed.; B&W; 1.66:1; 100 min.

THE ULTIMATE INDIGNITY: An Italian woman (Sophia Loren) and her daughter survive the horrors of war only to be raped shortly after combat ends in *Two Women*.

CAST:
Sophia Loren (*Cesira*); Jean-Paul Belmondo (*Michele Di Libero*); Eleanora Brown (*Rosetta*); Raf Vallone (*Giovanni*); Carlo Ninchi (*Padre Filippo*); Andrea Checchi (*A Fascist*).

Rating: *****

With the coming of war, Rome mother Cesira's main concern is her daughter Rosetta's well-being. They travel to Ciociaria, the woman's rural hometown in the southern mountain provinces, where she becomes fascinated with several men, including a Communist intellectual and a rugged worker. When the war finally ends, mother (woman) and daughter (girl) head for home. On the way, they are gang-raped by a detachment of soldiers. Now, they are two women. De Sica and Zavattini, who together helped create Neorealism, closed the curtain on that movement with this, the form's final classic. Loren won an Oscar for Best Actress. Riveting, yet with a final ray of hope. The central characters were fictional; Moravia based his 1958 novel on an incident referred to as *Marocchinate*.

VERBOTEN! (1959)

CREDITS:
Globe Enterprises; Samuel Fuller, dir.; Fuller, scr.; Fuller, pro.; Harry Sukman, mus.; Joseph F. Biroc, cin.; Philip Cahn, ed.; B&W; 93 min.

CAST:
James Best (*Sgt. David Brent*); Susan Cummings (*Helga Schiller*); Tom Pittman (*Bruno Eckart*); Paul Dubov (*Capt. Harvey*); Harold Daye (*Schiller*); Dick Kallman (*Strasser*).

Rating: *** 1/2

A naïve American falls for a fraulein while serving in the occupying army, soon initiating the long, difficult process of procuring the right to marry and bring her home. The viewer realizes what he doesn't grasp: while pretending to be an anti-Hitler bystander, she's a fervent Nazi, using her relationship with the duped GI to forward Allied plans to the Werewolves, an anti-American underground group. Strong example of the considerable quality that can be achieved on an ultralow budget; also exemplary of auteur theory, which insists "one man, one movie." Not, however, the masterpiece Fuller fanatics believe it to be. For a more balanced view, see *The Big Lift*.

WAKOLDA, aka *GERMAN DOCTOR, THE* (2013)

CREDITS:
Historias/Cine Ar; Lucia Palenza, dir.; Palenza, scr.; Palenza, Christian Cardoner, many others, prods.; Andres Goldstein, Daniel Tarrab, mus.; Nicolas Puenzo, cin.; Hugo Primero, ed.; 2.35;1; C; 93 min.

CAST:
Alex Brendemuhl (*Mengele*); Natalie Oreiro (*Eva*); Diego Peretti (*Enzlo*); Elene Roger (*Nora Eldoc*); Florencia Bado (*Lilith*); Guillermo Pfening (*Klaus*); Alan Daicz (*Tomas*); Nicolas Marsella (*Polo*); Ana Pauls (*Nurse*).

RATING: ****

In 1960, a large, loving, poverty-stricken Patagonian family moves to an isolated rural area, hoping to eke out a living in the hotel business. One of their first roomers is a soft-spoken, moody, well-educated European doctor (Brendemuhl), who takes great interest in the 12-year-old daughter's (Bado) stunted growth, offering to help without pay. Quickly it becomes obvious that he takes something more than a medical interest in the pubescent beauty and that she in turn develops a schoolgirl crush on her potential savior. But this is no simple Lolita tale; gradually, the parents realize the 'kindly' fellow is actually Josef Mengele, a Nazi monster who used Jewish prisoners for his obscene experiments in genetics. Fascinatingly offbeat and original film progresses at a purposefully slow pace, disappointing only at the end when all plot elements (including Israel agents searching for war criminals in Argentina) wrap up too fast and furiously for a truly satisfying resolution.

WHEN HELL BROKE LOOSE (1958)

CREDITS:

Dolworth Prods./Paramount; Kenneth G. Crane, dir.; Ib Melchior (source materials), Oscar Brodney, scr.; Brodney, Sol Dolgin, pro.; Albert Glasser, mus.; Hal McAlpin, cin.; Asa Boyd Clark, Kenneth G. Crane, ed.; B&W; 1.85:1; 78 min.

CAST:

Charles Bronson (*Steve Boland*); Violet Rensing (*Ilsa*); Richard Jaeckel (*Karl*); Arvid Nelson (*Ludwig*); Robert Easton (*Jonesie*); Dennis McCarthy (*Capt. Melton*).

Rating: ** 1/2

A confidence man joins the army in hopes of escaping prison and becomes involved with a German girl. Her brother, a hardened Nazi, joins the fascist underground, planning to assassinate Eisenhower. When the soldier tries to warn people, no one will take such a perpetual liar seriously. Variation on the boy-who-cried-wolf (in this case werewolf) theme might have clicked if the at-best-minor Dolworth company had had enough money to shoot it properly. Jaeckel, always worth watching, is the bad egg; Bronson sets in place his future superstar image as a rugged individualist. Title notwithstanding, there's little action.

Over "Over There": You Can't Go Home Again

ACT OF VIOLENCE (1948)

CREDITS:
Metro-Goldwyn-Mayer; Fred Zinnemann, dir.; Robert L. Richards, Collier Young, scr.; William H. Wright, pro.; Bronislau Kaper, mus.; Robert Surtees, cin.; Conrad A. Nervig, ed.; B&W; 1.37:1; 82 min.

CAST:
Van Heflin (*Frank R. Enley*); Janet Leigh (*Edith Enley*); Robert Ryan (*Joe Parkson*); Phyllis Thaxter (*Ann*); Mary Astor (*Pat*).

Rating: **** 1/2

Ordinary "Joe" Enley returns a decorated hero. Much loved in his small California town, he has an adoring wife and a sweet child, and owns a successful construction company. This family's quiet life is turned upside down when surly Parkson appears, announcing his plans to kill the soft-spoken lead. At the movie's midpoint, we suspect we may be rooting for the wrong man. Zinnemann shot exteriors on location, kicking off a new era for MGM. A film that begins as a realistic thriller by daylight transforms into a dark expressionistic noir without missing a beat.

HERO'S WELCOME: In *MacArthur*, the general (Gregory Peck) and his troops experience a glorious ticker tape parade; shortly they will experience a major letdown as Americans turn on another during the McCarthy era and The Korean War.

ALL MY SONS (1948)

CREDITS:

Universal-International; Irving Reis, dir.; Arthur Miller (play), Chester Erskine, scr.; Erskine, pro.; Leith Stevens, mus.; Russell Metty, cin.; Ralph Dawson, ed.; B&W; 1.37:1; 95 min.

CAST:

Edward G. Robinson (*Joe Keller*); Burt Lancaster (*Chris*); Mady Christians (*Kate*); Louisa Horton (*Ann Deever*); Howard Duff (*George Deever*); Arlene Francis (*Sue*); Harry Morgan (*Frank*).

Rating: ****

Loving son Chris discovers that during the war, his father sold defective materials to our military. This led to the unnecessary deaths of many GIs, possibly even the hero's younger brother. Contemporary version of a Greek tragedy about unintended sins within a single family, with plenty of Freudian jargon thrown in for the postwar Zeitgeist. Early (pre–*Death of a Salesman*) Miller at his most Ibsenesque. A social-problem play composed in three well-wrought acts. Naturalistic acting by the cast but uninspired direction in terms of bringing the stage piece to cinematic life.

APARTMENT FOR PEGGY (1948)

CREDITS:
20th Century Fox; George Seaton, dir.; Faith Baldwin (novel), George Seaton, scr.; William Perlberg, pro.; David Raksin, mus.; Harry Jackson, cin.; Robert L. Simpson, ed.; C; 99 min.

CAST:
Jeanne Crain (*Peggy Taylor*); William Holden (*Jason Taylor*); Edmund Gwenn (*Prof. Barnes*); Gene Lockhart (*Bell*); Griff Barnett (*Dr. Conway*).

Rating: *** 1/2

A war bride encourages her husband to take advantage of the recently passed GI Bill and pursue a college education. Cramped quarters in leftover wartime housing inspire the young woman to search for a more spacious place to live. She meets embittered Prof. Barnes, his son lost in combat, who takes them in. Baldwin's memoir provided fine material for the definitive movie on this postwar syndrome, despite lapses into soap opera and sitcom. The effect of such mature students on older, set-in-their ways educators is well depicted, as are the quiet moments of anguish for nearly impoverished scholars whose friends have opted for the business world. Crain and Holden make a charming couple. Gwenn, as always, steals the show.

BABY BLUE MARINE (1976)

CREDITS:
Columbia; John D. Hancock, dir.; Stanford Whitmore, scr.; Leonard Goldberg, Robert LaVigne, Aaron Spelling, pro.; Fred Karlin, mus.; László Kovács, cin.; Marion Rothman, ed.; C; 1.85:1 90 min.

CAST:
Jan-Michael Vincent (*Marion*); Glynnis O'Connor (*Rose*); Katherine Helmond (*Mrs. Hudkins*); Dana Elcar (*Sheriff*); Bruno Kirby (*Pop*).

Rating: *** 1/2

Modest, nostalgic minidrama imposes a late–Vietnam era shattered sensibility on its WWII setting. When a would-be hero can't make it in the service and leaves in disgrace, he wanders into a small town where everyone mistakes him for the great marine he'd always hoped to become. Engaging until the cop-out ending. Kovács's dazzling cinematography shrouds the piece in a *Saturday Evening Post* aura. A young Richard Gere impresses as a shell-shocked vet.

BAD DAY AT BLACK ROCK (1955)

CREDITS:
Metro-Goldwyn-Mayer; John Sturges, dir.; Howard Breslin (short story), Don McGuire, Millard Kaufman, scr.; Dore Schary, pro.; André Previn, mus.; William C. Mellor, cin.; Newell P. Kimlin, ed.; C; 2.55:1; 81 min.

CAST:
Spencer Tracy (*John J. Macreedy*); Robert Ryan (*Reno Smith*); Anne Francis (*Liz Wirth*); Dean Jagger (*Sheriff Tim Horn*); Walter Brennan (*Doc T. R. Velie, Jr.*); John Ericson (*Pete*); Ernest Borgnine (*Coley*); Lee Marvin (*Hector*).

Rating: *****

WHAT WENT WRONG?: Spencer Tracy realizes that residents of a small American town are actually brutal racists who killed a war hero owing to his ethnicity in *Bad Day at Black Rock*; in the 1950s Civil Rights dramas came to dominate American film.

One year after the end of the war, a one-armed man steps off a train in a small southwestern town and makes inquiries about a Japanese American who once lived here. The townspeople, led by a local rancher, conspire to keep the stranger from learning that man's fate. A contemporary version of *High Noon* with the interpersonal dynamics reversed, adjusted to make a civil rights statement, under the influence of liberal Schary. Sturges provides a perfect blend of generic thriller and message movie. Casting is exquisite, Marvin and Borgnine standouts. No one could have played the lead but Tracy, who performs some of the first martial arts stunts ever in a Hollywood movie. A rightly cherished classic.

BEST YEARS OF OUR LIVES, THE (1946)

CREDITS:
The Samuel Goldwyn Company; William Wyler, dir.; MacKinlay Kantor (novel), Robert E. Sherwood, scr.; Samuel Goldwyn, pro.; Hugo Friedhofer, mus.; Gregg Toland, cin.; Daniel Mandell, ed.; B&W; 1.37:1; 172 min.

AN AMERICAN COMMUNITY OF MEN: Three veterans (Dana Andrews, Fredrick March, Oscar winner Harold Russell) enjoy each other's company while flying home; disappointed with what each finds awaiting him, they meet in a bar to drown their sorrows.

CAST:

Myrna Loy (*Milly Stephenson*); Fredric March (*Al*); Dana Andrews (*Fred Derry*); Teresa Wright (*Peggy*); Virginia Mayo (*Marie*); Cathy O'Donnell (*Wilma*); Hoagy Carmichael (*Butch Engle*); Harold Russell (*Homer Parrish*).

Rating: *****

Domestic epic that defined the postwar American experience, focusing on a collection of vividly realized individuals. Three vets share a plane to their hometown: well-to-do banker Al, whose loyal wife Milly and daughter Peggy await; ice boy Homer from a middle-class neighborhood, his hands severed in combat; and upwardly mobile Fred from the wrong side of the tracks, whose wife Marie is unfaithful. The film treats their problems with such sensitivity that the piece stretches beyond the limits of high-level soap opera, becoming a work of dramatic art worthy of inclusion in a time capsule. The title proves ironic: though these men would have never associated before the war, they're happiest when getting together at a neighborhood bar, trying to grasp how the glorious dream of peace soured so quickly.

BLUE DAHLIA, THE (1946)

CREDITS:

George Marshall, dir.; Raymond Chandler, scr.; John Houseman, pro.; Arthur P. Schmidt, ed.; Lionel Lindon, cin.; Victor Young, mus.; Paramount; 96 min.; B&W; 1.37:1.

CAST:

Alan Ladd (*Johnny Morrison*); Veronica Lake (*Joyce Harwood*); William Bendix (*Buz Wanchek*); Doris Dowlng (*Helen Morrison*); Howard Da Silva (*Eddie Harwood*); Tom Powers (*Hendrickson*); Hugh Beaumont (*Copeland*); Howard Freeman (*Corelli*).

Rating: **** ½

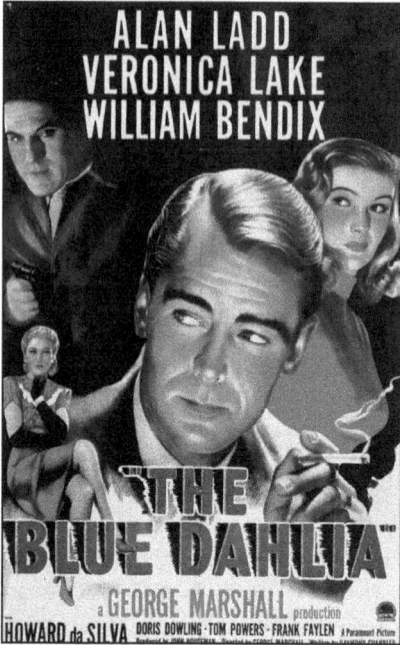

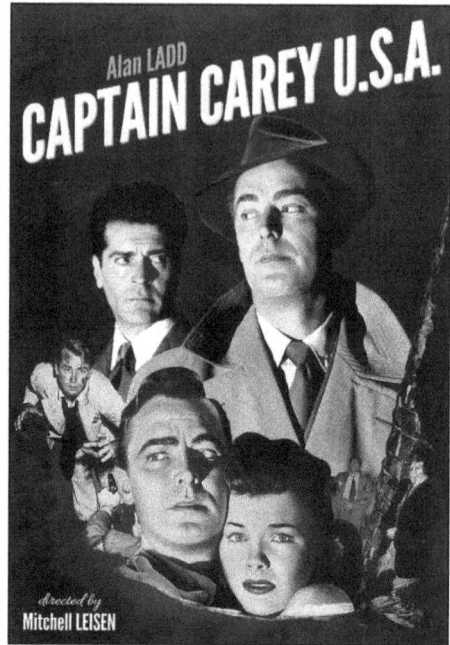

THE BIRTH OF NOIR: Alan Ladd, who played the all-American boy grown up during the war years, took on a more complex image as the anti-hero who walks America's dark alleys and mean streets in such films as *The Blue Gardenia* and *Captain Carey, U.S.A.*

In what would become a recurring image during the postwar era, a vet steps down from a bus (*Some Came Running*) or train (*Bad Day at Black Rock*) to encounter the existential ennui that has settled in to a once optimistic American community. Here it is Johnny Morrison, a Navy hero, who encounters the lonely crowd that L.A. has degenerated into, realizing his beloved wife is now mistress of a mob-connected club owner, Eddie Harwood. Her murder sets off a string of nasty encounters on mean streets and down dark alleys in a hard, cruel asphalt jungle. Lake is the mystery blonde of dubious intent and shady origins; Bendix another vet who suffers from unpredictable bursts of post-combat stress syndrome. Rare screenplay by noir novelist R.C. (*The Long Goodbye, Murder My Sweet*). The title references a notorious real-life murder known as 'The Black Dahlia' case.

BRIGHT VICTORY (1951)

CREDITS:

Universal; Mark Robson, dir.; Baynard Kendrick (novel), Robert Buckner, scr.; Buckner, pro.; Frank Skinner, mus.; William (H.) Daniels, cin.; Russell F. Schoengarth, Milton Carruth, ed.; B&W; 1.37:1; 96 min.

CAST:

Arthur Kennedy (*Larry Nevins*); Peggy Dow (*Judy Greene*); Julie (Julia) Adams (*Chris Paterson*); James Edwards (*Joe Morgan*); Will Geer, Nana Bryant (*Larry's Parents*).

Rating: ****

Based on the acclaimed 1945 social realist novel *Lights Out*. Larry takes a wound to the head from a sniper while serving in North Africa. The

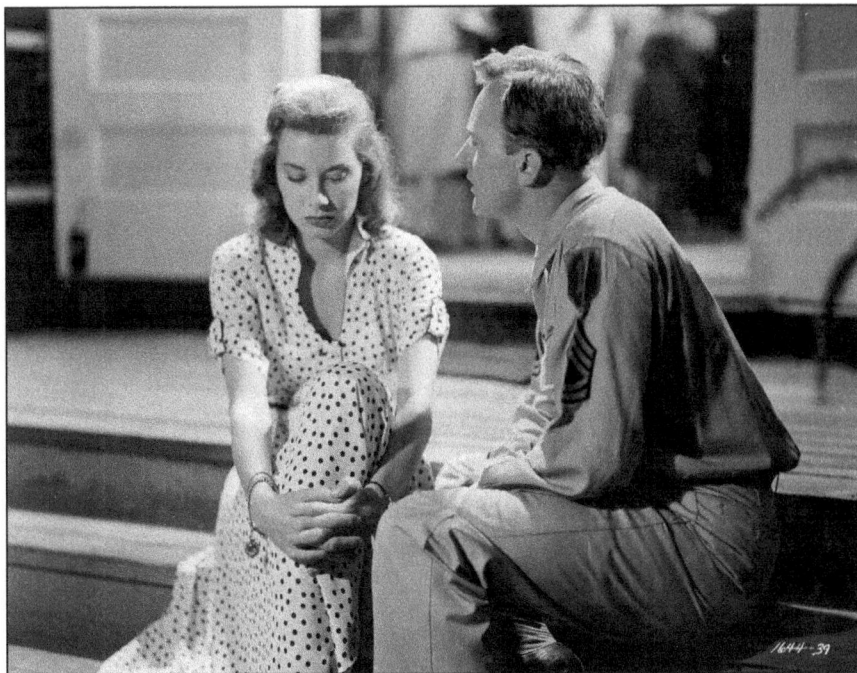

WHEN THE WORLD DARKENS: A blinded soldier (Arthur Kennedy) tries to reconnect with his fiancée (Peggy Dow) in Bright Victory;

focus is on the treatment he receives when interned in a military hospital. A civil rights theme materializes when the lead befriends fellow blind soldier Joe, whom the prejudiced Southerner does not realize is black. Often on the brink of slipping into sentimentality but managing to avoid that trap with a hopeful ending that refuses to see through rose-colored glasses. In a rare lead, character actor Kennedy received a Best Actor Oscar nomination. Filmed at the Valley Forge Army Hospital in Pennsylvania for total realism.

BUCK PRIVATES COME HOME (1947)

CREDITS:
Universal International; Charles (T.) Barton, dir.; Richard Macaulay, Bradford Ropes, John Grant, Frederic I. Rinaldo, Robert Lees, scr.; Robert Arthur, pro.; Walter Schumann, mus.; Charles Van Enger, cin.; Edward Curtiss, ed.; B&W; 1.37:1; 77 min.

CAST:
Bud Abbott (*Slicker Smith*); Lou Costello (*Herbie Brown*); Tom Brown (*Bill Gregory*); Joan (Fulton) Shawlee (*Sylvia Hunter*); Nat Pendleton (*Sgt. Michael Collins*).

Rating: ****

Those lovably incompetent GIs introduced in 1941 return, along with their crusty sarge and a six-year-old French orphan who stowed away in a duffel bag. Rare case in which a belated sequel is considerably better than the original. Humor (verbal and visual) is neatly balanced with effective emotions involving the vulnerable waif. "Inspired" is the only way to describe the decision to add racing cars to the mix, featuring the finest auto sight gags since Charlie Chaplin in *Kid Auto Races in Venice* (1914). Watch for the classic "Sawhorse Table" routine on the ship.

CAPTAIN NEWMAN, M.D. (1963)

CREDITS:

Brentwood Production; David Miller, dir.; Leo Rosten (novel), Richard L. Breen, Henry Ephron, Phoebe Ephron, scr.; Robert Arthur, pro.; Frank Skinner, mus.; Russell Metty, cin.; Alma Macrorie, ed.; C; 1.85:1; 126 min.

CAST:

Gregory Peck (*Josiah J. Newman*); Tony Curtis (*Cpl. Jackson Leibowitz*); Angie Dickinson (*Lt. Francie Corum*); Bobby Darin (*Cpl. Jim Tompkins*); Eddie Albert (*Col. Norval Bliss*).

Rating: ** 1/2

A stolid psychiatrist dealing with disturbed veterans is so shorthanded he must accept a conniving wise guy as his new assistant. The film combines elements of *Mister Roberts*, *Twelve O'Clock High*, and *Operation Petticoat*, as well as the upcoming *One Flew Over the Cuckoo's Nest*, but without success. Blame director Miller, utterly unqualified to transform Rosten's impressive black comedy into a film both dramatic and goofy. Bolstered by superb performances by Darin (Oscar nominee, Best Supporting Actor) and Albert as troubled returned veterans.

CHRISTMAS IN CONNECTICUT (1945)

CREDITS:

Warner Bros.; Peter Godfrey, dir.; Aileen Hamilton, Lionel Houser, Adele Comandini, scr.; William Jacobs, Jack L. Warner, pro.; Frederick Hollander, Adolph Deutsch, mus.; Carl E. Guthrie, cin.; Frank Magee, ed.; B&W; 1.37:1; 102 min.

CAST:

Barbara Stanwyck (*Elizabeth Lane*); Dennis Morgan (*Jefferson Jones*); Sydney Greenstreet (*Alexander Yardley*); Reginald Gardiner (*Sloan*); S. Z. Sakall (*Felix*); Una O'Connor (*Norah*); Frank Jenks (*Sinkewicz*).

BITTERSWEET: The homecoming of a genial hero (John Hodiak) who hopes to spend an old-fashioned holiday with a farm lady (Barbara Stanwyck) clashes with the fact that she is actually a cynical/sophisticated New Yorker in *Christmas in Connecticut*.

Rating: **** 1/2

Charming light comedy/sophisticated romance, just right for the war's final year. A pseudosophisticated career gal churns out a faux newspaper column, assuming the identity of a small-town New England housewife/mother. A returning war hero asks to spend the holidays with this prototypical American family, so an elaborate make-believe world must be created. Everything clicks in this cute though never cloying piece, its tone reminiscent of Capra's classics. Beloved members of the WB stock company bring their post-*Casablanca* personalities to the proceedings. Captures the era's mellow and bittersweet quality.

COURAGE OF LASSIE (1946)

CREDITS:
Metro-Goldwyn-Mayer; Fred M. Wilcox, dir.; Lionel Houser, scr.; Robert Sisk, pro.; Scott Bradley, Bronislau Kaper, mus.; Leonard Smith, cin.; Conrad A. Nervig, ed.; C; 1.37:1; 92 min.

CAST:
Elizabeth Taylor (*Kathie Merrick*); Tome Drake (*Sgt. Smitty*); Frank Morgan (*Harry MacBain*); Selena Royle (*Mrs. Merrick*); Harry Davenport (*Judge Payson*); George Cleveland (*Old Man*).

Rating: ****

Lassie, Come Home updated with a WWII background and a lonely girl (Taylor) praying for her pup's return. Bill (Lassie) is adopted by a sheep farmer's daughter who shares unconditional love with her pet. Eventually, a lost-again Bill is trained for combat service in the only Hollywood feature to depict that process. Shell-shocked, Bill becomes depressed, even vicious. A final speech makes clear the collie has been presented a metaphor for young men who would return scarred, not always visibly. Touching throughout, yet violent enough that this shouldn't be considered a kiddie film.

CROSSFIRE (1947)

CREDITS:
RKO Radio Pictures; Edward Dmytryk, dir.; Richard Brooks (novel), John Paxton, scr.; Dore Schary, Adrian Scott, pro.; Roy Webb, mus.; J. Roy Hunt, cin.; Harry W. Gerstad, ed.; B&W; 1.37:1; 86 min.

CAST:
Robert Young (*Capt. Finlay*); Robert Mitchum (*Sgt. Keeley*); Robert Ryan (*Montgomery*); Gloria Grahame (*Ginny*); Paul Kelly (*Tremaine*); Sam Levene (*Joseph Samuels*).

Rating: **** 1/2

Young plays a compassionate detective assigned to a bizarre case: a well-to-do man (Levene) was discovered beaten to death in his apartment by several GIs, recently returned and out for a good time. Is the murderer the level-headed sergeant (Mitchum), the group intellectual (Cooper), or the arrogant anti-Semite (Ryan)? Effectively combines the best qualities of postwar message movies with the emergent film noir thrillers, conveying the escalating sense of moral confusion in the late 1940s. As the victim put it, with our great enemies now gone, "you can feel the tension around you. We're too used to fighting, but we just don't know what to fight. So we start looking at each other again." In the novel *Brick Foxhole* (1945), the victim was a homosexual. This was considered too daring to include in a commercial film.

ENCHANTED COTTAGE, THE (1945)

CREDITS:
RKO; John Cromwell, dir.; Arthur Wing Pinero (play), DeWitt Bodeen, Herman J. Mankiewicz, scr.; Harriet Parsons, pro.; Roy Web, mus.; Ted Tetzlaff, cin.; Joseph Noriega, ed.; B&W; 1.37:1; 91 min.

CAST:
Dorothy McGuire (*Laura Pennington*); Robert Young (*Oliver Bradford*); Herbert Marshall (*Maj Hillgrove*); Mildred Natwick (*Abigail*); Spring Byington (*Violet*); Hillary Brooke (*Beatrice*).

Rating: *** 1/2

A once-handsome pilot returns terribly disfigured. He rents a small New England cottage, becoming a hermit who speaks to no one but the homely maid. Isolated, they fall in love, and in a seeming miracle, both transform into beauties. The "enchantment" exists only in their minds, thanks to the power of love. Wonderful premise undercut by Hollywood's mentality. As McGuire and Young were attractive stars as well as fine actors, the studio decided it would not be wise to make them appear *too* ugly. As a result, scenes that show them as (supposedly) not handsome compared to others fail to deliver the needed contrast.

FAITHFUL IN MY FASHION (1946)

CREDITS:
RKO; Sidney Salkow, dir.; Lionel Houser, scr.; Houser, pro.; Nathaniel Shilkret, mus.; Charles Salerno, Jr., cin.; Cotton Warburton, ed.; B&W; 1.37:1; 81 min.

CAST:
Donna Reed (*Jean Kendrick*); Tom Drake (*Jeff Compton*); Edward Everett Horton (*Hiram Dilworthy*); Spring Byington (*Mary Swanson*); Sig Ruman (*Prof. Riminoffsky*).

Rating: ***

A stuffy store manager (Horton) frets that when the boys return home, "most expect that they will come back to find nothing has changed." One easygoing vet, ready to assume his old job and marry "his girl," discovers she's now the manager and his boss, and also engaged to someone else. "I'm sure other girls are in the same position," a pal says. Indeed, millions of American women were. Though this becomes hopelessly contrived during the second half, the initial innocuous comedy/romance touches on a significant common problem during the immediate postwar years.

HAIL THE CONQUERING HERO (1944)

CREDITS:
Paramount; Preston Sturges, dir.; Sturges, scr.; Sturges, Buddy DeSylva, pro.; Werner R. Heymann, mus.; John F. Seitz, cin.; Stuart Gilmore, ed.; B&W; 1.37:1; 101 min.

CAST:

Eddie Bracken (*Woodrow Truesmith*); Ella Raines (*Libby*); Raymond Walburn (*Mayor Noble*); William Demarest (*Sgt. Heffelfinger*); Franklin Pangborn (*Reception Committee Chairman*).

Rating: *****

Honorably discharged from the Marines for chronic hay fever, a lovable loser passes himself off as a hero in his hometown with catastrophic results. Iconoclastic Sturges combined smart writing, absurd situations, accelerated or overlapping dialogue, slapstick sight gags, and a giddy madcap attitude to create a one-of-a-kind comedy. When simple patriotism reigned in Hollywood, Sturges dared spoof the excesses of flag-waving while poking good-natured fun at every revered institution, including small towns, family values, local politics, and American ethics. His stock company delivers inspired caricatures, including Demarest as a crusty sergeant and Pangborn as a notably fey cheerleader. The show, however, belongs to the sad-faced clown Bracken and radiant Raines. Their inspired silliness is relentlessly satirical while avoiding superficial cynicism.

HOMECOMING (1948)

CREDITS:

Metro-Goldwyn-Mayer; Mervyn LeRoy, dir.; Sidney Kingsley, Jan Lustig, Paul Osborn, scr.; Sidney Franklin, pro.; Bronislau Kaper, mus.; Harold Rosson, cin.; John D. Dunning, ed.; B&W; 1.37:1; 113 min.

CAST:

Clark Gable (*Maj. Ulysses "Useless" Johnson*); Lana Turner (*Lt. Jane "Snapshot" McCall*); Anne Baxter (*Penny Johnson*); John Hodiak (*Dr. Robert Sunday*); Ray Collins (*Col. Silver*).

Rating: *** 1/2

At war's end, a grim vet aboard a Navy transport recalls how the war changed him. He'd been a successful if smug doctor with a gorgeous wife until Pearl Harbor. In the military, he met a nurse whose caring attitude for others turned their tragic love affair into a life-altering experience. A bit thick on the suds; Gable's far too old for his part. Turner is at her snappiest. Melodramatics aside, the movie rates as an early attempt to explore problems many servicemen brought home as invisible baggage. Educates the moviegoing public about the New Normal via soap-opera-like entertainment. Derived from Homer's *Odyssey*, as the hero's name implies.

HOUSE ON TELEGRAPH HILL, THE (1951)

CREDITS:
20th Century Fox; Robert Wise, dir.; Dana Lyon (novel), Elick Moll, Frank Partos, scr.; Robert Bassler, pro.; Sol Kaplan, mus.; Lucien Ballard, cin.; Nick DeMaggio, ed.; B&W; 1.37:1; 93 min.

CAST:
Richard Basehart (*Alan Spender*); Valentina Cortese (*Victoria Kowelska*); William Lundigan (*Maj. Bennett*); Fay Baker (*Margaret*); Gordon Gebert (*Christopher*).

Rating: ** 1/2

Intriguing if ultimately unsuccessful attempt to revive the old Hitchcock-style thriller for the postwar audience. A Polish woman survives internment in a concentration camp. At war's end, she assumes a deceased girlfriend's identity, that woman's infant son earlier smuggled to America. The heroine arrives, marrying the boy's legal guardian, only to realize something strange—even evil—haunts the house. The opening looks and feels so realistic that the later twists appear ludicrous in context. Act One includes documentary footage of displaced persons, far too heartbreaking for the silly suspense ploys that follow.

I WAS A MALE WAR BRIDE (1949)

CREDITS:
20th Century Fox; Howard Hawks, dir.; Henri Rochard, Charles Lederer, Leonard Spigelgass, Hagar Wilde, scr.; Sol C. Siegel, pro.; Cyril J.

LIFE'S A DRAG: Cary Grant must disguise himself as a woman to reach the U.S. in the transgender comedy classic *I Was a male War Bride*.

Mockridge, mus.; Osmond Borradaile, Norbert Brodine, cin.; James B. Clark, ed.; B&W; 1.37:1; 105 min.

CAST:
Cary Grant (*Capt. Henri Rochard*); Ann Sheridan (*Lt. Catherine Gates*); Marion Marshall (*Kitty*); Randy Stuart (*Eloise*); Bill Neff (*Ramsey*); Russ Conway (*Chaplain*).

Rating: *****

The first Hawks comedy film shot on location in Europe boasts the same settings our postwar audience had seen in docudramas like *The Big Lift*: bombed-out buildings that resemble monstrous creations from a surrealist's imagination. Here, piles of rubble provide a backdrop for screwball fun, conveying an irony as dark as the gags themselves are light. The title refers to Grant, a recently retired French officer helping an American (Sheridan) reorient the German people. When they fall in love, they face a massive bureaucracy that could cope with a female spouse but had no idea how to handle this. Cross-dressing conclusion achieved classic status. As zesty and appealing as when it was first released.

IMPATIENT YEARS, THE (1944)

CREDITS:
Columbia; Irving Cummings, dir.; Virginia Van Upp, scr.; Van Upp, Cummings, pro.; Marlin Skiles, mus.; Joseph Walker, cin.; Al Clark, ed.; B&W; 1.37:1; 91 min.

CAST:
Jean Arthur (*Janie Anderson*); Lee Bowman (*Andy*); Charles Coburn (*Smith*); Edgar Buchanan (*Judge*); Charley Grapewin (*Pidgeon*); Phil Brown (*Henry*).

Rating: *** 1/2

"This isn't just one divorce," a father-in-law warns a sympathetic judge, "there's going to be a million more just like it." Prophetic words in the first movie to deal with the problems that war brides, many now mothers, faced when Johnny Came Marching Home: they and their spouses, wed in dreamy romantic excitement, have little in common. Young Janie and GI Andy grasp, after a one-and-a-half-year separation, that they are intimate strangers. Admirable, though the film falters during the second half when the couple heads back to San Francisco (where they met) to rekindle the romance. A wishful-thinking happy ending wraps things up too neatly. Still, this warns of what would become our swiftly skyrocketing divorce rate.

IT HAPPENED IN BROOKLYN (1947)

CREDITS:
Metro-Goldwyn-Mayer; Richard Whorf, dir.; Isobel Lennart, J. P. McGowan, scr.; Jack Cummings, pro.; Johnny Green, mus.; Robert H. Planck, cin.; Blanche Sewell, ed.; B&W; 1.37:1; 105 min.

CAST:
Frank Sinatra (*Danny Miller*); Kathryn Grayson (*Anne*); Peter Lawford (*Jamie*); Jimmy Durante (*Nick*); Gloria Grahame (*Blonde Nurse*); William Roy (*Leo Kardos*).

Rating: ***

Shy soldier Danny avoids a pretty blonde nurse in postwar England, thinking only of his beloved Brooklyn. Arriving home, he senses things have changed; people aren't as friendly as he recalled, nor are situations or places the same. Spirited cast in a slight story about his competition for music teacher Anne with Brit buddy Jamie. The Sammy Cahn/Jule Styne tune "Time After Time" is performed by the chairman-of-the-board-to-be. Even in a minor lighthearted musical, the postwar letdown is notably on display.

IT'S ALWAYS FAIR WEATHER (1955)

CREDITS:
Metro-Goldwyn-Mayer; Stanley Donen, Gene Kelly, dir.; Betty Comden, Adolph Green, scr.; Arthur Freed, pro.; Robert J. Bronner, cin.; Adrienne Fazan, ed.; C; 2.55:1; 101 min.

CAST:
Gene Kelly (*Ted Riley*); Dan Dailey (*Doug Hallerton*); Michael Kidd (*Angie Valentine*); Cyd Charisse (*Jackie Leighton*); Dolores Gray (Madeline); David Burns (*Tim*).

Rating: ****

Upon their return to New York, three former servicemen (Kelly, Dailey, Kidd) spend a deliriously happy evening at a local bar and then part to enjoy the lives each had fantasized about while overseas. They agree to meet here ten years hence. A decade later, each stumbles in, embittered, disappointed, his dreams turned to dust. Even the sense of community they once shared has dissipated, leaving them a trio of deeply unhappy rugged individualists—the case with so many real-life veterans who couldn't grasp what had gone wrong. Starts out like another gleeful MGM Kelly-Donen songfest only to grow depressingly downbeat as the show rolls on, perhaps explaining why this was not a box-office hit. Only liability: several weak songs.

JANIE GETS MARRIED (1946)

CREDITS:
Warner Bros.; Vincent Sherman, dir.; Agnes Christine Johnston, scr.; Alex Gottlieb, pro.; Friedrich Hollaender, mus.; Carl E. Guthrie, cin.; Christian Nyby, ed.; B&W; 1.37:1; 89 min.

CAST:
Joan Leslie (*Janie Conway*); Robert Hutton (*Dick*); Edward Arnold (*Charles Conway*); Ann Harding (*Lucille Conway*); Robert Benchley (*John Van Brunt*); Dorothy Malone (*Sgt. Spud Lee*).

Rating: ****

The appealing and underrated Leslie replaces Joyce Reynolds in this sequel to 1944's hit about a small-town girl who falls in love with an on-leave soldier (Hutton). Now, the war is over; he returns and marries the young woman. Postwar life turns out to be a nightmare. She's not satisfied with housewifery in the emergent suburbia; he hates his job. Their mutual melancholy takes a toll on the union when both face the fact that they have nothing in common. Their love, if that's was what it was, cannot survive the realities of everyday life. Malone shines in a strong early role as the husband's sexy wartime pal who shows up for a disturbing visit. Despite this supposedly light film's minor status, it provides sharp, smart commentary on why the new normal did not lead to the best years in anyone's lives.

KISS THEM FOR ME (1957)

CREDITS:
20th Century Fox; Stanley Donen, dir.; Luther Davis (play), Frederick Wakeman (novel), Julius J. Epstein, scr.; Jerry Wald, pro.; Lionel Newman, mus.; Milton R. Krasner, cin.; Robert L. Simpson, ed.; C; 2.35:1; 115 min.

CAST:
Cary Grant (*Cmdr. Andy Crewson*); Jayne Mansfield (*Alice Kratzner*); Leif Erickson (*Eddie Turnbill*); Suzy Parker (*Gwinneth Livingston*); Ray Walston (*Lt. McCann*).

Rating: **

Three stressed-out naval flyers receive a furlough in San Francisco. They want to pursue women and get drunk but find themselves exploited by a government PR man, businessmen, and a newshound, all out for personal profit. Potent idea results in one of the first films to portray a cynical side to war and the embitterment of sincere servicemen. Sadly, the presentation is spotty at best, done in by Mansfield's cartoon performance and, as Grant's love interest, classy Parker's inability to act (her voice had to be dubbed by Deborah Kerr). Bizarre tone shift from screwball silliness to deep sadness renders it all but unwatchable.

LOVE LAUGHS AT ANDY HARDY (1946)

CREDITS:

Metro-Goldwyn-Mayer; Willis Goldbeck, dir.; Aurania Rouverol (original characters), William Ludwig, Harry Ruskin, scr.; Robert Sisk, pro.; Robert Planck, cin.; Cotton Warburton, ed.; B&W; 95 min.

CAST:

Mickey Rooney (*Andy*); Lewis Stone (*Judge James Hardy*); Sara Haden (*Aunt Milly*); Bonita Granville (*Kay Wilson*); Lina Romay (*Isobel Gonzales*); Fay Holden (*Mrs. Emily Hardy*).

Rating: * ½

In the 15th and penultimate (until 1958) films in the Hardy Family saga, Carvel, CA's favorite son returns from service and re-enters college. The army changed Andy: no longer a skirt-chaser, he's dedicated to one girl (Granville) to the dismay of his over-protective mother (Holden). Dull, mundane, and lifeless; all the old charm is gone. Interesting only in revealing the changing social scene: advance in Civil Rights as Protestant Andy dates a Catholic girl (Romay) with no objection from his parents; the first film to note that new clothing choices of post-WWII youth (leotards for girls, hep jackets for boys) offended members of the older generation.

LOVE LETTERS (1945)

CREDITS:

Paramount; William Dieterle, dir.; Chris Massie (novel), Ayn Rand, scr.; Hal B. Wallis, pro.; Victor Young, mus.; Lee Garmes, cin.; Anne Bauchens, ed.; B&W; 1.37:1; 101 min.

CAST:

Jennifer Jones (*Singleton*); Joseph Cotten (*Allen Quinton*); Ann Richards (*Dilly Carson*); Cecil Kellaway (*Mac*); Gladys Cooper (*Beatrice*); Anita Louise (*Helen*).

Rating: *** 1/2

After recuperation, a badly wounded Brit becomes fascinated, obsessed even, with a mystery woman. While on the front, he wrote love letters to her for an all-but-illiterate friend who turned out to be a no-good bounder. Intent on tracking her down, the melancholy hero is shocked to learn she's in prison for murdering her abusive husband. Unlikely as the plot may be, the haunting romance mostly works owing to the craftsmanship of a team that would reunite several years letter for *A Portrait of Jennie*. Of considerable interest today owing to the unlikely choice for screenwriter, with bits of Rand's controversial philosophy present in the dialogue.

LOVE NEST (1951)

CREDITS:

20th Century Fox; Joseph M. Newman, dir.; Scott Corbett (novel), I. A. L. Diamond, scr.; Jules Buck, pro.; Cyril J. Mockridge, mus.; Lloyd Ahern, cin.; J. Watson Webb, Jr., ed.; B&W; 1.37:1; 84 min.

CAST:

June Haver (*Connie Scott*); William Lundigan (*Jim*); Frank Fay (*Charlie*); Marilyn Monroe (*Roberta*); Jack Paar (*Ed Forbes*).

Rating: *** 1/2

Young marrieds buy a run-down New York building and figure they'll enjoy the easy life, renting rooms to cover their mortgage. They learn the hard (if funny) way that whatever can go wrong in a tenement will. Biggest problem: his old war buddy comes to visit, the blonde Monroe (who lights up the screen). Charming adaptation of Corbett's appealing 1950 autobiographical novel *The Reluctant Landlord*. As in reality, the protagonist gives up his original literary project to jot down notes for a book on what's going on around him. Nicely captures the sensibility of young vets who used the GI Bill to negotiate a new lease on life.

MAN IN THE GRAY FLANNEL SUIT, THE (1956)

CREDITS:

20th Century Fox; Nunnally Johnson, dir.; Sloan Wilson (novel), Johnson, scr.; Darryl F. Zanuck, pro.; Bernard Herrmann, mus.; Charles G. Clarke, cin.; Dorothy Spencer, ed.; C; 2.55:1; 153 min.

CAST:

Gregory Peck (*Tom Rath*); Jennifer Jones (*Betsy Rath*); Fredric March (*Ralph Hopkins*); Marisa Pavan (*Maria*); Lee J. Cobb (*Judge Bernstein*); Ann Harding (*Helen*); Keenan Wynn (*Sgt. Caesar Gardella*).

Rating: *** 1/2

Wilson's 1955 novel defined a generation of American men. The story makes an uneasy transition to the screen in this glossy, overlong, intermittently effective adaptation. A decade after the war, Tom and his ambitious wife have achieved the postwar dream: a house in the upscale suburbs and three TV-addicted kids. Tom commutes by train from Connecticut to New York and wears a Brooks Brothers suit, which denies his individual identity, typing him as a Madison Avenue man. Why, he wonders, does he feel so empty and unsatisfied? Everything around Tom recalls the war; he suffers ongoing guilt over accidentally killing a friend (Kenneth Tobey) in combat. While in Italy, his affair with an Italian girl, he now learns, resulted in a child. The novel conveyed a sense of immediacy and universality, which the film flattens out into an expensive soap opera. Peck nicely captures the inner demons of an apparently content, deeply disturbed, representative suburbanite veteran.

MEN, THE (1950)

CREDITS:

United Artists; Fred Zinnemann, dir.; Carl Foreman, scr.; Stanley Kramer, pro.; Dimitri Tiomkin, mus.; Robert De Grasse, cin.; Harry W. Gerstad, ed.; B&W; 1.37:1; 85 min.

CAST:

Marlon Brando (*Ken*); Teresa Wright (*Ellen*); Everett Sloane (*Dr. Brock*); Jack Webb (*Norm*); Richard Erdman (*Leo*); Arthur Jurado (*Angel*); Dorothy Tree, Howard St. John (*Elle's parents*).

Rating: **** 1/2

One shot brings down an infantry lieutenant in Europe. He returns home a paraplegic, without hope of recovery. Terrified that the woman he loves will reject him (she does not), he grows remote, distant, mournful. Other than the leads, the forty-five men on view are portrayed by patients at the Birmingham Veterans Administration Hospital. Another of those early films shot on location for heightened realism during the postwar years, vividly realized by the same writer-producer-director team that would give us *High Noon* (1953). Stage star Brando made his screen debut in this indie project that, like all Kramer films, had something big to say. Intelligent, low key, rewarding.

MONKEY ON MY BACK (1957)

CREDITS:

Edward Small Productions; André De Toth, dir.; Barney Ross (book), Paul Dudley, Anthony Veiller, Crane Wilbur, scr.; Edward Small, pro.; Paul Sawtell, Bert Shefter, mus.; Maury Gertsman, cin.; Grant Whytock, ed.; B&W; 1.37:1; 94 min.

CAST:

Cameron Mitchell (*Barney Ross*); Dianne Foster (*Cathy Holland*); Paul Richards (*Rico the Pusher*); Jack Albertson (*Sam*); Kathy Garver (*Noreen*).

Rating: ***

A champion boxer, wounded during the war, is given morphine and returns a drug addict. With his wife's help, he tries to regain his once-happy life. Daring at the time, less so today. Packs a punch thanks to Mitchell's sincere performance (among his best) and De Toth's no-nonsense direction. Combat scenes are brief but memorable. Significant as one of Hollywood's first honest attempts to depict the endless ordeal of postwar addiction. Harrowing, though censorship of the time precluded a full depiction of the wide range of horrors described in Barney Ross's (1909–1967) autobiography *No Man Stands Alone* (1957).

MUDBOUND (2017)

CREDITS:
Armory Films/Artimage Ent.; Dee Rees, dir.; Rees, Virgil Williams, scrs., Hillary Jordan (novel); Tim Zajaros, many others, pros.; Tamar-kati, mus.; Rachel Morrison, cin.; Mako Kamitsuna, ed.; 2.39:1; C; 134 min.

CAST:
Carey Mulligan *(Laura McAllan)*; Garrett Hedlung *(Jamie)*; Jason Mitchell (Ronsel); Mary J. Bilge *(Florence Jackson)*; Dylan Arnold *(Carl)*; Jonathan Banks *(Pappy)*; Lucy Faust *(Vera)*; Bob Morgan *(Hap)*; Kerry Cahill *(Rose)*; Jason Clarke *(Henry)*.

Rating: **** ½

Late in 1945, all across America veterans returned to their home states only to discover that while the war might officially be over, dark dreams and frightful memories would continue to haunt their attempts to readjust. In the Deep South, Mississippi in particular, this was complicated by the race issue even as the modern Civil Rights Movement evolved. This fine little film focuses on two soldiers, a white land-owner and an African-American sharecropper, to present the larger historical and (here) cinematic canvas as hapless citizens of all social classes found themselves living in an era of Future Shock transition. Multiple Oscar winner; Bilge singled out for her outstanding work as an actress and songwriter. Feminist issues also addressed in a refreshingly non-didactic manner.

NEW YORK, NEW YORK (1977)

CREDITS:

United Artists; Martin Scorsese, dir.; Earl Mac Rauch, Mardik Martin, scr.; Robert Chartoff, Irwin Winkler, pro.; John Kander, Fred Ebb, mus.; László Kovács, cin.; Bert Lovitt, David Ramirez, Tom Rolf, ed.; C; 1.66:1; 155 min. (director's cut), 136 min. (original theatrical release), 163 min. (restored edition).

CAST:

Liza Minnelli (*Francine Evans*); Robert De Niro (*Jimmy Doyle*); Lionel Stander (*Tony*); Barry Primus (*Paul*); Mary Kay Place (*Bernice*); Georgie Auld (*Frankie*).

Rating: *** 1/2

Scorsese's ear-, eye-, and mind-boggling attempt to create an epic about modern music, from the end of WWII to the present, by focusing on a big-band girl singer caught in an abusive relationship with an edgy jazz artist. Various sequences alternate between ultrarealistic and clearly studio shot for no apparent purpose. The best bits reveal the director's genius, but the overall work rates as a disaster. Story begins on VE Day with one of those legendary parties that promised to go on forever, conveying the exuberant optimism at war's end. The melancholy that swiftly descended on society is reflected in the leads' relationship as everything sours, while the dreams of peace, prosperity, and plenty that sustained us through the war years dissipate before everyone's eyes. Contains great and diverse music that could and should go on endlessly. The film feels like it will never conclude.

THE BEST YEARS OF OUR LIVES?: A fictional musician (Robert De Niro) and his wife (Liza Minnelli) celebrate with Tommy Dorsey (William Tole) during a jubilant homecoming party; A veteran realizes that he has lost the ability to communicate with his wife (Myrna Loy) following his return in the ironically titled Oscar-winning Best Picture winner.

NO LEAVE, NO LOVE (1946)

CREDITS:

Metro-Goldwyn-Mayer; Charles Martin, dir.; László Kardos, aka Leslie Kardos, Charles Martin, scr.; Joe Pasternak, pro.; Calvin Jackson, George Stoll, mus.; Harold Rosson, Robert Surtees, cin.; Conrad A. Nervig, ed.; B&W; 1.37:1; 119 min.

CAST:

Van Johnson (*Mike Hanlon*); Keenan Wynn (*Slinky Edwards*); Pat(ricia) Kirkwood (*Susan Duncan*); Guy Lombardo (*Himself*); Edward Arnold (*Popsie*); Marie Wilson (*Rosalind*).

Rating: ** 1/2

Vet Mike asks investors to help create "the affordable home of tomorrow" (i.e., the suburban sprawl that overtook America in the late 1940s). He flashes back to the day he returned from the South Pacific, eager to see his hometown girl, unable to grasp the surprises life would have in store for him. Rather than have the leads break into song, this quasi-musical in the realist style offers specialty numbers by guest stars. Willie Best's appearance as a bug-eyed "boy" reminds us of the era's unconscious if prevalent racism. Highlight: Billy Preston as a child jazz great. Innocuous, uninspired, unmemorable. Shot during the war; the prologue was added before release to make the piece relevant.

NURA UNU, aka STRAY DOG (1949)

CREDITS:

Film Art/Shintoho; Akira Kurosawa, dir.; Kurosawa, Ryûzô Kikushima, scr.; Kurosawa, Sôjirô Motoki, pro.; Fumio Hayasaka, mus.; Asakazu Nakai, cin.; Yoshi Sugihara, Toshio Gotô, ed.; B&W; 1.37:1; 122 min.

CAST:

Toshirô Mifune (*Murakami*); Takashi Shimura (*Sato*); Keiko Awaji (*Harumi*); Eiko Miyoshi (*Harumi's Mother*); Noriko Sengoku (*Girl*); Isao Kimura (*Yusa*).

Rating: *****

Returning to Tokyo, veteran Murakami's backpack is stolen. This haunts the policeman, especially after his Colt automatic is taken by a thief. Hoping to locate the weapon, he embarks on a personal odyssey that takes him through all levels of postwar society. Determination becomes obsession when he realizes the gun is used by a mad-dog killer to murder innocent people. Murakami experiences a Hitchcock-like transference of guilt with the villain he's hunting. What begins as a predecessor to modern *policieurs* becomes at the midpoint a philosophical treatise on escalating nihilism in postwar Japan, as well as the world at large. Early proof Kurosawa would emerge as a noteworthy existential auteur.

SOME CAME RUNNING (1958)

CREDITS:
Metro-Goldwyn-Mayer; Vincente Minnelli, dir.; James Jones (novel), John Patrick, Arthur Sheekman, scr.; Sol C. Siegel, pro.; Elmer Bernstein, mus.; William H. Daniels, cin.; Adrienne Fazan, ed.; C; 2.35:1; 137 min.

CAST:
Frank Sinatra (*Dave Hirsh*); Dean Martin (*Bama*); Shirley MacLaine (*Ginnie Moorehead*); Martha Hyer (*Gwen*); Arthur Kennedy (*Frank Hirsh*); Nancy Gates (*Edith Barclay*).

Rating: ***

Adaptation of the 1957 novel concerns the big letdown many vets experienced upon their return, discovering the world they knew had become corrupted. Arriving in his Indiana hometown, Dave, an alcoholic writer—not unlike Jones—runs afoul of his brother Frank, a phony pillar of society. He charms creative writing teacher Gwen who inspires him, befriends no-account gambler Bama, and marries B-girl Ginnie. Memorable for some specific scenes (Sinatra stepping off the bus in the opening, Martin wearing his cowboy hat in the bathtub, sweaty all-night poker games) but less so for its overall impact, which tends toward

WECOME TO THE POSTWAR CESSPOOL: Frank Sinatra returns to his home town only to discover the once charming village has become a glitzy cesspool for life's hustlers in *Some Came Running*.

florid soap opera. A favorite among Minnelli devotees, less so among mainstream audiences.

SOMEWHERE IN THE NIGHT (1946)

CREDITS:
20th Century Fox; Joseph L. Mankiewicz, dir.; Mankiewicz, Howard Dimsdale, Lee Strasberg, W. Somerset Maugham, scr.; Anderson Lawler, pro.; Arthur Morton, mus.; Norbert Brodine, cin.; James B. Clark, ed.; B&W; 1.37:1; 110 min.

CAST:
John Hodiak (*George W. Taylor*); Nancy Guild (*Christy Smith*); Lloyd Nolan (*Det. Kendall*); Richard Conte (*Mel*); Josephine Hutchinson (*Elizabeth*); Fritz Kortner (*Anzelmo*).

Rating: ****

Somewhere in the South Pacific, a marine awakens in a hospital bed with no idea who he might be. After his recovery, he heads stateside, making his way to Los Angeles, where a George Taylor (the name in the identity papers found on him) had lived. When he goes into public places, everyone reacts strangely. Early example of the postwar antihero, a lone wolf who keeps his own counsel, almost always observed after midnight. Beautiful if potentially dangerous dames waltz in and out of his life whenever he's not being beaten to a pulp by gangsters. Strong stuff, even if nothing in the movie lives up to the spectacular opening sequence, shot from the protagonist's dizzy point of view.

STRANGER, THE (1946)

CREDITS:
International Pictures; Orson Welles, dir.; Welles, Victor Trivas, Anthony Veiller, scr.; Sam Spiegel, pro.; Bronislau Kaper, mus.; Russell Metty, cin.; Ernest Nims, ed.; B&W; 1.37:1 95 min.

CAST:
Edward G. Robinson (*Wilson*); Loretta Young (*Mary*); Orson Welles (*Rankin*); Philip Merivale (*Longstreet*); Richard Long (*Noah*); Konstantin Shayne (*Konrad*).

Rating: ****

Agent Wilson of the Allied War Crimes Commission tracks escaped high-ranking Nazi Rankin to a small college town, where he's created a new identity as a liberal-minded professor planning to marry innocent beauty Mary. Borrows from Hitchcock's *Shadow of a Doubt* while presaging *Vertigo*. Implication: Hitler's evil hasn't been eliminated and now infiltrates our most beloved institutions. Final sequence in a clock tower takes Welles-style suspense to the point of self-caricature. Well-crafted thriller, albeit mechanically plotted at times and devoid of thematic depth.

SUBJECT WAS ROSES, THE (1968)

CREDITS:
Metro-Goldwyn-Mayer; Ulu Grosbard, dir.; Frank D. Gilroy (play), scr.; Edgar Lansbury, pro.; Lee Pockriss, mus.; Jack Priestley, cin.; Gerald B. Greenberg, ed.; C; 1.85:1; 107 min.

CAST:
Patricia Neal (*Nettie Cleary*); Jack Albertson (*John Cleary*); Martin Sheen (*Timmy Clearly*); Don Saxon (*Club MC*).

Rating: ***

An Irish vet returns to his Bronx neighborhood only to sense, the morning after his parents throw him a welcome-home party, that any hope for a decent postwar life is doomed. His mother wants to dominate him as if he were still a child while his father remains unable to express paternal love. Onstage, Gilroy's intimate (one-set) domestic tragedy proved effective enough to win a Pulitzer Prize in 1965. On film, everything feels wrong. The apartment scenes are too claustrophobic; attempts to get the characters outdoors seem forced. Biggest mistake was including 1960s folk music (to make the movie "relevant") instead of the required mid-1940s swing sound. The acting is fine.

TERESA (1951)

CREDITS:

Metro-Goldwyn-Mayer; Fred Zinnemann, dir.; Stewart Stern, Alfred Hayes, scr.; Arthur M. Loew, Jr., pro.; Louis Applebaum, mus.; William (J.) Miller, cin.; Dave Kummins, Frank Sullivan, ed.; B&W; 1.37:1; 102 min.

CAST:

Pier Angeli (*Teresa Russo*); John Ericson (*Philip Cass*); Patricia Collinge (*Clara*); Richard Bishop (*Mr. Cass*); Peggy Ann Garner (*Susan*); Ralph Meeker (*Grissom*); Rod Steiger (*Frank*).

Rating: * 1/2

An Italian war bride arrives in America, hoping for a wonderful new life, only to be horrified by her young husband's slum home, as well as

THE TIMES THEY ARE A-CHANGIN': A young vet (John Ericson) realizes that he has nothing in common with his pretty Italian war-bride (Pier Angeli) in *Theresa*.

his oedipal relationship with a dominating mother. Here was a chance to make an important film, with on-location shooting. The premise and mostly impressive cast are wasted on an uninvolving tale about the pathetic (and unsympathetic) veteran, the title character shunted into the background. Supporting roles, including Steiger's psychiatrist, are poorly developed. The weakest film from a great director.

TILL THE END OF TIME (1946)

CREDITS:
RKO; Edward Dmytryk, dir.; Niven Busch (novel), Allen Rivkin, scr.; Dore Schary, pro.; Leigh Harline, mus.; Harry Wild, cin.; Harry Gerstad, ed.; B&W; 1.37:1; 105 min.

CAST:
Dorothy McGuire (*Pat Ruscomb*); Guy Madison (*Cliff Harper*); Robert Mitchum (*Bill Tabeshaw*); Bill Williams (*Perry*); Tom Tully (*Harper*); William Gargan (*Gunny*).

Rating: **** 1/2

From the bestseller *They Dream of Home* (1944) came this impressive precursor to *Best Years of Our Lives*. Returning servicemen, one (Williams) a paraplegic, have journeyed to hell and back only to discover that their once-routine lives can never be reclaimed. Each experiences disorientation, disappointment, and disillusion. The walking wounded include an all-American boy (Madison) unable to relate to his Norman Rockwellesque parents and an emotionally scarred war widow (McGuire), now a corner bar pickup. Along the way, this film touches on the GI Bill, job reorientation, small-town values giving way to an asphalt jungle, the formation of reactionary organizations that exploit naïve GIs, racial unrest in a recently integrated America, the emergence of the new musical form that would soon be called rock 'n' roll, and, with it, the creation of that unique postwar commodity—the American teenager. Shamefully underrated and little seen today.

TOMORROW WE LIVE (1942)

CREDITS:

Atlantis/PRC; Edgar G. Ulmer, dir.; Bart Lytton, scr.; Seymour Nebenzal, pro.; Leo Erdody, mus.; Jack Greenhalgh, cin.; Dan Milner, ed.; B&W; 1.37:1; 64 min.

CAST:

Ricardo Cortez (*The Ghost/Alexander Caesar Martin*); Jean Parker (*Julie Bronson*); Emmett Lynn (*Pop*); William Marshall (*Lt. Bob Lord*); Rose Anne Stevens (*Melba*).

Rating: ** 1/2

Veteran Lord returns to his small southwestern hometown in search of innocent girl Julie only to learn she's fallen under the spell of sleazy nightclub owner Martin. Bizarre Poverty Row trek into *Petrified Forest* territory. Enough of the cult director's stylistic flourishes are on view to satisfy Ulmer fans. Oddball item for its time, having more in common with 1930s gangster yarns and late 1940s noirs than early 1940s feel-good war-era home-front films. Sordid, anxiety-inducing pulp fiction; curiously engrossing.

WEEK-END AT THE WALDORF (1945)

CREDITS:

Metro-Goldwyn-Mayer; Robert Z. Leonard, dir.; Vicki Baum (play), Sam Spewack, Bella Spewack, Guy Bolton, scr.; Leonard, Arthur Hornblow Jr, pro.; Johnny Green, mus.; Robert H. Planck, cin.; Robert J. Kern, ed.; B&W; 1.37:1; 130 min.

CAST:

Ginger Rogers (*Irene Malvern*); Lana Turner (*Bunny Smith*); Walter Pidgeon (*Chip Collyer*); Van Johnson (*Capt. James Hollis*); Edward Arnold (*Edley*); Keenan Wynn (*Oliver*); Robert Benchley (*Morton*).

Rating: ****

A jaded journalist (Benchley, playing a variation of his own popular image) who resides at the upscale hotel year-round offers wise-guy commentaries on a single weekend's goings-on. Guests include a popular movie star (Rogers) who achieved commercial success yet remains lonely, a gold-digging secretary (Turner) hoping to use her brains and beauty to hit the big time, a world-weary combat reporter (Pidgeon) who has lost his sense of mission, and a self-serving businessman (Arnold) hoping to corner the postwar oil market. An appealing update of MGM's earlier triumph *Grand Hotel*, precisely the sort of breezy fluff this studio mounted better than any other. A transitional film revealing a growing if inexplicable sense of malaise.

WHITE CHRISTMAS (1954)

CREDITS:
20th Century Fox; Michael Curtiz, dir.; Norman Krasna, Norman Panama, Melvin Frank, scr.; Robert Emmett Dolan, pro.; Irving Berlin, mus.; Loyal Griggs, cin.; Frank Bracht, ed.; 1.85:1; 120 min.

CAST:
Bing Crosby (*Bob Wallace*); Danny Kaye (*Phil Davis*); Rosemary Clooney (*Betty Haynes*); Vera Ellen (*Judy Haynes*); Dean Jagger (*Gen. Thomas Waverly*); Mary Wickes (*Emma*).

Rating: *** 1/2

At Bastogne, two song-and-dance men (Crosby, Kaye) perform Berlin's holiday classic for GIs huddling in the ruins, cheered by a visit from their commanding officer (Jagger). Ten years later, now show-biz partners, they perform at a New England ski lodge owned by that elderly Eisenhower-like general while pursuing two pretty sisters (Clooney, Ellen). Hokey, glitzy, even garish; still, undeniably charming, and as such a sentimental favorite. One of numerous mid-fifties films that posited the war years as a warmly remembered, even preferable era in our collective lives.

HAVE YOURSELF A MERRY LITTLE CHRISTMAS: Two soldiers (Bing Crosby, Danny Kaye) sing 'White Christmas' to their comrades during the Battle of the Bulge while wishing they were back home; nearly ten years later, they perform the number again, surprised to realize that they miss "the good ol' days" of World War II…

Launched a nostalgia craze for a happier, simper time that existed only in our memories and in the movies from that sentimental era.

WITHOUT RESERVATIONS (1946)

CREDITS:
RKO Radio Pictures; Mervyn LeRoy, dir.; Mae Livingston (novel), Jane Allen, Andrew Solt, scr.; Jesse L. Lasky, Walter MacEwen, pro.; Roy Webb, mus.; Milton R. Krasner, cin.; Jack Ruggiero, ed.; B&W; 1.37:1; 107 min.

CAST:
Claudette Colbert (*Christopher "Kit" Madden*); John Wayne (*Rusty Thomas*); Don DeFore (*Lt. Dink Watson*); Anne Triola (*Connie*); Frank Puglia (*Ortega*).

Rating: *** 1/2

Following the war, novelist Kit pens a book in which a tough marine predicts that the way to a happy future is progressivism. She must find an unknown to play the part on film and bumps into a living incarnation of her hero, Rusty. Imagine Capra's *It Happened One Night* remade with a train rather than a bus, plus the jailhouse sequence from Hawks's *Bringing Up Baby* thrown in at the end. Made in 1945, released a year later, just before glorifying the "common man" disappeared from movies as communist witch hunting commenced. Cary Grant, Jack Benny, and columnist Louella Parsons play themselves. Fair.

Cinematic Medal of Honor: The Top 101

(in alphabetical order)

Air Force (1943)
Amarcord, aka *Fellini Amarcord* (1973)
Ashes and Diamonds (1958)
Attack (1956)
Au Revoir, Les Enfants (1987)
Bad Day at Black Rock (1955)
Ballad of a Soldier (1959)
Battle of San Pietro, (The) (1945)
Best Years of Our Lives, The (1946)
Big Red One, The (1980)
Boot, Das, aka *Boat, The* (1981)
Bridge, The (1959)
Bridge on the River Kwai, The (1957)
Casablanca (1942)
City of Life and Death (2009)
Closely Watched Trains (1966)
Come and See (1985)
Conformista, Il, aka *Conformist, The* (1970)
Cranes Are Flying, The (1957)
Dam Busters, (The) (1955)
December 7, aka *December 7, 1941* (1943)
Dirty Dozen, The (1967)
Downfall (2004)
English Patient, The (1996)

TAPS: In *From Here to Eternity*, 'Robert E. Lee Prewitt' (Montgomery Clift) blows the mournful bugle call after his best friend dies; the iconic vision can also be taken as a farewell to all those who served and died in World War II.

Four Days of Naples, The (1962)
From Here to Eternity (1953)
Garden of the Finzi-Continis, (The) (1970)
General Della Rovere (1959)
Great Escape, The (1963)
Guns of Navarone, The (1961)
Hail the Conquering Hero (1944)
Hill, The (1965)
Hiroshima, Mon Amour (1959)
Hope and Glory (1987)
Human Condition, The (1959–1961)
Imitation Game, The (2014)
Inglourious Basterds (2009)
In Which We Serve (1942)
Ivan's Children, aka *My Name is Ivan* (1962)
I Was a Male War Bride (1949)
Judgment at Nuremberg (1962)
Kanal (1957)
Lacombe, Lucien (1974)
Ladri di Biciclette, aka *Bicycle Thieves* (1947)
Lady Vanishes, The (1938)
L'armée des Ombres, aka *Army of Crime* (1969)
Last Metro, The (1980)
Letters from Iwo Jima (2006)
Life and Death of Colonel Blimp, The (1943)
Lifeboat (1944)
Life is Beautiful (1997)
Longest Day, The (1962)
Long Voyage Home, The (1940)
Lost Horizon (of Shangri-La), The (1937)
Matter of Life and Death, A, aka *Stairway to Heaven* (1946)
Meet John Doe (1941)
Mephisto (1981)
Miracle at Morgan's Creek, (The) (1944)
Mister Roberts (1955)
Night and Fog (1965)
Notorious (1946)
Nora Inu, aka *Stray Dog* (1949)
Objective Burma (1945)

One of Our Aircraft is Missing (1942)
Pan's Labyrinth (2006)
Pianist, The (2000)
Radio Days (1987)
Raiders of the Lost Ark (1981)
Remains of the Day (1993)
Roma Città Aperta, aka *Rome: Open City* (1945)
Sahara (1943)
Saving Private Ryan (1989)
Search, The (1948)
Shoah (1985)
Shop on High (Main) Street, The (1965)
Soldier of Orange (1977)
Sorrow and the Pity, The (1969)
Sound of Music, The (1965)
Stalag 17 (1953)
Story of GI Joe, The (1945)
Tea With Mussolini (1999)
They Were Expendable (1945)
Thin Red Line, The (1998)
Third Man, The (1949)
Tin Drum, The (1979)
To Be or Not To Be (1942)
To Have and Have Not (1944)
Triumph of the Will, The (1935)
Two Women (1962)
Untergang, Der, aka *Downfall* (2004)
Victors, The (1963)
Walk in the Sun, A (1945)
Way Ahead, The, aka *Immortal Battalion* (1944)
Way to the Stars, The (1945)
Why We Fight (1942–1945)
Yankee Doodle Dandy (1942)